DRAWINGS FOR PAINTINGS
IN THE AGE OF REMBRANDT

DRAWINGS FOR PAINTINGS

IN THE AGE OF REMBRANDT

Ger Luijten   Peter Schatborn   Arthur K. Wheelock, Jr.

with

Rhea Sylvia Blok, Wouter Kloek, Henriette Rahusen,
William W. Robinson, Cécile Tainturier, Ilona van Tuinen,
Gerdien Wuestman

SKIRA | NATIONAL GALLERY OF ART · U.S.A. · | FONDATION CUSTODIA · COLLECTION FRITS LUGT

The exhibition is organized by the National Gallery of Art, Washington,
and the Fondation Custodia, Collection Frits Lugt, Paris.
The exhibition in Washington is made possible
by Dr. Mihael and Mrs. Mahy Polymeropoulos,
and The Exhibition Circle of the National Gallery of Art.

Exhibition dates:
National Gallery of Art, Washington
October 4, 2016–January 2, 2017

Fondation Custodia, Collection Frits Lugt, Paris
February 3–May 7, 2017

Produced by the Fondation Custodia, Collection Frits Lugt, Paris,
in association with Skira editore Spa.
Designed by Wigger Bierma
English edition: Henriette Rahusen, project manager; Barbara Christen and Laura Jones
Dooley, editors; Lynne Richards, translator; John Long, production associate
Printed and bound in Italy. First edition

Distributed in USA, Canada, Central & South America by Rizzoli International Publications,
Inc., 300 Park Avenue South, New York, NY 10010, USA.
Distributed elsewhere in the world by Thames and Hudson Ltd., 181A High Holborn,
London WC1V 7QX, United Kingdom.

Library of Congress Cataloging-in-Publication Data
Names: Schatborn, Peter. | Robinson, William W. Drawing into painting. |
    Wheelock, Arthur K., Jr., Drawings and underdrawings. |
    Luijten, Ger. Reasons for drawing in seventeenth-century Holland. |
    National Gallery of Art (USA), organizer, host institution. |
    Fondation Custodia, organizer, host institution.
Title: Drawings for paintings in the age of Rembrandt / Ger Luijten, Peter
    Schatborn, Arthur K. Wheelock, Jr.; with Rhea Sylvia Blok, Wouter Kloek,
    Henriette Rahusen, William W. Robinson, Cécile Tainturier, Ilona van
    Tuinen, Gerdien Wuestman.
Description: Washington : National Gallery of Art, 2016. | "The exhibition is
    organized by the National Gallery of Art, Washington, and the Fondation
    Custodia, Collection Frits Lugt, Paris." | Includes bibliographical
    references.
Identifiers: LCCN 2016016707 | ISBN 978-0-89468-407-4 (National Gallery of Art
    and Fondation Custodia) | ISBN 978-88-572-3152-5 (Skira editore)
Subjects: LCSH: Drawing, Dutch–17th century–Exhibitions. | Artists'
    preparatory studies–Netherlands–Exhibitions. |
    Underdrawing–Netherlands–Exhibitions. | BISAC: ART / General.
Classification: LCC NC261 .D73 2016 | DDC 741.9492/074753--dc23 LC record available
at https://lccn.loc.gov/2016016707

Directors' Foreword

Drawings for Paintings in the Age of Rembrandt demonstrates the many ways in which seventeenth-century Dutch artists used drawings when composing and executing their paintings. The immediacy and realistic nature of their landscapes, still lifes, and genre scenes suggest that Dutch artists painted them from life. However, they actually executed such subjects, as well as biblical and mythological scenes, in their studios, often using preliminary drawings as points of departure. This fascinating exhibition, which consists of some ninety drawings and twenty paintings, demonstrates the varied ways in which this artistic process unfolded for Dutch artists throughout the course of the seventeenth century.

'Drawing,' wrote Karel van Mander in *Het Schilder-Boeck* (The Painter's Book), which was published in Haarlem in 1604, is 'the father of painting . . . and the portal to many of the arts.' A later Dutch theorist, Samuel van Hoogstraten, wrote in his treatise on painting, published in 1678, that pupils should postpone taking up the brush until they had fully mastered the art of drawing. Neither of these theorists, however, explained how the art of drawing could serve as a basis for paintings; understanding that process is the challenge that the curators have undertaken to address in this exhibition and catalog.

The range of drawings related to paintings is wide, and the exhibition includes numerous juxtapositions to demonstrate the variety of relationships that exists among these works. One sees here, for example, freely rendered chalk studies that Jan van Goyen made while traveling through the countryside, sketches that later served as inspiration for his landscape paintings; figure drawings in pen and ink or red chalk that Rembrandt van Rijn incorporated into biblical or mythological paintings; and construction drawings, executed with the aid of a compass and straightedge, that Pieter Saenredam explicitly made for paintings of church interiors. Sometimes artists utilized separate figure and landscape drawings in conceiving

their painted works, as did, for example, Aelbert Cuyp in his views of the Dutch countryside. Artists also utilized counterproofs to be able to depict objects in mirror image.

Another component of the exhibition examines how artists prepared their canvases and panels to plan their compositions before they began painting. Sometimes they made free sketches in chalk, sometimes they blocked in their compositions to create tonal relationships important for their composition, and sometimes they made elaborate construction drawings. A number of paintings in the exhibition have been studied with infrared reflectography, an examination technique that helps reveal the presence and character of underdrawings, information that adds greatly to our understanding of the integrated nature of drawings and paintings during the Dutch Golden Age.

The exhibition and catalog are the result of a close collaboration among Peter Schatborn, former head of the Rijksprentenkabinet, Amsterdam, who initiated the concept and was the driving force behind it; Ger Luijten, director of the Fondation Custodia/Collection Frits Lugt, Paris; and Arthur K. Wheelock, Jr., curator of northern baroque paintings at the National Gallery of Art, Washington. Their efforts have also greatly benefited from the coordination provided by Cécile Tainturier, curator at the Fondation Custodia, and Henriette Rahusen, researcher in the department of northern baroque paintings at the National Gallery.

The catalog, which is the first comprehensive study on this topic, contains three essays as well as entries on artists and works included in the show. Peter Schatborn and William W. Robinson, former Ian Woodner curator of drawings at the Harvard University Art Museums, provide an overview of the types of preliminary drawings that Dutch artists made for their paintings. Arthur Wheelock looks at the artists' utilization of drawings in the painting process, paying close attention to underdrawings as revealed through technical examinations. Ger Luijten explores the world of drawings in Dutch society, a field that extended well beyond the singular use of drawings made in preparation for paintings.

The National Gallery of Art and the Fondation Custodia/Collection Frits Lugt wish to acknowledge the support and cooperation of the many lenders to this exhibition, both institutional and private. Seed funding for the catalog was generously provided by the Kathrine Dulin Folger Publication Fund. We would like to thank Dr. Mihael and Mrs. Mahy Polymeropoulos, and The Exhibition Circle of the National Gallery of Art for their generous support of the exhibition in Washington.

This ambitious project reinforces, once again, the extraordinary generosity of Frits Lugt and his wife, To Lugt-Klever, who created the Fondation Custodia in 1947. They left to the art-loving community their remarkable collection of drawings and paintings, and a bequest that continues to provide funds for new acquisitions and exhibition support.

Earl A. Powell III
National Gallery of Art, Washington

Ger Luijten
Fondation Custodia, Collection Frits Lugt, Paris

Acknowledgments

Drawings for Paintings in the Age of Rembrandt, a truly collaborative project, has motivated a large number of colleagues from both sides of the Atlantic to examine how Dutch artists used drawings as part of the painting process. The concept of this exhibition, as well as the selection of objects, owes much to Peter Schatborn, whose lifelong fascination with this subject began with his groundbreaking exhibition, *Dutch Figure Drawings*, at the Rijksmuseum and the National Gallery of Art in 1981–1982.

For this catalog Schatborn teamed up with his long-time friend and collaborator William W. Robinson, former Ian Woodner curator of drawings at the Harvard University Art Museums, to write the introductory essay on the importance of drawings for Dutch artists. Both of these scholars, moreover, have written entries on artists whose works are included in this exhibition. The catalogue has also benefited from the contributions of other specialists who have written comparable entries, including Rhea Blok, Wouter Kloek, Henriette Rahusen, Cécile Tainturier, Ilona van Tuinen, and Gerdien Wuestman. Aside from her entries, Henriette Rahusen also compiled the extensive bibliography for the catalog.

Drawings for Paintings in the Age of Rembrandt could only have come about through the generosity of private collectors and museums, as well as through the dedication and expertise of many friends and colleagues. We would particularly like to thank Earl A. Powell III, director of the National Gallery of Art, for his support and encouragement. Among the many other colleagues who have kindly supported our efforts are: Stijn Alsteens, Susan Anderson, Marco van Baalen, Diederik Bakhuÿs, Holm Bevers, Peter de Boer, Hilde de Boer, Niels de Boer, Peter van den Brink, Stephanie Buck, Hans Buijs, Quentin Buvelot, An van Camp, Marianne Cavanaugh, Tara Cerretani, Keith Christiansen, Melanie Correia, John Delaney, Taco Dibbits, Simon Dickinson, Terry van Druten, Gaëlle Etesse, Robert Fucci, staff of the Getty Research Institute Library, Melanie Gifford, Emilie E.S. Gordenker, Michael Govan, Milou Goverde, Margaret Morgan Grasselli, S.A.C. Dudok van Heel, Lee Hendrix, Margreet van der Hut, Gregory Jecmen, Eddy de Jongh, Edouard Kopp, Bernd Lindemann, Erik P. Löffler, Yuri Long, Patrice Marandel, Petria Noble, Noelle Ocon, Elma O'Donoghue, Michiel C. Plomp, Timothy Potts, Lawrence Principe, Andrew Robison, Pieter Roelofs, Paul W.L. Russell, Jef Schaeps, Marijn Schapelhouman, Bernhard Schnackenburg, Stephanie Schrader, Christian Tico Seifert, Nicolette Sluijter-Seiffert, Miriam Stewart, Dominique Suhr, Ruben Suykerbuyk, Michael Swicklik, Lex van Tilborg, Neal Turtell, Jaap van der Veen, Robert Wald, Arie Wallert, Amy Walsh, Gregor Weber, Ernst van de Wetering, Marjorie Wieseman, Margreet Wolters, Elizabeth Wyckoff, Nancy Yocco.

In Paris we would like to thank Mariska de Jonge and Maud Guichané, assisted by Marie Abraini and Éléonore Dérisson, for the general organization of the project and administration of the loan requests and images. The librarians of the Fondation Custodia—Wilfred de Bruijn, Floortje Damming, Tony Grossin, and Cécile Raymond—were a great help. Regina Peixeiro critically commented on a number of entries and helped to improve them. Lynne Richards was responsible for the translation into English of the texts written in Dutch and in French. For the French edition we called on Véronique Crombé, who accomplished her task with great dedication. We would like to thank Marie-Noëlle Grison and Maud Guichané, who greatly assisted Cécile Tainturier with the editing of the French edition. At Skira Publishers in Milan, Giuseppina Leone and her team facilitated the production of this book, which has been artfully designed by Wigger Bierma.

In Washington, overall organization of the project and administration of the loan requests were ably carried out by D. Dodge Thompson, Naomi Remes, and Olivia Wood in the department of exhibitions. In the registrar's office, Michelle Fondas and Melissa Stegeman coordinated the transportation of the works of art, while Mervin Richard and Bethann Heinbaugh of the department of loans and exhibitions conservation supervised the packing and safe transport of the works of art. Mark Leithauser, Donna Kirk, Brian Sentman, and other members of the outstanding department of installation and design, developed the handsome installation of the exhibition. In the department of imaging and visual services, Alan Newman and, especially, Barbara Wood assembled the comparative figures for the catalog. In the publishing office, Judy Metro and Chris Vogel facilitated the English language edition of the catalog, ably assisted by editors Barbara Christen and Laura Jones Dooley and by production associate John Long. Susan Arensberg and Margaret Doyle in the department of exhibition programs enhanced the exhibition with insightful wall texts and a web feature. Anabeth Guthrie in the press office has worked diligently to provide information to the broader public, while Christine Myers in the development office and Julian Saenz in the office of the general counsel were instrumental. In the department of northern baroque paintings, Alexandra Libby, assistant curator, provided a range of support, and Jennifer Henel, curatorial associate, streamlined the complex logistics of the project.

To all those who have helped bring this project to its successful conclusion, we extend our deepest gratitude.

Ger Luijten and Arthur K. Wheelock, Jr.

Lenders to the Exhibition

Maida and George Abrams Collection, Boston
Albertina, Vienna
Amsterdam Museum
Ashmolean Museum, University of Oxford
Bayerische Staatsgemäldesammlungen,
    Alte Pinakothek, Munich
P. & N. de Boer Foundation
The British Museum, London
The Courtauld Gallery, Courtauld Institute
    of Art, London
Fondation Custodia, Collection Frits Lugt, Paris
Hamburger Kunsthalle, Hamburg
Harvard Art Museums / Fogg Museum, Cambridge
Koninklijk Oudheidkundig Genootschap, Amsterdam
The Leiden Collection, New York
Leiden University Library
Liechtenstein Museum, Vienna
Los Angeles County Museum of Art
The Metropolitan Museum of Art, New York
The Morgan Library & Museum, New York
Musée de Boulogne-sur-Mer, Boulogne-sur-Mer
Musée de Grenoble
Musée des Beaux-Arts, Rouen
Musée des Beaux-Arts et d'Archéologie, Besançon
Musée du Louvre, Paris, on loan to the Musée
    Bonnat-Helleu, Musée des Beaux-Arts de Bayonne
Musées royaux des Beaux-Arts de Belgique, Brussels
Museum Boijmans Van Beuningen, Rotterdam
Museum Mayer van den Bergh, Antwerp
National Gallery of Art, Washington
The National Gallery of Canada, Ottawa
The National Gallery of Denmark, Statens Museum
    for Kunst, Copenhagen

National Maritime Museum, Greenwich
Noord-Hollands Archief, Kennemer Atlas, Haarlem
The Orsay Collection, London, Paris
Otto Naumann Ltd., New York
Rose-Marie and Eijk van Otterloo Collection
Private Collections
Rijksmuseum, Amsterdam
The Royal Collection / HM Queen Elizabeth II
Staatliche Kunstsammlungen Dresden,
    Kupferstich-Kabinett
Staatliche Museen, Berlin, Gemäldegalerie
Staatliche Museen, Berlin, Kupferstichkabinett
Staatliches Museum Schwerin
Stadsarchief, Amsterdam
Saint Louis Art Museum
Teylers Museum, Haarlem

Note to the Reader

Works of art in this catalog are ordered as follows: Catalog numbers 1 through 13 introduce the overall theme of the exhibition and exemplify the various ways in which Dutch artists of the Golden Age used drawings when executing their paintings. These objects are discussed in the first two catalog essays, and eleven of them are also the subject of short entries immediately following the essays.

The catalog section offers case studies on the working methods of thirty-nine prominent and representative Dutch artists. Each artist is the subject of a single entry that describes his use of drawings, as illustrated by the exhibited object or objects. The entries are presented chronologically, based on the birth date of the artist, with the exception of Willem van de Velde the Elder, who is discussed in the entry on his son Willem the Younger.

Each exhibited drawing and painting is accompanied by a technical description, its exhibition history, and a selected bibliography. This information is included in the comprehensive checklist of works in the exhibition, organized alphabetically by artist on pages 275–315.

An alphabetical index of artists followed by pertinent catalog numbers appears on page XV.

List of Artists

Ast, Balthasar van der: cats. 38, 39, 40

Avercamp, Hendrick: cats. 27, 28, 29, 30, 31

Backer, Jacob Andriaensz: cats. 70, 71

Backhuysen, Ludolf: cat. 102

Bega, Cornelis: cats. 103, 104, 105

Berchem, Nicolaes Pietersz: cat. 4

Berckheyde, Gerrit Adriaensz: cats. 118, 119, 120, 121, 122, 123, 124, 125

Bloemaert, Abraham: cats. 16, 17, 18, 19, 21, 22, 20

Bosschaert, Ambrosius: cat. 12

Bray, Jan de: cat. 96

Bray, Salomon de: cats. 47, 48

Breenbergh, Bartholomeus: cats. 56, 57

Cooghen, Leendert van der: cat. 6

Coques, Gonzales: cat. 9

Cuyp, Aelbert: cats. 81, 82, 83, 84, 85, 86, 87

Dujardin, Karel: cat. 88

Eeckhout, Gerbrand van den: cats. 89, 90, 91, 92

Flinck, Govert: cat. 80

Gheyn II, Jacques de: cats. 14, 15

Goyen, Jan van: cats. 42, 43, 44

Graat, Baerend: cat. 97

Hagen, Joris van der: cat. 1

Hals, Dirck: cats. 34, 35

Heyden, Jan van der: cat. 11

Honthorst, Gerrit van: cat. 33

Jonson van Ceulen, Cornelis: cat. 7

Kessel, Jan van: cat. 3

Keyser, Thomas de: cats. 45, 46

Laer, Pieter van: cat. 37

Lastman, Pieter: cats. 24, 25, 26

Lievens, Jan: cat. 2

Maes, Nicolaes: cats. 111, 112, 113

Mieris, Frans van: cat. 114

Moeyaert, Claes Cornelisz: cat. 36

Molijn, Pieter: cat. 10

Musscher, Michiel van: cat. 13

Netscher, Caspar: cat. 8

Ostade, Adriaen van: cats. 72, 73, 74, 75, 76, 77, 78

Ostade, Isack van: cats. 93, 94

Palamedesz, Anthonie: cat. 58

Passe II, Crispijn de: cats. 5a, 5b

Poelenburch, Cornelis van: cat. 41

Potter, Paulus: cat. 95

Ravesteyn, Jan Anthonisz: cat. 23

Rembrandt van Rijn: cats. 59, 60, 61, 62, 63, 64, 65, 66, 67

Ruisdael, Jacob van: cats. 98, 99, 100, 101

Saenredam, Pieter Jansz: cats. 49, 50, 51, 52, 53, 54, 55

Saftleven, Cornelis: cats. 68, 69

Slingelandt, Pieter Cornelisz van: cats. 126, 127

Velde, Adriaen van de: cats. 115, 116, 117

Velde, Esaias van de, I: cat. 32

Velde, Willem van de, the Elder: cats. 108, 109

Velde, Willem van de, the Younger: cats. 106, 107, 110

Vliet, Hendrik Cornelisz van: cat. 79

DRAWING INTO PAINTING: AN OVERVIEW

William W. Robinson and Peter Schatborn

'Drawing,' wrote Karel van Mander in *Het Schilder-Boeck* (The painter's book, 1604), is 'the father of painting… and the portal to many of the arts.'[1] His views echoed those of Italian Renaissance writers on art and were endorsed in turn by later Dutch authors. 'He who wishes to become a good painter must endeavor to be a sure and accomplished draftsman,' wrote Willem Goeree in 1670 in his *Inleyding tot de Practijck der Algemeene Schilder-Konst* (Introduction to the practice of the general art of painting), and Samuel van Hoogstraten, in *Inleyding tot de Hooge Schoole der Schilderkonst* (Introduction to the high art of painting), published in 1678, admonished pupils to postpone taking up the brush until they had fully mastered the art of drawing.[2] Both Goeree and Van Hoogstraten underscored their advice by pointing out that many of the greatest artists continued to draw throughout their lives.[3] Whether or not a painter made use of preparatory studies in the design and production of pictures—and many did not—it was assumed that he should be a competent draftsman and maintain his skills through practice.

The training of a Dutch artist commenced with drawing. Goeree prescribed a four-step process that probably represents an idealized compilation of instructional exercises followed in many artists' workshops. The novice started out by copying prints and other drawings before graduating to copying paintings and sculpture and, finally, to making studies after live models.[4] Pupils drew from the model with their masters, and together they went outdoors with their sketchbooks to record landscapes, trees, farmhouses, and cattle. Many continued throughout their lives to draw for practice and to build a stock of motives that, preserved in albums in the workshop, could be consulted and used at any time. Among other purposes, drawings served as working material, as preparation for the creation of various kinds of artworks.

How did seventeenth-century Dutch painters use drawings in designing and executing their pictures? Most drawings related to paintings fall into two broad categories: compositions that show, often in a sketchy or summary manner, all or most of the image envisioned by the artist; and studies for prominent details in the finished work, such as figures, animals, hands, legs, landscapes, buildings, plants, trees, shells, or flowers. Within these general categories there are countless variations in the functions of drawings and painters' working methods. Artists developed practices that best suited their own style, workshop procedures, and the subjects they depicted. In establishing the relation between preparatory studies and paintings we should take several factors into account: the style of the drawings, the media with which they were executed, the technique (the way the artist used the media), the working process, and the dating.

Seventeenth-century Dutch writers on art offer little explicit information about our subject. They do, however, address such issues as the role of drawings in artistic training, media and techniques, and the various types of studies artists made, as well as studio practices that involved the use of drawings. Their texts clarify what we learn from the surviving artworks, which constitute our primary source for understanding the purposes served by drawings in the creative process of a Dutch painter. And let us emphasize at the outset that our source material is far from complete, comprising only the random sample of drawings that have survived from the seventeenth century, which represent a small fraction of those made by the artists. Although thousands of drawings have come down to us, most do not relate to known paintings, and it is virtually certain that time has taken a greater toll on working studies, especially sketchy ones, than on more finished works. We should also note that many artists who learned to draw during their apprenticeships did not, as mature masters, rely on drawings in the production of their paintings, choosing instead to work directly on the canvas or panel (see cat. 10 and p. 20). Last, there are numerous artists—and they include such major masters as Hendrick ter Brugghen, Johannes Vermeer, Pieter de Hooch, and Salomon van Ruysdael—to whom no drawings are securely attributed today. They, too, surely made drawings as part of their training, but we do not know how—or if—they used them in the creation of their paintings.

Seventeenth-century authors distinguished between works made from life (Dutch: *naer 't leven*) and those executed from the imagination (*uyt den geest*) or memory (*van onthout*).[5] These terms offer an insight into how the artists mentally classified the types of studies they made for paintings, but the conceptual distinction they represent also corresponds to a difference in the circumstances of the drawings' production. In a sketch made *uyt den gheest*, the artist used the pen or chalk to give material form on paper to the ideas in his mind. When drawing *naer 't leven*, by contrast, the draftsman worked after an existing model. Most compositions were drawn from the imagination. They include studies for literary narratives—those illustrating texts from the Bible, mythology, or history—but also those for portraits and scenes of daily life. Some landscapists drew compositions from the imagination, whereas others adapted the design of a painting from a sketch made from life. The large number of surviving detail studies serves as a reminder that the innovative naturalism characteristic of the pictorial arts of the period depended in part on the practice of drawing from life. This practice increased dramatically during the seventeenth century, as did the incorporation of studies made from life directly into paintings, and this is one of the developments in style and artistic practice that most clearly distinguishes seventeenth-century Dutch paintings from those by sixteenth-century Netherlandish masters. Of course, artists also drew inspiration from figures and compositions by earlier artists, which they could study in prints.

TRAVEL AND SKETCHBOOKS

Artists often traveled together, especially on longer trips, such as the journey up the Rhine to Cleves or to France or Italy. They sometimes drew each other at work, although this does not mean that every time we see a draftsman in a landscape that he was actually sitting there. The figure of an artist drawing could be included as an affirmation that what is represented in the image was observed from reality (cats. 1, 2). The inclusion of a draftsman in a topographical view—for example, in the panoramas of cities in Georg Braun and Frans Hogenberg's atlas *Civitates Orbis*

Fig. 1. Adriaen van Ostade, *A Painter in His Workshop*, 1663, oil on panel. Staatliche Kunstssammlungen, Gemäldegalerie Alte Meister, Dresden, 1397

Terrarum (Atlas of cities of the world, 1572–1617)—attests to the accurate, 'eyewitness' representation of the site.[6]

Seventeenth-century Dutch painters used sketchbooks to draw landscapes and other motives from life (fig. 2). This exercise trained the artist eventually to paint or draw the same kinds of motives from memory or imagination. Nine sketchbooks by Dutch draftsmen have survived intact from the seventeenth century, and two are included in this exhibition (cats. 3, 79).[7] Most contain sketches of landscapes in the Netherlands or Germany. Artists occasionally adapted images more or less directly from sketchbooks for compositions or details in paintings, prints, or finished drawings, but not every sketchbook served this purpose.

DRAWINGS FROM MODELS

Like studies in sketchbooks, drawings after sculpture or from the live model served both as exercises and as a collection of motives that could be incorporated into paintings, prints, or finished drawings. Artists attended sessions with models to maintain their drawing skills through regular practice and to create a stock of studies. Few drawings from live models have survived from the sixteenth

Fig. 2. Jan van Goyen, *View of Brussels*, c. 1648, black chalk. Dresden Sketchbook, Staatliche Kunstsammlungen, Kupferstich-Kabinett, Dresden, fol. 24

Fig. 3. Jan van Goyen, *View of Brussels*, 1652, oil on panel. Szépművészeti Múzeum, Budapest, 51.2968

century, and the question arises whether Netherlandish masters of that period drew more often after earlier works of art, or from the imagination, than from life. The biography of Karel van Mander published in the posthumous 1618 edition of *Het Schilder-Boeck* records that Van Mander, together with Hendrick Goltzius and Cornelis van Haarlem, 'established an Academy among themselves in order to study from life.'[8] Two drawings from life of nude female models by Goltzius, one dated 1594, have survived, but the activities of this Haarlem Academy might also have included making other types of *naer 't leven* studies, such as Goltzius's 1603 views of the local landscape.[9] In addition to figures, artists drew body parts, such as hands and arms, which portraitists, among others, used as preparatory studies. Artists without access to a model might use a mannequin, or lay figure, particularly for drapery studies.[10] Lay figures were articulated wooden dolls whose limbs could be manipulated to assume various positions. Adriaen van Ostade included a mannequin among the studio furnishings in his 1663 painting of an artist in his workshop (fig. 1), and Crispijn van de Passe II's *Van 't Light der Teken en Schilder-Konst* (On the light of the arts of drawing and painting, 1643) (cats. 5a, 5b)

includes engravings that illustrate the use of the lay figure for drawing draperies.[11]

COMPOSITION
PAINTINGS BASED ON STUDIES FROM LIFE

Some Dutch landscapists and architectural painters adapted *naer 't leven* studies for the composition of a picture. The incorporation of a topographical view into a painting, a practice that originated in the sixteenth century and became far more widespread in the seventeenth, helped to create the impression of an image based on observed reality.[12] Two sketchbooks by Jan van Goyen have survived intact, and four others can be partially reconstructed.[13] Studies from these volumes provided compositions for some of his paintings. A summary sketch of the Haringpakkerstoren, a medieval tower with a baroque spire in Amsterdam, supplied the central motif of an oil painting dated 1655, which shows a broader and more detailed prospect of the site (cat. 42 and p. 129, fig. 1), and a view of Brussels in a sketchbook was the basis for a painting dated 1652 (figs. 2, 3). Van Goyen also used material from his sketchbooks to compose the finished drawings he sold to collectors. A sketch of a

Fig. 4. Jan van Goyen, *View of a River Bank*, c. 1648, black chalk. Dresden Sketchbook, Staatliche Kunstsammlungen, Kupferstich-Kabinett, Dresden, fol. 25

Fig. 5. Jan van Goyen, *River Landscape with Cottages amid Trees*, 1651, black chalk with brown wash. British Museum, London, 1895 0915.1163

riverbank provided the point of departure for a more detailed drawing dated 1651 that includes additional houses, boats, and figures (figs. 4, 5). We know of only a few instances in which Jacob van Ruisdael adapted studies from life for the entire composition of a painting. His remarkable panoramic view over the densely built urban core and harbor of Amsterdam was based on a sketch in black chalk and gray wash made around 1665 from the scaffolding erected to construct the tower of the new town hall (cats. 99, 100). Pieter Saenredam produced various types of extremely precise preparatory works, including compositions made on the spot, sketches with measurements of architectural elements, ground plans, detail studies, and full-scale construction drawings that could be traced directly onto a panel (cats. 49–55). In 1661, Cornelis de Bie wrote that Saenredam depicted buildings 'in such a way, *naer 't leven*, that their essence and nature could not be shown to a greater perfection,' although he did not explicitly connect the artist's painstaking working process to the lifelike appearance of his paintings.[14] For his *View of the Nieuwezijds Voorburgwal in Amsterdam*, Gerrit Berckheyde made an exceptional design drawing (cat. 119) that only outlines the buildings, so that he could vary the fall of light and shadow in different versions of the painted composition (cats. 120, 121 and p. 262, fig. 1).

When landscapists and architectural painters adapted scenery and buildings studied from life for the composition of a picture, it might take only the addition of a few figures and other details to complete the work. Aelbert Cuyp's *Rhine Valley Stretching North toward the Elterberg* (cat. 83) provided the setting for a painting, to which he added only sheep, horses, and riders, one of whom has dismounted to draw.[15] For his *Group of Houses with a Church Tower in the Background* (cat. 94), Isack van Ostade referred to a study of the inn and church steeple, which he had worked up with colored chalks and watercolor. He revised the architectural composition on the canvas and completed the work by painting the figures, horse, and cart (p. 214, fig. 2). A drawing made in the countryside provided the basis for Adriaen van de Velde's *Landscape with Trees* (cat. 116). In the painting, he modified the format of the composition and added the staffage of farmers and cattle (p. 257, fig. 1).

FROM THE IMAGINATION

In the chapter on drawing in his didactic poem *Den Grondt der Edel Vry Schilderkonst* (The foundation of the noble and free art of painting), which forms part of *Het Schilder-Boeck*, Van Mander wrote that some artists first put down their thoughts in sketches and drawings and used them to set up their compositions on the lowest paint layer.[16] Numerous examples survive from the seventeenth century of studies, sketched from the imagination (*uyt den gheest*), that illustrate biblical and mythological subjects and that are preparatory for paintings. Claes Moeyaert's composition in black and white chalk on brown paper relates to his *Cloelia's Escape from Porsena's Camp*, a painting that depicts an episode from the early history of Rome (cat.

36 and p. 114, figs. 1, 2). While working on the picture, Moeyaert introduced a number of changes and refinements, which he regarded as improvements over the design in the sketch. Composition studies by Rembrandt's pupil Gerbrand van den Eeckhout show considerable variation in the choice of media and degree of finish. His two chalk sketches for *Jacob's Dream*, 1672 (cats. 91, 92), are less resolved than the pictorially finished composition design for *David Promises Bathsheba to Designate Solomon as His Successor*, 1646 (cat. 89). Yet, even in the latter picture, he introduced several changes in details while working on the canvas, some prepared in a study of an appropriately costumed model for the figure of *Seated Oriental* (cat. 90). Rembrandt usually painted his works directly on the canvas or panel, but an exception to this practice is his study in brown ink and brown wash for *The Rape of Ganymede*, 1635 (cat. 66), which, although summarily drawn with impetuous strokes, corresponds in most respects to the composition of the picture (p. 171, fig. 13). Samuel van Hoogstraten, who was Rembrandt's pupil in the 1640s, recommended ink and wash 'handled in a sketchy manner' to put down 'your first thoughts on paper' and 'thus to see in a rough way the main part of a whole [image] which you have in mind.'[17]

On occasion Rembrandt made studies after he had begun work on a painting to resolve specific poses or groupings of figures. He evidently sketched *Studies of Mary, the Mother of Christ, and Mary Magdalene* after he had established the composition on the canvas of *The Entombment* (cat. 65 and p. 168, fig. 11). Sketches related to the grisaille painting *St. John the Baptist Preaching*, 1634/1635 (cat. 61), were also executed during work on the canvas. They include two studies for the figure of John (cat. 62), but Rembrandt was especially interested in a vivid portrayal of his audience and the three Pharisees (scribes) or Sadducees standing in the foreground, for which he drew a number of studies (cats. 63, 64). We do not know whether any of Rembrandt's pupils followed this practice of making studies while working on a painting.

Genre painters also produced composition studies *uyt den gheest* for their scenes of daily life. Like studies for pictures of literary subjects, they vary widely in the choice of materials, the size and finish of the drawings, and how closely the artist followed the composition in the painting. For his *Lacemaker* of 1655 (cat. 111), Nicolaes Maes made a tiny sketch of the composition in ink and wash, leaving the details of the figure and setting to be worked out later (cats. 112, 113). When he executed his *Merry Company* in 1622, Gerard van Honthorst referred to a larger and more fully resolved preparatory drawing of the composition, but he still introduced changes to the revelers' poses and gestures (cat. 33 and p. 106, fig. 1). Adriaen van Ostade probably began his *Peasants Dancing in a Tavern*, 1659 (cat. 73), by roughly painting the composition on the panel from his imagination, but he produced a separate sketch for the group at the center of the work as well as studies for individual figures (cats. 72, 74, 75).

Painters of portraits and group portraits also made composition studies from the imagination. On occasion they might have shown these sketches to patrons for their approval, but in some examples that have survived, the compositions underwent considerable modification by the time the artist produced the painting. Two studies survive for Thomas de Keyser's *Militia Company of Captain Allaert Cloeck and Lieutenant Lucas Jacobsz Rotgans* of 1632 (cats. 45, 46 and p. 133, fig. 1). The trio of officers in the center remains the same in the studies and the painting, but De Keyser had to reconfigure the guardsmen at both sides into tighter groups to fit the format of the picture. Both drawings have been squared, or covered with a network of rectangular cells. The grid could have been drawn on a larger scale on the canvas, enabling the artist to control the enlargement of the composition on the new support by dividing it into compartments. In each of the three studies for Adriaen van Ostade's *Family Portrait*, the ten figures occupy different positions or strike varying poses, so that the artist or patron could choose from the sketches (cats. 76–78 and p. 186, fig. 1). None of the three comes very close to the composition of the painting, although in every one the number of figures is the same. Rembrandt's pupils learned to draw and paint in his manner so that they could participate in the production of his workshop. In some cases a student executed a painting from a drawing by the master. In 1644, an artist in the workshop, probably Carel Fabritius, produced the posthumous portrait of *Jan Cornelisz Sylvius, the Preacher*, taking as his point of departure a pen-and-ink composition by Rembrandt (cat. 67 and p. 174, fig. 15). For the face of the deceased sitter, the painter referred to the portrait of the preacher etched by Rembrandt in 1633, when Sylvius was still alive (p. 172, fig. 14).

Although sixteenth-century drawings of landscape motives studied from life and incorporated into pictures are rare, countless examples attest to this method of working in the seventeenth century. Hendrick Avercamp reproduced his *View of Kampen from outside the Walls* (cat. 30), a study in brown ink and watercolor, in the background of his *Winter Scene outside the Walls of Kampen* (cat. 31). Abraham Bloemaert's 1629 *Landscape with Dilapidated Buildings and Figures* (cat. 16) offers an exceptional example, in which most of the composition was assembled from four different studies of buildings and figures (cats. 17, 18 and p. 77, figs. 2, 3). The two studies of tumbledown cottages that he used in this painting recall a passage in Van Mander's life of Bloemaert in which the author singled out the attractive technique of such drawings and underscored how their remarkable naturalism contributed to the lifelike appearance of his paintings. Bloemaert's landscape paintings, Van Mander wrote, incorporate 'well-observed and droll peasant houses, peasants' implements, trees, and countryside—things which are to be seen in great variety round about Utrecht and which are drawn by him; for he does a great deal after life and he has a clever manner of drawing and penmanship to which he sometimes adds some watercolors so that it looks particularly good.'[18] Aelbert Cuyp also used studies from life of landscapes as well as figures for his paintings. The background of his *Landscape with Herdsmen* (cat. 81) reproduces a drawing with a view of the Rhine valley (cat. 82), while he adapted two figure studies for his *Landscape with Horseman, Herder, and Cattle* (cats. 84, 85 and p. 194, fig. 1).

In Adriaen van Ostade's 1663 picture of a painter at work, the artist has attached a drawing—evidently a figure study—to his easel and is incorporating it into the composition on the panel. Other studies, and the album from which they presumably came, lie on the floor (see fig. 1). Figure drawings from life that artists reproduced in paintings are hardly known at all from the sixteenth century, but the practice became commonplace in the seventeenth. Rembrandt's teacher Pieter Lastman produced a study in red chalk heightened with white on prepared paper for the reclining Rachel in his painting *Laban Seeking the Idols* (cats. 24, 25). For the figure of Jacob in the grisaille *Joseph Telling His Dreams* (cat. 60), Rembrandt used a finished model study in red chalk, while he painted the other figures, as far as we know, from the imagination (cat. 59). This is an exceptional instance of this practice in the oeuvre of Rembrandt, who rarely made figure studies in preparation for his paintings.

Genre painters employed a variety of media and techniques for their studies. Whereas Anthonie Palamedesz (cat. 58) and Dirck Hals (cats. 34, 35) used thinned oil paint on paper, an uncommon medium for figure drawings, Nicolaes Maes and Cornelis Bega chose the more conventional red chalk (cat. 113) and black and white chalk on blue paper (cat. 104). Some landscapists, including Hendrick Avercamp (cats. 27–29) and Esaias van de Velde (cat. 32 and p. 102, fig. 1), even made studies for figures that appear on a small scale in their paintings.

Portraitists occasionally drew studies from life to establish the poses of the sitters in their paintings. Both Govert Flinck and Barend Graat executed drawings from models in black and white chalk on blue paper in preparation for double portraits of married couples. Only studies for the husbands have survived. The sitter did not pose for Flinck's study, since the man in the painting has different facial features from those of the model in the drawing, but his stance and gesture are very similar to those in the portrait (cat. 80 and p. 193, fig. 1). Graat, too, followed

Fig. 6. Jacob Backer, *Weeping Woman Kneeling, Seen from Behind*, black and white chalk on blue paper. Metropolitan Museum of Art, New York, Rogers Fund, 1953 53.127.3

his study quite closely, although he adjusted the man's collar and the position of his legs (cat. 97 and p. 222, fig. 1). In this case the sitter evidently did pose for the drawing, because the face closely resembles the features of the man in the picture.

An artist could adapt a figure drawing from stock or, if necessary, produce a new one to suit the requirements of a composition. For his paintings of biblical and mythological subjects with large-scale figures, Adriaen van de Velde drew specific studies, whereas for the small-scale herdsmen that populate his pastoral landscapes, he could dip into his portfolios for a suitable model.[19] Van de Velde and Hendrick Avercamp occasionally reused the same figure study for different compositions.[20] When an artist adapted an existing drawing from his stock for a new work, the figure could be made to fit, depending on its place in the composition, for example by having him or her look in a different direction. An instructive example is the *Seated Man, Smoking* by Dirck Hals (cat. 34), which is reproduced, exactly as he appears in the drawing, in the painting *Figures at the Fireside* (p. 109, fig. 1), while in another picture he reappears without a pipe and playing a violin (p. 110, fig. 3). Hals anticipated reusing the study, because he drew variant versions of the legs and adapted one pair of legs for the pipe smoker and the other for the musician.

Some artists made counterproofs, offsets in mirror image of the original drawings, so that a figure could be used in more than one composition and facing in a different direction. In his *View of the Bank of the Rhine near Cologne*, Gerrit Berckheyde painted two figures studied from life in the foreground. He used a counterproof for the walking boy because he wanted the boy to walk to the left, not to the right, as in the original drawing (cats. 123, 124 and p. 267, fig. 3). Counterproofs could also be taken of whole compositions or other pictorial elements, such as those made from drawings of ships by Willem van de Velde the Elder (cat. 109) or from a sheet with studies of sheep and a cow by Nicolaes Berchem (cat. 4).

We know of a few instances where an artist used a figure study by another master. Bartholomeus Breenbergh borrowed a counterproof of a drawing by Jacob Backer, *Weeping Woman Kneeling, Seen from Behind*, which Breenbergh used for his painting *Alexander and the Family of Darius*, c. 1645 (figs. 6–8). Backer and Breenbergh knew each other well and must have attended sessions with other Amsterdam history painters who got together to draw from the model. Philips Wouwerman came into the possession of a drawing of a seated shepherd by Pieter van Laer—perhaps he acquired it after Van Laer's death—and adapted it for one of his pictures (cat. 37 and p. 116, fig. 1). Dirck van Bergen, a pupil of Adriaen van de Velde,

Fig. 7. Bartholomeus Breenbergh, *Alexander and the Family of Darius*, c. 1645, oil on canvas. Private Collection

Fig. 8. Detail of fig. 7

acquired his master's studio estate after his death in 1672, and thereafter regularly adapted Van de Velde's studies of figures and animals for his own compositions (cat. 117 and p. 259, fig. 2).

DRAWING FROM THE MODEL

Archival sources and surviving drawings attest that the practice of drawing in groups from the model increased in the Netherlands during the 1640s and 1650s.[21] One document records that in the late 1640s, the sisters Catrina, Margaretha, and Anna van Wullen posed nude for Govert Flinck.[22] In 1658, Flinck, Willem Strijcker, Ferdinand Bol, Nicolaes van Helt Stocade, and Jacob van Loo testified that Catharina Jans sat completely naked as a model for them and that they drew and painted her.[23] An engraving in Crispijn van de Passe II's *Van 't Light der Teken en Schilder Konst* shows a group of draftsmen working from a male model who assumes a pose based on an ancient image of the god Jupiter (cat. 5).[24] In many instances, of course, artists depicted figures in attitudes derived from antique sculpture, which represented a widely respected ideal.[25] There was also a tradition of drawing a figure in the pose struck by the protagonist in a biblical or mythological composition by an admired artist.[26] Goeree recommends that the artist, as one way to choose the model's pose, fol-

low 'some invention by a good master, from memory or by looking at prints and drawings,' since one finds such beautiful examples in the works of famous old masters.[27]

Most studies from models survive in only one version (cat. 6). In some cases, however, we have drawings that depict the same models from different angles, and these provide an instructive insight into the practice of working from life in the Netherlands during the seventeenth century. Govert Flinck's *Seated Female Nude*, 1648, shows the same woman in the identical pose as a drawing by Jacob Backer, who sat just to the left of Flinck (cat. 71 and p. 180, fig. 1). Among the many drawings of nude models by Rembrandt and his pupils are studies made simultaneously by the master and Arent de Gelder and Johannes Raven that represent the same model from different sides.[28] Haarlem artists, too, drew together from models. The male figure in a drawing dated 1666 by Leendert van der Cooghen (fig. 9) was studied at the same time by Cornelis Bega (fig. 10), while Bega and Gerrit Berckheyde simultaneously drew a standing woman from different angles, although in Bega's study she holds a glass (cat. 103), which is missing in the work by Berckheyde (cat. 125).

In addition to drawings of nude and clothed figures, artists also made detail studies of arms, hands, and legs. On the recto and verso of a sheet (cat. 20, pp. 78, 82), Abraham

Fig. 9. Leendert van der Cooghen, *Young Man Kneeling beside a Vase*, 1666, black and white chalk on blue paper. Museum Boijmans Van Beuningen, Rotterdam, LvdC 7

Fig. 10. Cornelis Bega, *Young Man Kneeling beside a Vase*, 1666, red chalk. Städtische Wessenberg-Gemälde Galerie, Sammlung Brandes, Konstanz, 34/78

Bloemaert drew various limbs and heads after he had established the composition of his painting *The Adoration of the Shepherds*, and he referred to the studies while completing the picture. Around 1650 Abraham's son Frederik made prints after studies such as these and published them in an album that served as a model book for draftsmen and connoisseurs.[29] Cornelis Jonson van Ceulen drew studies of hands in connection with his painted portraits. His *Study of a Woman's Hands* corresponds in many, though not all, details to one of his paintings (cat. 7), but he reproduced exactly another *Study of a Woman's Hands* in a portrait dated 1646 (figs. 11, 12). An album of drawings by Caspar Netscher in the Rijksmuseum, Amsterdam, contains mostly studies of limbs.[30] Netscher's *Studies of Two Female Arms* (cat. 8)—also in the Rijksmuseum, but not part of the album—was copied by one of his pupils, indicating that this kind of drawing served as instructional material in the workshop.[31]

ANIMALS

Animals, especially dogs and horses with riders, appear in many pictures, and some painters specialized in animal scenes. A sleeping dog in a drawing by Frans van Mieris the Elder rests in a chair in his painting *The Song Interrupted* (cat. 114 and p. 253, fig. 2). In his *River Landscape with Horseman and Peasants*, Aelbert Cuyp painted horses and cattle based on drawings (cats. 86, 87 and p. 201, fig. 2). Paulus Potter adapted his sketch *A Sow and Her Farrow* for a panel dated 1652 that depicts nursing piglets and cows in a pasture (cat. 95 and p. 217, fig. 1). Exotic animals make occasional appearances in paintings. Goeree advises artists to draw such rare creatures when the opportunity presents itself, because they can be used in biblical and mythological scenes.[32] Paintings by Roelandt Savery and his workshop incorporate his studies of a dodo into landscapes that feature a variety of rare animals and birds.[33]

TREES, PLANTS, AND SHELLS

Several Dutch artists made drawings of individual trees, and some of these served as studies for paintings.[34] Abraham Bloemaert reproduced the gnarled trunk at the left in his *Study of Trees (Studies of Two Pollard Willows)* in a painting of the holy family resting in a landscape, adding leaves to the bare branches in the study (cat. 19 and p. 81, fig. 4). Plants often served as motives in the foregrounds of landscape paintings, for example in Aelbert Cuyp's *Farm with Cottages and Animals* of c. 1639–1640, where he represented leaves, presumably of sorrel and butterbur, from a study in the British Museum, London.[35]

Painters of floral still lifes could find models in illustrated plant books or print series, but they also drew life studies of blooms cultivated in botanical gardens or by amateur growers. Tulips figured in most painted bouquets beginning in the first decades of the seventeenth century. In an allegorical picture dated 1603, Jacques de Gheyn II copied a study of a tulip that he had made in 1601 in an

Fig. 12. Cornelis Jonson van Ceulen, *Portrait of a Woman, Possibly of the Raphoen Family*, 1646, oil on canvas. Musées royaux des Beaux-Arts de Belgique, Brussels, inv. 2943

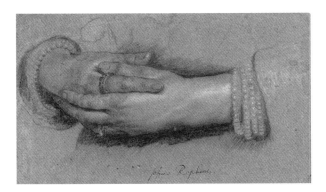

Fig. 11. Cornelis Jonson van Ceulen, *Study of a Woman's Hands*, 1646, black and white chalk on blue paper. J. Paul Getty Museum, Los Angeles

album of watercolors of flowers and small animals (cat. 14 and p. 75, fig. 1). Artists needed models of various sorts of flowers that did not bloom at the same time, so they compiled stocks of images. Balthasar van der Ast kept a large album of watercolor studies of flowers and shells, and he reproduced some of the shells in pictures, often as precious accessories to bouquets of rare blooms (cats. 38–40, p. 123 fig. 1).

SHIPS AND BUILDINGS

In addition to drawings of seascapes and naval battles, the marine painters Willem van de Velde the Elder and Willem van de Velde the Younger made exacting detail studies of ships, some of which they reproduced in pictures (cats. 107, 108, 110). Although the traditional identification of Willem van de Velde the Younger as the painter portrayed in Michiel van Musscher's *An Artist in His Studio with His Drawings* is not correct,[36] the man in this picture may well have been a specialist in seascapes (cat. 13). We cannot clearly distinguish the image on the easel, but it includes a boat with sails. As he prepares to resume work on the painting, the artist has laid out several drawings on the floor, some piled on top of the album in which they were stored. Those we can see are studies of ships and a bridge with three arches and two towers. Van Musscher's picture is a rare and evocative image of a Dutch artist's studio that shows the painter referring to his detail studies as he works.[37]

We of course encounter architecture in cityscapes and topographical views, but there are also 'portraits' of buildings that were prepared in drawings, such as Pieter Saenredam's 1641 *Old City Hall of Amsterdam*, which he used for a painting of 1657.[38] Other artists, too, made use of architectural motives studied in drawings. For his *Jewish Cemetery*, Jacob van Ruisdael used life studies of graves in the Jewish cemetery at Ouderkerk and the ruins at Egmond (cat. 101 and p. 231, figs. 2–4). The building in Cornelis van Poelenburch's *Houses in Italy* appears in a painting high on a hill surrounded by ancient ruins (cat. 41r and p. 124, fig. 1). Adriaen van de Velde's study in gray wash over black chalk of an isolated shepherd's hut in the woods became the centerpiece of his painting *The Hut* of 1671, in which he also used studies from life in red chalk for the shepherdess and cattle.[39]

Last, before completed paintings left the workshop, some artists drew copies of them to keep as an accurate visual record of the composition. These detailed copies constituted a workshop archive that a painter might consult when designing other works or show to prospective patrons.[40] Two generations of the De Bray family produced a considerable number of these record drawings, which, until 2001, were regarded as preparatory studies for the paintings.[41] Between 1652 and 1659, the Middelburg architectural painter Daniel de Blieck filled an album with copies after his pictures. It includes seventy line drawings in graphite after paintings of church interiors, many of which are known today.[42]

It is important to reiterate that many seventeenth-century Dutch artists, even some who were productive draftsmen, did not use drawings in the preparation and execution of their paintings or, like Rembrandt, did so only occasionally and by no means methodically. We should also recall that our understanding of the working methods of Dutch painters is inevitably skewed by vicissitudes of taste and other historical factors. Our sample of working studies by Dutch painters is surely biased in favor of those artists—Rembrandt, Abraham Bloemaert, Adriaen van de Velde—whose works have been preserved because collectors and experts of the eighteenth and nineteenth centuries admired them. Those connoisseurs generally favored finished drawings over summary sketches, so that many small or slight studies for paintings have undoubtedly been lost. The working drawings that have survived fall into two groups: studies of compositions and studies of details. Dutch painters devised a wide range of strategies in their use of both types—in the choice of media, the degree of finish of the drawing, and the ways they revised the studies on the canvas or panel. Most important, the innovative practice of making studies from life and reproducing them in pictures contributed in no small measure to the development of the distinctive naturalism of Dutch painting in its Golden Age.

1. Mander *Grondt*, I, 98–101.

2. Goeree 1670, 87; Hoogstraten 1678, 36.

3. Goeree 1668, 98; Hoogstraten 1678, 36.

4. Goeree 1668, 47–50.

5. Miedema 1981, 21, 24–25, 122–26, 140. Gerard Terborch the Elder wrote on a drawing by his son Harmen that the youth had made it '*van onthout*,' while he noted on other drawings by his children that they were done '*naer 't leven*.' Chapman 2007, 213, and Kettering 1988, I, no. H 51, H 60, H 69, H 70, H 80.

6. *View of Cabeças* (Las Cabezas de San Juan), etching, after a drawing made in 1565 by Joris Hoefnagel, in Braun and Hogenberg 1572–1617, V, 1598.

7. The nine sketchbooks that survive intact are: Nicolaes Berchem, Drawings in a sketchbook, mainly animal studies, c. 1644–1645, British Museum, London, 1920,0214.2.3-141 [Stefes 1997, no. I/7]; Gerard ter Borch the Younger, Drawings in a sketchbook, mainly landscapes and city views, 1631–1634, Rijksprentenkabinet, Rijksmuseum, Amsterdam, RP-T-1888-A-1797 [Kettering 1988, I, GrJ 93]; Anthonie van Borssom, Drawings in a sketchbook, mainly landscapes and animals, 1660s, British Museum, London, 1854.0628.111,1-43 [Davies 2014, nos. 122–177]; Jan van Goyen, Drawings in sketchbook, mainly landscapes, c. 1648, Staatliche Kunstsammlungen, Kupferstich-Kabinett, Dresden [Beck 1972, I, 271–283, no. 846]; Jan van Goyen, Drawings in a sketchbook, mainly landscapes, 1644–1649, Museum Bredius, The Hague [Beck 1966 is a facsimile of this sketchbook; Beck 1972, 265–270, no. 845]; Jan van Kessel, Drawings in a sketchbook, landscapes, 1659–1660, Fondation Custodia, Collection Frits Lugt, Paris, 2006-T.30 [Giltaij 2007], cat. 3 of the present catalog; Pieter Moninckx, Drawings in a sketchbook, landscapes, c. 1645–1646, Rijksprentenkabinet, Rijksmuseum, Amsterdam, RP-T-1976-29; Hendrick Cornelis van Vliet, Drawings in a sketchbook, portraits, church interiors, and figures, 1660s (?), Museum Boijmans Van Beuningen, Rotterdam, HvV1 [Rotterdam 1991, no. 73], cat. 79 of the present catalog; Jacob Willemsz

de Wet, Drawings and notes in sketchbook, figure studies and compositions, some landscapes, 1636–1671, Gemeentearchief, Haarlem, Hs 230 [Sumowski 1979, X, nos. 2354–2372].

8. Mander *Grondt*, II, 303.

9. For Goltzius's *Reclining Female Nude*, 1594, drawing (private collection, USA), and *Seated Female Nude*, drawing (Maida and George Abrams Collection, Boston), see London/Paris/Cambridge 2002, no. 24 and fig. 1. For Goltzius's drawings of landscapes near Haarlem dated 1603 (Museum Boijmans Van Beuningen, H 253; Fondation Custodia, Collection Frits Lugt, Paris, 2628), see Reznicek 1961, I, 430, no. 404, II, fig. 381, and I, 427–428, no. 400, II, fig. 380.

10. Chapman 2007, 189–190, 197–211. In his treatise on drawing published in 1636, Cornelis Biens provides instructions on how to construct a mannequin but does not discuss its use. Klerk 1982, 32–36.

11. Kleinert 2006, 288–289; Passe 1643, pt. 4.

12. For a sixteenth-century example, see Hans Bol's 1583–1585 metalpoint sketch of Delfgauw, which provided the composition for a miniature painting in gouache, dated 1586, to which he added groups of figures that enact the biblical story of Abraham Entertaining the Angels. Washington/London 2015, 154, 284–285, pl. 70.

13. Beck 1972–1991, I, 255–264, no. 843, 257–264, no. 844, 285–315, no. 487, III, 118–122, no. 844A.

14. De Bie 1661, 246. Translation from Arthur K. Wheelock, Jr., http://www.nga.gov/content/ngaweb/Collection/artist-info.1853.html?artobj_artistId=1853&pageNumber=1 (accessed October 15, 2015).

15. Aelbert Cuyp, *The Rhine Valley Stretching North toward the Elterberg*, Wooburn Abbey, Duke of Bedford. See Wouter Kloek in Washington/London/Amsterdam 2001, 261, cat. 93.

16. Mander *Grondt*, I, 254–255.

17. Hoogstraten 1678, 31.

18. Mander *Lives*, I, 450; Bolten 2007, I, 406.

19. Robinson 1979, 21, nos. D-3 and D-6, 22, no. D-15.

20. Robinson 1979, 10; Amsterdam/Washington 2009, 104–107, 116.

21. Manuth 2001, 47, 49–53; Sluijter 2006, 322–324.

22. Dudok van Heel 1982, 74; Manuth 2001, 53.

23. Bredius 1915–1922, IV, 1255; Manuth 2001, 49–50.

24. Passe 1643, pt. 2, frontis.; Bolten 1979, 16–25.

25. On this studio practice, see also Schatborn 2010b, I, under cat. 82, p. 213, where it is noted that the pose of a reclining female nude by Govert Flinck (Fondation Custodia, Collection Frits Lugt, Paris, 2969) derives ultimately from the antique marble *Sleeping Ariadne* but in the seventeenth century was adapted for life studies and compositions of various subjects. For example, Jacob Backer and Bartholomeus Breenbergh used such a pose in paintings of Cimon and Ephigenia; Sluijter 2006, 243–244.

26. Robinson and Anderson 2016, 135, under no. 36.

27. Goeree 1668, 33–34.

28. Los Angeles 2009, cats. 41.1, 41.2, 43.1, and 43.2.

29. Bolten 1979, 26–29.

30. Casper Netscher and pupils, Album of drawings, Rijksprentenkabinet, Rijksmuseum, Amsterdam, RP-T-1890-A-2282.

31. After Caspar Netscher, *Studies of Two Female Arms*, 1675 or later, drawing, Rijksprentenkabinet, Rijksmuseum, Amsterdam, RP-T-1890-A-2282.

32. Goeree 1670, 121.

33. Roelandt's orginal studies of a dodo are lost but are reflected in a drawing now attributed to his nephew Hans (Jan) Savery the Younger in the Crocker Art Museum, E.B. Crocker Collection, 1871.102 [Sacramento/Poughkeepsie 2010, no. 19]. The dodo at the left in the Crocker drawing appears in a painting by Hans Savery the Younger, possibly in collaboration with Roelandt Saverij, *Wooded Landscape with a Vista and Various Birds, among Which a Dodo*, c. 1625/1630, oil on panel, exhibited at TEFAF Maastricht in 2014 by Douwes Fine Art,

Amsterdam, http://www
.douwesfineart.com/object-profile/51
(consulted October 31, 2015).

34. For example, Hendrick Goltzius, *Study of a Tree*, c. 1600, drawing, Ashmolean Museum. Oxford, 1962.17.34; and Roelant Saverij, *Studies of Gnarled Trees*, 1606/1607, drawing, Rijksprentenkabinet, Rijksmuseum, Amsterdam, RP-T-2008-961. These are finished drawings and not studies for paintings.

35. British Museum, London, 1865, 0114.828; Washington/London/Amsterdam 2001, nos. 10, 96.

36. First identified as a portrait of William van de Velde the Younger in the catalog of the sale of J. van der Marck, Amsterdam, August 15, 1773, no. 469; Kleinert 2006, 155, 280. Merwe 2012, 66, identifies the artist as Adriaen van de Velde, but this, too, is doubtful, because he does not resemble known portraits of Adriaen.

37. Kleinert 2006, 141.

38. Pieter Saenredam, *The Old Town Hall of Amsterdam*, 1641, drawing, Stadsarchief, Amsterdam, Collectie Atlas Splitgerber; Saenredam, *The Old Town Hall of Amsterdam*, 1657, painting, Rijksmuseum, Amsterdam, on loan from the City of Amsterdam, C 1409.

39. Adriaen van de Velde, *Study of a Shepherd's Hut*, drawing, Private Collection, Boston; Adriaen van de Velde, *The Hut*, 1671, painting, Rijksmuseum, Amsterdam, SK-A-443. Schatborn 1975a, 159–165, and Amsterdam/Washington 1981, 116–117.

40. Giltaij and Lammertse 2001, 390–391.

41. Giltaij and Lammertse 2001, 367–387.

42. Rijksdienst voor de Monumentenzorg, Zeist; Rotterdam 1991, no. 70; Buijsen 1995.

DRAWINGS AND UNDERDRAWINGS: THE CREATIVE PROCESS IN DUTCH PAINTING

Arthur K. Wheelock, Jr.

All Dutch artists were trained in the art of drawing, not only because drawing was important in its own right, but also because its mastery was crucial for the art of painting.[1] This point was stressed by every seventeenth-century Dutch theorist, including Karel van Mander, Willem Goeree, Joachim Sandrart, and Samuel van Hoogstraten.[2] Nevertheless, only Van Mander in *Het Schilder-Boeck* (The painter's book, 1604), specifically discussed how artists could use preparatory drawings in the painting process.[3] As a result, how drawings actually functioned to guide seventeenth-century Dutch painters in creating their works is not well understood. In this essay I examine this question, paying particular attention to underdrawings that artists made on their panels and canvases to guide them in their work.

Van Mander emphasized that a well-designed preliminary drawing on the prepared support was crucial to a painting's success. So important were these preparatory drawings, he wrote, that only the master should be entrusted to make them.[4] Once these underdrawings were completed, workshop assistants could paint the first *doot-verven* layers ('dead color,' or blocked-in layers), which, Van Mander acknowledged, could occasionally be amended to improve on the initial concept. According to this important Dutch art theorist, such a carefully planned foundation would allow the master to achieve excellence once he applied his flowing paints, both to strengthen contours or to fill in well-defined forms.

Van Mander recommended that artists prepare full-scale cartoons and then trace them to make underdrawings on their panels, much as the Italians had done for their frescos. He wrote that his recent predecessors in the Northern Netherlands had followed this approach after preparing their panels with thick, white grounds. Many of these artists used black chalk or pencils in transferring these lines, but the underdrawings Van Mander most admired had been made with pulverized coal black mixed with water. Artists would then cover these lines with a thin primer, the color of flesh, through which the drawing could still be seen. After this layer had dried, they should apply paint thinly and sparingly, and add details with fine brushes.

Van Mander's comments came at the onset of the seventeenth century, before naturalism became a dominant concern for painters and theorists alike, transforming Dutch art in the following decades. Indeed, few Dutch artists seem to have followed Van Mander's recommendation to transfer a cartoon to the ground layer covering the support. The preeminent painter of church interiors, Pieter Jansz Saenredam, did make careful construction drawings that he would then transfer to his panels. Strikingly, other architectural painters, including Jan van der Heyden and Gerrit Berckheyde, apparently did not follow Saenredam's lead. These artists seem to have decided to forego making cartoons on separate sheets of paper and instead drew their carefully measured designs, or construction drawings, directly on their panel supports, as is discussed below.

Evolving attitudes toward painting encouraged artists to develop different approaches that would give them more flexibility in creating their compositions and fulfilling their pictorial goals. Thus, aside from construction drawings, artists made quick compositional sketches, nature studies, and figure drawings. Changes in painting techniques also occurred. Artists began to color their grounds and block in forms with broadly rendered oil sketches, sometimes in combination with underdrawings, to imbue their work with deeper and richer tonalities.

Information about the various ways in which Dutch artists used drawings for their paintings is unfortunately quite fragmentary, and much of it must be deduced from partial evidence garnered from such varied sources as Van Mander's treatise *Schilder-Boeck*, along with unfinished or thinly painted works, paintings depicting artists in their studios, and technical examinations of paintings, particularly through the use of infrared reflectography. Adding to the uncertainties in our interpretation of the artistic procedures is the fact that Dutch artists often hid their methods from others. For obvious economic reasons, artists kept secret the means by which they achieved unique effects in their paintings or managed to streamline production.[5] Moreover, as is evident in the oil stains on one of Hendrick Avercamp's drawings in this exhibition (cat. 30), many preliminary drawings were likely damaged during the painting process and discarded after use. With a few exceptions, as with Rembrandt van Rijn, such working drawings would not have been valued as collector's items.

VISUAL AND TECHNICAL EVIDENCE OF UNDERDRAWINGS

Unfinished paintings provide the clearest indications of the appearance of underlying preparatory drawings. One

Gonzales Coques (attributed), *Portrait of a Man Receiving a Letter from a Boy*, c. 1660. The Orsay Collection, London, Paris (cat. 9)

remarkable example is *Portrait of a Man Receiving a Letter from a Boy*, c. 1660, attributed to Gonzales Coques (cat. 9). In this unfinished portrait/genre scene the artist has painted the faces and laid in the background elements but has not yet filled in the figures' bodies, whose forms are indicated by a dark underdrawing on a light gray ground. The brushstrokes of the underdrawing, though quickly rendered, are quite specific: details of the figures' clothing, as well as the position of their hands and the letter passing between them, are all carefully indicated. The nature of this unfinished image suggests a sequential working procedure, where the master first drew in the composition on the panel support and then painted the sitters' portraits. Such a working process could allow for the participation of studio assistants, who might paint the still-life elements or the figures' clothing.

Partial information about underdrawings can often be gleaned from paintings that have been executed with thin, somewhat transparent paints. For example, a freely drawn black underdrawing is visible with the naked eye in many areas of *Landscape with Open Gate*, c. 1630/1635 (cat. 10), a monochromatic landscape from the early 1630s by the Haarlem artist Pieter Molijn. Nevertheless, the presence of the final paint layer makes it impossible to determine the full extent and character of this drawing by observation alone. Infrared reflectography largely eliminates the obscuring properties of this visual overlay (fig. 1) and reveals the full scope of the preparatory drawing on Molijn's panel.

Infrared reflectography registers the differences in temperature when light, directed at a painting, is reflected by the white ground and absorbed by the black lines of the underdrawing. It allows one to see through most paint layers, thereby revealing underlying drawings made with black chalk on a white ground.[6] This examination technique has proven to be particularly useful in investigations of fifteenth- and sixteenth-century Netherlandish paintings, where artists generally prepared their paintings in this manner. For Dutch paintings, however, its results are less predictable because these artists often made underdrawings with white or red chalk, neither of which registers in a reflectogram.[7] Although Dutch paintings have not yet been consistently examined in this way, the applicability of infrared reflectography to this area of study has become more broadly accepted in recent years.

Pieter Molijn, *Landscape with Open Gate*, c. 1630/1635 (cat. 10)

Fig. 1. Infrared reflectogram of Pieter Molijn, *Landscape with Open Gate*, c. 1630/1635 (cat. 10)

Fig. 2. Pieter Molijn, *Road between Trees near a Farm,* 1626, pen-and-ink on blue paper. Rijksprentenkabinet, Rijksmuseum, Amsterdam, RP-T-1920–76

Fig. 3. Infrared reflectogram of Pieter Lastman,
David Gives Uriah a Letter for Joab, 1619 (cat. 26)

Infrared reflectography was successful for the study of the underdrawing in Pieter Molijn's *Landscape with Open Gate* because he drew in carbon black on a light ocher-colored ground. The bold lines with which he defined the massive foreground tree with its rhythmic branches, the fence and its gate, as well as the ruts in the road and clouds in the sky, are all clearly visible. This freely executed drawing, with its searching lines, is comparable to Molijn's landscape drawings on paper (fig. 2), which suggests that, in his efforts to make a naturalistic painting, the artist drew directly on the panel rather than transferring a preliminary drawing in the manner that Van Mander had recommended.

When the overlying paint layer completely obscures an underdrawing made in black chalk, infrared reflectog-

raphy can be particularly informative. Such is the case with *David Gives Uriah a Letter for Joab*, 1619 (cat. 26), a compelling biblical scene by Pieter Lastman. A reflectogram reveals that Lastman here followed Van Mander's recommendation to make a complete underdrawing on the panel that outlines all of the painting's major compositional components (fig. 3). Given the free and expressive character of the underdrawing's black chalk lines, however, it seems unlikely that a cartoon for this panel ever existed, although Lastman may have first worked out the composition with a quick sketch. Lastman's style of underdrawing is similar to that seen in his figure drawings (cat. 24), and one wonders whether he made individual studies of David and Uriah in anticipation of this work.

26. Pieter Lastman, *David Gives Uriah a Letter for Joab*, 1619.
Oil on panel, 42.8 × 63.3 cm (16⅞ × 24¹⁵⁄₁₆ in). Private Collection
Washington only

Many of the investigations of Dutch paintings with infrared reflectography have focused on architectural and still-life paintings, and some of these results are discussed below. Genre paintings have also been examined, but less systematically and less successfully, in part because the artists' painting techniques often differ from those that can be registered with this method. Uncertainties surrounding the working procedures of Jan Steen demonstrate the questions that have confounded Dutch scholars with the study of many genre painters. Steen, for example, often repeated figures and motifs in his paintings, albeit with small variations in their poses and character. The frequent repetition of these pictorial elements suggests that he relied on a repertoire of drawn studies and used these drawings in a manner similar to that of

Adriaen van Ostade (see pp. 182–188). Nevertheless, no firm conclusions can be reached at this time about how he designed his paintings. Only one sheet, with figure drawings on the recto and verso, has been attributed to Steen, and that attribution is not universally accepted.[8] Most evidence indicates that the artist prepared his works with a quickly rendered monochromatic sketch and relied on his memory rather than a template when adapting motifs from earlier works.[9]

The issues surrounding Gerard ter Borch raise other interesting questions. Like Steen, Ter Borch often repeated motifs from one painting to another, but unlike Steen, these reused motifs are often identical, sometimes differing only in scale.[10] A case in point is the beautifully rendered white satin dress worn by the central female protag-

Fig. 4. Gerard ter Borch, *The Suitor's Visit*, c. 1658, oil on canvas. National Gallery of Art, Washington, Andrew W. Mellon Collection, 1937.1.58

Fig. 5. Gerard ter Borch, *A Lady at Her Toilet*, c. 1660, oil on canvas. The Detroit Institute of Arts, 65.10

onist in *The Suitor's Visit*, c. 1658, in the National Gallery of Art (fig. 4). Exactly the same dress, with identical folds and wrinkles, reappears in *A Lady at Her Toilet*, c. 1660, in the Detroit Institute of Arts (fig. 5), but larger. Ter Borch must have had a carefully drawn model for this dress that he transferred at a different scale by using a mechanical device, perhaps a pantograph. Although Ter Borch made many drawings throughout his career, no such cartoons or transfer drawings have been preserved.

THE USE OF CARTOONS IN DUTCH ARCHITECTURAL PAINTING

One Dutch artist who did make careful construction drawings intended for use as cartoons to be transferred to panel supports was Pieter Jansz Saenredam. He transferred the compositions of a number of these drawings by blackening their versos and incising the lines on their rectos— exactly the method recommended by Karel van Mander. One such cartoon is the elaborate construction drawing (cat. 51) Saenredam made for the painting of *The Choir of the Church of St. Bavo in Haarlem*, 1636, in the Frits Lugt Collection (cat. 50). With a straightedge and compass, Saenredam worked out the proportions of columns and

arches and the overall perspective system complete with vanishing point. Infrared reflectography demonstrates that the artist carefully followed the inscribed lines of his cartoon. The reflectogram, however, also reveals surprising information about a hitherto unknown earlier version of the composition on the Lugt panel. Initially, Saenredam painted graffiti and signed and dated the painting, 1636, on the face of the pillar at the left (figs. 6, 7). When he reworked his painting, he eliminated the graffiti and moved his signature and date to the base of the engaged column at the right.

The uppermost drawing on the pillar in this earlier version of the composition depicts an episode from the popular thirteenth-century French epic poem of the four sons of Aymon of Dordogne. They are shown escaping on their magic horse, Bayard, after one of them had killed Charlemagne's nephew. Below this drawing are a stick figure of a child and a larger depiction of a man with a raised arm. It is not known why Saenredam initially included this graffiti or why he decided to eliminate it and move his signature and date.[11] Nevertheless, the fact that he introduced two children playing marbles in the lower right of his final image must be significant. Not only do the children pro-

Fig. 6. Infrared reflectogram (detail) of Pieter Jansz Saenredam, *The Choir of the Church of St. Bavo in Haarlem*, 1636 (cat. 50)

Fig. 7. Detail of Pieter Jansz Saenredam, *The Choirs of the St. Bavo in Haarlem*, 1636 (cat. 50)

vide a human scale to the scene, but their size also emphasizes the enormity of the pier behind them. Dutch artists, moreover, often included depictions of children's games to allude to serious subjects, and Saenredam may have intended to contrast the game of chance that the boy and girl play with the certainty of the spiritual realm.[12]

Not all of Saenredam's construction drawings are blackened on the verso for transfer. Occasionally, as with the one he made on four separate sheets of paper—two of which are exhibited (cats. 53, 54)—for the enormous painting *The Interior of St. Bavo's Church, Haarlem (the 'Grote Kerk')*, in the Scottish National Gallery, Edinburgh (p. 146, fig. 2), these drawings were smaller in scale than the panels on which they were to be transferred. Instead of blackening the construction drawing for the nave, Saenredam squared it for transfer to a panel twice its size. Reflectograms reveal a complete underdrawing of the architecture as well as a grid of horizontal and vertical lines appropriately scaled for this larger support. Saenredam also drew orthogonals to define the recession of the architecture, and he carefully defined the church furniture, not included in the drawing, which he wanted to add to his painted image.[13]

Pieter Jansz Saenredam, *St. Bavo, Haarlem, View in the Choir*, 1636 (cat. 51)

[23]

Fig. 8. Infrared reflectogram (detail) of fig. 9

Fig. 9 Pieter Jansz Saenredam, *Cathedral of Saint John at 's-Hertogenbosch*, 1646, oil on panel. National Gallery of Art, Washington, Samuel H. Kress Collection, 1961.9.33

A different type of adjustment in the compositional design is seen in a comparison of the reflectogram of Saenredam's *Cathedral of Saint John at 's-Hertogenbosch* (fig. 8) with the final painting (fig. 9). Although Saenredam followed his extensive underdrawing almost exactly in his painting, he elongated the proportions of the apse: in the underdrawing the ribs join the keystone slightly below rather than at the top edge of the painting.

CONSTRUCTION DRAWINGS ON THE PAINTING SUPPORT

Construction drawings of the type that Saenredam made with a straightedge and compass are an anomaly in Dutch art, and even drawings squared for transfer are rare (for two of these, see the De Keyser and Backhuysen entries, cats. 45, 46, and 102). The question then arises how other painters of architectural scenes, some of whom clearly used straightedges and compasses when composing their paintings, prepared their compositions. This issue is particularly fascinating with Jan van der Heyden, for Arnold Houbraken wrote in 1721 that the artist 'was accustomed to draw everything from life, in order to transfer it later to panel.'[14] Despite Houbraken's assertion, no drawings by Van der Heyden have been preserved. A counterproof of a red chalk drawing, however, does exist (fig. 10), and it presents intriguing questions about the role of drawings in his paintings.

The red chalk counterproof records, in reverse, a preliminary study for the artist's *View of Oudezijds Voorburgwal with the Oude Kerk in Amsterdam*, c. 1670, in the Mauritshuis (fig. 11). Also seen on the counterproof are the color notations Van der Heyden wrote to serve as a guide when executing the painting. Despite these connections to the painting, the relation of the preliminary drawing to the finished work is unclear. To begin with, Van der Heyden made this red chalk drawing without the use of a straightedge or compass. It was also smaller in scale than the painting, and the proportions of the buildings and the spaces between them differ from those in the final composition.

The most likely explanation for these discrepancies between the drawing and the painting is that Van der Heyden, much like Saenredam, subsequently refined this freehand rendering of the site and enlarged its scale in a construction drawing. Unlike Saenredam, how-

Fig. 10. Jan van der Heyden, *View of Oudezijds Voorburgwal with the Oude Kerk in Amsterdam*, c. 1670, red chalk on paper, counterproof. Koninklijk Oudheidkundig Genootschap, Amsterdam (Atlas Amsterdam, Port. 14)

Fig. 11. Jan van der Heyden, *View of Oudezijds Voorburgwal with the Oude Kerk in Amsterdam*, c. 1670, oil on panel. Royal Picture Gallery, Mauritshuis, The Hague, 868

ever, he probably made these modifications on the panel itself rather than on a separate sheet of paper. Although no underdrawing is evident with infrared reflectography, presumably because Van der Heyden drew with red chalk, faint ruled lines can be seen in the buildings, such as would be found in a construction drawing.[15] This approach would have saved him a step in the creative process and increased the efficiency of his artistic production.

Technical examinations of Van der Heyden's paintings, however, indicate that he did not always work in this manner but employed a variety of approaches in designing his paintings. For example, infrared reflectography of his *View Down a Dutch Canal*, c. 1670, in the National Gallery of Art (cat. 11), records an extensive underdrawing in black chalk (fig. 12). As with the red chalk counterproof of the view along the Oudezijds Voorburgwal, this is not a careful construction drawing in which a straightedge was used to refine the image, and no ruled lines are visible on the panel. Unlike the Mauritshuis painting, however, this composition is focused largely on the leafy trees lining the canal, with the architecture of the buildings serving primarily as a backdrop. In the underdrawing Van der Heyden depicted the foliage quite freely, with bold, rhythmic strokes defining the trunks and branches of the trees, and only subsequently did he indicate the buildings with drawn lines. In the final painting Van der Heyden made no real adjustments to the trees or buildings but did eliminate a boat tied to the quay at the left.

An intriguing aspect of the painting is that the artist inserted the Romanesque church of Veere to this view along an Amsterdam canal, presumably basing his image of the church on a drawing he had made earlier in his career.[16] The reflectogram indicates that, in arriving at this composite composition, Van der Heyden did not make any adjustments to the buildings, other than slightly enlarging the church's tower, which leads one to believe that he initially worked out his design on a separate sheet of paper before drawing on the panel.

This ad hoc approach to compositional design is markedly different from the one Van der Heyden took in *An Architectural Fantasy*, c. 1670 (fig. 13). Here, instead of a freely rendered yet imaginary scene created from a composite of drawings made at different sites, Van der Heyden designed the entire composition from his imagination. The buildings and gardens surrounding them are completely fanciful. The composition's abstract character is evident in the mathematical precision of the underdrawing (fig. 14). Not only did Van der Heyden use a straightedge for every straight line and a compass for each circular shape, but these construction lines extend beyond buildings and into the sky as though he were establishing proportional relations among all the pictorial elements. Indeed, the design seems to be built on the ideal of the golden mean, with its fulcrum situated at the pinhole of the compass that he used to define the arched doorway of the gate in the lower right.

Jan van der Heyden, *View Down a Dutch Canal*, c. 1670 (cat. 11)

Fig. 12. Infrared reflectogram of Jan van der Heyden,
View Down a Dutch Canal, c. 1670 (cat. 11)

Fig. 13. Jan van der Heyden, *An Architectural Fantasy*, c. 1670,
oil on panel. National Gallery of Art, Washington, Ailsa Mellon
Bruce Fund, 1968.13.1

Fig. 14. Infrared reflectogram (detail) of fig. 13

Fig. 15. Infrared reflectogram (detail) of Gerrit Berckheyde, *The Grote or St. Bavokerk in Haarlem*, 1666 (cat. 118)

Gerrit Berckheyde, *The Grote or St. Bavokerk in Haarlem*, 1666 (cat. 118)

The differences in the approaches Van der Heyden took in designing *View of Oudezijds Voorburgwal with the Oude Kerk in Amsterdam*, *View Down a Dutch Canal*, and *An Architectural Fantasy* serve as a reminder that one must be careful about making too many generalized statements about artistic process on the basis of the few instances where reflectography has been successfully undertaken. While certain generalities may apply, one must assume that artists were not always consistent in their techniques.

Abstractions of reality such as those characteristic of Van der Heyden's paintings are not found in the work of Gerrit Berckheyde, who remained far truer to the physical character of the scenes he depicted than did his contemporary. Berckheyde made careful drawings of buildings and canals in Haarlem, Amsterdam, and The Hague, and he based many of his paintings on such studies. He was so interested in topographical accuracy that he even amended drawings at a later date when new buildings were constructed (cats. 119, 122). He also sought to portray the effects of sunlight at different times of the day by applying washes to his drawings to capture the impact of shadows on buildings and town squares. The strict geometry of Berckheyde's city views, and his devotion to following the laws of perspective, would seem to suggest that he made construction drawings. As with Van der Heyden, however, none exist.[17] It seems most likely that he made such preliminary designs only on the panels themselves.

Reinforcing this hypothesis is a reflectogram (fig. 15) of Berckheyde's imposing painting *The Grote or St. Bavokerk in Haarlem*, 1666 (cat. 118), where ruled construction lines and orthogonals demonstrate how carefully the artist designed the architectural elements. Much like Van der Heyden, he drew quick squiggles to indicate the foliage of the trees shading the vegetable market and did not draw the figures.

CONSTRUCTION DRAWINGS FOR
EARLY SEVENTEENTH-CENTURY
STILL-LIFE PAINTINGS

Infrared reflectography indicates that early seventeenth-century flower painters, particularly Ambrosius Bosschaert the Elder and his protégé Balthasar van der Ast, based many of their compositions on carefully conceived construction drawings, even though, yet again, none have survived. In *Bouquet of Flowers in a Glass Vase*, 1621 (cat. 12), for example, Bosschaert indicated the painting's central vertical axis, the tabletop, and the foreground plaque with ruled lines (fig. 16). He also made detailed underdrawings of all of his pictorial elements: leaves, blossoms, and insects.[18] The presence of this centering line as well as defined contour lines defining the shapes of the plants suggest that, like Saenredam, Bosschaert transferred a construction drawing onto the support.

Fig. 16. Infrared reflectogram of Ambrosius Bosschaert, *Bouquet of Flowers in a Glass Vase*, 1621 (cat. 12)

Ambrosius Bosschaert, *Bouquet of Flowers in a Glass Vase*, 1621 (cat. 12)

Another reason to conclude that Bosschaert used such drawings is that his bouquets generally include flowers that bloom at different times of the year. He must have composed his scenes by consulting drawings of individual plants he had put together in his portfolio. He likely also made counter-proofs of such drawings since the same blossoms occasionally appear in reverse in different paintings. Sadly, though, what must have been an extensive drawn oeuvre of individual blossoms and construction drawings is no longer extant.

Aside from drawings from life, Bosschaert consulted florilegia and model books such as Crispijn van de Passe II's *Hortus Floridus* (Utrecht, 1614). Van de Passe, who provided detailed instructions for coloring the images and lists more than thirty pigments that he believed were necessary to capture the great variety of colors found in blossoms, stems, and leaves, lived and worked in Utrecht,

where Bosschaert moved around 1616.[19] Van de Passe's publication was widely consulted and used as a model book by artists and designers, and images from his book have been pounced for transfer.[20] Interestingly, infrared reflectography seems to reveal pouncing in the white rose in one of Bosschaert's most beautiful paintings, *Bouquet of Flowers on a Ledge*, c. 1620, in the Los Angeles County Museum of Art, a blossom that is in many ways comparable to those in Van de Passe's florilegium.[21]

Like Bosschaert, underdrawings are visible in Van der Ast's paintings, sometimes with the naked eye, as in *Basket of Fruits*, c. 1622, in the National Gallery of Art, where distinctive contour lines define many of the fruits. Infrared reflectography has revealed that Van der Ast also used construction lines to center his compositions. Occasionally he used a ruler to draw large diagonals across the panel sur-

Fig. 17. Balthasar van der Ast, *A Still Life of Flowers in a Glass Vase*, 1624, oil on copper. Sarah Campbell Blaffer Foundation, Houston, BF.2007.4

Fig. 18. Infrared reflectography (detail) of fig. 17

face, and sometimes, as in his *Still Life of Flowers in a Glass Vase*, 1624 (fig. 17), he drew the horizontal and vertical axes of the composition before quickly rendering the leaves, stems, and blossoms of most of the plants (fig. 18).[22]

COMBINING UNDERDRAWINGS AND OIL SKETCHES IN LANDSCAPES AND GENRE PAINTINGS

One reason that Dutch theorists may not have stressed the importance of underdrawings is the emphasis they placed on capturing the immediacy of an artist's response to nature. A recommendation that an artist make a preliminary drawing on a painting's support would seem to distance the act of creation from a direct engagement with nature. This consideration may help place into a broader context Samuel van Hoogstraten's account in his treatise of 1678 about a contest among three landscape painters, Francois Knibbergen, Jan van Goyen, and Jan Porcellis, to see who could create the most naturalistic painting.[23]

In his chapter on the 'Handling or Manner of Painting,' Van Hoogstraten described how each of these masters constructed his painting, and in no instance does he mention the presence of an underdrawing. Van Hoogstraten writes that Knibbergen began at once to 'paint in such an accomplished fashion that everything he put on was at once finished. [All of the elements in his painting] were as though born from his paints.' Van Goyen, in contrast, worked 'in an entirely different way; by covering his whole panel at once, here light, there dark more or less like a variegated agate or marbled paper, he succeeded in creating various amusing drolleries, almost effortlessly, it would seem, with delicate touches. . . . In short, his eye, as though looking for forms that lay hidden in a chaos of paint, steered his hand and mind in true wise so that one saw a complete painting before one realized what he intended.' Last, Porcellis, who was judged the winner in this competition, stared for a long time at his panel before commencing to paint, 'first forming in his imagination the whole conception of his work.' In this way he was able to paint with 'well-chosen naturalness' that surpassed that of his competitors.[24] Whether such a contest ever occurred is unknown, but it could have taken place in The Hague around 1630, when all three artists were active in that city. Ernst van de Wetering has argued that Van Hoog-straten's descriptions of the artistic approaches of the three masters were related to an art theoretical topos: works created as a result of a preexisting 'Idea' (as by Porcellis) were superior to paintings conceived by 'Fortuna' (chance, as was the case with Van Goyen) or by 'Usus' (practice), in the manner of Knibbergen.[25] Van de Wetering rightly concludes that Van Hoogstraten's discussion of this artistic competition must be considered with caution: he may have slanted his text to support this theoretical argument.

The question of Van Goyen's method of painting is not straightforward. By the 1630s, the artist had, indeed, begun to design his compositions with freely rendered oil sketches, somewhat akin to the approach described by Van Hoogstraten. Nevertheless, Van Goyen also made rapid underdrawings in black chalk on his panels.[26] He painted his landscapes quite thinly, and much as in Pieter Molijn's *Landscape with Open Gate* (cat. 10), his quickly rendered black chalk lines are often visible through his translucent paint layers. These preliminary notations indicate basic

compositional elements of his works and are comparable to the numerous drawings he made in sketchbooks that he carried through the Dutch countryside.

By the 1630s, many Dutch artists, ranging from Dirck Hals (cats. 34, 35) to Rembrandt (cats. 59–67), had begun to block in their compositions with oil sketches rather than by composing them with underdrawings. For example, in her *Self-Portrait*, c. 1630 (fig. 19), Judith Leyster has shown herself with a completed oil sketch on the canvas on her easel, with the various colors of the final composition already indicated. Other artists began to combine these oil sketches with line underdrawings. The cottage scene on the easel in the delightful *Painter's Studio*, c. 1673 (fig. 20), by Adriaen van Ostade, is at a similar stage of completion. Here, however, the artist has painted fewer local colors on the prepared ground; instead, he has blocked in an ocher-colored oil sketch for the build-ing and deep green for the foliage, a layer comparable to the *doot-verf*, or blocking-in layer, mentioned by Van Mander. Certain contour lines on the cottage's façade suggest that Van Ostade gave further definition to this underlying oil sketch with a pen or fine brush.[27]

Fig. 19. Judith Leyster, *Self-Portrait*, c. 1630, oil on canvas. National Gallery of Art, Washington, Gift of Mr. and Mrs. Robert Woods Bliss, 1949.6.1

Fig. 20. Adriaen van Ostade, *The Painter's Studio*, c. 1673, oil on panel. Rijksmuseum, Amsterdam, SK-A-298.4

Technical examinations of the refined genre paintings of Frans van Mieris reveal that this Leiden *fijnschilder* worked in a similar manner, even though the subject matter and style of his paintings are totally different from those of Van Ostade. He seems to have started his paintings with a vigorous brush drawing and then elaborated on the details with thin lines. He also indicated shading with fine hatching. Even though Van Mieris did make preliminary drawings related to his paintings (cat. 114), the searching character of the brush and line modeling on his panels, along with the presence of construction lines, suggests that he used these drawings as points of reference but largely recomposed his scenes on his panel supports.[28]

Michiel van Musscher's *An Artist in His Studio with His Drawings,* which introduces this exhibition (cat. 13), provides a wonderful example of how Dutch artists integrated drawings and oil sketches in the creative process. Arrayed on the floor in front of the young painter are a number of elaborate drawings of ships on the open portfolio in which they have been preserved. Some of the longer, more horizontal sheets have folds so that they can fit comfortably within it. From this example one may deduce that the artist had not made these drawings specifically for the painting on the easel but that he had kept them in his portfolio for future use. It is also likely that he had made these careful drawings of ships from life and that he was incorporating these images into an invented landscape, perhaps an Italianate harbor. Van Musscher, however, does not show the artist in the process of translating these drawings directly to his painting support. Since he is mixing his paints with a palette knife and is holding brushes rather than a pen or a piece of chalk, he is clearly making a preliminary oil sketch, based on these drawings, that will serve as the foundation for his finished painting.

The approach to artistic creation suggested by Van Musscher's compelling painting, in which underdrawings and oil sketches were both instrumental in the painting process, seems to have been, with the exception of architectural painters such as Pieter Jansz Saenredam and Jan van der Heyden, the predominant way that Dutch artists worked after the early 1630s. The evidence of such an integrated working procedure ranges from the landscapes of Jan van Goyen to the refined genre paintings of Frans van Mieris. This approach allowed artists to use quick compositional drawings and careful figure drawings while also giving them the opportunity to exploit underlying tonalities to create deeper and richer harmonies and colors in their paintings. Although many questions remain about how Dutch artists used drawings in creating their paintings, recent investigations have revealed much about this aspect of artistic production. It is hoped that this exhibition will lead to an even deeper understanding of this fascinating story.

Michiel van Musscher, *An Artist in His Studio with His Drawings,* mid-1660s (cat. 13)

1. I thank Henriette Rahusen and Alexandra Libby for their thoughtful comments on this essay.

2. For a discussion of these early sources, see Amsterdam/Washington 1981, esp. 11–32.

3. Mander 1604, fols. 46v, 47r–v.

4. Mander 1604, fol. 46v, verse 4. For an excellent and thorough overview of materials used in underdrawings and different transfer techniques, particularly for fifteenth- and sixteenth-century northern European paintings, see Siejek and Kirsch 2004.

5. Many examples of the secrecy of Dutch artists could be cited, but see Houbraken 1718–1721, III, 81, for his musings about how Van der Heyden might have been able to paint such small and realistic-appearing bricks and mortar ('Waar omtrent men nu nog gelooft, dat hy een byzondere konstgreep, of middle heft uitgevonden gehad').

6. Infrared reflectography is an examination technique developed by J.R.J. van Asperen de Boer in the late 1960s. See Van Asperen de Boer 1970. In a forthcoming publication that Elma O'Donoghue, associate painting conservator at the Los Angeles County Museum of Art, has kindly shared with me, she writes that although 'the range of infrared is very wide, only a small portion (850 to 2000 nanometers [nm]) is useful for detecting underdrawings in paintings.' She also stresses that the upper paint layers have to be (somewhat) transparent in the infrared range of the IR (infrared) camera for an underdrawing to be visible.

7. Van Asperen de Boer understood the challenges of investigating seventeenth-century Dutch paintings with infrared reflectography, but he also felt that this examination technique could yield important results with certain artists, particularly Pieter Saenredam. See Van Asperen de Boer 1971.

8. Kloek 2005, 50. Kloek postulates that the drawings on this sheet, which relate to one of his early paintings, were made by an apprentice and not by the master. He writes: 'If Steen had studied all the elements of his work beforehand in this way, it would mean that literally thousands of drawings must have been lost. This is not likely.'

9. Palmer and Gifford 1997, 131–135. See also Kloek 2005, 54–55.

10. Arie Wallert, 'The Miracle of Gerard ter Borch's Satin,' in Washington/Detroit 2004, 35–36, discusses a possible scenario for a transfer process for a drawn template onto the support. That Ter Borch also rendered the dresses at different scales was discovered only during the course of that exhibition.

11. Saenredam depicted the four sons of Aymon of Dordogne as graffiti on a wall in the foreground of *The Interior of the Buurkerk at Utrecht*, 1644, oil on panel, National Gallery, London. Many interpretations have been advanced for explaining its appearance in that painting. For an overview, see Utrecht 2001, 201–202, cat. 40, esp. n. 6.

12. The inscription on the bandura in the emblem *Kinderspel* by Adriaen van de Venne in Jacob Cats, *Houwelijk*, 1642, reads: 'Ex nugis seria,' meaning 'From trifles, serious matters.' The accompanying text reads, in translation, 'Play, even if it appears without sense, contains a whole world therein.'

13. See Edinburgh 1984, 34–35, figs. 9, 10. For further discussion of Saenredam's drawings for this painting, see the entry to cats. 52–54.

14. Ariane van Suchtelen, 'Jan van der Heyden,' in The Hague/Washington 2008, 128, cat. 24. See also Houbraken 1718–1721, III, 81: 'Gewoon was, alles naar 't leven af te teekenen, om het naderhand op paneel te brengen.'

15. Information kindly provided by Petria Noble (pers. comm., October 13, 2015), who examined the painting in 2008 with infrared reflectography (with an Artist camera, 900–1,000nm) during her treatment of the painting at the Mauritshuis.

16. Although no drawing of the church at Veere is extant, Van der Heyden must have made one. The same church, seen from the same point of view, is shown in the artist's earlier painting *The Church of Veere*, n.d., oil on canvas, Royal Picture Gallery, Mauritshuis, The Hague.

17. See the discussion of Berckheyde, cats. 118–125.

18. The central axis was also discovered through infrared reflectography of the Rijksmuseum painting, *Still Life with Flowers in a Wan-li Vase*, 1619, oil on copper. See Wallert 1999, 48–51.

19. Van de Passe even suggested ways of giving some blossoms a glossy appearance by adding gum to the medium. For an excellent discussion of Van de Passe's recommendations for coloring the images in his book, see Murray and Groen 1994, 7–9.

20. A number of images in a copy of Van de Passe's book in the Folger Shakespeare Library, Washington, have been stippled for transfer. For a discussion of this matter, see Washington 1999, 28.

21. This information was kindly shared with me by Elma O'Donoghue, associate painting conservator at the Los Angeles County Museum of Art.

22. Murray and Groen 1994, 18, fig. 10.

23. Hoogstraten 1678, 237–238.

24. These translations from the Dutch are from Wetering 2000, 82–86.

25. Wetering 2000, 86.

26. Melanie Gifford, 'Jan van Goyen en de techniek van het naturalistische landschap,' in Leiden 1996, 76.

27. Van Ostade's *Painter's Studio* provides firm evidence that Dutch artists did not paint their landscapes from nature. The presence of a sketchbook on the floor near the artist's easel indicates that he likely derived the motif for his painting from images drawn from life, although he is not actively consulting any drawings while executing his painting. Indeed, one can imagine that Van Ostade, just like Paulus Potter, took such sketchbooks with him on his walks, jotting down whatever he found intriguing or enjoyable and would serve his purpose. See Houbraken 1753, II, 129.

28. Carol Pottash, 'Underdrawings in the Paintings of Frans van Mieris,' in The Hague/Washington 2005, 62–68.

Fig. 1. Pieter Codde (attributed), *The Young Artist*, c. 1630, oil on panel. Koninklijk Museum voor Schone Kunsten, Brussels, 4411

Fig. 2. Moses ter Borch, *Cast of Samson and the Philistine after Michelangelo*, c. 1657, brush and black ink, black chalk. Rijksmuseum, Amsterdam, RP-T-1887-A-1126

REASONS FOR DRAWING IN SEVENTEENTH-CENTURY HOLLAND

Ger Luijten

In an engaging painting attributed to Pieter Codde, we see a youthful artist, bare-headed and squatting on a low stool, examining his drawing of the Michelangelo-inspired plaster cast of the figure group *Samson and the Philistine* (fig. 1). His drawing paper lies on a firm cardboard base, and the three-dimensional model stands on the table before him. Other casts, as well as a lute, are in the room, and sheets of paper are strewn here and there.[1] The young man may be at the start of a career, but whether he was being trained as an artist is open to question: drawing was often part of the general curriculum for children. We know how this boy's drawing might have looked because one was actually made by Moses ter Borch at about the age of twelve (fig. 2).[2] Alongside various other drawings of classical and Renaissance sculpture, Moses made copies of prints by Rembrandt, Albrecht Dürer, Abraham Bloemaert, and Annibale Carracci, studies of horses, and lovingly executed portraits of his parents and other members of his family. He also made self-portraits with facial expressions practiced in the mirror (fig. 3).[3] Among his drawings are compositions with narrative scenes of his own invention—highly appropriate in the light of his name—*The Finding of Moses*, *The Judgment of Solomon*, the *Annunciation*, and more.[4] Moses's father, Gerard ter Borch the Elder, was always careful to preserve the studies made by his children. The estate of the Ter Borches—a dynasty of artists—was also treasured by later heirs and gives us a window on how drawing was taught in the seventeenth century.

Moses ter Borch was the son of an artist trained in drawing, unlike Constantijn Huygens, whose father could not draw but realized that drawing and painting—knowledge and understanding of it and also its practice as such—should be an essential part of an ideal education. Baldassare Castiglione had already stressed this in *The Book of the Courtier* (1528).[5] Undergirding the conviction that drawing was important lay the belief that it intensified the process of looking. An added advantage was that

someone with a trained drawing hand would benefit when wishing to record something while studying physics and mathematics.[6]

Huygens devotes a passage in his autobiography to his drawing training (around 1611). The overstretched Jacques de Gheyn was approached in vain, so Hendrick

Fig. 3. Moses ter Borch, *Self-Portrait with Open Mouth*, c. 1660, black chalk, some dark brown wash, heightened with white chalk, on blue paper. Rijksmuseum, Amsterdam, RP-T-1887-A-1063

Hondius became his teacher in The Hague. Huygens gave a shrewd account of Hondius's shortcomings as a draftsman, but he was nonetheless happy with Hondius's method of getting his pupils 'to draw the limbs of the human body one by one, life-size or slightly enlarged. Then he taught us to make combinations and to make a well-rounded composition, first of a child, then of an adult, and finally of a group of three or four people on a single sheet.' Huygens continued: 'My further progress can easily be illustrated, to my satisfaction, by the examples collected in my sketchbooks.'[7] None of these sketchbooks has survived, underscoring our awareness that a great deal of material that would have provided insight into how and what people drew in seventeenth-century Holland has been lost.

The motto *Nulla dies sine linea* (No day without a line), derived from Pliny's life of the classical painter Apelles, was popular in Holland in the seventeenth century. It was illustrated in emblem books like Justus Reifenberg's *Emblemata Politica* (fig. 4) and cited by Philips Angel in his *Lof der Schilder-Konst* (In praise of the art of painting,

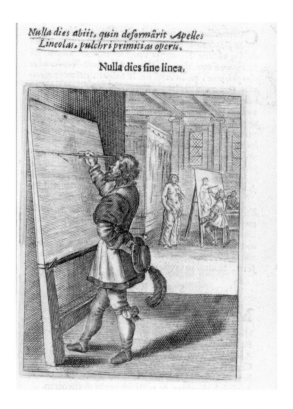

Fig. 4. *Nulla dies sine linea*, emblem from Justus Reifenberg, *Emblemata Politica* (Amsterdam, 1632). Fondation Custodia, Collection Frits Lugt, Paris, OBL-725

1642), in which Angel urges artists to draw every day: 'Never may a day pass by when a line is not drawn.'[8] In a collection of emblems by Gabriel Rollenhagen, dated 1612, a hand holds a pen, simply drawing a line; in *Van 't Light der Teken en Schilder Konst* (On the light of the arts of drawing and painting, 1643), Crispijn van de Passe II chose a hand drawing, distilling the essence of the motto.[9] In Reifenberg, a painter is at work on a canvas, and in a late seventeenth-century drawing that recently appeared on the market, bearing the inscription 'Geen dag zonder trek' (No day without drawing), we see Apelles at an easel, illustrating the motto (fig. 5).

The highest objective of the arts was to depict biblical and mythological stories, and countless painters aspired to this goal. The result was numerous drawings exploring a narrative subject, as Rembrandt must have repeatedly asked his various pupils to do. Hundreds of these drawings have survived, and they are part of this exhibition precisely because they show how artists drew for their paintings. Many of these drawings show small steps in the whole—studies of a hand, hands folded in prayer, a leg—elements that we can find in a subsequent painting. But mature, fully finished composition drawings in which a moment in a story has taken shape, such as Moses ter Borch's *Finding of Moses*, are in a category of their own. One exercise in Rembrandt's workshop must have been

Fig. 5. Anonymous, late seventeenth century, *Geen dag sonder trek,* pen and gray ink, gray wash. Fondation Custodia, Collection Frits Lugt, Paris, 2016-T.19

to draw an episode from a Bible story—a story that pupils and master may have read together. The idea was to create a deepened sense of the story and give the pupils a feeling for the staging, composition, and emotional dimension of a moment. During such a session Rembrandt most likely drew with his pupils. Something of the essence of this element of his teaching becomes clear when we compare various drawings by him and his pupils. In the strictest sense these are not drawings for paintings but exercises to stimulate the imagination (figs. 6, 7).[10]

Some years ago, a group of chalk drawings by the Haarlem artist Pieter de Grebber came to light. Carefully

executed, finished compositional drawings on blue paper, they appear to be a sort of catalog of motifs that could be ordered from him as paintings—drawings as *vidimus:* see, this is what I can do for you in oils. All that remained to be agreed on was the size, for that determined the number of hours needed for the painting (fig. 8).[11] The finished compositions by Moses ter Borch, Willem Drost, Carel Fabritius, and Pieter de Grebber have a certain kinship, but the intentions behind their creation were different. And this brings us to the question of the functions of drawings in the seventeenth century.[12]

Why people drew is difficult to answer, but the types and functions of drawing are much broader than the

Fig. 6. Willem Drost, *Eliezer and Rebecca at the Well,* c. 1650–1655, pen and brown ink, brown wash, and white gouache. Maida and George Abrams Collection, Fogg Art Museum, Harvard University, Cambridge, Massachusetts, 1999.136

Fig. 7. Carel Fabritius, *Eliezer and Rebecca at the Well,* c. 1640–1645, pen and brown ink, brown and gray wash, heightened with white, over black chalk. Fondation Custodia, Collection Frits Lugt, Paris, 9629

Fig. 8. Pieter de Grebber, *Christ among the Doctors,* black chalk on blue paper, heightened with white. Private Collection

focus chosen for this exhibition might suggest. A great many works of art in various techniques were conceived, considered, and designed with the aid of drawings. Sculptures are a case in point. As we have seen, drawing sculpture—from famous Renaissance statues to classical examples—was regarded as a fundamental exercise. Amateurs who made drawings of this kind often achieved impressive results. One such was Jan de Bisschop (fig. 9), who published a book of prints of statues to give Dutch art a classical foundation.[13]

Sculptors themselves studied the work of contemporaries and predecessors with great interest, as is evident in a drawing of a statue of a crucified, naked Christ with a strong emphasis on musculature and anatomy (fig. 10). Beside the figure's fully worked out arm, the draftsman wrote 'dit aldus': so, like this. This note, the careful and detailed mise-en-page of the studies, and the sculptor's need to record the statue from different vantage points reveal the importance given to the thorough understanding of the figure. Although the concept of 'sculpture drawing' was not used at the time with any consistency, this unpublished sheet is a telling example.[14] We know of only ten drawings by Adriaen de Vries, one of the most important sculptors of his generation, but these give us some idea of how he prepared his three-dimensional designs on paper.[15] These drawings betray the unmistakable influence of Bartholomeus Spranger and Hendrick Goltzius. The individual figures and figure groups of mythological personages he defined with bold outlines. He tried out the positions of the figures one to another, as, for instance, in *Hercules and the Centaur Fighting* of about 1615 (fig. 11).[16] Although the sculptor Hendrick de Keyser left no known drawings for statues, a small signed portrait drawing in profile may well be a self-portrait—with two mirrors it is possible to capture your own profile—and could have been a design for a relief portrait or a medallion (fig. 12).[17]

Trained artists were often asked to make drawings for tapestries and stained glass windows.[18] The large dimensions

Fig. 9. Jan de Bisschop, *Crouching Venus*, pen and brown ink, brown wash. Fondation Custodia, Collection Frits Lugt, Paris, 6696

Fig. 10. Anonymous, Dutch school, *Studies of Christ on the Cross*,
pen and brown ink, brown wash. Private Collection

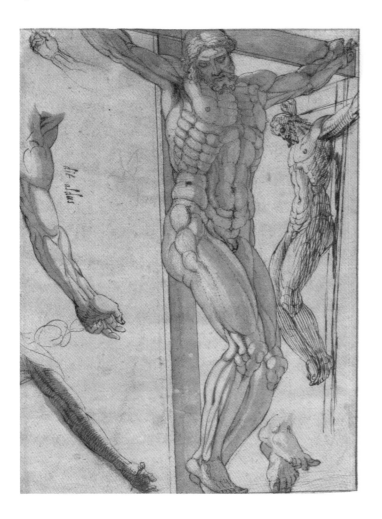

Fig. 12. Hendrick de Keyser, *Self-Portrait*, pen and brown ink.
Pierpont Morgan Library, New York, 2001.17

Fig. 11. Adriaen de Vries, *Hercules and the Centaur Fighting*,
c. 1615, pen and brown ink, brown wash. Szépművészeti
Múzeum, Budapest, 379

Fig. 13. Pieter Lastman, *King Cyrus Returns the Treasures
of the Temple*, 1611, pen and brown ink, brown wash.
Staatliche Museen, Berlin, Kupferstichkabinett, KDZ 3793

Fig. 14. Pieter Jansz, *Design for a Stained Glass Window*, pen and
brown ink, brown wash over a sketch in red chalk. Fondation
Custodia, Collection Frits Lugt, Paris, 3953

of such works made it necessary to create cartoons for
the craftsmen to work from. This working procedure
was an established tradition in the sixteenth-century
Northern Netherlands and is well documented in the
records of commissions, particularly those for the Sint-
Janskerk (Church of St. John) in Gouda.[19] A number
of seventeenth-century examples exist, including the
windows in Amsterdam's Zuiderkerk, for which David
Vinckboons and Pieter Lastman, and possibly Joachim
Anthonisz Wtewael, all made designs.[20] The finished
drawings by Vinckboons and Lastman can be regarded

as a vidimus, presented to the clients for approval, here
the guild of tanners and cobblers and the goldsmiths'
guild, respectively. Lastman's drawing of *King Cyrus
Returns the Treasures of the Temple* (fig. 13) shows that he
had divided the window into compartments in anticipation of the work in the stained-glass artist's workshop.[21]
The stained glass was removed from the church around
1658, either because it took away too much light, as
one eighteenth-century historian believed, or, perhaps
more likely, because orthodox Calvinists objected to the
insistent presence of Old Testament scenes. Thanks to

Fig. 15. Nicolaes Berchem, *Air*, from a series of *The Elements*, 1658, black chalk, black and gray wash. Albertina, Vienna, 9824

Fig. 16. Gerbrand van den Eeckhout, *Design for the Title-Page of 'Verscheyde Aerdige Compartementen en Tafels,'* 1655, black chalk, gray wash. École Nationale Supérieure des Beaux-Arts, Paris, Mas.2511

a 1660 painting by Thomas de Keyser in the Fondation Custodia, we have an idea of what the window looked like.[22]

Many stained-glass artists were proficient at drawing in their own right, men like the Haarlem-born Jan van Bouchorst and Pieter Jansz. Jansz made designs for stained glass that he executed in glass himself (fig. 14). He also had an ingenious way of drawing cartouches for decorating maps, atlas pages, and the title pages of books.[23] In the description of a cover in the collection of the renowned Amsterdam art dealer Jan Pietersz Zomer dating from about 1720 we read: 'A cover in which lie 136 fine decorative and finished compartments, with many images, nicely pictured, and 90 excellent drawings, comprising many histories, symbols, and witty scribbles, in all sorts, many also with fine washes, by Mr. Pieter Jansz, skilled stained-glass artist, also with colors.'[24] Other artists, among them David Vinckboons, Adriaen van de Velde, Nicolaas Berchem, and Gerard de Lairesse, created drawings for map publishers.[25] Berchem, for instance, supplied Nicolaes Visscher with four drawings of allegories of the elements, with cleverly conceived iconography, for a map of the world that saw the light of day in 1658 (fig. 15).[26] The word 'Compartementen'—compartments—appears on the title page of a set of ornament prints with auricular cartouches by Pieter Hendricksz Schut, published in 1655, to a design by Rembrandt's pupil Gerbrand van den Eeckhout; the drawing for it has survived (fig. 16).[27] This set was also published by Visscher, whose name is referenced by the prominently placed fisherman.[28]

These examples lead us to the domain of designs for decorative and applied art, in which models and proto-types were often distributed by way of ornament prints. A design was produced in print first, and wide circulation ensured that it had an influence. We have to assume that, almost without exception, all of these ornament prints were based on drawings—a fundamental function of drawing in the seventeenth century. Superb examples from the first half of the century can be found in a large album in the British Museum. It contains collected sheets by the silversmith Arent van Bolten with designs for cartouches, tazze, tableware, and the like, as well as highly inventive drolleries, some of which also appeared in print (fig. 17).[29] A group of bronze fantasy figures—grotesques—is clearly related to these drawings and prints, but whether Van Bolten, who worked in Zwolle, made them remains unclear.[30]

Some designs for decorative art objects involved major artists, as with the important design for a salt, dated 1603 or 1608, by the painter Joachim Anthonisz Wtewael (fig. 18). It demonstrates just how refined and elegant silversmithing was in Utrecht at the time of mannerism.[31] Adam van Vianen worked in the same milieu, while his brother Paulus tried his luck abroad and was attached to the court of Rudolph II in Prague.[32] Paulus had a gift for drawing landscapes and woodland—figures, too— and drawings by him survive that are connected with his work as a silversmith: bridges and stands of trees, poses of biblical and mythological figures, and finished designs like the one for the 1607 *Judgment of Paris* tazza in the Rijksmuseum.[33] The circular drawing for the tazza was closely followed in the positioning of the figures and the structure of the composition, though the extensive washes make it hard to say whether Paulus had also planned out in advance how the relief would go (fig. 19).[34] There are a number of sheets in Stockholm by other members of the Van Vianen silversmithing dynasty, Adam or Christiaen, of the type that we have to assume were made in vast numbers: working drawings in which the ornament is worked out in precise detail, drawings with an aesthetic all their own (fig. 20).[35] Salomon de Bray made designs for silver dishes and a drinking horn with evident delight.[36] Architects like Jacob van Campen and Pieter Post made meticulously worked out drawings for churches, town halls, and houses and sometimes branched out to related areas. Post, for example, was involved in building a States yacht, supplying designs of an uncommon type (fig. 21).[37]

Then, as now, most of what we use every day and gather around us, including the most prosaic objects, was drawn first: cutlery, clothespins, plates, buckets, brooms, tables, cupboards, and chairs were all based on drawn

Fig. 17. Arent van Bolten, *Grotesque*, pen and brown ink, brown wash. British Museum, London, SL 5217.156

Fig. 18. Joachim Anthonisz Wtewael, *Design for a Salt*, 1603 or 1608, black ink, gray wash, and white body color, on gray-prepared paper. British Museum, London, 1872, 1012.3322

Fig. 19. Paulus Willemsz van Vianen, *The Judgment of Paris*, c. 1607, pen and brown ink, brown wash, traces of red wash. École Nationale Supérieure des Beaux-Arts, Paris, Mas.705

Fig. 20. Adam or Christiaen van Vianen, *Design for Part of a Tazza*, pen and brown ink, black chalk, on brown paper. Nationalmuseum, Stockholm, NIMH 131/1973

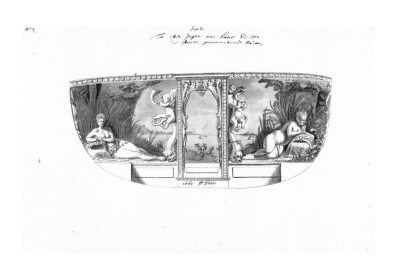

Fig. 21. Pieter Post, *Interior Decoration for the Statenjacht van Holland*, 1663, pen and gray ink, gray wash, watercolor. Rijksmuseum, Amsterdam, RP-T-1976-3

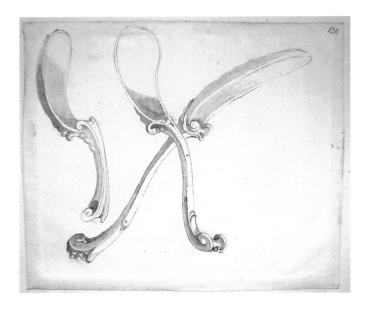

Fig. 22. Arent van Bolten, *Designs for Spoons*, pen and brown ink, gray wash, over black chalk. British Museum, London, SL, 5217.130

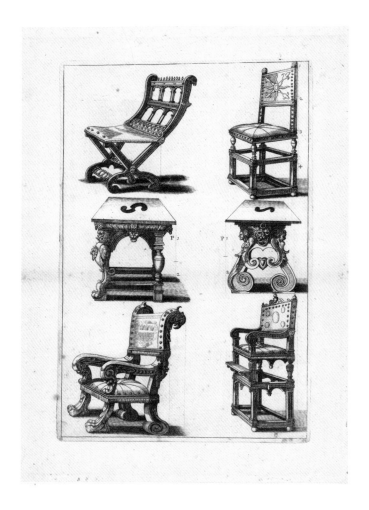

Fig. 23. Anonymous, after Crispijn van de Passe II, *Six Chairs and Three Stools*, 1621, etching. Rijksmuseum, Amsterdam, RP-P-1964-3315

prototypes. One finds, for example, drawings of spoons by Arent van Bolten (fig. 22) and designs published in print form for knife handles and candlesticks, for gold, silver, and brass fittings, and for watch faces, carved coats of arms, and patterns for gold leather. Specialist fields include staircases, fireplaces, and garden designs with the indispensable ornamental urns, not to mention the architecture itself. Drawn models turned into prints served as inspiration for artists and craftsmen. Peter Fuhring's three-volume *Ornament Prints in the Rijksmuseum: The Seventeenth Century* (2004) is a superb means of accessing this material, which is dizzying in its creativity and in the whirling, writhing interplay of lines that dominate the prints.[38] In 1621 (Utrecht), 1642 (Amsterdam), and 1651 (Amsterdam), the twenty copper plates of furniture and ornament by Crispijn van de Passe II hit the presses. Beneath the title *Oficina Arcularia* on the title page is a subtitle in Dutch that explains the idea behind the publication. We are presented with a catalog for furniture makers of chairs and cupboards, beds and cartouches. The chair models remained in fashion throughout the seventeenth century (fig. 23).[39]

The category of designs for cartography and ornament prints brings us to a fundamental function of drawing in the seventeenth century—the preliminary stage in the production of prints. The output of woodcuts, engravings, and etchings as independent works and as illustrations in books was so vast that it is almost impossible to comprehend the importance of supplying preliminary drawings for such works.[40] The demand for prints was stimulated in the sixteenth century by Antwerp print publishers like Hieronymus Cock and Gerard de Jode and book publishers like Christoffel Plantijn and Johannes Moretus.[41] Cock invited Pieter Bruegel the Elder, along with Frans Floris, Lambert Lombard, and Maarten van Heemskerck, to make drawings that would be turned into prints. Other established

Fig. 24. David Vinckboons, *Beggars Carousing*, 1608, pen and brown ink, brown wash. Ashmolean Museum, Oxford, WA.1863.218

painters, such as Johannes Stradanus and Maarten de Vos, supplied hundreds of often iconographically sophisticated and detailed drawings that professional engravers then transferred to copper plates.

Painters who made their own prints also used drawn designs to transfer onto their copper plates. The number of drawings made as models for professional engravers or etchers in the seventeenth century is well-nigh infinite. The generation of Claes Jansz Visscher and David Vinckboons made many drawings specifically designed to be turned into prints. Vinckboons's *Beggars Carousing* (fig. 24), which was converted into an etching by Pieter Serwouters in 1608, is a good example.[42] The print denounces the behavior of beggars who pretend that they need money to survive and then spend it in the evening. They throw their sticks aside and dance, enjoying the food and drink served at the inn. The figures to the side, sitting near the gate, are also beggars. They have started to search

one another for lice. Beggars and lice were proverbially linked, as, for instance, in the saying 'Be kind to a beggar and you'll be rewarded with lice.'[43] The two protagonists strolling toward the church in the background may be the antithesis of the carousing beggars, instead representing down-and-outs who have been reduced to begging through no fault of their own. The print tackles a key theme in the seventeenth-century worldview: charity is a great boon, but the honesty of someone asking for alms is not always what it seems. Serwouters followed the drawing faithfully, other than that it is more obviously evening in the print.

Some preliminary drawings are very linear, with heavily emphasized outlines, as if to make things easier for the printmaker, as in Willem Buytewech's drawing of *Summer*, with fully laden hay wagons and countryfolk walking through the landscape (fig. 25).[44] Gillis van Scheyndel, who turned this drawing into a print, filled in the shadows and added gradations of tone in the pattern of lines, so

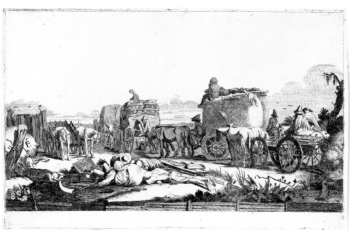

Fig. 25. Willem Buytewech, *Summer*, c. 1622, pen and brown ink, black chalk. Staatliche Museen, Berlin, Kupferstichkabinett, KDZ 11745

Fig. 26. Gillis van Scheyndel, after Willem Buytewech, *Summer*, 1622, etching and engraving. British Museum, London, s.5914

that the print looks much richer than the drawing from which it was taken (fig. 26).[45] Jan van de Velde the Younger, who also worked from Buytewech's drawings, made a huge number of landscape prints of his own invention. In those cases where preparatory drawings by his own hand have survived, it is striking that they could be less linear and built up with washes. Perhaps this was all he needed to work up the design on the plate, as we see in the fluidly executed *Landscape with Ruins and a Monumental Gateway* (fig. 27), the title page for a series of landscape etchings.[46]

A number of *peintres-graveurs* were accustomed to making preparatory drawings for their etchings. In 1640, for example, Rembrandt made a powerful red chalk study for his etching *Portrait of Cornelis Claesz Anslo* (fig. 28). He scored the outlines on the drawing to transfer the figure to the copper plate in the correct proportions. In this masterly drawing he was studying both the likeness of the minister and his pose. In this period Rembrandt also painted a portrait in which Anslo turns movingly toward his wife, Aeltje Gerritsdr Schouten (Gemäldegalerie, Berlin). Before embarking on the painting, he made a pen-and-ink study in which he focused on expressing the

Fig. 27. Jan van de Velde the Younger, *Landscape with Ruins and a Monumental Gateway*, 1616, pen and brown ink, blue and brown wash, traces of black chalk. Museum Boijmans Van Beuningen, Rotterdam, H 175

vitality of the model and the surface and texture of the fabrics in the clothes.[47]

Adriaen van Ostade's *Peasant Kermis* is another example of an artist making a preparatory drawing for his own etching (fig. 29).[48] In the sixteenth century, pictures of this subject were often composed from a perspective that gave the impression that the viewer was observing the scene from a distance. Here, however, Van Ostade has chosen a vantage point very close to the action, as if to suggest that we are among the revelers. Van Ostade borrowed this conceit from an etching by Jan van de Velde. When we compare the drawing and the print, created some forty years earlier, one sees that the logs in the foreground are in the same place, that the houses and church tower are in the same position, and the distribution of the figures is similar.[49] Despite the connection to Van de Velde's prototype, Van Ostade carefully crafted his drawing so that he could sell it as a work of art in its own right.

The market for drawings grew rapidly in the seventeenth century, but collectors continued to admire drawings of varying degrees of finish.[50] Elaborated drawings and watercolors by Adriaen van Ostade were sought-after collectibles, as were a great many other worked-up drawings of that period, including colored landscapes by Philips Koninck. Gouaches with imaginary subjects and cityscapes by Gerrit Battem that look like

Fig. 28. Rembrandt Harmensz van Rijn, *Portrait of Cornelis Claesz Anslo*, 1640, red chalk with some red wash, heightened in oil. British Museum, London, 1848, 0911.138

Fig. 29. Adriaen van Ostade, *Peasant Kermis*, c. 1670, pen and black and brown ink over black chalk, brown and gray wash. Fondation Custodia, Collection Frits Lugt, Paris, 8233

Fig. 30. Gerrit Battem, *View of Rotterdam from the North*, c. 1665,
gouache. Albertina, Vienna, 10789

Fig. 31. Anthonie Waterloo, *View of the Sint-Antoniessluis in
Amsterdam*, c. 1670, black chalk, gray wash. Amsterdam Museum,
A10370

Fig. 32. Bartholomeus Breenbergh, *Ruins of the Villa Maecenas in Tivoli*, 1627, pen and brown ink, brown wash over a sketch in black chalk. Fondation Custodia, Collection Frits Lugt, Paris, 3032

small paintings were highly regarded, as, for example, Battem's *View of Rotterdam from the North* (fig. 30).[51] More sketchlike renditions of a topographical subject, a place in the world, were also popular. One such, without doubt, is Anthonie Waterloo's superb drawing of a *View of the Sint-Antoniessluis in Amsterdam* (fig. 31).[52] We see the lock surrounded by trees and in the distance the step gable of the first house in Sint-Antoniebreestraat, next door to the house Rembrandt bought (now the Rembrandt House Museum). At that time this knowledge added nothing to the importance of the large sheet, but a location could contribute to the value of a drawing, as in the case of the *Ruins of the Villa Maecenas in Tivoli*, by Bartholomeus Breenbergh (fig. 32). According to the inscription on the verso it had once belonged to the artist Philips Koninck, who wrote: 'This is a prime drawing by Bredenberg. Anyone who does not buy it as that makes an incorrect calculation. Philips Koning Ao. 1680.'[53] This is proof, were it needed, that a drawing such as this was highly sought after in collectors' circles, as Koninck himself also was. The way Breenbergh signed his drawings suggests

that he was making them with a view to the burgeoning market for drawings.[54] Exactly what seventeenth-century buyers valued in a drawing is not clear: a recognizable motif, if it was a picture of an informal corner of an insignificant farmyard, or the distinctive hand of a maker who could transform a group of trees into something typical, something that was unmistakably connected to his style.[55]

Countless portrait drawings were obviously made as works in their own right—as the drawn equivalent of a painted likeness. Among the specialists in this field were Johannes Thopas and Pieter Cornelis van Slingelandt, but artists like Albert Cuyp, who owed his fame to art of an entirely different kind, also produced impressive drawn likenesses.[56] The same applies to the portrait drawings by the Haarlem artist Leendert van der Cooghen, which are of a rare precision (fig. 33).[57]

In seventeenth-century Holland there were far more reasons to draw than as preparations for paintings. It was a culture in which people appreciated the quality of drawings as much as of paintings. Even though they valued and collected drawings on a large scale, a large number have regrettably been lost. We simply have to accept this in reconstructing the artistic reality of the era. Many drawings were not even made on paper but on a white wall in the studio, as we can see in *Young Painter in a Workshop* by Barent Fabritius, where we also find a sheet of paper with a sketch tacked to the wall as working material, a piece not likely to have survived (fig. 34).[58] Fortunately, there is a magnificent record of the dialogue about drawing and of how albums were used in the formation of a painting in a work attributed to Pieter Codde in which two people converse in a studio (fig. 35). One of the figures, likely an artist, enveloped in a smock with an album of drawings in his lap, is speaking. We can never know what they are discussing, but the painting is a fine testimony to the circumstances in which such a conversation—right there in an artist's workshop—would have occurred. It is a conversation that we keep alive by reflecting on the reasons why drawings were made at the time that this painting was created.[59]

Fig. 34. Detail of Barent Fabritius, *Young Painter in a Workshop*, c. 1655, oil on panel, Musée du Louvre, Paris, R.F. 1993-17

Fig. 33. Leendert van der Cooghen, *Portrait of a Girl or a Boy*, c. 1665, black chalk. Städel Museum, Frankfurt, 3342

1. For this painting, see Plietzsch 1960, 30, fig. 21, and Pauwels 1984, 61.
2. Kettering 1988, I, 308–309, no. M 41.
3. Kettering 1988, I, 286–351; for the *Self-Portrait* pictured, see 338–339, no. M 103.
4. On *The Finding of Moses*, see Kettering 1988, 350–351, no. M 129.
5. Castiglione 1980, 96–101. For the widespread fame of *Il Cortegiano* in Europe, see Burke 1995. Allan Ellenius examined the role painting took on in children's upbringing in the sixteenth and seventeenth centuries; see Ellenius 1960, 223–263.
6. See Huygens 1987, 72, and Frans Blom in his annotation of the translation of Huygens's autobiography, Huygens 2003, II, 62–63.

Fig. 35. Pieter Codde (attributed), *An Artist and Another Man in Conversation in a Workshop*, c. 1630, oil on panel. Fondation Custodia, Collection Frits Lugt, Paris, 7335

7. 'Om de ledematen van het menselijk lichaam stuk voor stuk op ware grootte of iets vergroot te laten uittekenen. Daarna leerde hij ons combinaties te maken en tot een afgeronde voorstelling te komen, eerst van een kind, dan van een volwasse-ne en tenslotte tot een groepje van drie of vier personen op één vel'; 'Mijn verdere vorderingen laten zich tot mijn voldoening gemakkelijk illustreren aan de hand van de voorbeelden die in mijn schetsboeken bijeengebracht zijn'; Huygens 1987, 72.

8. Reifenberg 1632, 51. 'Dat noyt dach voor-by mach gaen, Of daer wordt een trek gedaen'; Angel 1642, 57–58.

9. Rollenhagen 1613, no. 24; see Rollen-hagen 1983, 260–261. Passe 1643, 13; for his drawing book, see cat. 5.

10. For Willem Drost's version, see Green-wich 2011, 118–119, no. 40. And for the drawing attributed to Carel Fabritius in the Fondation Custodia, see Schatborn 2010a, 199–202, no. 77; see also Amster-dam 2014, 69, no. 18, for a related drawing attributed to Fabritius with the same in Edinburgh, Scottish National Gallery, inv. D1338. For a series of confrontations between drawings by Rembrandt and those of his pupils, see Los Angeles 2009.

11. There is a similar drawing in the Rijksmuseum; see Schapelhouman and Schatborn 1998, I, 95, no. 202, and Andrews 1984.

12. For an initial analysis of drawings in the sixteenth century, see William W. Robin-son and Martha Wolff, 'The Functions of Drawings in the Netherlands in the Six-teenth Century,' in Washington/New York 1986, 25–40, and Ger Luijten, 'Functions of Drawing,' in Paris/Rotterdam/Washing-ton 2014, 28–32.

13. Gelder 1972, 19, fig. 56. See Gelder and Jost 1985, I, 164–166, nos. 78–80. De Biss-chop drew the statue from three different angles and included it in his *Signorum Veterum Icones* (1668–1669). See also Shoaf Turner and White 2014, I, 30–31, nos. 23.9, 23.10.

14. See Boston 2014.

15. Thomas DaCosta Kaufmann in Amster-dam/Stockholm/Los Angeles 1999, 84–89, 248–267, nos. 45–55.

16. Amsterdam/Stockholm/Los Angeles

1999, 262–263, no. 52; Gerszi and Tóth 2012, 149–150, no. 56.

17. Shoaf Turner 2006, I, no. 110.

18. For tapestry, the six surviving designs for subjects from the Eighty Years' War by Leonaert Bramer are a good example; see Schapelhouman and Schatborn 1998, I, 28–30, nos. 59a–e, with literature on the sixth design in the city archives in Leiden.

19. For the cartoons made for the Sint-Janskerk in Gouda, see Ruyven-Zeman 2011b.

20. See Marijn Schapelhouman in Amsterdam 1993b, 571–572, no. 244.

21. Peter Schatborn in Amsterdam 1993b, 572–573, no. 245; Berlin 2011, 51–52, no. 29.

22. Hans Buijs in The Hague 2002, 110–115, no. 17 with ill.

23. Schapelhouman 1985; see also Von Oven 1992 and Ruyven-Zeman 2009. For the drawing illustrated here, see Schapelhouman 1985, 74–75, fig. 3; for the window, see Ruyven-Zeman 2011a, I, 336.

24. 'Een Omslagje daar in leggen 136 Aardige Sierade en Uytgevoerde Compartementjes, in meenigte Verbeeldinge, net uytgebeeld, en 90 stuks zoo kapitale Tekeningen, bestaande in veel Historien, Zinnebeelden, en geestige Crabbelinge, in alderhande sortement, veele mede braaf gewassen, van myn Mr. Pieter Jansz., konstig Glasschryver, ook met koleuren.' Schapelhouman 1985, 71.

25. See 'Ontwerptekeningen voor Kaartdecoraties in de Zeventiende Eeuw,' in Amsterdam 1989b, 65–94.

26. See Schaar 1958, 239–243, and Amsterdam 1989b, 76–80.

27. See Mària van Berge-Gerbaud in Paris/Ajaccio 2012, 78–80, no. 19.

28. For references to the figure of the fisherman by successive members of the print publishing house founded by Claes Jansz Visscher, see Leeflang 2014.

29. See Peter Fuhring in Amsterdam 1993a, 408–409, no. 65. For all the material collected in a black album dating from 1637, see the British Museum website.

30. For a bronze figure that closely resembles the drawings, see, e.g., Peter Fuhring in Amsterdam 1993a, 410–411, no. 67.

31. See Reinier J. Baarsen in Amsterdam 1993a, 441, no. 100.

32. See Utrecht 1984.

33. Gerszi 1982, 211, no. 70, fig. 77; Paris/Hamburg 1985, 224–225, no. 116.

34. Utrecht 1984, 45, no. 20.

35. Utrecht 1984, 102, no. 93.

36. Schapelhouman and Schatborn 1998, I, 45, no. 66, with further literature.

37. Terwen and Ottenheym 1993, 174–176.

38. Fuhring 2004. See also the catalog to the exhibition staged in the Rijksmuseum during the preparations for this publication, with various examples of the applications of ornament prints, Fuhring 1998.

39. Peter Fuhring in Amsterdam 1993a, 417–419, no. 76.

40. See Leeflang 2003.

41. For Hieronymus Cock's publishing house, see Leuven/Paris 2013. Marjolein Leesberg is working on a complete reconstruction of the De Jode family's print and map publishing business for the *New Hollstein*.

42. See Ger Luijten in Amsterdam 1997a, 111–114, no. 17. For the drawing, see Wegner and Pée 1980, 73, no. 33. The Fondation Custodia has recently acquired an impression of the very rare first state of Serwouters's print.

43. 'Doe een bedelaar goed en je wordt met luizen beloond.'

44. Rotterdam/Paris 1974, 23, no. 23.

45. Hollstein Dutch and Flemish XXIV, 199, no. 3. The set of seasons to which this print belongs was previously erroneously attributed to Jan van de Velde; see Rotterdam/Paris 1974–1975, 148–151, nos. 155–158.

46. Ger Luijten in New York/Fort Worth/Cleveland 1990, 84–85, no. 27. For the print, see Hollstein Dutch and Flemish XXXIII, 75, no. 232, and XXXIV, 120 (ill.).

47. See Martin Royalton-Kisch, 'The Role of Drawings in Rembrandt's Printmaking,' in Amsterdam/London 2000, 64–81, 196–200, no. 45.

48. Schnackenburg 1981, I, no. 71.

49. Ger Luijten in Amsterdam 1997a, 307–310, no. 63. For Jan van de Velde's print, see Konrad Renger in Munich 1982, 39–40.

50. See Held 1963 and Haarlem/Paris 2001b, which focuses on the eighteenth century but also has a great deal of material on the early collection of drawings.

51. Marian Bisanz-Prakken in Vienna 2009, 310–311, no. 146.

52. Broos and Schapelhouman 1993, 218–219, no. 171.

53. 'Dit is van Bredenberg een Allerbeste Tekening. Wie hem daar niet voor koopt die maakt verkeerde rekening. Philips Koning Ao. 1680.'

54. Brussels/Rotterdam/Paris/Bern 1968, I, 29–30; Amsterdam 2001, 71–72, 205, n. 18.

55. For Van Borssom's drawing, see Schatborn 2010a, I, 117–118, no. 38; for Adriaen Verboom's sheet, see Jeroen Giltaij in Paris 2014, 200–201, no. 90.

56. Wouter Kloek in Washington/London/Amsterdam 2001, 276–277, nos. 108–109; Berlin 2011, 56, no. 34.

57. Frankfurt 2000, 186–187, no. 80, considers the difficulty of determining the gender of the sitter; see Coenen 2005, 64, no. A62.

58. See Kleinert 2006, 224–225, no. 22.

59. For the painting, see Hans Buijs in The Hague 2002, 80–83, no. 1.

CATALOG

JORIS VAN DER HAAGEN

c. 1615–1660

1. *View in the Vicinity of Doorwerth*, 1650
   Black chalk and gray wash, pen and brown ink
   on paper
   19.5 × 25.9 cm (7^{11}⁄₁₆ × 10³⁄₁₆ in.)
   Rijksmuseum, Amsterdam, RP-T-1884-A-342

Joris van der Haagen spent his youth in Arnhem and settled in The Hague in 1640. A painter, he mostly drew landscapes on white and blue paper, except for three drawings that he completed on vellum in an album.[1] In his early years he depicted some imaginary mountain landscapes, while the rest of his drawn oeuvre consists of views of different towns and landscapes in the Netherlands.[2] He traveled down the Rhine, drawing at Rhenen, around Arnhem, the Elterberg, Emmerik, and Cleves. The hilly countryside made this an attractive journey, and one popular with artists as a source of inspiration. Once Van der Haagen established himself in The Hague, he often drew in the woods around the city and in the dunes. This scene of an artist who is drawing the landscape, while being observed by an old man leaning on a stick (cat. 1), presents a view of Doorwerth Castle, on the Rhine near Arnhem, looking west. It is possible that the artist depicted a companion, who also drew the view, but Van der Haagen may have included both the artist and the old man to indicate that the scene was drawn from life, as stated by the inscription.   [PS]

1. Robinson 2015, 12, fol. 5v; 39, fol. 37r; 49, fol. 48r.
2. Robinson 1990; Robinson 2000; Robinson 2015, 49, fol. 48r.

JAN LIEVENS

1607–1674

2. *Forest Interior with a Draftsman*, 1660s
Pen and brown ink and brown wash on paper
24 × 36.2 cm (9⁷⁄₁₆ × 14¼ in.)
Maida and George Abrams Collection, Boston

In the second half of the 1620s Jan Lievens and Rembrandt van Rijn were both working in Leiden. Rembrandt left for Amsterdam at the end of 1631, and the next year Lievens went to England, where he remained until 1635. He then worked in Antwerp, before settling in Amsterdam in 1643. The versatile Lievens made paintings, prints, and drawings of countless subjects and in different styles.

In 1632 and 1633 the Antwerp-born artist Anthony van Dyck was also in England, and Van Dyck's pen-and-ink landscapes of this period influenced Lievens in many ways.[1] For instance, Lievens echoes his colleague's work in his rendering of trees and wooded areas, and especially in the relationship between open, brightly lit passages and evocative shadows that Lievens indicated with pen-and-ink hatching. While Lievens was working in Antwerp, after his stay in England and his contact with Van Dyck, he drew landscapes in a sketchbook. This volume has not survived, but it was listed in 1686 in the estate of Philippus Happart in Antwerp.[2]

Among the landscapes attributed to Lievens, only a handful were most probably made out of doors.[3] Because of their sketchy execution, it is likely that two drawings on the same sheet—*Large Tree at the Edge of a Forest* (recto) and *Wooded Landscape* (verso) (Kupferstich-Kabinett, Dresden)—were done on the spot.[4] *Forest Path with Large Tree* of 1650–1660 (also in Kupferstich-Kabinett, Dresden) is a finished, altered version of the loosely sketched recto image, and it must have been created in the studio with the sketchy drawing on hand as a reference.[5]

Like most of Lievens's drawings, *Forest Interior with a Draftsman* (cat. 2) is a finished version based on an earlier sketch. Lievens made a second version of this drawing on Japanese paper, c. 1664 (Kupferstich-Kabinett, Dresden).[6] The artist shown sitting among the trees must also have been present in the original sketch, which suggests that this unknown colleague and

Lievens were drawing this spot together. The artist's presence also serves to emphasize the realism of the scene.

In general, Lievens's finished drawings are dated to the 1650s and 1660s. The paper on which *Large Tree at the Edge of a Forest* is drawn has a watermark that suggests that this drawing was made around 1664.[7]   [PS]

1. Antwerp/London 1999, cats. 12–18.
2. Schneider and Ekkart 1973, SZ 444.
3. Sumowski 1979, VII, nos. 1666[x]–1668[x], 1692[x].
4. Jan Lievens, *Large Tree at the Edge of a Forest* (recto) and *Wooded Landscape* (verso), drawing, 1635–1643, Kupferstich-Kabinett, Dresden, C 1436; Sumowski 1979, VII, nos. 1667[x]; Amsterdam 1988, nos. 52, 53.
5. Jan Lievens, *Forest Path with Large Tree*, drawing, 1650–1660, Kupferstich-Kabinett, Dresden, C 1896–30; Sumowski 1979, VII, no. 1693[x].
6. Jan Lievens, *Forest Interior with a Draftsman*, drawing, c. 1664, Kupferstich-Kabinett, Dresden, C 1432; Sumowski 1979, VII, no. 1689[x].
7. Sumowski 1979, VII, 3710–3711.

JAN VAN KESSEL

1626–1679

3. *Sketchbook*, 146 pages, 1659–1660
Black chalk and gray or brown wash on paper (closed): 9.9 × 16 cm (3⅞ × 6⁵⁄₁₆ in.)
Fondation Custodia, Collection Frits Lugt, Paris, 2006-T.30

Panorama of Deventer, fols. 91v/92r

This sketchbook containing studies of landscapes, trees, ships, and animals was discovered several years ago. After thorough research and comparison with other drawings, it was convincingly attributed to Jan van

Kessel.[1] His work is so heavily influenced by Jacob van Ruisdael (cats. 98–101) that we may safely assume that Van Kessel must have been one of his pupils—at the same time as Meindert Hobbema, likewise a landscape painter and godfather to Jan's son, Thomas van Kessel.[2] At the beginning of the sketchbook Van Kessel used only black chalk, but later we find brush washes in gray or brown (cat. 3, fol. 126). Most of the drawings are views in the west of Holland, and assuming that the sequence is chronological, we can follow Van Kessel on his travels, as some locations have been identified. At the beginning of the book, for instance, is Noordwijk Binnen (fols. 8, 9, 57), while further on we find Brederode Castle (fol. 34) and Egmond Castle (cat. 3, fols. 58, 59), both very popular subjects for artists. There are drawings in the vicinity of Alkmaar (fols. 60–62, 74, 75) and a landscape with the St. Bavo Church in Haarlem (fol. 81). The unidentified places resemble the landscape in the same region of Holland.

Van Kessel also went to the east of the Netherlands, where he drew panoramas of Deventer across two pages (cat. 3, fols. 91v/92r, 92v/93r) and made other drawings (fols. 86–91). Inspired by his master's drawings, Van Kessel visited places that Ruisdael had drawn. Accompanied by Nicolaes Berchem, Ruisdael had visited Bentheim in Westphalia in 1651. No drawings of that trip have survived, but Bentheim Castle features in several of Ruisdael's paintings, one of which is dated 1651.[3] Van Kessel did make a drawing of Bentheim, but we do not know when he was there.[4] Since the earliest signed and dated painting by Jan van Kessel dates from 1661, the drawings in the sketchbook must be slightly earlier, around 1659–1660.   [PS]

1. The attribution was made by Jeroen Giltaij; see Giltaij 2007.
2. Davies 1992, 14–16.
3. Slive 2001, 23–27, cats. 10–26.
4. Jan van Kessel, *View of Bentheim*, c. 1660–1665, drawing, Private Collection; Buvelot 2010, 33–34, fig. 1.

Egmond Castle, fol. 58

Study of Landscape, fol. 126

NICOLAES PIETERSZ BERCHEM

1620–1683

4. *Four Sheep and a Cow*, c. 1652
Red chalk on laid paper with counterproof
13 × 19.5 cm (5⅛ × 7¹¹⁄₁₆ in.)
National Gallery of Art, Ailsa Mellon Bruce Fund,
2002.141.1

Nicolaes Berchem, who was born and raised in Haarlem, joined the St. Luke's Guild of that city in 1642. He was one of the most popular and successful Italianate landscape painters of his day. Aside from views of Italy, his extensive oeuvre of paintings, drawings, and etchings consists of depictions of the hunt and biblical and mythological scenes. Berchem began his career by depicting scenes of his native landscape, sometimes in collaboration with Jacob van Ruisdael. He then became inspired by Italianate painters who had returned to the Netherlands in the previous two decades, among them Pieter van Laer, Jan Both, and Jan Asselijn. He probably visited Italy in the mid-1650s; thereafter, he became one of the most sensitive interpreters of the pastoral qualities of the Roman Campagna.

Berchem was an astute observer of livestock—particularly sheep, goats, and cattle—in drawings, paintings, and prints. In the mid-1640s he devoted an entire sketchbook, now at the British Museum, to black and red chalk studies of animals. This red-chalk drawing, with attached counterproof (cat. 4), was probably part of another sketchbook of animal drawings that dates from the early 1650s. By making counterproofs of his drawings Berchem provided models for these images facing in opposite directions. He included one of the ewes in this sheet in an etching that was part of a print series depicting sheep, and it is likely that the animals shown here also provided him with models for his paintings.   [AKW]

CRISPIJN VAN DE PASSE II

1594/95–1670

5. *A Drawing School in the Evening (or 'Roman Academy or Drawing School'*), in *Van t' Light der Teken en Schilder Konst* (Amsterdam 1643)
Engraving
33 × 39.8 cm (13 × 15¹¹⁄₁₆ in.)
National Gallery of Art Library, Washington (cat. 5a)
Fondation Custodia, Collection Frits Lugt, Paris
(cat. 5b)

Crispijn II was the son of Crispijn van de Passe the Elder (1564–1637), an important printmaker who left a very considerable oeuvre. He was born in Cologne in 1594/1595, but the family had to leave the city in 1611; they settled in Utrecht, where Crispijn the Younger trained as an engraver in his father's workshop. He moved to Paris in 1618, attended a renowned drawing academy there, and stayed until 1630. He returned to Utrecht, moving to Amsterdam in 1639 and remaining there until his death.

The book on the theory and practice of drawing that Crispijn the Younger published in 1643 is lavishly illustrated with prints and contains lengthy articles in four languages (Italian, Dutch, German, and French) aimed at aspiring artists. Most of the prints and preparatory sketches were made by Crispijn himself, although there is a group of prints by and after other artists. The texts, in many cases taken from earlier authors, treat various aspects of art under five headings.

The first section illustrates geometric figures and parts of the body and the face. The second part is prefaced by a print of a drawing class in the evening, known as the *Roman Academy or Drawing School*, in which pupils draw a model representing Jupiter (cat. 5a and 5b). Following this, the proportions of the male figure are presented in the form of foreshortened bodies and body parts.

The third section deals with the proportions of the female figure. The fourth illustrates the use of a lay figure or manikin—a jointed wooden figure that can be placed in a variety of positions and used for drapery studies. These aids were seldom, if ever, mentioned in drawing books. This part also contains different types of figure studies, such as allegorical female figures and religious scenes. Part five, finally, covers animals of all kinds, starting with the horse and ending with insects.

A sketch for the title page print of the book is held in Braunschweig.[1] Minerva, in her role as patroness of painting and drawing, is seated on a throne surrounded by eight figures who can be identified as portraits of Utrecht artists.[2] Abraham Bloemaert is certainly one of them and can also be identified on the left of the print of the *Roman Academy or Drawing School*. Although it is described as a 'Roman academy,' the scene is actually set in Utrecht, where in 1612 Bloemaert was one of the founders of the drawing academy that Passe attended in his youth.[3] [PS]

1. Crispijn de Passe, *Pallas Athena as Patroness of Painting and Drawing*, drawing, 1643, Herzog Anton Ulrich–Museum, Braunschweig, z.1288. See also Veldman 2001, fig. 178 (print).
2. Utrecht/Schwerin 2011, 28.
3. Sluijter 2006, 213–214.

LEENDERT VAN DER COOGHEN

1632–1681

6. *Study of a Nude Man, Seated Three-Quarters Length on a Cushion* [n.d.]
Black chalk on paper
39.1 × 26 cm (15⅜ × 10¼ in.)
Fondation Custodia, Collection Frits Lugt, Paris, 6634

Like many Dutch artists, Leendert van der Cooghen practiced art as an amateur. Unlike many, however, he did so not to supplement his income from some other profession but as a true dilettante. Coming from a wealthy family, Van der Cooghen did not need to work in order to support himself. Only three of his paintings have survived; thus, he is known mainly for his fourteen etchings and his many high-quality drawings. In 2005, Baukje Coenen conclusively attributed sixty-six sheets to him, most of them portraits and figure studies.

Van der Cooghen drew from life, most probably in the company of professional artists in Haarlem, where he

lived. Arnold Houbraken mentioned in his biography that Van der Cooghen and his friend Cornelis Bega sometimes had models pose for them (see pp. 236–237). Although no tangible evidence exists of such sessions, it is nevertheless very likely that Van der Cooghen sketched in the company of Salomon and Jan de Bray (see pp. 136–139 and 219–221) because of the way he depicted the curves and hollows of the bodies with long hatching lines, which is very similar to the way the De Brays, both father and son, worked. He also seems to have adopted their very precise way of inscribing dates on drawings.   [CT]

CORNELIS JONSON
VAN CEULEN

1593–1661

7. *Study of a Woman's Hands*, c. 1652
Black chalk, heightened with white on blue paper
23 × 38.8 cm (9 1/16 × 15 1/4 in.)
Musée de Grenoble, MG D 230

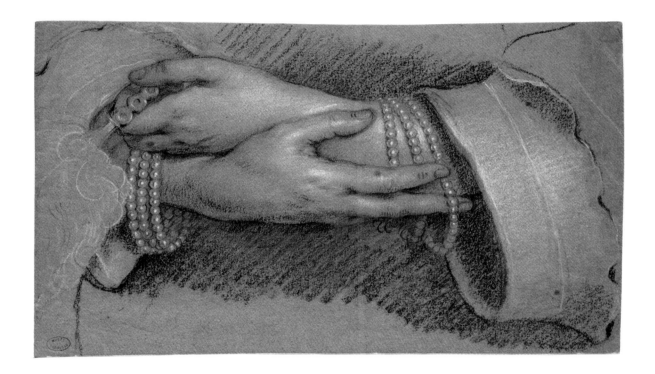

Cornelis Jonson van Ceulen was born in London to an émigré couple from the Southern Netherlands. He might have trained for some time in Amsterdam before returning to London, where he worked as a portraitist. In 1643 he went to the Low Countries, where, after a short stay in Middelburg, he settled in Amsterdam, from about 1646 to about 1652. Later, he worked in Utrecht.

Only a few drawings by Jonson van Ceulen are known: *Self-Portrait* of c. 1650 (British Museum, London), *Study of the Head of a Woman*—inscribed *Joffroù Poelenburg*—of c. 1650? (Kupferstichkabinett, Berlin), and *Portrait of a Young Woman* of 1650 (University Libraries, Leiden).[1] Some studies of hands also survive: *Study of a Woman's Hands* (cat. 7) in Grenoble and the *Study of a Man's Hand*, which was used for the *Portrait of the Amsterdam Burgomaster Jan Cornelisz Geelvinck* of 1646 (Rijksmuseum, Amsterdam).[2]

The hands shown in the Grenoble drawing correspond somewhat to those of a woman in a portrait whose whereabouts are unknown.[3] In the drawing, she holds an ostrich-feather fan, whereas, in the painting, she poses with a smaller fan, her forearms are uncovered, and the sleeves of her gown are different. The artist probably made a separate study of the hands for each of his portraits and wrote the sitter's name on the corresponding drawing. The inscription on the verso of the drawing indicates that these are the hands of a member of the Hinloopen family. One may only speculate here as to whether the artist changed his mind about the hands when he started to paint or, given the differences between the two works, the hands were drawn in preparation for a different portrait.   [PS]

1. Cornelis Jonson van Ceulen, *Self-Portrait*, black chalk, heightened with white, on blue-gray paper, c. 1650(?), British Museum, London, 1856, 0112.379; Hearn 2015, 66, fig. 51. Cornelis Jonson van Ceulen, *Study of the Head of a Woman*, black and white chalk on blue paper, Kupferstichkabinett, Berlin, KDZ 1381; Hearn 2015, 66, fig. 52. Cornelis Jonson van Ceulen, *Portrait of a Young Woman*, black and white chalk on blue paper, 1650, University Libraries, Leiden, PK-T-AW-1183; Amsterdam 2014b, no. 33.

2. Cornelis Jonson van Ceulen, *Study of a Man's Hand*, black and white chalk on blue paper, 1646, Rijksmuseum, Amsterdam, RP-T-1950-101. Cornelis Jonson van Ceulen, *Portrait of Jan Cornelis Geelvinck*, oil on canvas, 1646, Rijksmuseum, Amsterdam, C 1179.

3. Cornelis Jonson van Ceulen, *Portrait of a Woman*, oil on canvas, whereabouts unknown. See Grenoble 2014, 173–174, no. 81, fig. 81.3. In 1922, this painting was at the Arthur Kay Gallery in London.

CASPAR NETSCHER

1639–1684

8. *Studies of Two Female Arms*, 1675
Black and white chalk, some brush in black on blue paper
24.2 × 22.4 cm (9½ × 8¹³⁄₁₆ in.)
Rijksmuseum, Amsterdam, RP-T-1890-A-2375

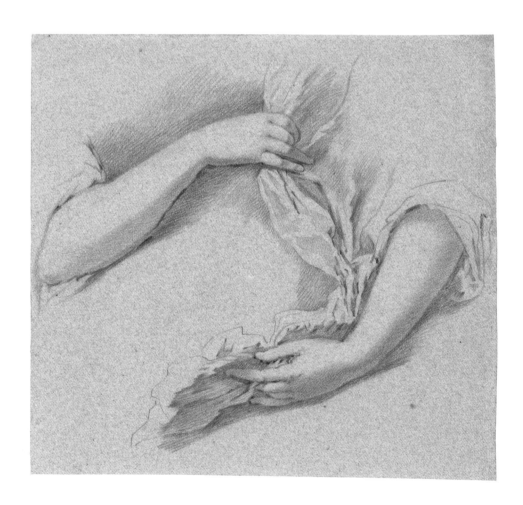

As a pupil of Gerard ter Borch, Caspar Netscher began his career as a genre painter. Setting out for Italy in 1658 or 1659, he got no further than Bordeaux, where he met and married Margaretha Godijn. In October 1662, back in the Netherlands, he joined Pictura, a painters' society in The Hague, where he became a successful portraitist with a large workshop. Two sons, Theodoor and Constantijn, and others assisted in executing commissions.

Netscher's drawn oeuvre is not large. It consists of sketchy compositions and portraits made as preparations for his paintings, drawings that could be shown to clients, and copies of his own paintings to serve as reminders of his work.[1] Among the drawings there are also a number of studies of arms and hands that could be used for portraits—sometimes more than once—by him and his assistants. The drawing shown here (cat. 8) was the starting point for the sitter's arms in the *Portrait of Elizabeth van Bebber* of 1677(?) (Mauritshuis, The Hague), although the fingers of her left hand were not copied exactly from the drawing.[2] The last number of the year is difficult to read, but given that the drawing is dated 1675, it is safe to assume that the painting was done in that year or soon after.

The 1694 inventory of Margaretha Godijn's estate lists numerous albums of drawings and prints, including 'drawings of little value for pupils to copy.'[3] One of these is in the Rijksmuseum.[4] An album attributed to Netscher and his pupils, probably compiled at a later stage by Mattheus Verhagen, one of Constantijn Netscher's students, is also in the Rijksmuseum. It contains numerous drawings of portraits, costumes, arms, legs, and hands, some by Netscher himself, but many others are the work of pupils.[5]　[PS]

1. Wieseman 2002, 112.
2. Caspar Netscher, *Portrait of Elizabeth van Bebber*, 1677?, oil on canvas, Mauritshuis, The Hague, 714.
3. The inventory reads: 'teykeningen van weinigh waarde dienende voor disipelen om na te teykenenen'; Bredius 1887, 273.
4. Caspar Netscher, *Studies of Two Female Arms*, copy, 1675 or later, black and white chalk on blue paper, Rijksmuseum, Amsterdam, RP-T-1890-A-2282.
5. Caspar Netscher and pupils, *Album of Drawings*, Rijksmuseum, Amsterdam, RP-T-1893-3720. Several drawings from the album are now attributed to other artists.

GONZALES COQUES (attributed)

1614/18–1684

Gonzales Coques was a master of small-scale portraits, often of a group, which he painted in a delicate and graceful manner. Little is known about his artistic training. On the basis of his elegant manner, it seems that he was closely associated with Anthony van Dyck probably between 1629 and 1632, after Van Dyck returned to Antwerp from Italy and before he moved to London to become a court painter for King Charles I. Coques probably again worked with Van Dyck when that master returned to Flanders for a few years in the mid-1630s. Coques may have returned to England with Van Dyck, for he also painted for the English king. By 1640 Coques was back in Antwerp, where he joined the city's St. Luke's Guild.

9. *Portrait of a Man Receiving a Letter from a Boy,* c. 1660
Oil on panel
55.9 × 44.2 cm (22 × 17⅜ in.)
The Orsay Collection, London, Paris

Coques's small single and group portraits were very much to the taste of Antwerp's rich bourgeoisie, but they also appealed to an international audience, including the English aristocracy. The Dutch stadholder Frederick Hendrick, Prince of Orange, presented Coques with a gold chain in 1646 in appreciation for portraits and a pastoral scene that the artist had presented to him in The Hague. Coques subsequently received commissions

to decorate the prince's hunting castle at Honselaarsdijk, and was later invited to participate in the decoration of the Oranjezaal in the Huis ten Bosch, the country house of the stadholder's widow, Amalia von Solms.

Coques's *Portrait of a Man Receiving a Letter from a Boy*, which he probably painted around 1660, reflects experiences he would have gained from his work in and around the Dutch court. The concept of a gentleman receiving a letter from a page is directly related to Thomas de Keyser's celebrated *Portrait of Constantijn Huygens and His Clerk*, 1627 (National Gallery, London), while the delicacy of touch and human interactions of the two figures reflects the manner of Gerard ter Borch.   [AKW]

PIETER MOLIJN

1595–1661

10. *Landscape with Open Gate*, c. 1630–1635
  Oil on panel
  33.6 × 47.9 cm (13¼ × 18⅞ in.)
  National Gallery of Art, Washington, Ailsa Mellon
  Bruce Fund and Gift of Arthur K. and Susan
  H. Wheelock, 1986.10.1

In this small work, so evocative of the windswept coastal landscape near Haarlem, Pieter Molijn has captured the essence of early seventeenth-century landscape painting. His bold and fluid brushstrokes create a vigorous and animated scene. Molijn situates the viewer below the horizon, facing a road with neither beginning nor end; in this way, the vista remains limited, and the sky becomes an active element in the scene. The painting appears to be a spontaneous record of a view that the artist happened upon while traveling along a sandy road near the Dutch coast, but he executed it in his studio after first freely sketching the composition on his panel.

Molijn was one of the most innovative landscape artists of his day, ushering in the tonal phase of Dutch landscape painting by limiting his range of motifs and color tonalities. He also combined an unprecedented sense of realism with powerful diagonal compositions and strong effects of light and dark. Molijn's distinctive drawing and painting style influenced the work of Jan van Goyen.   [AKW]

JAN VAN DER HEYDEN

1637–1712

11. *View Down a Dutch Canal*, c. 1670
Oil on panel
32.5 × 39 cm (12¹³⁄₁₆ × 15⅜ in.)
National Gallery of Art, Washington, Gift of George
M. and Linda H. Kaufman, 2012.73.2
Washington only

Jan van der Heyden's oeuvre is composed largely of cityscapes and depictions of country mansions. Some of these works are relatively faithful representations of an actual location, but many others are architectural fantasies. Whether real or imaginary, Van der Heyden typically bathed his scenes in a brilliant, crisp light of almost unnatural clarity. As in *An Architectural Fantasy* (p. 27, fig. 13), he rendered bricks with the greatest precision, and yet he never allowed this technique to interfere with the creation of a balanced and harmonious composition.

Among Van der Heyden's greatest strengths was his ability to convey the flavor and feeling of such urban centers as Amsterdam, even in fancifully conceived images such as in *View Down a Dutch Canal* (cat. 11). He captured the mood of the city gained by wandering along its waterways, in the glimpses of imposing buildings behind trees lining canals, and in witnessing the human activities found on the quays. He introduced marvelous effects of light that enliven a city so defined by its topography, including reflections in the water that mirror the physical reality above. Quite remarkably, the massive stone church tower rising just beyond the brick dwellings in this painting is not an Amsterdam building at all, but rather a church from the city of Veere.

Unlike *View Down a Dutch Canal*, which is an amalgamation of pictorial elements, *An Architectural Fantasy* is a product of the artist's imagination, despite its resemblance to other paintings of country estates that he painted for his patrons among the urban elite. The alternative approaches he took in these two paintings is reflected in the entirely different underdrawings found on their panel supports: a freely executed preliminary design in *View Down a Dutch Canal* and a carefully ruled underdrawing in *An Architectural Fantasy*.   [AKW]

AMBROSIUS BOSSCHAERT

1573–1621

12. *Bouquet of Flowers in a Glass Vase*, 1621
   Oil on copper
   31.6 × 21.6 cm (12⁷⁄₁₆ × 8½ in.)
   National Gallery of Art, Washington, Patrons'
   Permanent Fund and New Century Fund, 1996.35.1
   Washington only

Ambrosius Bosschaert, who spent most of his career in Middelburg and Utrecht, was a pioneer in the history of Dutch still lifes. He had an unerring awareness of composition, and delighted in combining flowers with a wide variety of colors and shapes to create a pleasing and uplifting visual experience. As in this exquisite work, painted in the year of his death, Bosschaert usually arranged his blossoms symmetrically. Here, a spectacular yellow iris and a red-and-white-striped tulip surmount a bouquet composed of numerous other types of flowers, among them roses, fritillaria, grape hyacinth, lily of the valley, and a sprig of rosemary. Even though this bouquet is fanciful and consists of flowers from different seasons of the year, it looks naturalistic because of the soft, velvety textures of the flowers' petals.

Although no drawings by this master are known, he certainly must have made careful flower studies and used them for his paintings. He sometimes depicted individual flowers in reverse, which also suggests that he made counterproofs of his drawings. The extensive underdrawing he made on the copper support demonstrates the care with which he composed this work.   [AKW]

MICHIEL VAN MUSSCHER

1645–1705

From 1660 on, Michiel van Musscher worked in Amsterdam, where he painted chiefly portraits and some genre scenes. Few drawings by him are known. The finished *Artist's Studio with the Painter at Work*, 1665 (Teylers Museum, Haarlem) was inspired by a painting and an etching by Adriaen van Ostade (p. 6, fig. 1), and those three works all create the impression of a painter's actual workshop.[1]

Van Musscher's corollary painting, by contrast, shows a different sort of artist in a much more elegant setting (cat. 13 and catalog cover). In a room with a tiled floor, the artist sits at an easel bearing a canvas. Given the easel's acute angle, however, the painting at hand cannot be identified. In the background, a mantelpiece with fluted columns is partly visible, and on the right, the lid of a painter's box is propped open. Framed paintings are displayed on the wall, while several canvases are propped against it. Light enters the scene from the right, but no window is visible. A curtain frames the composition at the top—perhaps a reminder that, as on a stage, reality is a mere suggestion. This studio scene conveys a whole new status to the life of an artist.

Drawings lie on the floor in the foreground, as they do in Van Musscher's drawing of a studio. At center right is an album in which stock drawings are kept and from which the painter can select preliminary studies for his paintings. Most of the drawings in *An Artist in His Studio with His Drawings* depict ships, although one portrays a round tower along a river with a triple-arched bridge. A painting in the background shows a hilly landscape with a river, beside which we discern a man walking with a stick over his shoulder. It would seem that the artist was a landscape painter, although the ship drawings suggest his familiarity with seascapes.

At the sale of J. van der Marck's collection in 1773, the subject in the painting was identified as the marine artist Willem van de Velde the Younger.[2] However, a portrait of Van de Velde by Lodewijk van der Helst, 1660–1672 (Rijksmuseum, Amsterdam), does not really resemble this man.[3] Since then, it has also been suggested that Van Musscher depicted Jan Rietschoof, an artist from Hoorn.[4] It is possible, though, that this is not a portrait at all, but a genre scene of a painter at his easel. Regardless of the level of reality or the identity of the artist, the painting beautifully illustrates the close relationship between drawings and paintings.   [PS]

1. Michiel van Musscher, *The Artist's Studio with the Painter at Work*, drawing, 1665, Teylers Museum, Haarlem, inv. R^x 14a; Thiel 1969, 4, fig. 3.
2. Amsterdam, August 15, 1773, no. 469.
3. Lodewijk van der Helst, *Portrait of Willem van de Velde the Younger*, Rijksmuseum, Amsterdam, SK-A-2236; see also Thiel 1969, 14, fig. 10. The sitter holds a drawing of a seascape signed 'W v Velde.'
4. Thiel 1969, n. 25.

13. *An Artist in His Studio with His Drawings,* mid-1660s
     Oil on panel
     47 × 36 cm (18½ × 14³⁄₁₆ in.)
     Collections of the Prince of Liechtenstein,
     Vaduz-Vienna, GE 23 97

JACQUES DE GHEYN II

1565-1629

14. *Three Flowers: A Double Carnation, a Tulip,*
and a Liverwort or Liverleaf, 1601
Gouache and tempera on vellum, probably over
a sketch in metalpoint (silverpoint?)
(fol. 6 from an album)
22.8 × 17.6 cm (9 × 6¹⁵⁄₁₆ in.)
Fondation Custodia, Collection Frits Lugt, Paris,
5655-6

The album containing the gouache drawing (cat. 14) is almost certainly the 'little book in which De Gheyn had, in the course of time, drawn some little flowers from life in gouache with many small animals too,' as Karel van Mander described in his *Schilder-Boeck* of 1604.[1] The album consists of twenty-two drawings of flowers and small creatures, including butterflies, beetles, a crab, and a mouse, that are—unsurprisingly—regarded among the finest nature studies of the sixteenth and seventeenth centuries. The drawings attest to the artist's scientific as well as artistic interests. De Gheyn depicted his subjects with extraordinary precision, while also having an eye for light, texture, and shadow. This allowed the artist to convincingly depict details such as the luster of a petal and the shadows that sheer insect wings cast on the ground.

It is difficult to imagine today how extraordinary some of these flowers were in De Gheyn's own time. Many of his contemporaries, for example, would never have seen

a blooming tulip. Although this species had been introduced into the Low Countries shortly before the artist created his small album, the tulip was cultivated in very few places. Charles de l'Écluse (also known as Carolus Clusius), the director of the botanical gardens in Leiden, was involved in tulip cultivation in that city and was an acquaintance of the artist.[2] Contemporary sources note that most of the flowers depicted by De Gheyn were growing in Leiden's botanical gardens, so it is safe to assume that he drew them there.[3] He undoubtedly began with sketches on paper, which he then later, in his studio, used to create gouache on vellum, probably over silverpoint drawings.[4]

De Gheyn would not have made these meticulously executed nature studies specifically as models for his paintings, but he clearly used the drawings for this purpose. He compiled one of his earliest known flower still lifes entirely from the drawings in this album.[5] De Gheyn's repeated use of other flowers, not represented in

1. Van Mander writes: 'een cleen Boecxken daer de Gheyn metter tijt eenige bloem-kens van Verlichterije nae t' leven in hadde ghemaeckt met oock veel cleene beestkens.' See Mander 1604 *Lives*, I, fol. 294v. For the Fondation Custodia album, see Boon 1992, I, 132–147, no. 80, and II, pls. 162–183, and Swan 2005, 66–94. For De Gheyn as a draftsman, see Regteren Altena 1983, Paris 1985, and Rotterdam/Washington 1985.

2. For the relationship between De Gheyn and Clusius, see Regteren Altena 1983, I,

66–69; for engravings that De Gheyn made on commission or in collaboration with Clusius, see Filedt Kok and Leesberg 2000, 67, no. 213; 99, no. 241; and 119, no. 58.

3. Hopper 1991, 21, 31–36. Brennink-meijer-De Rooij 1996, 42–43, argued that in a number of cases De Gheyn did not work from a living specimen but from examples by Jacques Le Moyne de Morgues.

4. The suggestion that De Gheyn used silverpoint in these drawings was made by

Karel Boon in Boon 1992, I, 133. The sketch of three dragonflies in the Fogg Art Museum in Cambridge (Mass.) may have been made in preparation for a page in the Fondation Custodia album. See William W. Robinson in London/Paris/Cambridge 2002, 84–85, no. 29.

5. Current whereabouts unknown; Hopper-Boom 1975 and Regteren Altena 1983, II, 20, no. 31, III, pl. 1. See Washington 1999, 33–36 (fig. 26), 83, no. 14, for an addition to the flower still lifes by De Gheyn included in Regteren Altena 1983.

JACQUES DE GHEYN II

15. *Democritus and Heraclitus*, 1602/1603
   Black and white chalk on light brown paper
   23.7 × 28 cm (9¹⁵⁄₁₆ × 11 in.)
   Stichting P. & N. de Boer, Amsterdam, B 509

this album, in his still lifes indicates that he must have had more examples at hand.[6] Although contemporary sources sometimes mention flower still lifes that were supposedly painted from life, it was standard practice to work from drawings of individual flowers.[7] This process was actually unavoidable, as artists liked to depict a variety of species—preferably exotic—which meant that they had to contend with expensive, perishable specimens and with different flowering cycles. After all, a spring flower like the tulip could in reality never share a vase with roses and lilies, which bloom later.

De Gheyn's album proved its value again for his allegory of human vanity of 1603, one of the earliest known vanitas paintings (fig. 1).[8] At left, the tulip in the vase is almost identical to the central flower in the gouache drawing. Like the skull, the coins, and the smoke that spirals out of the vase on the right, the valuable but rapidly wilting tulip is a symbol of transience. The two figures above the niche represent Democritus and Heraclitus, classical philosophers who observed earthly struggles with laughter and tears, respectively.[9] Even more interesting is the survival of a second drawing related to this painting; although De Gheyn left behind an incredibly large drawn oeuvre, only a few sketches can be identified as preliminary studies for paintings, so to have two drawings for the same painting is an exceptional occurrence. The second drawing is a study of the two philosophers in black chalk on light brown paper (cat. 15), produced specifically for the still life.[10] These figures appear in the painting as stone statues, albeit with some changes, chiefly in the pose of Heraclitus. The ball, reminiscent of a globe, on the ground in the drawing, seems to have been transformed in the painting into a floating bubble that shows the reflection of a window and some symbols that are part of the iconography of transience, including a burning heart and a crown with swords.[11] To paint this unusual image the artist drew upon his detailed studies

made from nature and his powers of invention, making this work a perfect illustration of Van Mander's observation that De Gheyn endeavored to work 'from life' as well as 'from imagination.'[12]   [GW]

Fig. 1. Jacques de Gheyn II, *Vanitas Still Life*, 1603, oil on wood. Metropolitan Museum, New York, Charles B. Curtis, Marquand, Victor Wilbour Memorial, and The Alfred N. Punnett Endowment Funds, 1974, 1974.1

6. Some examples are illustrated in Bergström 1956, 51.
7. Mander 1604 *Lives*, I, fol. 294v, for example described 'een clee Bloempotken nae t'leven' (a little pot of flowers from life) by De Gheyn. For this phenomenon see Brenninkmeijer-De Rooij 1990.
8. Bergström 1970.
9. Blankert 1967, 113, no. 80.
10. See also Regteren Altena 1983, II, 38, no. 137, which is possibly a second preliminary study for these figures.
11. For the iconography of this painting, see Bergström 1970 and Liedtke 2007, I, 213–223.
12. Mander 1604 *Lives*, I, fol. 294v.

ABRAHAM BLOEMAERT

1566–1651

16. *Landscape with Dilapidated Buildings and Figures*, 1629
   Oil on canvas
   91.5 × 135.5 cm (36 × 53⅜ in.)
   Hamburger Kunsthalle, Hamburg, 732
   Washington only

Fig. 1. Abraham Bloemaert, *Tobias and the Angel*, c. 1610, black chalk, pen and brown ink, brown wash, white bodycolor. Albertina, Vienna, 8105

Abraham Bloemaert, who worked chiefly in Utrecht, left a great many drawings. They give us a clear idea of how he built up his paintings, although he did not always approach the task along the same lines.[1] In his Caravaggesque period he would lay in whole compositions, in the manner of Gerrit von Honthorst, with large areas of wash and highlights put in with a brush, preparing for the chiaroscuro.[2] He conceived his clear, bright late canvases, mostly altarpieces, with the aid of detailed compositional drawings that could be shown to clients for their information and approval. Especially Bloemaert's paintings of figures in a landscape setting made for the open market enable us to see how drawings were the building blocks for an inventively evoked reality.

A good example of this is *Landscape with Dilapidated Buildings and Figures* of 1629 (cat. 16). The picture space is almost entirely occupied by picturesque, tumbledown buildings, described by Karel van Mander as 'pretty, quaint peasants' houses,' of which, he said, 'there are a great number and variety around Utrecht which were

painted by him.'[3] Tobias and the angel are striding by in the background, looking rather wraithlike, as if they are apparitions. Without a doubt, Bloemaert created this significant effect by falling back on an early mannerist drawing (fig. 1) that, before 1610, he had already used in a painting.[4] He based the 'quaint peasants' houses' on carefully worked out drawings—colored, as Van Mander

1. For Bloemaert the draftsman see Bolten 2007, I, 2–9, and Albert J. Elen, 'A Gifted and Practical Draughtsman: Creativity and Utility in the Working Process,' in Utrecht/Schwerin 2011, 31–38.
2. For example, in the *Supper at Emmaus*

in the collection of the Stichting en N. de Boer, Amsterdam. See Bolten 2007, I, 77, no. 176; II, 99 (ill.), and Rhea Sylvia Blok, 'Abraham Bloemaert,' in Paris 2014, 134–135, no. 60 (ill.).
3. Van Mander cites: '*aerdighe en drollighe*

boeren huysen'; '*om Wtrecht seer veel en verscheyden te sien en van hem gheconterfeyt zijn.*' Mander 1604 *Lives*, fol. 298r.
4. Bolten 2007, I, 39, no. 61; II, 37 (ill.). For the painting, see Roethlisberger and Bok 1993, I, 141–143, no. 98; II, figs. 171–173.

Fig. 2. Abraham Bloemaert, *A Tumbledown Shed*, 1595–1605, pen and brown ink, colored wash. Hermitage, St. Petersburg, 25310r

Fig. 3. Abraham Bloemaert, *A Sitting Woman and a Standing Woman*, 1595–1600, black chalk, green wash, white bodycolor. Hermitage, St. Petersburg, 23505v

Abraham Bloemaert, *Studies of Arms, Hands, and Heads* (cat. 20), verso

says, 'with some watercolors' (cat. 17 and fig. 2)—which were likewise much earlier. These he put together to create a single dilapidated farmhouse with barns.⁵ In other words he did not start drawing when he was about to embark on a painting but unearthed studies, some-times decades old, that he must have kept in some sort of order. The dovecote, erected on stilts and towering above the buildings, also came from existing drawings.⁶ The non-biblical figures that populate the foreground of the scene are based on red chalk studies of a type that Bloemaert made in the hundreds. He went back to three different sheets, two of which are seen here (cat. 18, fig. 3), to weave the figuration together.⁷ He made drawings

of the dog lying down and looking at us (this animal appears in print in the *Tekenboek*), the foreshortened, recumbent dog on the right, the farming implements, and the wicker baskets lying in the corner.⁸

Bloemaert also browsed his drawings to serve as sources for paintings that were chiefly landscapes. The *Landscape with Willow and the Rest on the Flight into Egypt* of 1631 (fig. 4) is a good example. It is based on a superior drawing in which there are two studies of willow trees (cat. 19).⁹ In this work, subtly colored in shades of green, the trees are leafless; in the painting, for which the tree on the left was the model, the branches bear slightly stereotypically painted foliage that looks like an afterthought. On the verso of the sheet there is an indication in black chalk of a dune landscape crossed by a path that is reminiscent of the gently rolling landscape in the painting.¹⁰ By using the two landscape impres-sions, he could compose the painting, placing the figure group of the Virgin, the Christ Child, and Joseph in the rural setting to create a narrative. For the figures he could turn to his collection of studies of a woman swathed in robes with a child on her lap and for the arrangement of Holy Family groups to the exercises he had done from the start of his career—drawings that have much in common with the work of Hendrick Goltzius. The figure of Joseph calls to mind Goltzius's set of apostles.

In some instances, while working on a picture, Bloe-maert did not turn to his portfolios full of ready-to-use sheets but created new studies instead. After he had established the composition of his painting *The Adoration of the Shepherds,* 1612 (Landesgalerie, Hannover), he drew various limbs and heads on the recto and verso of a sheet (cat. 20), and he made use of the studies while complet-ing the picture.¹¹   [GL]

5. Van Mander cites: 'met eenighe sappighe verfkens.' For fig. 2, see Bolten 2007, I, 422, no. 1424; II, 429 (ill.).
6. See the drawing in Centraal Museum, Utrecht, inv. 23526, Bolten 2007, I, 182, no. 513; II, 235 (ill.). The dovecote, pic-tured from more or less the same vantage point, is a recurring element in Bloemaert's paintings and drawings (see, for example, the *Landscape with Tobias and the Angel* of c. 1630 in Centraal Museum, Utrecht,

Utrecht/Schwerin 2011, 173–174, no. 70; Bolten 2007, I, 25, no. 27 and 420, no. 1413; II, 21 (ill.) and 427 (ill.).
7. For fig. 3, Bolten 2007, I, 316, no. 962; II, 360 (ill.). The boy sitting on the right occurs in a drawing in a private collection in Amsterdam, see Bolten 2007, I, 426, no. 1443; II, 434 (ill.).
8. Bolten 2007, I, 394, no. 1302; II, 411 (ill.).

9. Roethlisberger and Bok 1993, I, 316–317, no. 492; II, fig. 674.
10. Bolten 2007, I, 439, no. 1493, noted that the drawing was used by Frederick Bloemaert in plate 12 of a series of etchings after designs by his father; see Roethlisberger and Bok 1993, I, 307, no. 474; II, fig. 656.
11. Amsterdam/Washington 1981, 38–39.

ABRAHAM BLOEMAERT

17. *Ruins of a Farmhouse,* c. 1571–1629
    Black chalk, brushed in red and light green, on paper
    15.2 × 20.8 cm (6 × 8³⁄₁₆ in.)
    Rijksmuseum, Amsterdam, purchased with the
    support of the Vereniging Rembrandt,
    RP-T-1886-A-1159

ABRAHAM BLOEMAERT

18. *Two Seated Boys with Studies for Hands and Feet*, c. 1620–1629
   Pen and brown ink, red chalk, heightened with white gouache on beige paper
   14 × 18 cm (5½ × 7⁄16 in.)
   Musée du Louvre, Paris (on long-term loan to Musée Bonnat-Helleu,
   Bayonne), RF 50861
   Washington only

ABRAHAM BLOEMAERT

19. *Study of Trees (Studies of Two Pollard Willows)*, [n.d.]
Pen and brown ink, watercolor, traces of black
chalk on paper
21 × 31 cm (8¼ × 12³⁄₁₆ in.)
Metropolitan Museum of Art, New York,
Rogers Fund, 1970, 1970.242.3

Fig. 4. Abraham Bloemaert, *Landscape with Willow
and the Rest on the Flight into Egypt*, 1631, oil on canvas.
Hermitage, St. Petersburg, 9911

ABRAHAM BLOEMAERT

20. *Studies of Arms, Legs, and Heads*, [n.d.]
   Red and white chalk, some pen in brown on paper
   25.7 × 16.7 cm (10⅛ × 6⁹⁄₁₆ in.)
   Rijksmuseum, Amsterdam, RP-T-1886-A-686 (verso)

ABRAHAM BLOEMAERT

21. *Head of an Old Man Turned and Looking to Right*, 1625–1635
Black chalk, with gray wash, white body color, heightened
with white (partly oxidized), on gray prepared paper
41.5 × 29.7 cm (16⁵⁄₁₆ × 11¹¹⁄₁₆ in.)
The British Museum, London, PD A, 17.65

ABRAHAM BLOEMAERT

22. *Head of an Old Man*, 1630–1640
   Oil on panel
   48.3 × 36.3 cm (19 × 14⁵⁄₁₆ in.)
   National Gallery of Art, Washington, Joseph
   F. McCrindle Collection, 2010.93.41

Fig. 5. Frederick Bloemaert after Abraham Bloemaert,
Head of an Old Man, c. 1650, engraving.
The British Museum, London, L, 83.105

Fig. 6. Maarten van Heemskerck, *Head of an Old Man*,
c. 1560–1570, red chalk. Kupferstichkabinett,
Staatliche Museen, Berlin, 8485

There are countless drawings of half-length figures and
character heads in Bloemaert's oeuvre. There are also
examples of study heads (*tronies*) with different expressions, distilled from drawings and paintings Abraham
made to practice drawing, in the *Tekenboek* (*Artis Apellae
liber*), which appeared in print for the first time, published by his son Frederick, around 1650. They include
a *Head of an Old Man* (fig. 5), which was made after the
Head of an Old Woman. The former is a good example of
an invention by Bloemaert that exists as both a drawing
and a painting (cats. 21, 22). It would seem obvious to
assume that the large drawing in the British Museum
preceded the painted *tronie*. It has been suggested that
the head was not necessarily drawn from life, although
that is difficult to prove.[12] The position of the head and
the upturned eyes resemble those of the dying Seneca,
the Roman statue in the Louvre.[13] However, the likeness
to *Old Age* in a series of engravings by Maarten van
Heemskerck is greater, particularly the preparatory
drawing (fig. 6).[14] Bloemaert concentrated on the same
taut muscles in the face and on the lines in the neck. He
also relied on the similar effect of a classical bust. In his
painting and the engraving, great pains have been taken
with the suggestion of the coat, and the expression of its
texture and surface: in paint it became cloth, and in the
engraved lines fur.   [GL]

12. Bolten 2007, I, 277, no. 816.
13. Haskell and Penny 1981, 303–305,
no. 76, figs. 160–161.
14. See Ger Luijten in Amsterdam 1986,
325–326, no. 205, and Veldman 1993,
257–261, nos. 595–598.

JAN VAN RAVESTEYN

1572–1657

23. *The Hague Magistrate Receiving the Officers
of the St. Sebastiaansdoelen,* 1618
Pen and black ink, brown wash, heightened
with white gouache, on paper
24.8 × 51.7 cm (9¾ × 20⅜ in.)
Fondation Custodia, Collection Frits Lugt, Paris,
3845

Fig. 1. Jan van Ravesteyn, *The Hague Magistrate Receiving the Officers of the St. Sebastiaansdoelen*, 1618, oil on canvas. Haags Historisch Museum, The Hague, 0000-0025-SCH

In the seventeenth century, the military protection of The Hague and the maintenance of public order were in the hands of two distinct militia groups. Except for the central area that contained the Stadholder's Court, the buildings of the provincial government of Holland, and those of the Republic's central government, the safety of The Hague was in the hands of the militia of the St. Sebastiaansdoelen.[1] Named after its patron saint (St. Sebastian) and the company's headquarters with the adjacent field used for target practice (*doelen*), the St. Sebastiaan's militia operated under the auspices of the municipal government, so its command was always in the hands of a senior city official with the rank of colonel. It was organized into four 'banners'—Orange, White, Blue, and the triple-hued Orange/White/Blue—each banner responsible for one of the town's four quarters. Each banner comprised residents of its respective quarter, led by a captain. He was assisted by an ensign, who had the honor of bearing the banner's flag and who traditionally wore a colorful costume.

Jan van Ravesteyn, the foremost portraitist in The Hague in the early decades of the century, was commis-sioned to depict the officers of the Saint Sebastiaan's militia on November 20, 1617, and completed the painting by October 18, 1618 (fig. 1). The timing of the commission suggests that it commemorates the formal annual reception of the militia's officers by the city officials following the reorganization of the militia in 1617.[2] Van Ravesteyn's preparatory drawing for this large group portrait, the only drawing firmly attributed to him, reveals a revolutionary and dynamic composition that sweeps the eye from left to right. Earlier militia paintings depicted a company of guardsmen in fairly rigid rows or clustered around a table, while civic group portraits often showed the leadership of a municipal institution in its board room. Here, however, Van Rave-steyn successfully combined these distinct types of group portraits into a unified whole while maintaining the portrait-like quality of the individual likenesses of those who participated in this celebratory event.[3]

1. The St. Joris (George) militia was responsible for the protection of the town's historic core.

2. Servaas van Rooijen 1881, 334–335. Van Ravesteyn was paid 500 guilders for the large painting; the work was deemed so successful that the magistrates also granted the artist lifelong exemption from further militia duties.

3. The Hague 1998, 233.

Fig. 2. Infrared reflectogram of a detail of the painting, revealing the underpainting of the window. Photo by Restauratieatelier Redivivus, courtesy of the Haags Historisch Museum.

Van Ravesteyn's lively drawing depicts The Hague's municipal leaders seated around a massive table in the Burgomasters' Room of the militia headquarters, as they receive the officers of all four banners of the St. Sebastiaan's *doelen*. The four captains and other city officials are all clustered on the right side of the room. The colonel, a senior magistrate appointed to head the militia, sits at the center of the table and has doffed his hat in greeting. In the drawing's relatively spacious left side, the reeve, representative of the Count of Holland, has turned to engage the viewer. In the foreground corners, two servants pouring wine from large pitchers hint at the festive purpose of the gathering and impart further movement to the scene. Two windows flank the fireplace on the rear wall, yet most of the light seems to enter from the left, giving the room and the drawing an airy feel.

With a diagonal composition, the drawing of the gathering is incredibly lively. Van Ravesteyn, who was an active member of the militia, probably worked on it in several stages. His initial sketch in black chalk with traces of red chalk could well have been made while witnessing the proceedings. He later elaborated on this sketch with pen and dark-brown ink, and added subtle white highlights to the faces and costumes of the principal figures that greatly contribute to the scene's dynamic feel.

The subject of the drawing and painting are the same, yet the two compositions differ significantly. The painting is more crowded and stilted than the drawing, because Van Ravesteyn not only added the portraits of four ensigns and his own, for a total of twenty-six men, but also because he reverted to a more traditional line-up in order to give equal weight to the likeness of every man.[4] He depicted the captains and ensigns of the Orange, White, and Blue banners as having just entered the room on the right, while the colonel and the officers of the Orange/White/Blue banner stand at the far left side, resulting in a more horizontal than diagonal composition. The most important local dignitaries, including the reeve and the city's three serving burgomasters, make up the 'inner circle' at the head of the table. By placing two men back to back in front of the table, Van Ravesteyn created two distinct circles of interaction, perhaps in an attempt to increase the painting's sense of action.[5]

Restoration of the painting in 2011 led to several interesting discoveries about Van Ravesteyn's painting process.[6] Infrared photography revealed the underdrawing of a window to the right of the fireplace, indicating that Van Ravesteyn initially adhered to his original concept but that he covered up that window at a later stage (fig. 2). By removing this second source of light he could illuminate all the faces uniformly. Several pentimenti, including the existence of a 'third' eye on the forehead of the second man from the right, point to further adjustments.[7] Little is known about the workshop practices of Van Ravesteyn, but over the course of his active career he had at least sixteen students, and six of them could have been in the studio around the time of the commission.[8]　[HR]

4. See Domela Nieuwenhuis 2012, 102–103, for an explanation of the belated inclusion of the four ensigns; and 105–106 for a discussion about the event depicted.

5. Martin 1923, 193–198. See 196–197, Appendix 1, for the identification of the 26 men. Van Ravesteyn has portrayed himself standing fifth from the left in the second tier, wearing a relaxed ruff collar. Seven aldermen complete the center portion of the painting, while one servant is now positioned in front of the fireplace, above which we can just discern the bottom of a chimney piece depicting the martyrdom of St. Sebastian.

6. The pre-restoration frame covered about 1.5 more inches (4 cm) of the canvas at both the top and bottom, which effectively had hidden the arrow and the bloody wound in St. Sebastian's leg, details that identify the subject of the chimney piece.

7. Haags Historisch Museum, treatment report by Restauratieatelier Redivivus 2011, 2–3, fig. 4, for Sebastian's legs; 9–10, figs. 19 and 20 for the third eye in Willem van Neck's forehead.

8. Jan van Ravesteyn's biography in the RKD database lists sixteen boys/men with the years in which they were registered as his students. https://rkd.nl/en/explore/artists/Ravesteyn,%20Jan%20van (accessed August 20, 2015).

PIETER LASTMAN

1583–1633

Few drawings by Pieter Lastman have survived, although the inventory of his possessions drawn up in 1632—the year before his death—lists ten albums of drawings, red chalk drawings, and drawings of horses.[1] Rembrandt, who had studied with Lastman for six months in 1625, also owned a book of pen-and-ink sketches and one of the red chalk drawings by his former teacher, as revealed in Rembrandt's own inventory of 1656.[2]

Eight figure studies are known to have been drawn by Lastman in red chalk, sometimes with touches of black and white chalk, on paper prepared with an orange hue. Lastman must have come across this technique when he was in Italy between 1603 and 1607.[3] The drawings he made in this mode were probably intended as preliminary studies for paintings. Three figure studies appear almost exactly reproduced in paintings, while the others correspond to varying degrees. In the painting *Laban Seeking the Idols* (cat. 25), Lastman adopted *Reclining Woman, as Rachel* (cat. 24) very closely, save for a few folds in her clothes.[4] The handling of the drawing is quite fine and flowing, with stronger accents in red chalk here and there. The shaded side of her left arm is emphasized with black chalk, and points of light are heightened with white.

The painting illustrates the story in Genesis 31, which recounts how Jacob fled with Laban's daughters, Rachel and Leah, to Canaan, the land of Jacob's father, Isaac. Laban followed Jacob, looking for the idols that Rachel had secretly taken away with her and had hidden in a saddle. Rachel lay on the saddle while he was searching, as the drawing illustrates, so that Laban could not find what he sought. Eventually he made a covenant with Jacob and departed.

The reclining woman also appears in a later painting, *St. John the Baptist Preaching*, 1625 (Art Institute of Chicago), where Lastman adapted the figure's pose to the subject.[5] She sits slightly more upright, looking up at John with her face in profile and her entire ear visible, and no longer supports her head on her right arm. A resemblance to the figure of Mary Magdalene in *The Crucifixion* (c. 1628, Virginia Museum of Fine Arts, Richmond) has also been noted.[6] There she holds the cross with both hands and sits almost upright, while her legs are placed a little closer together. The skirt covering her legs is modeled with lively folds. Such folds are also found in the depiction of a similar figure in *The Anointing of Christ*, c. 1622 (whereabouts unknown).[7]

Given the dates on related paintings, Lastman probably made the group of eight chalk figure studies in the 1620s, although earlier drawings in the same technique may have been lost.[8] A figure bearing some likeness to Rachel, seen more from the side and looking up, appears in a much earlier painting of *Hagar and the Angel*, 1614 (Los Angeles County Museum of Art).[9]

Lastman's only surviving compositional sketch for a painting is *Balaam and the Ass*, 1622 (National Galleries of Scotland, Edinburgh), which he similarly used for a panel in Jerusalem (1622, Israel Museum Collection).[10]

1. Freise 1911, 21, nos. 71, 72, 75; Amsterdam 1991b, 132; Seifert 2011, 177.

2. Strauss and Van der Meulen 1979, no. 1656/12, nos. 263, 264.

3. Seifert points to drawings by Tanzio da Varallo; Seifert 2011, 195.

4. Bauch associated the drawing with the painting; Bauch 1960, 107, fig. 70, 257, n. 81; Seifert 2011, 204, fig. 223, 210–211.

5. Inv. no. 1998.4 (loan), panel, signed 'P. Lastman 1627.' Seifert examines in depth the relationship between the different figures in all the known drawings and paintings.

6. Inv. no. 97.127, panel; Seifert 2011, 204, fig. 224.

7. Seifert 2011, 204, n. 1248, fig. 225.

8. Amsterdam 1991b, 135; Seifert 2011, 209.

9. Inv. no. M 85.117, panel, signed 'PL/1614'; Seifert 2011, 207, 210, fig. 227.

10. The drawing is inv. no. D 2955, in red and some black chalk, pen and black ink. The attribution to Lastman was made by K. Andrews 1985, I, no. D 2955, and II, fig. 306; Seifert 2011, 182–190, fig. 195. The Jerusalem panel is inv. no. B97.0069, which is signed 'PLastman fecit 1622'; Seifert 2011, 182–190, fig. 196.

Others may have been lost. There is one surviving design for a stained glass window in the Zuiderkerk in Amsterdam, *King Cyrus Returning the Vessels of the Temple to the Jews*, 1611 (Kupferstichkabinett, Berlin).[11]

Lastman would certainly not have needed drawings for all the figures in his paintings. Throughout his life he depicted countless figures in history compositions, and he was perfectly capable of painting figures and other motifs from memory and from his imagination without a direct example. For this, he might simply have relied on underdrawings, drawings that he made directly in black chalk on the panel. The reflectogram of *David Gives Uriah a Letter for Joab*, 1619 (cat. 26 and fig. 3, p. 20) reveals not only that Lastman here followed Van Mander's recommendation to make a complete underdrawing on the panel but, furthermore, that his style of underdrawing is similar to that seen in his figure drawings.

After his return from Italy in 1607 Lastman became a leading history painter who later included Rembrandt van Rijn and Jan Lievens among his pupils. One technique that they learned from him was the use of prepared paper for figure studies (see, for example, cat. 59), albeit in less strikingly bold colors.   [PS]

11. KdZ 3793, pen and brown ink, brown wash. Amsterdam 1991b, no. 28; Seifert 2011, 41, fig. 26.

PIETER LASTMAN

24. *Reclining Woman, as Rachel*, 1622
Red and some black chalk, heightened with white,
on orange prepared paper
22.9 × 20.2 cm (9 × 7¹⁵⁄₁₆ in.)
The Ashmolean Museum, Oxford, WA1953.114

PIETER LASTMAN

25. *Laban Seeking the Idols*, 1622
    Oil on panel
    110 × 152 cm (43¹⁵⁄₁₆ × 59¹³⁄₁₆ in.)
    Musée municipal, Boulogne-sur-Mer, 147/13
    Paris only

HENDRICK AVERCAMP

1585–1634

27. *A Standing Girl with Her Hands under Her Apron*,
c. 1620
Black and red chalk on paper
26 × 13.2 cm (10¼ × 5³⁄₁₆ in.)
The Royal Collection/HM Queen Elizabeth II,
906506

Fig. 1. Hendrick Avercamp, *Numerous Figures on the Ice Outside a Town*, c. 1620, pen and brown ink, brush and brown ink, and watercolor, over a sketch in graphite. The Royal Collection/ HM Queen Elizabeth II, 6472

Born in Amsterdam, Hendrick Avercamp spent most of his life in Kampen, where his family moved in 1586 after his father was appointed town apothecary. This business was taken over by Avercamp's mother after his father's death. Early documents indicate that Hendrick was a deaf mute, which must have had an enormous impact on his artistic career.[1]

Around 1607 Avercamp went to Amsterdam for his artistic training. There he soon came under the influence of Flemish mannerist landscape painters who were then living in the city, notably Gillis van Coninxloo and David Vinckboons. Avercamp was back in Kampen by the beginning of 1613, where he remained until his death in 1634. He devoted his career almost entirely to depicting winter scenes, often with crowds of people engaging in a wide range of activities on frozen waterways. He was a keen observer of daily life, and his paintings and drawings are filled with human vignettes that capture human interactions of old and young, rich and poor.

Avercamp was a prolific draftsman. The Dutch marine painter Jan van de Cappelle owned three portfolios containing no fewer than 880 of his drawings.[2] Sadly, however, many of Avercamp's drawings have been lost through the vagaries of time. Those that remain are quite varied, from quick pen and chalk sketches seemingly made from life (fig. 1) to careful chalk figure drawings—probably made from models posing in his studio (cats. 27, 28)—to elaborate finished compositional drawings executed in a complex combination of materials, including chalk, pen-and-ink, watercolor, and bodycolor (fig. 2).

The functions of these drawings seem to have been quite varied. Most of Avercamp's drawings served as part of a continuum of ideas that helped him formulate engaging paintings.[3] He clearly sketched out of doors, even in the cold of winter, where he rapidly jotted down images of skaters and others enjoying the ice. He would

---

1. For Avercamp's biography, see Jonathan Bikker, 'Hendrick Avercamp "The Mute of Kampen,"' in Amsterdam/Washington 2009, 11–21.

2. Jonathan Bikker, 'The Early Owners of Avercamp's Work,' in Amsterdam/ Washington 2009, 122.

3. For an overview of Avercamp's drawings, see Marijn Schapelhouman, 'The Drawings: Reflections on an Oeuvre,' in Amsterdam/Washington 2009, 85–117.

Fig. 2. Hendrick Avercamp, *Winter Games on the Frozen River IJssel*, c. 1626, pen and black and gray ink with watercolor, gouache, and graphite. National Gallery of Art, Washington, Woodner Collection, Gift of Andrea Woodner, 2006.11.3

make these rapid sketches with graphite, and then subsequently work them up in pen-and-ink and watercolor in his studio (see fig. 1). In his studio, as well, he would pose figures in attitudes and costumes that he anticipated using in his paintings. Two of the most engaging of such works are a large black and red chalk drawing, *A Standing Girl with Her Hands under Her Apron*, and a more modestly scaled pen-and-ink drawing, *An Elegantly Dressed Youth Skating*, both of which are in Windsor Castle (cats. 27, 28). Avercamp depicted these figures in

a number of his paintings. Both appear in a skating scene in the Los Angeles County Museum of Art (fig. 3), where the woman is shown having her fortune told by a gypsy and the skater—who is dressed in vivid red—skates while holding the hand of his female companion.

In the National Gallery of Art's painting (cat. 29), the young woman stands by herself as she intently watches an elegant horse-driven sled passing nearby. As is characteristic of his working procedure, Avercamp slightly adjusted the figure's pose when painting her figure. He provided the woman with skates and revealed her gloved hands instead of having them tucked under her apron. Although the scenarios he created in his paintings are entirely imaginary, his depictions of the figures' ward-

Fig. 3. Hendrick Avercamp, *Winter Scene on a Frozen Canal*, c. 1620, oil on panel. Los Angeles County Museum of Art, Mrs. Edward W. Carter Collection, L.2005.16.1

HENDRICK AVERCAMP

28. *An Elegantly Dressed Youth Skating*, c. 1620
    Pen and brown ink over graphite, shaded with graphite
    on paper
    17.1 × 11.5 cm (6¾ × 4½ in.)
    The Royal Collection/HM Queen Elizabeth II, 906477

HENDRICK AVERCAMP

29. *A Scene on the Ice*, c. 1625
   Oil on panel
   39.2 × 77 cm (15⁷⁄₁₆ × 30⁵⁄₁₆ in.)
   National Gallery of Art, Washington,
   Ailsa Mellon Bruce Fund, 1967.3.1

HENDRICK AVERCAMP

30. *A View of Kampen from outside the Walls*, c. 1620
Pen and brown ink with watercolor over graphite
on paper
12.2 × 31 cm (4¹³⁄₁₆ × 12³⁄₁₆ in.)
The Royal Collection/HM Queen Elizabeth II,
906507

HENDRICK AVERCAMP

31. *Winter Scene outside the Walls of Kampen*, c. 1613–1615
   Oil on panel
   44.5 × 72.5 cm (17½ × 28⁹⁄₁₆ in.)
   Private Collection, The Netherlands

robes are remarkably accurate; for example, the red band of cloth braided into the woman's hair indicates that she is unmarried.[4]

Avercamp occasionally made delicate renderings of the land, water, and buildings, as in the marvelous view of Kampen he drew from outside the city's walls (cat. 30). The artist then worked up the drawing in his studio with pen and brown ink and watercolor. The discolored spots in the sky were probably caused by drips of linseed oil that the artist used to mix his oil paints, an accident that must have occurred when the artist consulted this drawing while painting his *Winter Scene outside the Walls of Kampen* (cat. 31).[5] In Avercamp's painting the fields surrounding the city's walls have become flooded, and he has depicted figures of all ages and classes enjoying the frozen landscape—skating, playing kolf, traveling in horse-drawn sleds, or just standing around chatting with friends and neighbors. It is probable that the artist composed this scene by consulting a number of drawings arrayed near his easel, much as is seen in Musscher's painting of an artist at work in his studio (see cat. 13).

Infrared reflectography of this painting indicates that Avercamp defined a number of the figures with careful contour lines before painting them, occasionally adjusting their forms so that they functioned effectively in the painting's overall composition.[6] Not all of his preliminary drawings are visible in infrared reflectography, however, because he often created contours of the figures in colors that relate to those of their costumes.[7] Interestingly, it is likely that the artist portrayed himself as one of the three kolf players in the lower left, where he has even scratched the kolf score into the ice with the blunt end of the brush.

Avercamp must have made elaborately finished drawings, such as *Winter Games on the Frozen River IJssel* (fig. 2), for the open market as a less expensive alternative to his paintings. One seventeenth-century inventory lists 'four drawings by the Mute of Campen behind glass,' a clear indication that these drawings were conceived to be hung as framed works of art.[8] Such a grouping suggests that Avercamp intended these particular drawings to be kept together, perhaps as a series of the four seasons. In creating such finished drawings, which he carefully colored with gouache and watercolor, Avercamp also drew upon his stock of quick sketches from life and his carefully rendered figure studies. As with his paintings, Avercamp often adjusted the poses and clothing of the figures from these studies for compositional purposes. For example, the elegant couple behind the kolf player in *Winter Games on the Frozen River IJssel* wear clothing fashionable in the late 1620s, quite different in style from the clothing of the figures in the drawing on which he based this group, a drawing that he had executed around 1620.[9]   [AKW]

4. Bianca M. du Mortier, 'Aspects of Costume: A Showcase of Early 17th-Century Dress,' in Amsterdam/Washington 2009, 143–144.
5. Schapelhouman in Amsterdam/Washington 2009, 115.

6. Arie Wallert and Ige Verslype, 'Ice and Sky, Sky and Ice: Technical Aspects,' in Amsterdam/Washington 2009, 132, fig. 156.
7. This observation was kindly shared with me by Elma O'Donoghue, associate painting conservator at the Los Angeles County Museum of Art.

8. Schapelhouman in Amsterdam/Washington 2009, 102.
9. Schapelhouman 1995, 250. Avercamp based this figure group on a similar one appearing in a drawing now in Dresden.

ESAIAS VAN DE VELDE

1587–1630

32. *Standing Couple Seen from the Side*, c. 1617
Black chalk with gouache highlights on blue paper
23.5 × 16.5 cm (9¼ × 6½ in.)
Rijksprentenkabinet, Rijksmuseum, Amsterdam,
RP-T-1886-A-569

Esaias van de Velde was one of the most innovative artists of the early seventeenth century and a pioneer in the evolution of Dutch naturalistic landscape painting. Probably trained in Amsterdam by David Vinckboons, he started his career in Haarlem around 1610 and finally settled in The Hague in 1618. A very prolific artist, Van de Velde left a large body of work despite his relatively short lifespan of forty-three years. Approximately 180 paintings, more than 200 hundred drawings and some 30 prints by him survive today, as well as around 120 prints made after his designs. Although many of his works are landscapes, he also depicted merry companies, fighting bandits, and other figure compositions. In the 1620s he collaborated with Bartholomeus van Bassen and others by adding figures and other staffage to their paintings.[1]

Remarkably few of Van de Velde's extant drawings relate directly to his paintings or prints; those that do all date to his early career between about 1614 and 1619. This discrepancy can partially be ascribed to loss or usage. The contents of his sketchbooks, for instance, have been preserved fragmentarily.[2] Also, only about a handful of preparatory studies survive for prints after Van de Velde's designs that were executed by other printmakers, whereas one can assume that Van de Velde produced a drawing for each print made.[3] When it came to preparing his own work, however, it is possible that Esaias rarely used drawings.[4] The scarcity of repeated motifs in Van de Velde's oeuvre attest to his great inventiveness.

This black chalk and gouache drawing of an elegant couple (cat. 32), one of Van de Velde's very few figure

Fig. 1. Esaias van de Velde (and unknown artist?), *Beached Sperm Whale between Scheveningen and Katwijk*, 1617, oil on canvas. New Bedford Whaling Museum, New Bedford, Mass., O 378

1. For a list of paintings on which Van de Velde collaborated, see Keyes and Briels 1984, 169–184.
2. For a general discussion of Van de Velde's sketchbooks, see Keyes 1987; for the technical information, see Keyes and Briels 1984, nos. D105, D78 (see also William Robinson in London/Paris/Cambridge 2002, 42, no. 9, and Marleen Ram in Amsterdam/Paris 2015, 54–57, no. 18, for two additions to this group), D68, D100.
3. Keyes and Briels 1984 lists seven, nos. D5, D64, D65, D105, D109, D147, and D154.
4. Keyes lists three preparatory drawings for Van de Velde's own work: a quick pen sketch from life of Spaarnwoude of c. 1615, now at the Rijksmuseum, which Van de Velde etched in reverse with some additions (Keyes and Briels 1984, no. D133, and for the etching no. E12); his drawing *Large Square Tower to the Left of a Frozen River* of c. 1614 (Keyes and Briels 1984, nos. D66 [drawing] and E30 [etching]); and a chalk drawing of *Riders in a Forest* that corresponds almost entirely to a 1619 painting with the same subject (Keyes and Briels 1984, nos. D165 and 156).

studies, has long been recognized as his preparatory drawing for the couple in the right foreground of the painting *Beached Sperm Whale between Scheveningen and Katwijk* from around 1617 (fig. 1).[5] The figures are richly dressed in the fashion of the mid-1610s, which is especially noticeable in the man's wide breeches, sable fur, and tall hat.[6] Executed in bold and accurate lines, the drawing fits well within Van de Velde's drawn oeuvre of around 1617–1618. During this period, he had just started to use black chalk and was developing an original, minimalist style that would come to fruition after his move to The Hague in 1618 and would have a great influence on his student Jan van Goyen (see pp. 127–131).[7] This is one of very few drawings executed on blue paper, a type of paper Van de Velde appears to have experimented with only around this time.[8] Just a few small differences exist between the drawing and the painting. In the latter, Van de Velde eliminated the glove in the man's left hand, covered the man's face with his hair billowing in the wind, and turned the woman's face more toward the whale.

The painting appears to record the historical event of a sperm whale that washed ashore in January 1617, but it actually contains a striking inaccuracy.[9] Compared to the engraving by Willem Buytewech of the same beaching of 1617, it is clear that the animal was actually lying on its left side, and not—as depicted in the painting—on its right side.[10] Scholars have rightly pointed to the reliance on previous depictions of the same subject, most notably Jacob Matham's print after Goltzius's 1598 drawing of the stranded whale near Berckhey and Jan Saenredam's 1602 print of a similar event near Beverwijck (fig. 2).[11] The position of the whale and the curve of the dunes in the background of the painting are so similar to the older depictions that the artist seems to have created an amalgam of the existing pictorial traditions without necessarily having witnessed the scene.

Compared to Van de Velde's keen interest in other whale beachings, as attested by his engraving after the

5. Amsterdam/Washington 1981, 43 and 144, no. 96. For the painting, see Keyes and Briels 1984, 124–125, no. 19.
6. Compare, for instance, *Elegant Couple on a Terrace* of c. 1616–1620 by Van de Velde's contemporary Willem Buytewech in the

Rijksmuseum, Amsterdam. See Everhard Korthals Altes in Bikker 2007, 98, no. 41.
7. Keyes 1987.
8. Keyes and Briels 1984 further lists *Two Horses Drawing a Large Canopied Wagon*, black chalk on blue paper, c. 1619,

Rijksprentenkabinet, Leiden, D 46; and *Riders in a Forest*, black chalk on blue paper, c. 1619, Kupferstichkabinett, Kassel, D165.
9. Keyes and Briels 1984, 124–125, no. 19.
10. For the drawing, now in the Kupferstichkabinett in Berlin, see

event of 1614 at Noordwijk and his drawing of the 1629 beaching, again at Noordwijk, this painting is atypical.[12] In fact, the flatly painted dunes and stiff waves, which create an unnatural opening around the whale's head, are hard to reconcile with the fluid, crisp scenery in Van de Velde's landscape painting of that time.[13] One wonders whether this painting might represent an early collaboration between Van de Velde and another artist, to which Van de Velde perhaps contributed the figures and the boats.[14] In that case, *Standing Couple Seen from the Side* is a unique example of a studio drawing by Van de Velde for staffage work that can be connected to a painting. Perhaps the very few other figure drawings in his oeuvre had the same function.[15] The small differences between this drawing and the painting moreover indicate that Van de Velde could adjust the figures depending on which painting he used them for.[16]   [IVT]

Rotterdam/Paris 1974, 36–37, no. 36, and for the engraving, in the same direction as the drawing, 98–100, no. 124.

11. Amsterdam/Washington 1981, 43 and 144, no. 96; Keyes and Briels 1984, 124–125, no. 19; Schapelhouman and Schatborn 1998, 148, no. 313.

12. For a discussion of Van de Velde's depictions of beached sperm whales in 1614 and 1629, see Niemeijer 1964.

13. Compare, for instance, his *Fighting Bandits in a Landscape*, 1616, Rijksmuseum, Amsterdam, SK-C-1533.

14. See Keyes and Briels 1984, 124–125, no. 19, who raises the same question.

15. See Keyes and Briels 1984, for the *Pilgrim*, black chalk and gray wash, Musée du Louvre, Paris, D59; *Standing Man*, black chalk and gray wash, lost in Bremen during World War II, D53; and *Young Men Seated on a Stool* and *Young Man Standing*, black chalk, British Museum, London, D57 and D58, respectively.

16. Interestingly, technical research carried out on the canvas in 1987 revealed that the boats were painted over and moved around considerably during the painting process. If this was indeed a collaboration piece, Van de Velde was clearly not limited to any set composition provided by the other artist. Many thanks to Melanie Correia at the New Bedford Whaling Museum for supplying information on the 1987 conservation treatment at the Fogg Art Museum (email correspondence, September 2015).

GERARD VAN HONTHORST

1592–1656

33. *Merry Company*, 1621/1622

Pen and black-brown ink, white chalk highlights, over
a preliminary sketch in black chalk, on paper
18.3 × 27.1 cm (7³⁄₁₆ × 10¹¹⁄₁₆ in.)
Albertina, Vienna, 8437

Gerard van Honthorst occupies a singular place among
the Dutch Caravaggisti. Whereas other artists of his
generation such as Hendrick ter Brugghen, Dirck van
Baburen, and Jan van Bijlert left virtually no drawings,
close to one hundred of his survive, and sources suggest
that there used to be more.[1] Van Honthorst's outstanding talent as a draftsman was recognized early. Italian
scholar Giulio Mancini, who must have known the artist
personally when he was in Rome, noted then that the
studies Van Honthorst made in life classes testified to his
excellence in drawing.[2]

Following the example of his teacher, Abraham Bloemaert, Van Honthorst used elaborate sketches to prepare
for his paintings. Carefully composed designs have
survived both for his prestigious commissions for the
English and Danish courts and for some genre and
history paintings. Despite the level of detail in these, he
seldom—if ever—adopted the compositions exactly. In
known instances where a drawing and related painting
have both survived, Van Honthorst always made changes—some major, some less so—when he started to
paint: he moved figures, changed their poses, and sometimes censored his original design by covering a bare
shoulder or knee exposed too daringly.[3]

In the composition drawing for his *Merry Company*
(cat. 33) Van Honthorst concentrated primarily on the

way candlelight illuminated the men and women around
the table. He sketched the figures in pen-and-ink in his
rather nervy and angular style, indicating the position of
light and dark areas with washes. He hatched some
details with a pen, as in the face and sleeve of the man in
the foreground. The parts of the composition that had to
be most brightly lit were accentuated with highlights and
white chalk lines in a manner reminiscent of his former
teacher's technique.

Fig. 1. Gerard van Honthorst, *Merry Company*, 1622, oil on
canvas. Bayerische Staatsgemäldesammlungen, Alte Pinakothek,
Munich, 1312

1. For Van Honthorst's drawn oeuvre
see Judson and Ekkart 1999 and, for
supplements to it, dealer cat. Bréton 2014,
and Gert Jan van der Sman, 'I disegni di
Gerrit van Honthorst' in Florence 2015,
103–119. For the group of eighty-nine
drawings said to have been taken from
the workshop by Van Honthorst's pupil
Joachim von Sandrart, see Van der Sman,
op. cit., 119, n. 39, and Fischer 1936, 55.
2. Giulio Mancini's manuscript *Trattato
della Pittura*, cited from Judson and Ekkart
1999, 8. See Reznicek 1972, 169–172,
for one of Van Honthorst's few known
figure studies.
3. Compare the preliminary study and the
painting *The Liberation of St. Peter*; Judson
and Ekkart 1999, pls. 32, 33.

As was his custom, Van Honthorst adjusted some aspects of the drawn composition in his painting (fig. 1).[4] As well as correcting an awkward detail (for example, the old woman's left hand, which, in the drawing, is completely concealed behind the hand of the man in front), the artist was principally concerned with making the scene more animated and emphasizing the main figural group.[5] He altered the direction of gaze and gestures of some of the figures around the table so that the couple in the foreground attracts the viewer's attention. By adding the candlestick, salt cellar, and other objects on the table, Van Honthorst was able to play with the reflections of the candlelight in the shiny metal surfaces. The chiaroscuro is particularly convincing in the faces of the three figures at left. As carefully measured as the lighting effects may seem, however, they are not entirely correct: the young woman on the right, for example, catches far more light than is justified by her distance from the light source.

These and similar sketches could create the impression that Van Honthorst conceived his compositions in their entirety in his imagination, put them down on paper in one pass, and then painted them with only a few adjustments. It is more likely, however, that the elaborate sheets created in the final preparation stage are the ones that have primarily been preserved, whereas the studies and sketches of details leading up to those have only rarely survived. From Mancini's comment that Van Honthorst drew from life it is safe to assume that the artist used figure studies and detailed sketches as well as his composition studies, even though only a few studies from life are known.[6]

The assumption that Van Honthorst did not always prepare for his paintings with just a single sketch is confirmed by the recent discovery of a group of dozens of drawings that came from his workshop and have always been kept together.[7] These sheets, some with signs of use, such as paint splashes, traces of indenting, or squaring lines, date from different periods. Some of them show how the painter was seeking the right composition by making more than one sketch for the same painting.[8] Artistic considerations will surely have been a factor, but clients would also have expressed their wishes regarding a painting's composition. Some studies for portraits in which models are shown in different poses, standing or seated, beside a fountain or leaning on one arm on a plinth, may well have been made to offer his clientele various options from which to choose.[9] Van Honthorst kept his composition drawings, and occasionally even reused an old design.[10] Because he and later owners always found it worthwhile to preserve drawings, this visual documentation provides a unique insight into the workshop practices of one of the most successful figure painters and portraitists of the first half of the seventeenth century.   [GW]

4. For the painting in Munich, see Judson and Ekkart 1999, 219–220, no. 238, pl. 168.

5. The differences were described by Mieke Vermeer in Utrecht/Braunschweig 1986, 288, and Judson and Ekkart 1999, 346.

6. Judson 1988, 115, points to a study of a female head in the Staatliche Kunstsammlungen, Dresden, C 1180 (fig. 158), with a facial type and expression that resemble the second woman from the right in Van Honthorst's *Merry Company* of 1622.

7. For this group see Bréton 2014.

8. Bréton 2014, n.p., nos. 4, 5, 11.

9. Bréton 2014, n.p., nos. 14, 16.

10. Leonard Slatkes in Haboldt 2001, 60–62, no. 26.

DIRCK HALS

1591–1656

Nowadays Dirck Hals is not as famous as his older brother, Frans, but he was an immensely successful artist in seventeenth-century Holland. His merry company paintings appear very often in contemporary inventories.[1] To satisfy the considerable demand for such work, Dirck Hals developed an effective technique for making many variations to his compositions and turning them out quickly. The characters—who occupy a central place in his work—no doubt all originate from a fairly limited repertoire of figures that he combined variously and adapted to suit any given scene. These figures were sketched first in oil on paper, resulting in such drawings as those now in the Rijksmuseum (cat. 34) and the Fondation Custodia (cat. 35). Hals used these two particular works as the basis for figures in *Figures at the Fireside* now in Berlin (fig. 1). The Rijksmuseum smoker is reproduced almost identically in the painting, whereas the Fondation Custodia's *Seated Man, Leaning Backwards* is recognizable on the left. A few differences, however, are evident in the painted figure's attitude: his chin is lifted in a haughty pose and his right leg rests on his left knee. Hals may have altered him as he painted, although it is possible that a second sketch existed of this same man in another pose.

These two figures appear again in the Dirck Hals painting now in the California Palace of the Legion of Honor (fig. 2): the Rijksmuseum smoker is referenced on the far right and the Fondation Custodia's figure is seen behind the table. The latter is in the same pose as that shown in the drawing (hand on hip, with elbow raised), but his body is turned toward the viewer. Again, it should be assumed that either the figure was modified

Fig. 1. Dirck Hals, *Figures at the Fireside*, 1627, oil on panel. Staatliche Museen, Berlin, Preussischer Kulturbesitz, Gemäldegalerie, Berlin, 816A

Fig. 2. Dirck Hals, *Merry Company*, oil on panel. California
Palace of the Legion of Honor, San Francisco, 1957.160

Fig. 3. Dirck Hals and Dirck van Delen, *Merry Company
in a Renaissance Hall*, 1628, oil on panel. Frans Hals Museum,
Haarlem, on loan from the Instituut Collectie Nederland,
os 75-318

DIRCK HALS

34. *Seated Man, Smoking*, 1622–1627
   Brush and brown ink with oil containing paint,
   heightened with white, over a sketch in black chalk
   on paper
   27.7 × 17.8 cm (10⅞ × 7 in.)
   Rijksmuseum, Amsterdam, RP-T-1965-180

DIRCK HALS

35. *Seated Man, Leaning Backwards*
Brush in brown and gray oil containing paint
on paper
22.6 × 19.4 cm (8⅞ × 7⅝ in.)
Fondation Custodia, Collection Frits Lugt, Paris,
1796

as the painting was created, or that a third sketch might have influenced the final oil composition.

The group in the San Francisco painting (fig. 2) turns out to be based on several other drawings. The seated man on the left, in particular, appears in a second sketch in the Rijksmuseum, and one of the women is based on a drawing in the Fitzwilliam Museum, Cambridge.[2] The man standing in the foreground, with his back to the viewer, cannot be associated with a sketch known to be by the artist, but the same figure is included on the far right of the Berlin painting (fig. 1). He is also recognizable, albeit in a slightly different form, in the features of a backgammon player on the far left of the large panel in the Frans Hals Museum in Haarlem (fig. 3).[3] Again, this figure was probably created initially in an oil sketch that has since disappeared. On the far right in the Haarlem painting, Hals used the smoker figure once more, this time exchanging the man's pipe for a violin, and making him look a bit younger by removing his beard and prominent moustache.

It is clear that Dirck Hals did not sketch these figures in preparation for a specific painting but reused them again and again in different compositions. The Rijksmuseum's drawing (cat. 34) shows two extra legs, dressed not in hose and shoes (as in the Berlin and San Francisco paintings) but in turned-down boots (as in the Haarlem scene), thus providing the artist with the options that he might need later. Furthermore, Dirck Hals's figures were always about the same size in his paintings—between 20 and 25 centimeters[4]— which corresponds to the size of his figures in oil sketches. This way of working meant that figures were ready to be incorporated into various compositions created by this 'super-specialized' artist.[5]

Today, fourteen of his drawings have been identified.[6] The naturalism and speed of his technique seem to suggest that the painter recorded details of most figures in contemporary clothes, using models who probably posed in his studio. He may have sketched others from memory, however, such as the Fitzwilliam Museum's *Seated Man Playing the Violin*, whose face portrays stereotypical features.[7] This sketch, which is much more complete than others, is the only one to bear the monogram 'DH' and a date (1629). Thus, it may be a work in its own right and not a study.[8]

The oil-on-paper technique Hals chose for his sketches was quite rare in the Northern Netherlands of the seventeenth century.[9] Although this technique was employed from the sixteenth century onward by such artists as Dirck Barendsz in Amsterdam and Otto van Veen in Antwerp, it was used for entire compositions and not only for studies of individual figures. The choice of this technique—halfway between drawing and painting—was not accidental as far as Dirck Hals was concerned. Because of its pictorial qualities, sketching with oil on paper enabled him to work more closely toward the end result, which was a wise choice for efficient production.   [CT]

1. Kolfin 2005, 172–173.

2. Schatborn 1973, 109–110.

3. Dirck Hals painted the figures in this painting, and the architecture was done by his colleague, Dirck van Delen, with whom he sometimes collaborated. See Köhler 2006, no. 174; on the figures found in Hals's other paintings, compare with David Scrase, in Munich/Heidelberg/Braunschweig/Cambridge 1995, no. 87.

4. Kolfin 2005, 146. In inches, Hals's figure studies measure between 7⅞ – 9¹³⁄₁₆ in.

5. On Dirck Hals's 'super-specialization' as a result of the art market in Haarlem, see Kolfin 2005, 173.

6. It was Peter Schatborn who first identified twelve drawings previously attributed to other artists; see Schatborn 1973. Carlos van Hasselt added one drawing in the Victoria and Albert Museum, in New York/Paris 1977, under no. 57 (see Schatborn in Amsterdam/Washington 1981, 137; Shoaf Turner and White 2014, I, no. 82). Nehlsen-Marten, though she paraphrased the whole of Schatborn's article, does not mention this drawing in her catalogue raisonné (Nehlsen-Marten 2003, 223–227, 318–320). Today, the *Study of a Standing Youth in a Hat* that was in Michael Ingram's collection can be included (sale London, Sotheby's, December 8, 2005, no. 20, ill.).

7. Dirck Hals, *A Seated Man Playing the Violin*, oil on paper, Fitzwilliam Museum, Cambridge, PD.401-1963.

8. David Scrase rightly notes, however, that a figure with the same facial features can be seen in a painting by Dirck Hals (sale New York, Sotheby's, July 8, 1981, no. 29). Scrase in Munich/Heidelberg/Brunswick/Cambridge 1995, no. 87.

9. Schatborn 1973, 107.

CLAES CORNELISZ MOEYAERT

1591–1655

36. *Cloelia's Escape from Porsena's Camp*, 1640
Black and white chalk, on brownish cartridge paper
23.1 × 38.4 cm (9¹⁄₁₆ × 15¹⁄₈ in.)
Fondation Custodia, Collection Frits Lugt, Paris,
1994-T.9

In 1605 Moeyaert moved with his family from Durgerdam to nearby Amsterdam, where he and Pieter Lastman (see pp. 90–91) became important history painters. During his long career, Moeyaert is known to have produced more than three hundred paintings, many drawings, and a number of prints. Among his drawings for historical scenes are preliminary studies for paintings, the earliest of which date from the mid-1620s.[1]

Cloelia's Escape from Porsena's Camp (cat. 36) is a preliminary study for a painting of 1640 in St. Petersburg

remain hostage. Cloelia was one of them. She and some of her companions were not prepared to submit to their fate, so they hoodwinked their guards and escaped, reaching Rome by swimming across the Tiber, the southern border of the Etruscan territory. This feat broke the terms of the peace treaty, so the Romans sent the young people back. Cloelia then begged Porsena to keep only her and release the other hostages. Porsena was so impressed by the nobility of her proposal that he let her and five others go.

Fig. 1. Claes Cornelisz Moeyaert, *The Escape of Cloelia from Porsena's Camp*, 1640, oil on canvas. The State Hermitage Museum, St. Petersburg, 706

Fig. 2. Claes Cornelisz Moeyaert, *The Escape of Cloelia from Porsena's Camp*, 1642, pen and brown ink, gray wash, heightened with white, black chalk, on brownish paper. Szépművészeti Múzeum, Budapest, 1917-196

(fig. 1).[2] Cloelia's flight represented an episode in the war between the Romans and Etruscans in 508 BC.[3] At peace negotiations with the Romans and as a condition for his withdrawal, Etruscan king Lars Porsena had demanded that several young men and women—the sons and daughters of prominent Roman families—would

In Moeyaert's composition Cloelia and some of her female companions have reached the Tiber on horseback. Some of them, naked in the water, are about to begin swimming, and others are disrobing, preparing to make the night crossing. Right of center, the woman on the horse and with a companion is probably Cloelia. She

is still fully clothed, while the woman on horseback to Cloelia's right is being helped off her mount by a nude woman.

Moeyaert achieved the effect of a nocturnal event by using brownish paper and accentuating highlights with white chalk. Many differences exist between the drawing and painting. The figures on the extreme right do not appear in the painting, while a woman on horseback in the right foreground of the painting does not appear in the drawing. Moeyaert moved some other figures and cast their glances in different directions.

Moeyaert often depicted subjects more than once, sometimes after a long interval. He pictured *Cloelia's Escape from Porsena's Camp* in a painting of 1642 in the Nationalmuseet, Oslo, and a preliminary drawing for that painting in Budapest (fig. 2). He featured the same figures and motifs in the drawing, but altered the composition. He also created the effect of darkness by brushing in heavy washes. In the painting Moeyaert added a silhouetted, kneeling figure in the middle foreground that does not appear in the Budapest drawing.[4]   [PS]

1. The drawings associated with paintings, both preliminary studies and related compositions, are listed by Tümpel 1974, 247–290.

2. Inv. no. 706; Tümpel 1974, 110, figs. 149, 267, no. 184.

3. Livy, *Ab Urbe Condita*, book II, 13.

4. The Oslo painting is inv. no. 322, panel, signed and dated lower right 'CL.M f 1642'; Tümpel 1974, 112, figs. 152, 267, no. 185. The Budapest work is discussed in Tümpel 1974, 267, fig. 260; and Gerszi 2005, no. 165.

PIETER VAN LAER

1599–after 1641

37. *Two Studies of a Seated Shepherd*, c. 1630–1637(?)
   Black and white chalk on blue paper
   18.6 × 26.2 cm (7⁵⁄₁₆ × 10⁵⁄₁₆ in.)
   Musée des Beaux-Arts et d'Archéologie, Besançon,
   D 805

At first glance, it would seem that the drawing of a seated shepherd, with a partially depicted second figure without a hat, was completed as a preliminary study for Philips Wouwerman's *Landscape with a Seated Herdsman near a House*, c. 1640–1643 (fig. 1). It is likely, however, that the two works are by different artists. Wouwerman, a landscape painter who incorporated genre scenes of various types, left a large, wide-ranging oeuvre, but few drawings by him are known. The drawing of the shepherds is inscribed 'Bamboots,' in the hand of the art dealer Jan Pietersz Zomer.[1] *Bamboots* is a Dutch translation of the Italian word *bamboccio*—a bumpkin—the nickname Pieter van Laer was given in Rome. The artist lived in that city between around 1625 and 1637, and was a member of the Bentvogels—the society of Dutch artists. In 1639, he was recorded to be living in Haarlem again. Van Laer painted landscapes with animals and genre scenes, both in the countryside and in town. He, too, left few surviving drawings.

Wouwerman was generally influenced by Van Laer in his paintings, perhaps because he owned drawings such as the one from Besançon (cat. 37). In his biography of Wouwerman, Arnold Houbraken writes that the painter and art dealer Jan (or Jacob) de Wet obtained Van Laer's drawings after that artist's death: De Wet 'acquired for Wouwerman [Van Laer's] chest of models, drawings, and sketches, before anyone stuck their nose in, of which precious stock (one man's death is another's gain) Wouwerman managed

Fig. 1. Philips Wouwerman, *Landscape with a Seated Herdsman near a House*, c. 1640–1643. Oil on panel. Private Collection

to avail himself without anyone knowing how he came by it. These were the drawings I have mentioned, which [Wouwerman] had burned before his eyes as he lay on his deathbed, so that the world should not know after his death with whose beasts he had ploughed.' Houbraken heard this story from Michiel Carree, who, in turn, had heard it from the painter Pieter van Roestraten, an acquaintance of Van Laer, Wouwerman, and De Wet. 'And I simply repeat it . . . without adding or omitting anything,' adds Houbraken.[2]

1. Plomp 1997b, 17–18, fig. 10. Jan Pietersz Zomer's handwriting appears on a number of drawings.
2. 'Hy maakte zig voor Wouwerman Meester van van zyn Koffer met Modellen, Teekeningen en Schetzen, eer iemand de Neus daar in stak, van welken kostelyken voorraad (des eenen Dood is des anders Brood) Wouwerman zig wel heeft weten te bedienen, zonder dat ymant wist hoe hy ér aan kwam. Dit waren nu de Teekeningen waar ik van gemeld heb, die hij op zijn sterfbed leggende voor zyn oogen deed verbranden; op dat de Warelt niet weten zoude na zyn dood, met wiens kalveren hy geploegt had. . . . En ik geef het weder zuiver over . . . zonder daar iets af of toe te doen.' Houbraken 1718–1721, II, 75.

Although this tale has been called into question in art historical literature, the fact that a drawing inscribed with 'Bamboots' was used in Wouwerman's painting suggests that there is a kernel of truth in it.[3] Two other figure studies on blue paper bear Zomer's inscription 'Bamboots.' They are *Standing Man with a Hat* (1660s, Rijksmuseum, Amsterdam) and *Seated Man with a Hat, Smoking* (c. 1645, Hamburger Kunsthalle, Hamburg).[4] The Hamburg drawing bears a strong resemblance to Van Laer's painted figures. This visual connection seems to support the attribution to Van Laer made by Zomer, but this art dealer did occasionally make mistakes.[5] Moreover, if the story is to be believed that, before he died, Wouwerman burned all of Van Laer's drawings, the sheet in Besançon must have escaped this fate.

An attribution to Van Laer is supported by the fact that the drawing's style does not resemble that of Wouwerman's drawings. Nevertheless, it should be emphasized that no comparable drawings can be attributed to Laer either. The attribution to Van Laer of the drawing in Besançon consequently remains a special case. If the inscription of 'Bamboots' is accurately connected to Van Laer, and Wouwerman used the drawing in his painting, Houbraken's story would have some credence. While the nucleus of the story that Wouwerman procured and utilized Van Laer's drawings might be correct, it may also have been exaggerated over time to make it even more believable. History writers in this period were not averse to embellishing facts with examples of their own invention or borrowed from others.[6] Thus, the attribution of the drawing to Van Laer could be correct. [PS]

3. Blankert 1986, 129–130.
4. Pieter van Laer (attributed), *Standing Man with a Hat*, 1660s, black and white chalk on blue paper, Rijksmuseum, Amsterdam, RP-T-1905-183; Amsterdam/Washington 1981, 62, no. 61. The watermark in the paper used for this drawing, a foolscap with seven points, does not occur before 1651 and most closely resembles watermarks of the 1660s; Laurentius 2008, vii. Barend Graat (attributed) *Seated Man with a Hat, Smoking*, c. 1645, drawing, Hamburger Kunsthalle, Hamburg, 22095. Stefes 2011, no. 388, as attributed to Barend Graat.
5. Plomp 1997a gives several examples.
6. See Blankert 1986, 120–127.

BALTHASAR VAN DER AST

1593/94–1657

The vibrant realism and beautiful calligraphy of the inscriptions of Balthasar van der Ast's many drawings of tulips are reminiscent of the tulip books commissioned by bulb growers for their sales catalogs in the seventeenth century (cat. 38).[1] But in Van der Ast's case it is clear that—at least in part—he made such works for his own use: motifs found in his drawings appear in various paintings.[2] For instance, he used the study of the red, white, and yellow flame Admirael Pottebacker variety for the tulip in the upper left corner of the flower still life pictured here (cat. 39).[3] The flowers are virtually the same. For the purposes of the painted composition the tulip is depicted slightly more closed, but the curling edges of the petals, the irregularly shaped edge of the left petal, and the small gap at left which allows a view of two stamens, are identical.

Van der Ast was thus no different from other flower painters in the early seventeenth century, for his teacher Ambrosius Bosschaert and Jacques de Gheyn II (see pp. 69, 72–75) also worked with studies of individual flowers. Unusual, however, compared to the works of those flower painters, is the number of Van der Ast's sheets that have survived. A collection of seventy-one watercolors of flowers, shells, insects, and other small creatures (currently in Paris) has survived from a group that must have numbered at least 483 sheets.[4] Other drawings in this series, a studio stock which the artist must have built up over a lengthy period of time, are known only from copies, are scattered among various collections, or are in the hands of art dealers.[5] Lot descriptions in old sale catalogs tell us that, originally, drawings of fruit must have been part of this group as well.[6]

Exotic shells appear in several dozen of the studies in this series (cat. 40). Like tulips, such shells were expensive collectibles to which an artist did not necessarily have access, although some painters are known to have had their own collections.[7] Van der Ast, using his drawings as sources, gave shells a significant—if not starring—role in many of his still lifes. He put the baroque form of the adusta murex (*Chicoreus brunneus*) virtually unchanged, shadow and all, in his *Still Life with Flowers and Shells* (fig. 1).[8] The same shell—sometimes reversed—appears in other paintings by him.[9] In some of them it is depicted from a different angle, suggesting that the artist made more than one drawing of this specimen.[10]

1. For more about these tulip books, see Segal 1987 and Sam Segal, 'De Tulp in de Gouden Eeuw,' in Amsterdam 1994, 78–83.

2. The likelihood that the drawings were part of Van der Ast's workshop stock is also suggested by the cursory outlines of tulips in black chalk (attempts by pupils?) on the back of the two sheets illustrated here and various others in the series.

3. The derivations in the works illustrated here were noted by Peter Schatborn (written communication, 2015).

4. For the series, see Michiel C. Plomp, 'Tulip', 'Lizard and Shell,' and 'Pansy and Shell,' in New York/London 2001, 445–447, under nos. 96–98; Stijn Alsteens, 'Merveille Delphius de Hollande,' in Paris 2004, 108, 305, under no. 41;

and Martina Dlugaiczyk in Aachen/Gotha 2016, no. 40 a-k (in print). The attribution of this series, which for a long time was credited to Bartholomeus Assteyn, was made by Segal in Amsterdam 1994, 96.

5. Alsteens in Paris 2004, 305, nn. 2, 16.

6. See, for example, sale [Beudeker] Amsterdam (Jan Cloppenburg and Hendrik de Leth), July 27, 1751, 18, book V: '20 Stuks Vruchten van Van der Ast. . . . Alle konstig met Waterverf geschildert' ('20 Fruit Works by Van der Ast . . . . All skillfully painted in Watercolor').

7. Meyere 2006, 20. On collecting shells in the seventeenth and eighteenth centuries see H. E. Coomans, 'Schelpenverzamelingen,' in Amsterdam 1992, 192–203.

8. *Still Life with Flowers and Shells*, 1635–1640, oil on panel, 23.8 × 34.5 cm (9⅜ × 13⁹⁄₁₆ in.), Private Collection. See Amsterdam/Cleveland 1999, 157, n. 1, for the identification of the *Chicoreus brunneus*. The shell at the bottom can be identified as *Conus magus*. Both are found in the Indian and Pacific Oceans.

9. See, for example, the painting in sale London (Sotheby's), April 1, 1992, no. 59 (ill.), and in the Staatliche Kunstsammungen, Gemäldegalerie Alte Meister, Dresden, A 654.

10. The possibility that Van der Ast made more than one drawing of some shells was previously put forward by William W. Robinson, 'Pica Shell' and 'Feathered Cone Shell,' in London/Paris/Cambridge 2002, 230, under nos. 102a and 102b.

BALTHASAR VAN DER AST

38. *Study of a Tulip (*Admirael Pottebacker*) and a Fly*,
    1620–1630
    Gouache, watercolor, and tempera on paper
    31.3 × 20.2 cm (12⁵⁄₁₆ × 7⁵⁄₁₆ in.)
    Fondation Custodia, Collection Frits Lugt, Paris,
    6534/42

BALTHASAR VAN DER AST

39. *Flower Still Life*, c. 1630

 Oil on panel

 37.2 × 24.5 cm (14⅝ × 9⅝ in.)

 Rose-Marie and Eijk Van Otterloo Collection

BALTHASAR VAN DER AST
40. *Two Shells*, 1620–1630
  Gouache, watercolor, and tempera on paper
  31.4 × 20.2 cm (12⅜ × 7¹⁵⁄₁₆ in.)
  Fondation Custodia, Collection Frits Lugt, Paris,
  6534/49

Strikingly, even though numerous studies by Van der Ast of individual flowers or shells such as these have survived, no compositional drawings exist for his paintings.[11] Surely with a complex composition such as *Still Life with Flowers and Shells*, one would expect him to have made a preliminary design on paper, as some later flower painters did.[12] However, this was almost certainly not

Fig. 1. Balthasar van der Ast, *Still Life with Flowers and Shells*, 1635–1640, oil on panel. Private collection

the case. Van der Ast, along with most other early specialists in the genre, worked out his compositions at the easel. Infrared reflectography has revealed extensive underdrawing in several of his paintings, which helps to understand how he gradually built up the composition, making occasional changes, both during the drawing and in the painting process.[13] Underdrawings reveal that he began a number of still lifes by placing two crossed diagonal lines, originating in the four corners, on the ground layer of his panel, after which he arranged certain objects in the composition along these lines.[14]

In his underdrawings, which can sometimes actually be seen through the paint layer with the naked eye, Van der Ast tended to limit himself to the outlines. Some details were drawn freehand, others with a somewhat searching line, which suggests that, in these cases, he was working from drawn models, either by copying or by transferring the outlines by means of indentation. Once the detailed underdrawing was finished he began painting with the watercolor studies at hand in order to capture the proper colors and textures. The strongly delineated outlines led one author to remark, tongue in cheek, that it is like 'painting by numbers,' or, in other words, something that could be left to a pupil or assistant.[15] This process, however, was more than a coloring-in exercise. It took a skilled hand to make the delicate petals of a rose look different from the robust petals of a tulip, and a practiced eye to create three dimensionality by using light and shadow. For all Van der Ast's reliance on drawings as sources for his paintings, his flower pieces and other still lifes in no way give the impression that they were actually compiled from individual studies, which is proof of his mastery.   [GW]

11. There is only one known drawn still life by Van der Ast, but given its elaborate finish and the flamboyant signature it is more likely to be a work of art in its own right. British Museum, London, 1906.11.28.1; Plomp in New York/London 2001, 444–445, no. 95.

12. We know of various composition sketches by Jan van Huijsum; for instance, see White 1964 and Delft/Houston 2007.

13. An unpublished infrared reflectogram of a still life by Van der Ast (52.9.197) in the North Carolina Museum of Art in Raleigh not only reveals a number of corrections in the underdrawing but also shows that Van der Ast made several adjustments while painting. The author wishes to thank Noelle Ocon for sharing this reflectogram. See also Weller 2009, 7.

14. Some paintings by Van der Ast in which diagonal composition lines were found were described by Sam Segal, 'Still-Life Painting in Middelburg,' in Amsterdam 1984, 25–62, 56, 58, and Groen and Murray 1991, 152, pl. 82 (also illustrated in Taylor 1995, 94–95). On the composition principles in some of Van der Ast's still lifes see Gemar-Koeltzsch 1995, I, 44.

15. Arie Wallert, 'Methods and Materials of Still-Life Painting in the Seventeenth Century,' and Willem de Ridder et al., 'Still Life with Flowers,' in Amsterdam 1999, 7–24 and 57–59, respectively. For Van der Ast's working method, see also Arie Wallert, 'Balthasar van der Ast: Materialien und Techniken,' in Aachen/Gotha 2016, 81–93.

CORNELIS VAN POELENBURCH

1594/95–1667

41. *Houses in Italy* (recto), c. 1620–1625
Pen and brown ink and wash over black chalk
on paper
Putto Carrying an Urn (verso)
Counterproof in red chalk
18.7 × 23.2 cm (7⅜ × 9⅛ in.)
Private Collection

When one considers how much Cornelis van Poelen-burch had in common with Gerrit van Honthorst—they were almost exact contemporaries who trained in the same Utrecht workshop and then traveled to Italy—one might expect them to have prepared their paintings in the same way. Yet their approaches could hardly have been more different. While Van Honthorst made elabo-rate compositional sketches that he transferred to canvas or panel, Van Poelenburch worked with a large stock of drawings that he called upon piecemeal for his paint-ings.[1] This stock, part of which he had built up during his time in Rome between 1617 and around 1625, included landscapes, classical ruins, figure studies, and views in and around the city, such as a sun-drenched Italian street lined with houses (cat. 41 recto).[2]

Shepherds with Their Flocks in a Landscape with Roman Ruins (fig. 1), dating from the early 1620s, is a good illustration of Van Poelenburch's working method.[3] Some of the details in this work have been identified as buildings that stood in the Forum Romanum in Rome, among them the fountain at left and the ruins of a

Fig. 1. Cornelis van Poelenburch, *Shepherds with Their Flocks in a Landscape with Roman Ruins*, c. 1620–1625, oil on copper. Royal Collection Trust/© Her Majesty Queen Elizabeth II, RCIN 404819

classical temple at right.[4] However, the artist was not endeavoring to paint an accurate picture of the situation; he instead selected motifs from different drawings to create the scene. Van Poelenburch placed large elements as repoussoirs in the landscape to the left and right, creating a distant view between them—a tried and tested template that Karel van Mander had recommend-ed in his *Schilder-Boeck* of 1604.[5]

1. For Van Poelenburch as a draftsman see chiefly Chong 1987 and Peter Schatborn, 'Cornelis Poelenburch,' in Amsterdam 2001, 57–65.
2. The framing line was put in before the small figure in the foreground was drawn, so it was not by a later hand. As a result, the drawing evokes associations with a

design for a print. Another version, which is regarded as a copy, is in the Städel Museum, Frankfurt am Main, 3145.
3. For this painting see Shawe-Taylor 2010, 132–133, no. 28; White 2015, 276–278, no. 141; and Sluijter-Seijffert 2016, 361, no. 214.

4. Schaar 1959, 35–36, identified the ruins on the right as part of the Temple of Castor and Pollux, but it looks more like a compressed version of the ruined Temple of Vespasian and Titus.
5. Mander 1604 *Grondt*, I, 130–131 (V, verses 11–12).

One of the motifs Van Poelenburch used in *Shepherds with Their Flocks* was the house with the striking roof that is depicted in the exhibited drawing.[6] He incorporated the house into the painting with few changes, but located it in a completely different setting by siting it on a rock with classical ruins. He probably used a drawn example of this particular site, too, because the rock—with the two cavernous openings and ruins—calls to mind the Acropolis in Tivoli, one of the places where he was known to draw.[7] Some other elements, such as the ruin of a classical temple at right and the strangely shaped rock in front of it, appear in other works and must likewise have been taken from sketches made in situ.[8]

During his time in Italy Van Poelenburch's focus was not confined to the landscape and buildings; he also took an interest in the work of his predecessors. He studied works by Raphael and Michelangelo, among others, and sometimes copied figures that he later used in his own work. Figure studies in red chalk or counterproofs of them on the back of a number of his drawings are evidence of this interest.[9] The back of *Houses in Italy*, for instance, was used for a counterproof of a drawing of a standing putto with an urn (cat. 41 verso), possibly after an example by Annibale Carracci, which the artist featured in his painting *Moses Striking Water from the Rocks* in Florence in, or before, 1621.[10]

Once back in Utrecht, Van Poelenburch continued to make extensive use of the material that he had collected in Italy. He also made new drawings based on the ones he had brought back: several dozen gray-washed Italianate landscapes, believed to have been made in the flat lands of the north, survive.[11] It seems highly likely that Van Poelenburch made them so that his workshop could produce painted works as efficiently as possible. He had pupils and assistants who copied his paintings and used his drawings to create compositions in the master's style. These landscapes, which often include classical ruins, functioned as settings for historical or mythological scenes.[12] It was a successful formula: fifty years after his death Van Poelenburch was still being praised for his 'delightful discrimination' and 'clever additions of old ruins.'[13]   [GW]

6. Alan Chong in Le Claire 1998, n.p., no. 11. The house also appears in a painting sold at auction in London (Christie's), December 13, 1996, no. 210 (ill.), which, according to Nicolette Sluijter-Seijffert, is not an autograph work (email, August 2015).

7. A drawing made in this location is in the Rijksmuseum, Amsterdam, RP-T-1989-90(R). This rock appears in similar form in two sheets from a series of drawings in the Uffizi, Florence, nos. 772, 774; Kloek 1975, n.p., nos. 741, 742. Until recently this series was attributed to Van Poelenburch, but it has now been established that it cannot be by him because one of these drawings is of an architectural feature that did not exist until 1628–1629, or, in other words, years after he had left Italy. See Peter Schatborn in Kloek and Meijer 2008, 128–129.

8. Albert Blankert in Utrecht 1965, 66, observed that the rock on the right in this painting was also used in Van Poelenburch's painting in the Toledo Museum of Art, inv. no. 56.52. See further Sluijter-Seiffert 2016, 361, no. 214.

9. Chong 1987, 27–28, no. 17; 31, no. 29; 31–32, no. 32. See also Joaneath A. Spicer, 'Feast of the Gods,' in San Francisco/ Baltimore/London 1997, 293–297.

10. Palazzo Pitti, Florence, inv. no. 1890, n. 1220; Chiarini 1989, 247, saw similarities to Annibale Carracci's nudes in the gallery of the Palazzo Farnese in Rome.

11. Chong 1987, 11–13.

12. For examples see Ger Luijten in Rotterdam 1988, 103–104, nos. 62–63; Shoaf Turner and White 2014, 195–200, nos. 147–149; and Jane Shoaf Turner, 'Italianate Landscape with Ruins,' in Amsterdam/Paris 2015, 62, no. 21.

13. Houbraken 1718–1721, I, 128.

JAN VAN GOYEN

1596–1656

During his own lifetime, Jan van Goyen was already recognized as a virtuoso and as one of the most famous landscape artists of the seventeenth century.[1] Born in Leiden, Van Goyen trained with Esaias van de Velde (see pp. 102–105) in Haarlem around 1617–1618. Deeply influenced by his master's naturalistic landscape paintings, Van Goyen developed his own distinctive and efficient painting style toward the end of the 1620s, characterized by few pigments and paint layers.[2] His prolific output of paintings made them affordable for the middle class, but wealthy collectors also sought them out for their artistic merit.[3] In 1632, Van Goyen moved to The Hague, where he was based until his death.

Van Goyen was also an avid draftsman, as the more than one thousand surviving drawings attest.[4] Many of them are signed and dated, and no doubt intended as finished works of art for sale. There are also numerous drawings in his sketchbooks that Van Goyen executed in the open air. His early drawings are executed in pen, but around 1626 he switched to black chalk.[5] Although he started using black chalk almost eight years after working under the tutelage of Van de Velde, there is no doubt that the latter's minimal and quick black chalk landscape drawings were an important example. In his later sketches, especially those of the 1650s, Van Goyen was often even more succinct than his master, jotting down only bare contours with stenographic virtuosity.

Van Goyen's sketches from life provided rich source material throughout his career. Back in the studio he used them extensively in his finished drawings and paintings, repeating motifs in a variety of inventive ways and creating new compositions with relatively few pictorial means.[6] Two of Van Goyen's sketchbooks survive more or less intact: the so-called Bredius-Kronig Sketchbook, which Van Goyen used between 1644 and c. 1650 in and around Haarlem and Delft, and the Dresden Sketchbook (see p. 7, fig. 2 and p. 8, fig. 4), which he carried with him in 1648 on his travels to Antwerp, Brussels, and Zeeland.[7] A third sketchbook—the so-called Lilienfeld Sketchbook that Van Goyen used in 1650–1651 on a trip along the Rhine to present-day Germany and later in Amsterdam—is no longer intact. It was taken apart in 1918 and the sheets were sold separately in 1957 by art dealer Karl Lilienfeld.[8]

This drawing of the *Haringpakkerstoren* (cat. 42), which at the time stood on the corner of the Singel and the IJ in Amsterdam, originally came from the Lilienfeld Sketchbook and was probably made in the spring of 1651.[9] With an astonishing economy of line and a modest use of gray wash, Van Goyen depicted the tower with its

1. For the contemporary reception of Jan van Goyen's work, see Sluijter 1996.
2. On the development of Van Goyen's painting technique in the 1620s and the rest of his career, see Gifford 1996.
3. See Sluijter 1996.
4. Beck 1972–1991, I, lists 841 separate drawings and a few hundred more in Van Goyen's sketchbooks, either intact or dissembled.
5. For Van Goyen's pen drawings, executed until around 1629–1631, see Beck 1972–1991, I, 6–17, nos. 1–45. For his earliest dated black chalk drawing of 1626, see Beck 1972–1991, I, 22, no. 56.
6. See Beck 1996, 193, for the observation that Van Goyen used his drawings more extensively than his contemporaries. For a general discussion of Van Goyen's drawings as preparatory studies, see Beck 1957.
7. For the entirely intact so-called Bredius-Kronig Sketchbook, preserved at Museum Bredius in The Hague, see Beck 1972–1991, I, 265–270, no. 845, and Buijsen 1993. For the Dresden Sketchbook, preserved at the Kupferstichkabinett in Dresden, from which a few pages are missing, see Beck 1972–1991, I, 271–283, no. 846. For a general overview of Van Goyen's sketchbooks, see Buijsen 1996.
8. For the Lilienfeld Sketchbook, see Beck 1972–1991, I, 285–315, no. 847, and Buijsen 1996, 28–31.
9. Some of Van Goyen's drawings in the Lilienfeld Sketchbook reveal that he was in Amsterdam just after the Diemerdijk had broken in early March 1651. See Buijsen 1996, 31.

JAN VAN GOYEN

42. *The 'Haringpakkerstoren' in Amsterdam*, c. 1651
Black chalk, gray wash, on paper
9.9 × 15.7 cm (3⅞ × 6³⁄₁₆ in.)
Fondation Custodia, Collection Frits Lugt, Paris,
2997G

distinctive multilayered spire and the surrounding buildings. This sketch provides an interesting illustration of Van Goyen's working method, since it is a rare example in Van Goyen's oeuvre that can be connected to both a finished drawing as well as a painting.[10] Back in the studio shortly after his trip, he apparently used this sketch to make a separate finished drawing, monogrammed and dated 1651.[11] In the finished drawing, Van Goyen fleshed out the buildings and ships that he had indicated cursorily in the sketch, and added more wash. In the foreground of the drawing, which he had left almost entirely empty on the sketchbook page, he added a little rowboat.[12] In the painting (fig. 1) that Van Goyen executed after this same view he simply added more staffage: several rowboats on the left and right that are secondary to the main subject. Curiously, the painting is dated 1655, four years after the two drawings. Considering the time gap and the differences in staffage between the finished drawing and the painting, it seems likely that the rudimentary sketch—and not the finished drawing—functioned as the starting point for the later painting.[13] It is telling that Van Goyen's sketches were so significant: the staccato sketch provided sufficient information for the artist to develop, even years after it was made.

In 1653, Van Goyen executed the finished drawing *Sailing Ships* (cat. 43). This drawing depicts a rowboat in the left foreground, and two sailing boats flanked by two small barges just right of the center. These two motifs appear in the same relation to one other in Van Goyen's painting *Ships under a Cloudy Sky* from 1655 (cat. 44).

With just slight variations in the people's activities on the boats and in the size of the clouds, Van Goyen managed to create two different compositions and moods. It is likely that the artist again used a sketch that contained both motifs—or a combination of sketches

Fig. 1. Jan van Goyen, *View of Amsterdam with the Haringpakkerstoren*, 1655, oil on panel. Private Collection

each with individual motifs, now lost—as the starting point for both works. He had probably created the initial sketch, or sketches, some years before. The two motifs also appear together in Van Goyen's two earlier paintings from the late 1640s in which he incorporated distinct topographical elements of Dordrecht, namely *Sailing Boats with a Distant View of Dordrecht* from c. 1647 and *The Oude Wachthuis on the River Kil*, 1649.[14]   [IVT]

10. Beck 1957, 246.
11. For the drawing, last seen at an auction at A. Beurdeley in Paris on June 8, 1920, no. 182, see Beck 1972–1991, I, 83, no. 230 (11 × 20 cm, black chalk with gray wash). The drawing is monogrammed and dated 1651 at bottom right. Also reproduced in *Oud Holland*, 1957/4, 248.
12. Beck 1972–1991, II, 204, no. 421. The painting, currently in an unidentified private collection, is monogrammed and dated 1655 on the rowboat in the right foreground.

13. Beck 1957, 246, on the other hand, believes that the finished drawing represents an intermediary phase in the process from drawing to painting. For an image of the painting, see https://rkd.nl/explore/images/241684.
14. For the painting *Sailing Boats with a Distant View of Dordrecht*, c. 1647, formerly in the Arthur Kay Collection in Glasgow, see Beck 1972–1991, II, 408, no. 905. This connection was also made by Vogt in Brussels/Amsterdam/Aachen 2007a and 2007b, 113–114, no. 35. For *The Oude*

Wachthuis on the River Kil, 1649, last seen at an auction at Christie's London on July 10, 1987, no. 4, see Beck 1972–1991, III, 205, no. 534A. Bakhuÿs in Paris 2009b, 67–70, no. 17, tentatively suggested that, considering the strong similarities between the two works exhibited here, this might be a rare case in which a finished drawing served as preparatory study for a painting. This seems unlikely considering that the motifs appeared in earlier paintings and that Van Goyen was inventive enough to create different combinations with them.

JAN VAN GOYEN

43. *Sailing Ships*, 1653
   Black chalk, gray wash, on paper
   11.4 × 19.5 cm (4½ × 7¹¹⁄₁₆ in.)
   Musées royaux des Beaux-Arts de Belgique, Brussels,
   4060/1407

JAN VAN GOYEN

44. *Ships under a Cloudy Sky*, 1655

Oil on panel

32.5 × 32 cm (1 2¹³⁄₁₆ × 1 2⅝ in.)

Musée des Beaux-Arts, Rouen, 1 8 1 1.35

THOMAS DE KEYSER

1596–1667

---

45. *Company of Allaert Cloeck*, 1630
Pen and brown ink, violet wash, over black
chalk, squared, on paper
20.4 × 40.9 cm (8¹⁄₁₆ × 16¹⁄₁₆ in.)
Albertina, Vienna, 9246

The citizen's militia of Amsterdam was not only responsible for the city's protection and the maintenance of public order but also provided military pomp at important ceremonies. Following the upheavals of the early years of the Dutch Revolt against the Spanish Empire, the municipal government reorganized the medieval militia companies in 1580. Remarkably, the opening paragraph of the *Great Ordinance* of 1580 already anticipates Amsterdam's meteoric rise as economic powerhouse in the first half of the seventeenth century. The document advised that, in addition to the militia's traditional roles, it should also 'guarantee the smooth operation of commerce and the overall [city] economy.'[1]

In 1580, Amsterdam was divided up into eleven administrative districts, which each mustered its eligible men into a militia 'banner' that was led by a captain. To commemorate their service, many officers commissioned group portraits of their banner to decorate the walls of the militia headquarters. In the sixteenth and seventeenth centuries, Amsterdam's civic guard companies commissioned no fewer than 57 of the 135 documented Dutch militia paintings.

In 1630, the company of Captain Allaert Cloeck and Lieutenant Lucas Jacobsz Rotgans commissioned Thomas de Keyser to paint its group portrait (fig. 1), likely to celebrate Cloeck's appointment to the captaincy.[2] The company of sixteen men includes not only Allaert's younger brother Claes Cloeck Nanningsz—the ensign carrying the orange/white/blue banner—but also Thomas Jacobsz Hoyngh, son of the district's captain who was depicted in an earlier militia portrait.

De Keyser probably signed the contract shortly after the completion of the new Great Hall of the Kloveniersdoelen (the militia headquarters), and the painting seems to have been the first in a long series of imposing group portraits—all painted between 1630 and 1643—destined for the hall.[3] Of the two preparatory drawings of De Keyser's composition that have survived, the Albertina drawing (cat. 45) carries the date November 27, 1630, on the pediment of the building in the background. The exact date suggests that the drawing was part of the formal contract between De Keyser and the guardsmen.[4]

1. Knevel 1994, 99.
2. District III covered a seven-block area near the Oude Kerk in the city's medieval core. In 1616, the banner's previous leaders had commissioned Paulus Moreelse to paint their group portrait: *Officers and Guardsmen of District III, Led by Captain Jacob Gerritsz Hoyngh and Lieutenant Nanningh Florisz Cloeck*, Rijksmuseum, Amsterdam, SK-C-623.
3. For a reconstruction of the Great Hall of the Kloveniersdoelen, see Dudok van Heel 2009, 5–41. Originally, De Keyser's painting was probably 15 cm (5⅞ in.) taller. At some point, the list of names

Fig. 1. Thomas de Keyser, *The Militia Company of Captain Allaert Cloeck and Lieutenant Lucas Jacobsz Rotgans*, 1632, oil on canvas. Amsterdam Museum, SA 7353, on long-term loan to Rijksmuseum, Amsterdam, SK-C-381

THOMAS DE KEYSER

46. *Officers and Other Civic Guardsmen of the IIIrd District
of Amsterdam, under the Command of Captain Allaert
Cloeck and Lieutenant Lucas Jacobsz Rotgans*, c. 1630
Pen and deep brown ink, gray brown wash over black
chalk, squared, on paper
20.2 × 40.8 cm (8¹⁄₁₆ × 16¹⁄₁₆ in.)
Statens Museum for Kunst, Copenhagen,
KKSgb7824

Compared to the relatively well defined Albertina drawing, the Statens version (cat. 46) comes across as more spontaneous and freely drawn, which may indicate that the latter was De Keyser's initial concept drawing which he then refined for the contract. The two drawings are virtually the same width and almost equal in height. Both feature a grid, in graphite, of 16 × 8 squares, which undoubtedly helped De Keyser transfer the drawn concept to canvas, but also facilitates the comparison between concept and execution.

The center of the painting hews closely to both preparatory drawings. The three main figures—Captain Cloeck, holding his command staff; Ensign Cloeck with the banner; and Lieutenant Rotgans carrying the partisan, a thrusting weapon that by this time had become a ceremonial weapon[5]—stand on a broad landing, while three junior officers make their way up the steps behind them. The wings of the painting, however, differ significantly from those in the drawn compositions. The drawings prove that De Keyser's original design envisioned a much wider composition—with ample room on the sides—as compared to the finished canvas. The changed dimensions suggest that sometime between the execution of the drawings and the conversion to canvas, the leadership of the Kloveniersdoelen switched the space allotted to the painting to a narrower wall.[6]

The painting also differs from the preparatory drawings in the increased prominence of the three junior officers moving up the steps, to the detriment of the two groups of five guardsmen on each side. The junior officers take up one-third of the painting's width as opposed to about one-fifth of the corollary space in the drawings. At the same time, the area occupied by the groups to each side is diminished from approximately half the composition's width in the drawings to a mere one-third in the painting.[7] The reduced width of the canvas forced De Keyser to create a second tier in order to adequately depict every individual. On the lower left side, he portrayed three men in full, but this decision resulted in an awkward spatiality. In the two drawings, the landing obscures the lower part of the legs of the men on the left, resulting in a sense of movement that is lacking in the painting. The men occupying the lower right tier seem slightly more at ease because, as the drawings show, De Keyser had conceptualized them as full figures from the start. The two drawings show the extent to which the artist was forced to compromise in the painting. As noted by an earlier critic: 'This eternal conflict between the truest possible likeness and the pictorial conception has here been resolved in favor of the former.'[8]   [HR]

identifying the guardsmen on the larger sheet was cut short, removing three names. The lost names later returned to the painting by way of a second sheet with comparatively larger lettering that might, at first glance, lead a viewer astray into thinking that Schülenborch, Hoingh, and Van den Bergen were the central figures in the group instead of Captain Allaert

Cloeck, his cousin the ensign, and Lieutenant Rotgans.
4. Adams 1985, II, 346–367; III, 84–94. Egbert Haverkamp-Begemann first connected the Albertina drawing and the contract (see Adams 1985, III, 94).
5. Partisans were usually carried by senior officers. Haarlem 1988, 234, no. 53.

6. Haarlem 1988, 377–378, no. 192, fig. 182.
7. The relative space taken up by the three central figures increased only marginally, from roughly 30 percent of the area in the drawings to 34 percent in the painting.
8. Henkel 1931, 37.

SALOMON DE BRAY

1597–1664

Few individual portraits of very young children exist from the Dutch Golden Age. Those that survive were usually commissions that depicted children who had died in infancy.[1] Such an interpretation has been suggested for Salomon de Bray's painting in Edinburgh (cat. 48).[2] But it is more likely that this double portrait was painted on the occasion of the infants' baptism. Each baby has a medal around its neck, and together they lie in an elaborate crib whose shell motif could allude to baptismal symbols.[3] This portrait depicts the twins Clara and Albert, children of the artist's nephew, Simon de Bray.[4] The De Bray family was Catholic, and thus would have endowed the sacrament of baptism with particular importance, perhaps explaining why this event might have been considered worthy of celebration with a likeness.[5]

This probably explains the special place that the babies' portrait occupies in De Bray's painted oeuvre. Painted in or just after 1646, it was completed when the artist focused almost exclusively on history painting and *tronies*.[6] During this period, he painted far fewer portraits, a genre on which he had concentrated at the start of his career.[7] The picture, created within the private context of the family, was unsigned, unlike most of De Bray's other work, which was destined for the art market or outside clients. The lack of signature had the consequence that the link to the double portrait's true creator was lost in the nineteenth century, and it was thought to be by Jacob Jordaens. The drawing in the Morgan Library (cat. 47) made it possible to reattribute the painting correctly.[8]

If the New York drawing was indeed used in preparation for the picture, when he came to paint it, De Bray made significant changes to the scene. The drawing was clearly made from life shortly after the twins' birth, showing them in a simple cradle with a wicker frame.[9] By contrast, in the painting, the twins are depicted in their elaborate bed and, most notably, with their eyes open. They also wear different clothes and are in a different position. In preparing these changes, intermediate versions may have been created, but they are not known today. For a long time it was thought that a preliminary oil sketch, smaller than the finished Scottish painting, existed.[10] Recent research revealed, however, that there never was one.[11]

Besides, Salomon de Bray, brilliant portrait painter that he was, may not have needed to do a second drawing of the children recording the details of their baptismal finery and their faces when they were awake. Perhaps he simply had seen the babies once more when they were awake, allowing him to give Clara, at left, her dimple and the contours of her cheeks around her mouth and chin, and to remember the shape of her open eyes and those of her brother's, before incorporating these features directly into the painting.

1. See Ariane van Suchtelen and the references given in London/The Hague 2007, no. 7.
2. Franklin W. Robinson in Washington/Denver/Fort Worth 1977, no. 25.
3. Felice Stampfle in Paris/Antwerp/London/New York 1979, no. 61, and Felice Stampfle in Shoaf Turner 2006, no. 44, puts forth an interpretation that is judiciously reiterated by Van Suchtelen in London/The Hague 2007, no. 7.
4. Simon de Bray was a lawyer in Haarlem and the son of Simon, Salomon's brother. De Bray, however, spelled his nephew's name as 'Symon' on the drawing. See Stamfle in Shoaf Turner 2006, no. 44.
5. Van Suchtelen in London/The Hague 2007, no. 7.
6. *Tronies* are character heads based on the features of live models, but they are not considered formal portraits.
7. Friso Lammertse, 'Schilder, bouwmeester en theoreticus,' in Haarlem/London 2008, 12–13.
8. Moltke 1938, no. z 104.
9. The drawing—dated precisely—was done nine months and one day after the parents' wedding. See Haarlem/London 2008, no. 6, 146.
10. Stampfle in Paris/Antwerp/London/New York 1979, no. 61, and Stampfle in Shoaf Turner 2006, no. 44; information reproduced in Haarlem/London 2008, no. 6.
11. This information was based upon two errors made by Von Moltke. In his publication, the author mentioned two painted versions based on the New York drawing (Moltke 1938, nos. 95, 95a). It now appears that these two paintings are one and the same: when Von Moltke

Fig. 1. Salomon de Bray, *Portrait of a Seated Woman with a Cushion and a Book on Her Lap*, black chalk, heightened with white, on paper tinted yellow. Rijksprentenkabinet, Rijksmuseum, Amsterdam, RP-T-1954-200

De Bray's use of preparatory drawings for his paintings appear to confirm this hypothesis. De Bray's few preparatory drawings were done quickly in pen, and it appears to have been his habit to include other details later when painting, as he must have done for the portrait of the twins. We know now that the very elaborate drawings—most often in black and red chalk—that were long thought to be preparatory works, are, in fact,

more likely to be *ricordi* of his paintings, made either by himself or by his sons.[12]

Aside from this technical similarity to De Bray's other known preparatory drawings, the Morgan Library's drawing has some very different characteristics. First, it is a life study, and second it was done in preparation for a portrait instead of a history painting. Furthermore, the artist did use red chalk, a dry technique, which he usually only utilized for his *ricordi*. To prepare for most of his painted compositions, De Bray seems to have preferred pen, sometimes with wash.[13] Furthermore, these drawings, carefully signed and dated, would appear to be from a sketchbook. Two sheets showing stages in the conception of *Eliezer and Rebecca at the Well* in the Musée de la Chartreuse, Douai provide a fine example of this practice.[14]

Only the *Portrait of a Seated Woman with a Cushion and a Book on Her Lap* in the Rijksmuseum (fig. 1) has distinctive features similar to those in the Morgan Library's drawing: it was completed in chalk—albeit black and not red—and it was drawn from life.[15] There must certainly be other similar drawings Salomon de Bray made in preparation for his portraits and for figures in his paintings, but some may still be known under other artist's names. It is possible that the catalogue raisonné of Salomon de Bray's drawings (forthcoming) will confirm the black chalk drawing of *Study of a Young Man*,[16] and the black and red chalk drawing of *An Oriental* both probably drawn using models, as autograph works.[17]   [CT]

referred to the portrait published in the third volume of the *Arundel Club*, he re-transcribed the dimensions given in inches as centimeters, without converting them back to the metric system. Furthermore, he described the children as dozing (*beide schlummern*), whereas in the photographic reproduction, they had their eyes open. See *Arundel Club* 3 (1906): no. 9. The picture was then in the possession of the Carfax & Co. Gallery in London, information which should now be included in its provenance.

12. Giltaij and Lammertse 2001.

13. The small study for a *Baptism of the Eunuch* bought by Frits Lugt in 1921, and which he, probably correctly, attributed to Salomon, is the artist's only known composition sketch in black chalk (Fondation Custodia, Collection Frits Lugt, Paris, 773). However, it could not be linked to a painting.

14. See Friso Lammertse in Rotterdam/ Frankfurt 1999a and b, under no. 11, figs. 11a, 11b.

15. Schapelhouman and Schatborn 1998, no. 65. However, the authors found no

painting associated with this sketch.

16. Amsterdam 1967, no. 6.

17. Sale Paris, Christie's, December 15, 2004, no. 259 (Moltke 1938, z 111); Friso Lammertse is preparing a catalogue raisonné of Salomon de Bray's drawings. I would like to thank him for confirming the exceptional nature of the Morgan Library drawing in the context of the artist's overall work.

SALOMON DE BRAY

47. *The Twins Clara and Albert de Bray*, August 12, 1646
   Red chalk, over faint indications in black chalk,
   on paper
   16 × 15.2 cm (6⁵⁄₁₆ × 6 in.)
   The Morgan Library & Museum, New York,
   Gift of J. Morgan, Jr., 1924, acc. no. III, 176

SALOMON DE BRAY

48. *The Twins Clara and Albert de Bray*, 1646 or after
Oil on canvas
82.6 × 64.8 cm (32½ × 25½ in.)
Private Collection, on loan to the National Galleries
of Scotland, Edinburgh, NGL 002.95

PIETER JANSZ SAENREDAM

1597–1665

---

49. *Choir and High Altar of Sint-Janskerk
at 's-Hertogenbosch*, 1632
Pen and brown ink with gray wash and watercolor,
over black chalk, on paper
40.7 × 32 cm (16 × 12⅝ in.)
The British Museum, London, PD 1895,0915.1300

The drawings of no other Dutch artist are as clearly related
to paintings as are those of Pieter Jansz Saenredam.
Fortunately, because so many of his remarkable architectural drawings and paintings have been preserved, one can
trace his creative process with remarkable assurance.[1]

Saenredam was born in the village of Assendelft in
1597, but after the death of his father, Jan, an important
late mannerist engraver and draftsman, the family moved
to nearby Haarlem. After receiving his artistic training
from Frans Pietersz de Grebber, he became a master in
the St. Luke's Guild in 1623.[2] Saenredam's interest in
architecture was probably encouraged by two painter-
architects active in Haarlem, Jacob van Campen
and Pieter Post, although he likely learned the art of
perspective from the Haarlem mathematician and
engineer Pieter Wils.[3]

As Cornelis de Bie wrote in 1661, by the late 1620s
Saenredam 'devoted himself entirely to painting perspectives, churches, halls, galleries, buildings and other
things from the outside as well as the inside, in such a
way, after life, that their essence and nature could not be
shown to a greater perfection.'[4] His earliest known
church interior is a drawing of the Grote Kerk, or the
church of St. Bavo, that he made for Samuel Ampzing's
city history of Haarlem, published in 1628.[5] Pieter Wils
also contributed to Ampzing's book, publishing there

Fig. 1. Pieter Jansz Saenredam, *Cathedral of Saint John
at 's-Hertogenbosch*, 1646, oil on panel. National Gallery of Art,
Washington, Samuel H. Kress Collection, 1961.9.33

St. Bavo's measurements, elevations, and ground plan.
Wils explained that this information would be 'of use
to anyone wishing to draw (the Grote Kerk) in
perspective.'[6]

The idea that architectural painting ought to be based
on precise measurements was entirely new, and one that
Saenredam quickly embraced. When he traveled to
's-Hertogenbosch in June 1632 to paint its cathedral of

1. Saenredam's oeuvre consists of approximately fifty paintings, some 150 drawings,
and a few prints executed early in his
career.
2. He was an officer in the guild in 1635 and
1640, and a *deken* (board member) in 1642.

3. Ruurs 1987, 87–92, was the first to
propose that Wils may have taught
Saenredam the art of perspective.
4. De Bie 1661, 246.
5. Saenredam's design was reproduced
in an etching by Jan van de Velde for

Ampzing's *Beschryvinge ende Lof der Stad
Haerlem in Holland* (Haarlem, 1628).
6. Ampzing 1628, 503. For an English
translation and analysis of Wils's list, see
Ruurs 1987, 87.

St. Jan, he first made a floor plan of that church.[7] He utilized knowledge gained from making this floor plan in subsequent drawings of the church's interior. The most significant of these was a freehand study in chalk, pen-and-ink, and watercolor of the church's imposing choir (cat. 49), which he made three days after he drew the floor plan.

This drawing includes a green curtain over the high altar, the reasons for which relate to the complex political and religious struggles then consuming the Dutch Republic. Saenredam had traveled to 's-Hertogenbosch shortly after the successful siege of the city by Frederik Hendrik, the Prince of Orange. With the capitulation of the Spanish forces, the church was cleansed of papist influence. Frederik Hendrik allowed the retreating Spanish forces to take valuables from the church, including the altarpiece; hence, the presence of the curtain. As Saenredam indicated in his detailed inscription at the lower left, he made this pen drawing from life. He carefully rendered the curtain, the altar, the sculpture, and the apse's architecture, while also indicating the flow of light with washes and watercolor.

Although Saenredam made this drawing in 1632, for various political reasons he did not paint an image of the interior until 1646 (fig. 1).[8] Although the drawing and the painting are quite similar, a number of differences do exist. In the painting the interior soars more than in the drawing, and the perspective recedes more rapidly. Most strikingly, however, Saenredam provided a painting for the high altar, Abraham Bloemaert's *The Adoration of the Shepherds*, 1612, a work that, in fact, had never hung there. He also depicted the altar as though it were prepared for a Catholic service, an impossibility in 1646. Such modifications of reality serve as a reminder that Saenredam often adjusted reality for compositional and thematic reasons.

After working in 's-Hertogenbosch, Saenredam returned to Haarlem for a major campaign depicting the Grote Kerk (St. Bavo). One of the most beautiful paintings he made of this church is a panel (cat. 50) in the Collection Frits Lugt.[9] Here Saenredam has situated himself in a side chapel and has painted the view across the choir and into the sourthern ambulatory. He carefully framed the composition with two large pillars, and used single-point perspective to reinforce the sense of scale and depth to the scene. Small figures enliven his interior: a group of men gathered at a long bench in front of the choir screen, another seated near them in a pew, and, high above, a man walking along the triphorium. Two children playing marbles in the foreground lessen the solemnity of the scene and, by their scale differential, emphasize the enormity of the large piers enframing the composition.

Saenredam generally began his artistic process with preliminary drawings made at the site. He then refined these images by making elaborate construction drawings with the help of straightedge rulers and compasses to work out the proportions of columns and arches and the overall perspective system.[10] These construction drawings then became the basis for his paintings. In the construction drawing for this work (cat. 51), remnants of perspective lines recede to a vanishing point at the right edge of the sheet—the 'eye' ('oog') point.

Saenredam provided amazingly precise information in notations inscribed on his drawings and paintings. The inscription on this sheet, reads, in translation: 'Finished this drawing the 3rd of January 1636 and finished painting the 23rd of May in the year 1636. This is as big [as the painting] and is a view in the Great Church in Haarlem.'[11] To transfer the drawing Saenredam blackened the verso of the sheet and traced the ink lines, thereby creating an underdrawing on the panel to guide the painting process (see Wheelock essay pp. 22–23). While the architectural elements in the drawing and painting are identical, Saenredam made the church seem larger in the painting by changing the character and placement of the figures. Aside from the addition of the

7. See Schwarz and Bok 1989, 55, fig. 56, 269, cat. 98.

8. For a full examination of the painting and its commission, see Arthur K. Wheelock, Jr., 'Pieter Jansz Saenredam/Cathedral of Saint John at 's-Hertogenbosch/1646,' *Dutch Paintings of the Seventeenth Century*, NGA Online Editions, accessed September

8, 2015, http://purl.org/nga/collection/ artobject/46132.

9. For a more extended discussion of this painting see Quentin Buvelot's entry in Paris 2004, 86–87, cat. 31.

10. No such drawing of St. Janskerk has survived, but it seems probable that one once existed.

11. This text and translation are taken from Utrecht 1961, 87. 'Dit geijndicht met teijkenen den 3. Januarij 1636 ende geijndicht met Schilderen den 23 maijus Int Jaer 1636. Dito even dus groot ende is een gesicht inde grootte kerck binnen Haerlem.'

PIETER JANSZ SAENREDAM

55. *Organ of the St. Bavo, Haarlem*, [n.d.]

Pen and brown ink, pencil and watercolor, on paper

30.9 × 17.3 cm (12³⁄₁₆ × 6¹³⁄₁₆ in.)

Fondation Custodia, Collection Frits Lugt,

Paris, 2218

PIETER JANSZ SAENREDAM

51. *St. Bavo, Haarlem, View in the Choir*, 1636

Pen and gray wash on paper

48 × 37 cm (18⅞ × 14⁹⁄₁₆ in.)

Haarlem Municipal Archive, 53-001702 G

PIETER JANSZ SAENREDAM

50. *The Choir of the St. Bavo in Haarlem*, 1636
   Oil on panel
   49 × 36.6 cm (19⁵⁄₁₆ × 14⁷⁄₁₆ in.)
   Fondation Custodia, Collection Frits Lugt, Paris, 396

children, he eliminated a man seen in the drawing walking before the central column.[12]

Saenredam's creative process often took many years to complete, and it is evident that he kept a store of his drawings for future use. For example, in 1635 he made a number of drawings of the nave of the Grote Kerk that he later used when executing an enormous painting in 1648, which is now in Edinburgh (fig. 2).[13] Saenredam began the process with a large freehand pen and black chalk drawing on blue paper (cat. 52), which he signed and dated August 25, 1635, on the capital of the column at the right. Here he positioned himself on the north side of the choir, looking west down the nave, with part of the south transept visible on the left. He carefully rendered the architectural elements, paying particular attention to the soaring vault over the crossing and down the nave.

Fig. 2. Pieter Jansz Saenredam, *The Interior of St. Bavo's Church, Haarlem (the 'Grote Kerk')*, 1648, oil on panel. The National Galleries of Scotland, Edinburgh, NG 2413

His perspective system, however, was curiously flawed. For example, the arcade at the right of the nave is much lower than that at the left, and the windows on the end wall are far too small. He recognized some of these mistakes, and even indicated where revisions needed to be made with additional lines and markers.[14]

In December 1635 Saenredam made a large construction drawing of this composition that consisted of a number of separate sheets, two of which still survive, the left section depicting the south transept (cat. 53), and the view down the nave (cat. 54).[15] In this instance, however, he did not darken the back of the sheet and

12. The role of such figures in determining scale is also evident in the drawing, where Saenredam initially sketched in a large man standing next to the pillar at the right.

13. Saenredam may have executed the enormous Edinburgh painting to celebrate the signing of the Treaty of Münster. Saenredam offered this painting to the Stadholder William II, the Prince of Orange, on May 21, 1648—only six days after the prince had attended the signing of the treaty. Although the prince did not purchase the painting, the powerful burgomaster of Amsterdam, Andries de Graeff, did, suggesting that others responded to its nationalistic appeal. See Schwartz and Bok 1989, 206.

14. See Martin Kemp, 'Construction and Cunning: The Perspective of the Edinburgh Saenredam,' in Edinburgh 1984, 30.

15. Saenredam most likely prepared the design of the vault surmounting the crossing in a similar fashion, joining another sheet along the top edges of the Woodner and Haarlem sheets.

PIETER JANSZ SAENREDAM

52. *St. Bavo, Haarlem, Part of the Nave*, 1635
Pen and chalk on blue paper
54.5 × 39 cm (21⁷⁄₁₆ × 15³⁄₈ in.)
Haarlem Municipal Archive, 53-000435 G

PIETER JANSZ SAENREDAM

53. *South Transept of St. Bavo in Haarlem*, 1635
Pen and brush, gray wash, squared in red chalk, on paper
49 × 35.5 cm (19⁵⁄₁₆ × 14 in.)
Haarlem Municipal Archive, 53-001726 G

54. *Interior of Saint Bavo's Church*, Haarlem, 1635
   Pen and brown ink with gray wash and touches of red chalk
   over graphite, squared in red chalk, on paper
   49.1 × 35.8 cm (19⁵⁄₁₆ × 14⅛ in.)
   National Gallery of Art, Washington, Gift of Dian Woodner, 2015.149.1
   Washington only

incise the lines to transfer the composition. Instead, he created a grid in red chalk, which allowed him to transfer the image at a larger scale. Indeed, infrared reflectography examination of the Edinburgh panel reveals a comparable grid pattern, although with intervals twice as large.[16]

As is characteristic of his construction drawings, Saenredam refined his initial drawing with the aid of a straightedge and compass, and paid careful attention to the laws of linear perspective.[17] Rob Ruurs has demonstrated that Saenredam based his proportions on measurements that Pieter Wils provided in Ampzing's publication of 1628.[18] As seen in his view down the nave, Saenredam began by laying out his elaborate perspective system in graphite, locating the vanishing point on the horizon to the right of the foreground group of figures (the point is circled in ink). He determined the rate of recession with his distance point, which he located with a pin hole and the number '30' on the base of the column to the left of the nave on the portion of the construction drawing (cat. 53) now in Haarlem. After locating the vanishing and distance points, Saenredam could situate his columns correctly in space and construct the proper arch for the vaulted ceiling, which he

drew in graphite with the aid of a compass. Saenredam then applied gray washes to capture the play of light across the forms, and drew in his staffage figures with pen and wash. Once he had completed this stage, but before he added the brown pen lines, he squared the drawing in red chalk.

In addition to these large construction drawings, Saenredam also executed a careful watercolor study of St. Bavo's great organ (cat. 55).[19] The organ rests on a five-sided wooden projection, which has at its base a carved head with a shaggy beard. It is probable that this head of a wild man moved when wind from the organ bellows activated a small 'windmill' mechanism.[20] Far less carefully rendered than the organ are the architectural elements of the church's interior, including the rib vaulting, which indicates that this study functioned separately from the squared construction drawings.

Saenredam, who was interested in organs and how they functioned, must have made this careful study at about the same time, in 1635, because of the organ's importance to the composition, but he slightly simplified its shape in the painting to give it a flatter and less three-dimensional character.   [AKW]

16. See Edinburgh 1984, 34–35, figs. 9, 10.
17. This discussion is drawn from Arthur Wheelock's entry on the drawing in Washington 1995, 253–255.
18. Ruurs 1987, 140–141.
19. This drawing is discussed in New York/ Paris 1977, 146–148, cat. 99.
20. Peter Williams, 'The Organs of St. Bavo's Haarlem,' in Edinburgh 1984, 38.

BARTHOLOMEUS BREENBERGH

1598–1657

Bartholomeus Breenbergh specialized in paintings of Italianate landscapes with shepherds or small figures enacting scenes from the Bible or Greco-Roman mythology. Beginning 1619, he spent a decade in Rome, and the majority of his approximately two hundred surviving drawings of the city and the Italian countryside date from that period.[1] The poetic sensibility and ink-and-wash technique of his studies and those of Cornelis van Poelenburch inspired Claude Lorrain, Jan Asselijn, and generations of northern European draftsmen who sought to evoke the light of Italy and its effects on the architectural monuments of ancient and modern Rome.[2] Breenbergh produced most of his 125 known paintings and his entire oeuvre of more than thirty etchings after he returned to Amsterdam in 1629.[3]

In his 1969 monograph on Breenbergh's drawings, Marcel Roethlisberger conjectured that the artist must have made studies for some of the larger figures in his paintings of the 1640s and 1650s.[4] The Harvard Art Museums' male nude (cat. 56), the first such study to be identified, came to light in 1995. Sold in an Amsterdam auction as a work by Jan van Noordt, it was acquired by the art dealer Bob P. Haboldt, who later observed, to his astonishment, that it had served as a study for a picture in his own inventory: Breenbergh's *Venus Mourning the Death of Adonis* (cat. 57) of 1646.[5]

The painting depicts an episode from Ovid's *Metamorphoses* (book 10, lines 708–739). Venus's mortal lover Adonis ignored her plea to avoid the pursuit of dangerous game, and he was gored by a wild boar. The goddess descended from her swan-drawn chariot and, with her son, Amor, grieves over her lover's body. She memorialized Adonis by creating the anemone—one of her sacred flowers—from his blood, which, in Breenbergh's picture, flows conspicuously from the gash in Adonis's side. During work on the panel the artist introduced changes to the composition: he added drapery over Adonis's genitals, adjusted his feet and shod them with sandals, altered the angle of the foreshortened arm, and turned the head so that Adonis's profile is more clearly visible. The hand that rests on the model's chest in the study was omitted to make way for the arm and hand with which Venus caresses Adonis's face. Areas of highlight and shadow in the painting follow closely—if not exactly—the modeling in the drawing.

Breenbergh's choice of oiled charcoal and white chalk on blue paper for this drawing links his practice to that of Jacob Backer and others who preferred black and white chalks on blue paper for figure studies. Backer and Breenbergh were well acquainted and were very likely to have attended the same sessions where Amsterdam history painters met to draw from models.[6] In at least one instance, Backer gave, or loaned, one of his studies to his colleague. For his painting *Alexander and the Family of Darius* of c. 1645, Breenbergh adapted, in reverse, a drawing by Backer of a kneeling woman, seen from behind (see Robinson and Schatborn essay, p. 11, figs. 7, 8).[7] That Breenbergh painted the figure in reverse suggests that he worked from a counterproof of Backer's study.   [WWR]

1. Roethlisberger 1969, 1–2; Roethlisberger 1981, 3, 5, 13.
2. Roethlisberger 1969, 17–19; Roethlisberger 1968, I, 30–31; Amsterdam 2001, 57–59, 66–67, 78, 83.
3. Roethlisberger 1981, 5, 13.
4. Roethlisberger 1969, 15.
5. Haboldt 2012, 10, 199.

6. Backer painted pendant portraits of Breenbergh and his wife in 1644, and pictures by Breenbergh can be traced to Backer's estate. In paintings dated 1644 and 1647, Breenbergh repeated the sleeping female nude in Backer's *Cimon and Iphigenia* of c. 1642; Amsterdam/Aachen 2008, 21, 25, 54, 237, under no. A95.

7. Jacob Backer, *Weeping Woman Kneeling, Seen from Behind*, The Metropolitan Museum of Art, New York, 53.127.3; Sumowski 1979, I, 48–49, no. 17x; Plomp 2006, 34, fig. 41. For Breenbergh's painting *Landscape with Alexander and Family of Darius*, see Roethlisberger 1981, 88, no. 227, and figs. 227, 228.

BARTHOLOMEUS BREENBERGH

56. *Reclining Male Nude (Study for Venus Mourning
the Death of Adonis)*, 1646
Oiled charcoal and white chalk on blue laid paper
24.8 × 35.7 cm (9¾ × 14¹⁄₁₆ in.)
Harvard Art Museums/Fogg Museum, Cambridge,
Anonymous fund in honor of John and Anne Straus,
and through the generosity of the Fifth Floor Foundation, Howard and Sally Lepow, Leena and Sheldon
Peck, Maida and George Abrams and Kathryn
and William W. Robinson, 1996.303

BARTHOLOMEUS BREENBERGH

57. *Venus Mourning the Death of Adonis*, 1646
  Oil on panel
  38.7 × 49.5 cm (15¼ × 19½ in.)
  Harvard Art Museums/Fogg Museum, Cambridge,
  Kate, Maurice R., and Melvin R. Seiden Special
  Purchase Fund, Janine Luke, The Louis Agassiz
  Shaw Bequest, and William and Ami Danoff in honor
  of Seymour Slive, 1997.5

ANTHONIE PALAMEDESZ

1601–1673

58. *Seated Officer Holding a Glass*, c. 1635
 Brush and brown ink and darker brown oil paint,
 slightly heightened with white gouache, on paper
 20.5 × 15.5 cm (8¹⁄₁₆ × 6⅛ in.)
 Leiden University Library, PK-T-AW-1102

This cavalier, drawn by Anthonie Palamedesz with great
energy, was the starting point for a central figure in his
painting *Elegant Company in Conversation, Drinking, and
Playing Music in an Interior*, c. 1635 (fig. 1). By subtly
altering the position of the arms, legs, and sword, Palamedesz toned down the figure's very dynamic, original
pose. This decision was surely a question of etiquette, as
the setting is an elegant interior and not a guardroom,
another of Palamedesz's pictorial genres. Although no
other picture has yet to be found in which the painter
used this sketch, it is quite possible that he employed it
as the basis for a horseman in a military scene. Indeed,
like his senior colleague, Dirck Hals, Palamedesz
probably adapted his sketches of figures according to the
subject matter he was depicting (see cats. 34, 35).[1]
Just like Hals, Palamedesz must have made the changes
to the position of the figure as he painted, possibly in the
underpainting on the ground layer and mostly in shades
of brown.[2]

 In the subject's face, a curved line extends the outline
of the head, allowing the artist to place the nose and then
the rest of the face. This technique was often used by
draftsmen and was also taught in some drawing books
(see cat. 5) as an easy way to construct faces.

 The Leiden sketch is characterized by an extraordina-
rily free touch, particularly as far as the hands are
concerned, leaving them imprecisely defined. However,
Palamedesz appears to have reworked his drawing in
preparation for changes he was to make to the subject's
dress and sword in the painted version. Details were
added with a pen or a fine brush and darker ink at a later
stage to the lace collar, the sword hilt, and the shoulder

Fig. 1. Anthonie Palamedesz, *Elegant Company in Conversation,
Drinking, and Playing Music in an Interior*, c. 1635, oil on panel.
Hallwylska Museet, Stockholm, B.73

strap: in some places these changes cover his initial
sketch.

 The artist did not always work in this manner, as
shown by a drawing at the Fondation Custodia (fig. 2).
It has previously been noted that Palamedesz used this
work as a basis for the soldier in the center of a guardroom painting now in Copenhagen.[3] The changes made
to this figure are very minor. However, this sketch was
also used as a model for another soldier—playing a
secondary role this time—in a painting of a guardroom
scene in the Liechtenstein collection, Vienna. In this
case, changes to the painted figure were not worked out
first in the drawing. In recent decades, the number of
studies of sketched figures once attributed to Anthonie
Palamedesz has been considerably reduced.[4] Many

[154]

Fig. 2. Anthonie Palamedesz, *Standing Soldier,* brush and brown ink and darker brown oil paint. Fondation Custodia, Collection Frits Lugt, Paris, 1997-T.2

drawings that previously went under his name proved to be preparatory studies for paintings by his pupil Ludolf de Jongh or Simon Kick.[5] These are mostly studies of figures done in black chalk, sometimes highlighted in white chalk. Today, the drawings associated with Anthonie Palamedesz are in a very different medium.[6] The brush technique the artist used for his sketches was not at all common in seventeenth-century Holland.[7] He used both brown ink and another brown pigment that was darker, thicker, and oil based. He made it only slightly more fluid, in order to obtain a thick paint that adhered well to the roughness of the paper ground.

These oil sketches on paper are of course reminiscent of those by Dirck Hals, who depicted the same type of merry companies. It is unclear, however, whether there was any direct link between the two artists. Although it has been suggested that Anthonie Palamedesz might have been apprenticed in Dirck Hals's workshop,[8] no documentation has yet been found to substantiate this hypothesis.[9] Furthermore, Hals's technique in his sketches was generally more pictorial than that of Palamedesz; the former often used light shades—whites and grays—which are not simply highlights (see cat. 35). On the other hand, the way both artists used sketches to prepare their paintings is quite similar, leaving many questions about the relationship between the two men.   [CT]

1. On the use made of sketches by painters of merry companies see Kolfin 2005, 146.
2. See Kolfin 2005, 150–151.
3. Michiel Plomp, 'Drawing and Print-making in Delft during the Seventeenth Century,' in New York/London 2001, 478.
4. Peter Schatborn was first able to attribute cat. 58 as well as a second drawing, also held in the print collection of Leiden University, to the artist by identifying that they both appeared in paintings known to be by Anthonie Palamedesz; see Schatborn 1975b, 79–85, and Schatborn 1990. He was then able to include in the artist's body of drawn work two drawings in the École nationale supérieure des Beaux-Arts: Amsterdam/Washington 1981, 141, under no. 76. Finally, as far as the sketches in the Metropolitan Museum of Art and the

Fondation Custodia are concerned, they were published in 2001 by Plomp in New York/London 2001, nos. 120, 478. To the body of work attributed with some certainty to the artist, we can now add a sketch which came to Worcester Art Museum in 1988 (see Acton 1998, no. 27).
5. See Schatborn 1975b and Schatborn 1990.
6. Peter Schatborn does not rule out the possibility that certain black chalk draw-ings may be by Anthonie Palamedesz, but these are ones that are neither signed nor linked with any of the painter's known works. See Schatborn 1975b, 84. The drawing in the Fogg Art Museum's *album amicorum* is quite different: drawn on one of the album's vellum pages, this graphite drawing is monogrammed. It shows a

gallant scene that is definitely not a preparation for a painting; it is a finished work intended to show off his technical skills. See Plomp in New York/London 2001, 180–181, fig. 194; Robinson 2015, 30–32, repr. 31 as fig. 27.
7. Schatborn 1975b, 84, and the entry on Dirck Hals in this catalog (see p. 109–113).
8. See Thieme/Becker 1907–1950, XXVI; Amsterdam/Washington 1981, 74, 76, 142; Plomp is more cautious in New York/London 2001, 477; similarly Leonore van Sloten in Amsterdam 2014a: no. 20.
9. In her study of the Haarlem painters, Marion Goosens provides no record of Palamedesz being in Dirck Hals's studio. See Goosens 2001, particularly for the apprentices and artists who worked in Haarlem in Hals's and Palamedesz's time.

REMBRANDT HARMENSZ VAN RIJN

1606–1669

After an apprenticeship with Jacob Isaaksz van Swanenburg in Leiden and six months in 1625 with Pieter Lastman in Amsterdam, Rembrandt worked in his native city of Leiden until 1631. There he was in close contact with Jan Lievens (see pp. 56–57). His ambition was to become a history painter, making biblical and mythological compositions.

Rembrandt drew throughout his career. From life he depicted figures, portraits, animals, and landscapes, and from his imagination he portrayed biblical and mythological scenes, throughout taking his inspiration for these from earlier works by renowned printmakers. Alongside his more than three hundred paintings are more than three hundred prints and some seven hundred drawings, which were used as study materials by his many pupils.

Most of the drawings from Rembrandt's Leiden period are figure studies. Few of these are preliminary to specific paintings and prints because Rembrandt was then in the habit of drawing compositions directly onto the ground of a panel or canvas, or onto the etching plate, although exceptions to this method exist. One outstanding example of his drawing style from the Leiden period is *Old Man Seated*, dated 1631 (cat. 59), which he executed in the very year he moved to Amsterdam.

A drawing dated 1630 that depicts the same model indicates that Rembrandt drew *Old Man Seated* while he was still in Leiden.[1]

While Rembrandt's black chalk figure studies of this period are quite linear, those drawn in red chalk have far greater tonality. He rendered faces carefully and precisely, but he sketched the body in a freer manner. Rembrandt used the study of this old man for the figure of Jacob in the grisaille *Joseph Telling His Dreams* (cat. 60), painted in gray, brown, and white.[2] In this painting Joseph tells his father, Jacob, that he had dreamed that his brothers—who were jealous of him because he was Jacob's favorite—would one day bow down before their sibling (Genesis 37:1–11). Although the grisaille was not painted until some years later, Rembrandt probably already had the figure of Jacob in mind in 1631 when he made the drawing.

Rembrandt made four grisailles as designs for prints that Jan Gillesz van Vliet executed in the 1630s,[3] although only two of these were made in collaboration with the master: *The Descent from the Cross*, 1632/1633, which Uylenburgh published in 1633, and *Christ before Pilate*, 1635/1636.[4] Rembrandt's collaboration with Van Vliet came to an end after the publication of this latter print.[5]

1. The same model is depicted in Rembrandt, *Old Man Seated*, 1630, red chalk on laid paper, Washington, National Gallery of Art, Rosenwald Collection, 1943.3.7047; see Benesch 1973, no. 37. A second figure study of a *Seated Old Man* dating from 1631, red and black chalk, is in the Teylers Museum, Haarlem, o*50; see Benesch 1973, no. 40.
2. Rembrandt Corpus II 1986, no. A 66;

Rembrandt Corpus VI 2014, no. 108.
3. Rembrandt Corpus VI 2014, 176–187, under nos. 108–112.
4. Rembrandt's painting *The Descent from the Cross*, 1632/1633, oil on panel, is in the collection of Alte Pinakothek, Munich, 395; see Rembrandt Corpus II 1986, no. A 65; VI 2014, no. 107. For the etching, *The Descent from the Cross*, 1635/1636, two plates, see Hinterding, Rutgers, and

Luijten 2013, I, nos. 118/119. Regarding Rembrandt, *Christ before Pilate*, 1634, grisaille, London, National Gallery, 1400, see Rembrandt Corpus II 1986, no. A 89; VI 2014, no. 112. For etching, 1635/1636, see Hinterding, Rutgers, and Luijten 2013, I, no. 155.
5. The end of their collaboration is possibly related to the fact that Van Vliet married well in 1636; Amsterdam 1996, 12.

REMBRANDT HARMENSZ VAN RIJN

59. *Old Man Seated*, 1631
Red and some black chalk on pale yellowish
prepared paper
22.9 × 15.9 cm (9 × 6¼ in.)
Private Collection
Washington only

REMBRANDT HARMENSZ VAN RIJN

60. *Joseph Telling His Dreams*, 1633
    Grisaille on paper
    55.8 × 39.7 cm (22 × 15⅝ in.)
    Rijksmuseum, Amsterdam, purchased with the support of the Vereniging Rembrandt
    and the Stichting tot Bevordering van de Belangen van het Rijksmuseum, SK-A-3477

Fig. 1. Rembrandt Harmensz van Rijn, *Joseph Telling His Dreams to Jacob*, 1638, etching, second state. National Gallery of Art, Washington, Rosenwald Collection, 1943.3.7198

Fig. 2. (verso) Rembrandt Harmensz van Rijn, *Joseph Telling His Dreams to Jacob*, 1638, red chalk. Museum Boijmans Van Beuningen, Rotterdam, MB 1958/T 32

No print of the grisaille *Joseph Telling his Dream* was ever done, but in 1638 Rembrandt made a small portrait-format etching of the same subject (fig. 1), in which Jacob appears in mirror image.[6] Here Joseph stands in the center, and a woman with a book on her lap has been added at center right. Rembrandt drew a cursory design for this print (fig. 2), on the verso of the drawing of *Ruth and Naomi*, 1638 (Museum Boijmans Van Beuningen, Rotterdam).[7]

Rembrandt sometimes made drawings for a painting or print after he had already embarked on it, as a way of finding the most appropriate version of a figure, a group, or an overall composition. Among such studies are sketches that relate to his grisaille *St. John the Baptist Preaching* (cat. 61), a composition that Rembrandt might have originally designed to be executed as a print.[8] The initial stage of the grisaille, which Rembrandt executed on canvas around 1634/1635, was about the

6. Hinterding, Rutgers, and Luijten 2013, II, no. 167.
7. The verso drawing of Rembrandt, *Joseph Telling His Dreams*, 1638, Museum Boijmans Van Beuningen,

is no. MB 1958/T 32 verso. See Giltaij 1977, 1–9. The recto drawing *Ruth and Naomi*, 1638, pen-and-ink, is no. MB 1958/T 32, recto. See Benesch 1973, no. 161.

8. Rembrandt Corpus III 1989, no. A 106; Rembrandt Corpus V 2011, 176–185; and Rembrandt Corpus VI 2014, under nos. 107–112.

same size as two of his later prints.[9] He subsequently enlarged his grisaille in an extremely complex fashion and, in the process, radically changed and expanded his composition. The result was an expansive landscape with many more figures than he had originally conceived.[10] Rembrandt also painted a dark border around the finished composition. In the 1650s, after Jan Six had acquired this grisaille, Rembrandt designed a frame for the composition in a drawing that is now in the Musée du Louvre (fig. 3).[11]

In Rembrandt's grisaille, John the Baptist calls the multitude to come to be baptized in the River Jordan (Mark 1:4–8). A remarkable number of preparatory drawings have survived for this complex composition. In one drawing, a red chalk study sheet now in the Courtauld Gallery, Rembrandt sought to determine the best pose for St. John (cat. 62). He drew him twice, with the figure at the left corresponding most closely to St. John's pose in the painting. In the grisaille, however, the saint's face is shown in profile and the fingers of the hands are spread (fig. 4). The head on the verso of the Courtauld sheet bears some resemblance to that of the girl, with a small child on her lap, in the foreground of the grisaille.[12]

9. See cat. 60, 159.

10. It is generally accepted that the work was enlarged soon after the first version was finished; see Bevers 2006. Van de Wetering assumes that the enlargement was not done until around 1640; Rembrandt Corpus VI 2014, no. 110.

11. Six's ownership was recorded in a deed of September 13, 1658; Strauss and Van der Meulen 1979, 1658/18. The Louvre drawing (fig. 3), is cited in Benesch 1973, no. 969, fig. 1250, and Paris 2006a, no. 57.

12. Martin Royalton-Kisch sees this as a possible first attempt at John the Baptist's head. See *The Drawings of Rembrandt: A Revision of Otto Benesch's Catalogue Raisonné*, no. 142a, http://rembrandtcatalogue. net (accessed February 10, 2016).

Fig. 3. Rembrandt Harmensz van Rijn, *St. John the Baptist Preaching* in a frame, c. 1652, pen and brown ink, brown wash, corrections in white. Musée du Louvre, Paris, RF 4667

Fig. 4. Detail of Rembrandt Harmensz van Rijn, *St. John the Baptist Preaching*, 1634/1635 (cat. 61).

REMBRANDT HARMENSZ VAN RIJN

61. *St. John the Baptist Preaching*, 1634/1635
Oil on canvas, attached to panel
63 × 81.3 cm (24¹³⁄₁₆ × 32 in.)
Staatliche Museen, Berlin, Gemäldegalerie, 828 K
Paris only

REMBRANDT HARMENSZ VAN RIJN

62. *Two Studies of St. John for the Painting*
   'St. John the Baptist Preaching' (recto), 1634/1635
   Small Head of a Girl (verso)
   Red chalk on paper
   17.6 × 18.6 cm (6¹⁵⁄₁₆ × 7⁵⁄₁₆ in.)
   Courtauld Gallery, Seilern Collection, London, D 1978PG.182
   Paris only

REMBRANDT HARMENSZ VAN RIJN

63. *Studies of Standing Scribes for the Painting*
  'St. John the Baptist Preaching,' 1634/1635
  Pen and brown ink on paper
  16.7 × 19.5 cm (6⁹⁄₁₆ × 7¹¹⁄₁₆ in.)
  Staatliche Museen, Berlin, Kupferstichkabinett,
  кdz 3773
  Paris only

Fig. 5. Detail of Rembrandt Harmensz van Rijn, *St. John the Baptist Preaching*, 1634/1635 (cat. 61).

REMBRANDT HARMENSZ VAN RIJN

64. *Listeners for the Painting 'St. John the Baptist Preaching,'*
1634/1635
Pen and brown ink, brown wash, and some opaque white, on paper
18.9 × 12.5 cm ($7^{7}/_{16} × 4^{15}/_{16}$ in.)
Staatliche Museen, Berlin, Kupferstichkabinett, KdZ 5243
Paris only

Four other drawings—two of which are included in the exhibition—relate to the group of scribes listening critically and debating in the foreground of the painting (fig. 5). Rembrandt evidently considered it important to establish distinctive characters for these figures. In a sheet (fig. 6) for *St. John the Baptist* in Chatsworth, Rembrandt presents a half-length figure of a woman, two scribes in conversation, and a third scribe listening, although their arrangement differs somewhat from that in the grisaille.[13] Among the several sketchily rendered figures on a horizontal sheet from Berlin (cat. 63) are two scribes, seen at the left of center. Standing between them is a man wearing a tall hat, a figure Rembrandt more fully elaborated upon at the right of the drawing. Among the various figure groups in the upper center of the Berlin drawing is another rendering of the two scribes conversing.[14] Another variation on the motif of a scribe wearing a tall hat is found in a drawing in New York: *Head of a Scribe with a Tall Hat* (fig. 7).[15] This scribe also reappears on the verso of the Chatsworth sheet, where his head, however, is partly cut off at the bottom edge of the paper (fig. 8).

A vertically oriented drawing in Berlin (cat. 64) contains studies for figures who sit at the feet of the Baptist and listen to his words (see fig. 4). In this sheet, Rembrandt depicted two groups of seated figures, one above the other, the bottom group consisting of four figures and the upper group consisting of three. Above these seated figures Rembrandt depicted a standing man and some vegetation. This leafy plant is similar to one in grisaille to the left of St. John. Rembrandt adapted two of the seated figures in the lower group—as well as the man in the upper group resting his chin on his hand— when painting this grisaille. The latter figure closely

Fig. 6. (recto) Rembrandt Harmensz van Rijn, *Studies of Scribes for St. John the Baptist Preaching and a Woman Half Length*, 1634/1635, pen and brown ink, brown wash. The Devonshire Collection, Chatsworth, 1018

resembles the pensive man seated to the left of the Baptist in the grisaille.

Another drawing related to the painting, *Three Studies of an Archer* (fig. 9), in Stockholm, shows three variations of a man wearing the same feathered hat as two figures to the left of John the Baptist in the grisaille.[16] One of these men lies on the ground with the quiver on his back (see fig. 5); another archer stands to the right of St. John.

In the drawings and the grisaille Rembrandt depicted all manner of ways of listening and responding to John's words—from serious to skeptical, from benevolent and sympathetic to uncomprehending and indifferent. The range of expressions attests to Rembrandt's talent for conveying different emotions with pinpoint precision.

13. These two drawings are figs. 6 and 8 in this entry. Also see Benesch 1973, no. 142, figs. 169, 170.

14. The man drawn in strict profile in the upper right of this sheet is recognizable as the actor Willem Ruyter. Rembrandt depicted this actor in a number of life studies. See Schatborn and De Winkel, 1996. The hat he wears appears in

Rembrandt Workshop, *Portrait of Rembrandt*, National Gallery of Art, Washington, Widener Collection, 1942.9.63. Bredius and Gerson 1969, no. 39; Arthur K. Wheelock Jr., 'Anonymous Artist, Rembrandt van Rijn/Portrait of Rembrandt/1650,' *Dutch Paintings of the Seventeenth Century*, NGA Online Editions, http://purl.org/nga/collection/artob-

ject/1209 (accessed February 6, 2016).

15. The head on the left of the sheet (fig. 7) is regarded as a self-portrait. Benesch 1973, no. 336, fig. 406; Shoaf Turner 2006, no. 204.

16. Fig. 9 in this entry is cited in Benesch 1973, A 20, fig. 628, and Stockholm 1992, no. 135.

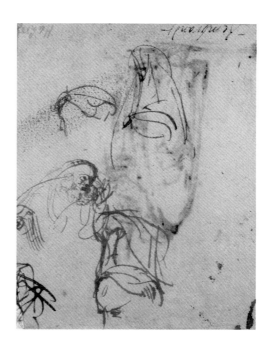

Fig. 7. Rembrandt Harmensz van Rijn, *Head of One of the Scribes with a Tall Hat for 'St. John the Baptist Preaching,'* 1634/1635, pen and brown ink, on light prepared brown paper. Morgan Library & Museum, New York, I 174a

Fig. 8. (verso) Rembrandt Harmensz van Rijn, *Sketches of Figures for 'St. John the Baptist Preaching,'* 1634/1635, pen and brown ink. The Devonshire Collection, Chatsworth, 1018

Fig. 9. Rembrandt Harmensz van Rijn, *Three Studies of an Archer,* 1634/1635, pen and brown ink. Nationalmuseum, Stockholm, NMH A 2/2004

In May 1635 Rembrandt left Hendrick Uylenburgh's workshop and set up his own studio as an independent artist. In the early 1630s he had been awarded a commission by Stadholder Frederik Hendrik, through his secretary Constantijn Huygens, for a series of paintings depicting the Passion of Christ.[17] No preliminary studies for these paintings survive, with the exception of sketches of the Virgin Mary and Mary Magdalene (cat. 65), which Rembrandt used for their respective figures in *The Entombment of Christ*, 1635/1639 (Alte Pinakothek, Munich, figs. 10, 11).[18] Rembrandt drew them while he was working on the painting, but only after the overall composition had been fixed. At the center of the sheet, he sketched Mary Magdalene in pen-and-ink—first with numerous searching lines, and then, slightly to the right and above, with fewer lines, more directly and with greater assurance. In the painting, she stands at the foot of Christ's tomb. Rembrandt borrowed this figure from a print by the German artist Lucas Cranach the Elder (fig. 12), and, indeed, he often took inspiration from earlier artists.[19]

17. Rembrandt Corpus VI 2014, 178.
18. Rembrandt Corpus III 1989,
 no. A 126; Rembrandt Corpus VI 2014,
 no. 162.
19. Hollstein German 1959, VI, 20–21,
 no. 21; Schapelhouman 2006, 77.

Fig. 10. Rembrandt Harmensz van Rijn, *The Entombment of Christ*, 1635–1639, oil on canvas. Alte Pinakothek, Munich, 396

Fig. 11. Detail of fig. 10

Fig. 12. Lucas Cranach the Elder, *The Lamentation*, 1509, woodcut. National Gallery of Art, Washington, Rosenwald Collection, 1950.1.50

REMBRANDT HARMENSZ VAN RIJN

65. *Studies of Mary, the Mother of Christ,*
   and Mary Magdalene, 1635/1636
   Pen and brown ink, red chalk, on paper
   20.1 × 14.3 cm (7¹⁵⁄₁₆ × 5⅝ in.)
   Rijksmuseum, Amsterdam, RP-T-1947-213

REMBRANDT HARMENSZ VAN RIJN

66. *The Rape of Ganymede*, 1635
  Pen and brown ink, brown wash, on paper
  18.3 × 16 cm (7⁵⁄₁₆ × 6⁵⁄₁₆ in.)
  Kupferstich-Kabinett, Staatliche Kunstsammlungen
  Dresden, C 1357
  Washington only

He twice drew the Virgin Mary with red chalk. The version at left in the drawing, where Mary has turned her head to the right, corresponds to her seated position in front of the tomb in the painting, where a woman kneels to her right (see fig. 11). It is not clear who is represented by the two cursory red chalk sketches at the upper right on the sheet.

The drawing is one of only seventeen to bear an

Fig. 13. Rembrandt Harmensz van Rijn, *The Rape of Ganymede*, 1635, oil on canvas. Gemäldegalerie, Dresden, 1558

autograph inscription; this sheet conveys Mary Magdalene's feelings: 'Een dijvoot tgheesoor dat in een / fijn harte bewaert weert / tot troost haerer / beleevende siel' (A devout treasure held in a fine heart to the comfort of her compassionate soul).[20] Rembrandt wrote these words to make it clear, particularly to his pupils, whom he had depicted and what he wanted to express.

As a history painter, Rembrandt also pictured mythological stories in paintings, drawings, and prints. In 1635 he painted *The Rape of Ganymede* (Gemäldegalerie, Dresden) (fig. 13).[21] Ganymede, the son of King Tros, founder of Troy, watched over his father's cattle until Zeus became fascinated by the young man and assumed the form of an eagle to abduct him. The story is told in Ovid's *Metamorphoses* (11.765), which Rembrandt must have known in the translation by Karel van Mander.[22] The artist also would have been familiar with the scene from various earlier prints.[23] The drawing (cat. 66) and the painting (fig. 13) correspond in many respects, making this one of the rare examples in Rembrandt's oeuvre of a complete composition used as a preliminary study for a painting. The drawing is very sketchy, except where Rembrandt used increasingly heavier outlines to shape the child's buttocks and legs in an anatomically correct manner. The eagle's feathers are likewise strongly defined, whereas Ganymede's parents at lower left are roughly indicated with very loose lines. It appears that the boy's father has a weapon aimed at the eagle.

Several differences can be noted between the drawing and the painting. In the latter, only the mother appears, her arms are flung upward, and she is much smaller than either of the two parents in the drawing, where Rembrandt probably concluded that they occupied too much space relative to the main subject of the work. The child in the painting is shown urinating, holding a bunch of cherries (a symbol of purity), and a tassel hangs in front of his belly.[24] These motifs are absent in the drawing. Furthermore, the child's face in the painting reflects a classical type, a form on which Rembrandt and other artists often relied in their work.[25]

The painting, therefore, is quite unusual: other artists generally depicted Ganymede as a youth and not as a small child relieving himself while in a state of shock.[26]

20. Schatborn and Dudok van Heel 2011, 347–351; Schatborn 2011, 320–321; Royalton-Kisch and Schatborn 2011, nos. 16, 20, 33.
21. Rembrandt, *The Rape of Ganymede*, 1635, oil on canvas, Gemäldegalerie, Dresden, 1558. Rembrandt Corpus II 1986, no. A 13; Rembrandt Corpus VI 2014, no. 137; Dresden 2006, cat. 1.
22. Dresden 2006, cat. 19.
23. Dresden 2006, cats. 5–6, 8–12.
24. Russell 1977, 11.
25. See, among others, Schatborn 1975c, 8–19.
26. For an overview of the interpretation of the subject, see Hecht 1997.

Johannes Cornelisz Sylvius was a late sixteenth- and early seventeenth-century Dutch Reformed minister, first in Friesland and then in Amsterdam; in 1610 he was attached to the Gasthuiskerk, moving to the Oude Kerk in 1622.[27] He was married to Aeltje Pietersdr Uylenburgh, a cousin of Hendrick Uylenburgh, the art dealer for whom Rembrandt worked in the early to mid-1630s. It was there that Rembrandt met Aeltje's much younger first cousin Saskia Uylenburgh, whom he married in 1634.[28]

Rembrandt and Saskia were very close to Sylvius and Aeltje, who, among other things, stood witness to the baptism of some of their children, all but one of whom died in infancy. Rembrandt painted a portrait of Aeltje in 1632.[29] In 1633 he made a simple, beautifully characterized portrait print of Sylvius (fig. 14), and in 1637 made a portrait print of their son Petrus Sylvius, who was also a clergyman.[30]

Various suggestions have been put forth regarding the attribution of painted pendant portraits of Sylvius and

Fig. 14. Rembrandt Harmensz van Rijn, *Portrait of Johannes Cornelisz Sylvius*, 1633, etching. National Gallery of Art, Washington, Rosenwald Collection, 1943.3.7093

Aeltje, dated 1644, but recently it has been determined that the artist was Carel Fabritius (figs. 15, 16).[31] Fabritius, who painted portraits in the 1640s under Rembrandt's name on more than one occasion, based his composition on Rembrandt's posthumous drawing of the preacher (cat. 67).[32]

27. I am most grateful to S. A. C. Dudok van Heel, Jaap van der Veen, and Ernst van de Wetering for their contributions to this entry.
28. On the Uylenburgh family see London/ Amsterdam 2006.
29. Rembrandt, *Portrait of Aeltje Uylenburgh*, 1632, oil on panel, private collection. Rembrandt Corpus II 1986, no. A 63; Rembrandt Corpus VI 2014, no. 75. The portrait was identified by Jaap van der Veen in the catalog of sale London, Christie's, December 13, 2000, no. 52. It is stated in the catalog that two portraits of his parents are listed in the 1681 will of the oldest son, Cornelius Sylvius.

30. The portrait prints of *Johannes Cornelisz Sylvius* and *Petrus Sylvius* were published, respectively, in Hinterding, Rutgers, and Luijten 2013, I, no. 124, and *ibid.*, II, no. 164. The latter identification is based on a seventeenth-century inscription on an impression of the second state, formerly in Lausanne; Hinterding 2008, under cat. 196.
31. Carel Fabritius, *Portrait of Jan Cornelisz Sylvius, the Preacher*, 1644, oil on canvas, Wallraf-Richartz-Museum & Fondation Corboud, Cologne, WRM 2527.
32. Rembrandt Corpus VI 2014, under 191b, 581. There is no record of Fabritius

in Amsterdam in 1644; he is documented in Middenbeemster before June 1643 and in April 1646. The Hague/Schwerin 2004, 18–19. Fabritius was not the first pupil to make a painting based on a Rembrandt drawing. In 1636 Govert Flinck most probably painted a second version, after a drawing by Rembrandt, of the master's *Sacrifice of Isaac*, dated 1635, in The State Hermitage Museum, St. Petersburg, ГЭ-727.

REMBRANDT HARMENSZ VAN RIJN

67. *Johannes Cornelisz Sylvius, the Preacher* (recto), 1644
Small Head of a Horse (verso)
Pen and brown ink on laid paper
13.3 × 12.2 cm (5¼ × 4¹³⁄₁₆ in.)
National Gallery of Art, Washington,
Rosenwald Collection, 1959.16.12

[173]

Fig 15. Carel Fabritius, *Portrait of Jan Cornelisz Sylvius, the Preacher*, 1644, oil on canvas. Wallraf-Richartz-Museum & Fondation Corboud, Cologne, WRM 2527

Fig. 16. Carel Fabritius, *Portrait of Aeltje Uylenburgh Seated in an Armchair*, 1644, oil on canvas. Art Gallery of Ontario, Toronto

The style of Rembrandt's portrait drawing corresponds closely to one of the two preliminary studies[33] that he made for his etched portrait of Sylvius of 1646 because they share the same cursory sketchiness.[34] Sylvius's face in Fabritius's painting is a mirror image of Rembrandt's etched portrait of the sitter that he made in 1633 (fig. 14). Rembrandt's portrait etching of 1646 depicts Sylvius as a rather older man, presumably reflecting the preacher's appearance prior to his death in 1638.

Aeltje died on February 20, 1644, and although it is possible that Fabritius painted her likeness before her death, it is more likely that the artist's portrait of her was a posthumous image (fig. 16).[35] Fabritius probably based her likeness on Rembrandt's portrait of 1632.[36] Her features in these two portraits are strikingly similar, and she wears the same cap in both. In Fabritius's portrait, however, she is no longer shown looking directly at the viewer, but rather toward the pendant of her husband, which would have been placed to her right. These pendant portraits, probably signed and dated by Rembrandt himself, are noted in the 1681 will of the couple's eldest son, Cornelius.[37]   [PS]

33. Rembrandt, *Posthumous Portrait of Johannes Cornelisz Sylvius,* 1646, pen and brown ink, Nationalmuseum, Stockholm, 137/1973; Benesch 1973, no. 762a, fig. 961; Stockholm 1992, no. 148; and Amsterdam/London 2000, under no. 54, fig. b.
34. Hinterding, Rutgers, and Luijten 2013, II, no. 235, shows this preliminary study. A second preliminary study for this print was very broadly executed in pen-and-ink and probably also a brush and some white: Rembrandt, *Posthumous Portrait of Johannes*

Cornelisz Sylvius, 1646, pen and brown ink with white heightening, British Museum, London, 1874, 0808.2272. Benesch 1973, no. 763; Royalton-Kisch 2009, no. 37.
35. Carel Fabritius, *Portrait of Aeltje Uylenburgh*, 1644, oil on canvas, Art Gallery of Ontario, Toronto. The work was first attributed to Fabritius in Berlin/ Amsterdam/London 1991a, no. 75. The dates on the portraits have erroneously been read as 1645. This information was kindly supplied by Ernst van de Wetering.

36. S. A. C. Dudok van Heel has suggested that it might represent a *post obitum* portrait, based on a likeness of Aeltje Uylenburgh on her deathbed.
37. Rembrandt's signature and date are noted in Ernst van de Wetering in Amsterdam/Berlin 2006, 318, under nos. 39 and 40. Regarding Cornelius's will, see note 29, above. Van der Veen suggests that the 1632 portrait of Aeltje, with an unknown pendant, could be one of the portraits noted in the will of 1681.

CORNELIS SAFTLEVEN

1607–1681

Approximately five hundred drawings by Cornelis Saftleven have survived. They represent an exceptionally diverse array of subjects, ranging from biblical, mythological, allegorical, social, and political themes to nudes, figures, heads, animals, barn interiors, farmyards, scenes from daily life, landscapes, and topographical views. Many are signed, and about a third bear dates. Dated works are known from almost every year from 1625 to 1677.[1]

The largest group of Saftleven's drawings consists of studies of single male or female figures. Nearly all of these are executed in black chalk, often elaborated with gray wash, and about half of them, including *Sleeping Hunter* (cat. 68), carry the artist's monogram and a date.[2] The models in these drawings represent a broad spectrum of social types and they strike poses ranging from the motionless lethargy of slumber to violent movement. They sit, stand, recline, smoke, drink, and play musical instruments, among other activities. A patrician gentleman preens in his fine clothes, a monk reads a book, a heavily draped woman runs away, and a wild-haired peasant youth stands with a protruding belly and beer glass held at a jaunty angle. Although many are finished, fully resolved works supplied with the artist's monogram and a date, it is unclear whether Saftleven made them all for sale or kept some or all of them in the workshop as sources of motifs for use in paintings. Only a few of those known today were adapted for pictures.[3]

Sleeping Hunter is one of the rare surviving studies of this type that Saftleven reproduced in a painting. The figure appears in the panel *Sleeping Hunter in a Landscape* (cat. 69), also in the Maida and George Abrams Collection, which depicts a hunter dozing against an earthen bank beneath a large tree that occupies most of the upper half of the composition. The man's head lolls farther back in the painting than in the drawing, and Cornelis Saftleven made a slight adjustment to his left hand, which rests limply on the stock of his gun in the oil. His hat has slipped off his head and it lies on the ground beside a felled duck, while the rest of his quarry—a hare—is stretched over the bank behind him. A watchful greyhound sits by his side, and another dog peeks over the top of the bank. While Cornelis painted the figure, the greyhound, the dead game, and the hat in the foreground, the rest of the picture—the tree, sky, and distant panorama—is the work of his younger brother, Herman, a landscape specialist. It is one of a handful of works from the 1630s and early 1640s to which Herman contributed the landscape and Cornelis the figures and animals.[4] The signature 'Saft-Levens,' notably written in the plural, confirms the collaboration.[5] The final digit of the date on the painting is illegible, but one may tentatively assume that, on the basis of the year inscribed on the drawing, it should be read as '1642.' However, in at least one instance, Cornelis Saftleven may have adapted for a painting a figure study executed several years earlier.[6]   [WWR]

1. Schulz 1978, 40–45.

2. Schulz 1978, 80–115, nos. 30–207.

3. Schulz 1978, 42, 63.

4. Schulz 1978, 27–28.

5. Amsterdam/Boston/Philadelphia 1987, 476, no. 96. My thanks to Susan Anderson for closely examining the signature and date.

6. It is worth noting that a drawing dated 1636 in the Maida and George Abrams Collection (London/Paris/Cambridge 2002, 186–187, no. 80) was used by Cornelis in a painting said to have been dated 1645 (sale, Dobiaschofsky Auktionen, Bern, May 12, 2004, lot 298; 'Cornelis Saftleven,' RKD Nederlands Instituut voor Kunsthistorische Documentatie, The Hague, image database, last modified October 23, 2013, https://rkd.nl/explore/images/61708). If the date on the painting is 1645, Cornelis reverted to a study that he executed nearly a decade earlier.

CORNELIS SAFTLEVEN
68. *Sleeping Hunter*, 1642
   Black chalk and gray wash on paper
   16.9 × 23.8 cm (6⅝ × 9⅜ in.)
   Maida and George Abrams Collection, Boston

CORNELIS and HERMAN SAFTLEVEN
69. *Sleeping Hunter in a Landscape*, 1642 or later
   Oil on panel
   36.8 × 52 cm (14½ × 20½ in.)
   Maida and George Abrams Collection, Boston

JACOB ANDRIAENSZ BACKER

1608–1651

70. *Seated Female Nude (Study for Venus)*, c. 1650
   Black and white chalk on blue laid paper,
   double framing line in brown ink on paper
   32.3 × 23.2 cm (12 11/16 × 9 1/8 in.)
   The Maida and George Abrams Collection, Fogg Art
   Museum, Harvard University, Cambridge, Massachusetts,
   Gift of George S. Abrams in appreciation of William
   Robinson's services as Curator of Drawings,
   1988–2013, 2013.170
   Washington only

Jacob Backer probably studied painting in Amsterdam, but his first teacher remains unidentified. In 1626, at the age of eighteen, he entered the workshop of the history painter Lambert Jacobsz in Leeuwarden, presumably as an advanced student or trained assistant. His employ-ment lasted about six years, during which Govert Flinck (pp. 192–193, cat. 80), seven years Backer's junior, was Lambert Jacobsz' pupil. By 1633 Backer returned to Amsterdam and quickly established himself as a portraitist and painter of biblical and mythological subjects.[1] He and Flinck became leading exponents of the classicizing style adopted by many Dutch history painters in the 1640s.[2]

Studies in black and white chalk on blue paper of single figures—nude and clothed—constitute the great major-ity of Backer's surviving drawings.[3] It is noteworthy that Arnold Houbraken, who rarely refers to works on paper in his biographies of Dutch painters, wrote that he could not do justice to Backer's reputation without mentioning 'his outstanding way of drawing. Certainly he [Backer]

drew his Academy figures, especially the women, so artfully on blue paper with black and white chalk, that he took the crown from all his contemporaries.'[4] Backer not only excelled at this technique for studies from the model but likely invented it after having seen drawings of single figures in black and white chalks on gray or brown paper by Peter Paul Rubens.[5] It was adopted by several Amsterdam painters who specialized in historical sub-jects and portraits, including Flinck, Bartholomeus Breenbergh (pp. 151–153, cat. 56), Gerbrand van den Eeckhout (pp. 206–211), Jacob van Loo, and Backer's pupils Abraham van den Tempel and Jan van Noordt.

Only a few figure drawings are securely attributable to Backer either because they were signed by the artist or served as studies for paintings.[6] *Seated Female Nude (Study for Venus)* (cat. 70) is one of two female nudes that he translated into a painting and, as such, provides a valuable reference for distinguishing studies from Backer's hand from those by Flinck and others, all of whom drew from live models in the same media and

1. Amsterdam/Aachen 2008, 14–18, 29–34.
2. For the date of Flinck's return to Amsterdam and his stay of about one year in Rembrandt's workshop, see Schatborn 2010a, 4.
3. Sumowski 1979, I, 16–186, nos. 1–86.

4. 'Ik had byna vergeten (en zou dus zyn roem by verzuim benadeeld) van zyne uitstekende wyze van teekenen te melden. Zeker hy heeft zyne Academiebeelden, inzonderheid de vrouwtjes zoo konstig op blaau papier met zwart en wit kryt geteek-ent, dat hy daar door de kroon van alle zyne

tydgenooten heeft weg gedragen.' Houbraken 1718–1721, I, 338.
5. De Witt 2006, 164.
6. Sumowski 1979, I, 16–39, nos. 1–12; Amsterdam/Aachen 2008, 69–78; Robinson 2010, 57–58.

Fig. 1. Jacob Backer, *Venus, Adonis, and Amor*, c. 1650–1651, oil on canvas. Schloss Fasanerie, Kurhessische Hausstiftung, Eichenzell, B 495

Fig. 2. Govert Flinck, *Seated Female Nude*, 1648, black and white chalk on blue paper. Staatliche Museen, Berlin, Kupferstichkabinett, KDZ 1327

occasionally during the same session.[7] The other seated nude (cat. 71), which is neither signed nor preparatory for a painting, displays the idiosyncrasies of Backer's draftsmanship that inform the Venus study: nervous, undulating contours, scattered light accents, and characteristic strokes used to render the figure's hair, face, and breasts. When Backer drew this nude, Flinck sat to his right and studied the model from a different angle (fig. 2).[8] Flinck's drawing is signed and dated 1648, which thus provides a date for Backer's work.

Backer executed *Seated Female Nude (Study for Venus)* in preparation for painting the nearly life-size goddess in *Venus, Adonis, and Amor* of c. 1650–1651 (fig. 1).[9] The subject is from Ovid's *Metamorphoses* (X.708–739). Venus pleads with her mortal lover Adonis not to pursue his favorite pastime of hunting. She holds his hand and

looks longingly up at him, while Amor pushes him toward Venus and away from his weapons. Adonis, however, ultimately ignored his lover's entreaties and was killed by a wild boar (see cat. 56). Backer posed his studio model nearly exactly as Venus would appear on the canvas, including the position of Amor's right arm, which reaches up to grasp Adonis's hand. In the painting, the artist moved Venus's hand slightly closer to her head, adjusted her legs, and added a swath of drapery to cover her lower body. In the drawing, she leans on her left arm, but on the canvas it disappears behind Adonis's back. These are minor changes, and the correspondence between the figure in the study and in the painting— albeit rendered on a different scale—is remarkably close.   [WWR]

7. For Backer's studies of female nudes, see Amsterdam/Aachen 2008, 69–72, nos. 53–55, 193–199. For the other study of a female nude used by Backer in a painting, see Robinson 2010, 57–58.

8. Govert Flinck, *Seated Female Nude*, 1648, black and white chalk on blue paper, Staatliche Museen, Berlin, Kupferstichkabinett, KDZ 1327. Sumowski 1979, IV, 1960–1961, no. 899; Amsterdam 1981, 90–91.

9. Jacob Backer, *Venus, Adonis, and Amor*, c. 1650–51, oil on canvas, Kurhessische Hausstiftung, Schloss Fasanerie, Eichenzell, B 495. Amsterdam 2008, 168–169, no. 37, and 248–49, no. A133. Christopher White was the first modern art historian to establish the connection between the drawing and the painting *Venus and Adonis*. See London/Birmingham/Leeds 1962, 18, no. 80. This relationship was also known to an eighteenth-century owner of the

study, who inscribed its verso 'Jacob Bakker het Schilderij bij Rapoen' (Jacob Backer the painting with Rapoen). It has not been possible, however, to identify the collector with the surname Rapoen or Raphoen who owned the picture before its acquisition by the ruling family of Hesse-Cassel, where it was first documented in 1749. On the provenance of the painting, see Kassel 2006, 243, no. B10.

JACOB ANDRIAENSZ BACKER
71. *Seated Female Nude*, 1648
    Black and white chalk on blue paper
    28.8 × 22.8 cm (11⁵⁄₁₆ × 9 in.)
    Maida and George Abrams Collection, Boston

ADRIAEN VAN OSTADE

1610–1685

ADRIAEN VAN OSTADE
72. *Dancing Man*, c. 1659
   Black and white chalk on light brown paper
   14.4 × 7.5 cm (5¹¹⁄₁₆ × 2¹⁵⁄₁₆ in.)

Rijksmuseum, Amsterdam, purchased with the
support of the F.G. Waller-Fonds, the Belport
Familienstifung and a contribution from
J.A.Z. Count van Regteren Limpurg Bequest,
RP-T-1981-237

Haarlem painter Adriaen van Ostade specialized in the depiction of peasant life and was extremely productive.[1] Aside from a large number of paintings, more than four hundred of his drawings have also survived.[2] They include approximately fifty detailed watercolors, made between 1672 and 1684, which were intended as works of art in their own right.[3] Other works done by him include composition drawings, figure studies, and small sketches with one or more figures.[4]

At the start of his career, in order to prepare for his paintings, Van Ostade chiefly used composition drawings, in which he indicated the placement of the figures, including their relations to each other and to the surroundings. They are executed in pen-and-ink with gray or brown wash over sketches in graphite, black chalk, or charcoal.[5] In 1645 he increasingly made use of figure studies.[6] In his painting of an artist's studio, Van Ostade depicts an artist who has fixed such a study above his easel so that he could copy it (see p. 6 fig. 1).[7] These studies, executed in black chalk and heightened with white chalk, on blue or brown paper, serve to capture poses and gestures, while sometimes giving the viewer information about the subjects' occupations.[8]

Van Ostade tried to render his figures as naturally as possible and was interested in clothing and lighting. One particular characteristic is that his figures are often shown in action, such as a man dancing (cat. 72). These studies, probably unlike others devoted to the figure, would not have been drawn from a posed model.[9]

Only a few composition drawings dating from after 1645 can be linked to his paintings,[10] even though Van Ostade continued to make carefully executed composition drawings for his etchings and watercolors, which he incised for transfer to the etching ground or the paper.[11]

Dancing Figures (cat. 74) is one rare known composition drawing that was used for a painting. It is a preparatory work for *Peasants Dancing in a Tavern* (cat. 73), dated 1659. The drawing was executed in graphite or black chalk in an extremely sketchy manner.[12] Only the seated man and the couple standing in the center were worked out in pen and brown ink.[13] In the painting, one can see that most figures were taken from the drawing.

1. For a biography see Irene van Thiel-Stroman, 'Biographies 15th–17th Century,' in Köhler 2006, 258–261, and Ebert 2013, 19–36.

2. For an overview of the drawings, see Trautscholdt 1959; Trautscholdt 1967; and Schnackenburg 1981.

3. Schnackenburg 1981, I, 41, and Ebert 2013, 125–126.

4. Schnackenburg 1981, I, 42–45, and Amsterdam/Washington 1981, 80–81.

5. Schnackenburg 1981, I, 43.

6. Schnackenburg 1981, I, 43.

7. Staatliche Kunstsammlungen Dresden, Gemäldegalerie Alte Meister, inv. no. 1397.

8. Schnackenburg 1981, I, 44, and Amsterdam/Washington 1981, 80–81.

9. See also Amsterdam/Washington 1981, 27–29, and Stefes 2011, I, under no. 765.

10. Schnackenburg 1981, I, 43.

11. Schnackenburg 1981, I, 43–44. For drawings as preparations for prints see p. 47, and Trautscholdt 1929; Schnackenburg 1981, I, 45–47; Amsterdam/Washington 1981, 80–81; Slatkes 1987; Athens 1994, Appendix 1; and Tom Rassieur, 'Adriaen van Ostade, the Methodical Artist: Preparatory Drawings, a Chronology, and Rembrandt,' in Amsterdam 1998b, 31–53.

12. Schnackenburg pointed out that there may have originally been more sketchy composition drawings, but fewer have survived because early collectors would have had less interest in them (Schnackenburg 1981, I, 43).

13. They were worked up even further in black ink by a later hand, see Schnackenburg 1981, I, no. 123, and Stefes 2011, I, no. 765.

ADRIAEN VAN OSTADE

73. *Peasants Dancing in a Tavern*, 1659
Oil on panel
44.1 × 60.3 cm (17⅜ × 23¾ in.)
Saint Louis Art Museum, Friends Fund, 147:1966

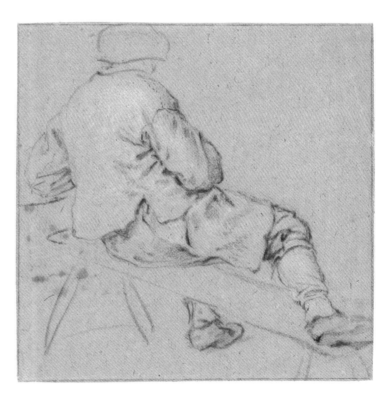

ADRIAEN VAN OSTADE

74. *Dancing Figures*, c. 1659
   Black chalk, pen and brown ink, on paper
   13.2 × 26.7 cm (5³⁄₁₆ × 10½ in.)
   Hamburger Kunsthalle, Hamburg, 22304

ADRIAEN VAN OSTADE

75. *Seated Man from Behind*, c. 1659
   Black chalk, heightened with white,
   on light brown paper
   20 × 19.2 cm (7⅞ × 7⁹⁄₁₆ in.)
   Rijksmuseum, Amsterdam, RP-T-00-209

[185]

However, the woman and child near the fire do not correspond to the group of figures in the drawing at far right, nor do the figures standing by and on a staircase correspond to the drawing's center background group.[14]

As was his custom at this stage of his career, Van Ostade mostly used individual figure studies to prepare for his paintings. We know of studies like this for six of the twenty-six figures represented in this painting.[15] Two drawings shown here convey the artist's skill in capturing peasants in poses that are natural, yet by no means simple. One drawing (cat. 75), on a relatively large sheet, depicts a peasant lying partially on a bench.[16] In *Peasants Dancing in a Tavern*, where his hat was further elaborated, he serves as a repoussoir figure. The male figure in the other drawing (cat. 72) appears in the center background of the painting, where he dances with a woman. In so doing, one of his legs is bent further back than it is in the drawing.

Even more exceptional are three preparatory sketches (cats. 76–78) in which the composition was worked out for a painting of 1654: the portrait of an unidentified family (fig. 1).[17] Van Ostade made few such portraits and evidently worked quite meticulously on the composition of this complex group.[18] The three drawings were swiftly sketched in graphite and then worked out with flowing lines in pen and brown ink, with areas of shadow indicated by ink wash.[19]

In these sketches Van Ostade concentrated on the placement of the figures and their mutual relationships; the faces are indicated in only a cursory fashion. However, the painting does not entirely correlate to

Fig. 1. Adriaen van Ostade, *Family Portrait*, 1654, oil on panel. Musée du Louvre, Paris, INV. 1679

any of the preparatory works.[20] Only the young man and woman at the rear center can be found in all three sketches and in the painting, almost in the same place and in the same poses.

Other figures were included in the painting in altered forms, such as the children in the center foreground, who were borrowed in mirror image from *Drawing for a Group Portrait* (cat. 76). To suggest more contact with the other sitters, Van Ostade had the young child—still unsteady on its feet—lean against its mother's knee, as can also be seen in another such sketch (cat. 77). Consequently, Van Ostade seems to have been seeking a coherent composition with an animated interaction between the sitters. In addition to these sketches, the artist would likely have made more drawings for this commission, although no others are known. It is not clear whether he made drawn portrait studies of the subjects or painted their likenesses from life. [RSB]

14. There are figure studies for the woman and child in the De Grez Collection; see n. 15.
15. Two in the Rijksmuseum (cats. 72, 75); Brussels, Musées royaux des Beaux-Arts de Belgique, Jean De Grez Collection, inv. nos. 4060/2549 and 4060/2550; Hamburg, Hamburger Kunsthalle, inv. nos. 22277 and 22285; see Schnackenburg 1981, nos. 124–128;

Brussels/Amsterdam/Aachen 2007, nos. 72–73; Stefes 2011, II, nos. 765 and 766 (see also under no. 764).
16. Stefes maintains that figure studies on larger, brownish, paper are model studies, unlike the small sketches 'from life' on blue paper. See Stefes 2011, I, under no. 765.
17. Paris 1970, no. 153; Foucart 2009, 195.
18. We know of only one other group portrait: *The De Goyer Family and the*

Painter, c. 1650/1655, Museum Bredius, The Hague, 86-1946. For his portraits see Ebert 2013, 128–129.
19. Schnackenburg pointed out that thanks to the date of the painting, the drawings give an indication of the artist's drawing style in the 1650s; Schnackenburg 1981, I, 40.
20. In one drawing (cat. 77) there are actually eleven figures, whereas only ten appear in the painting.

ADRIAEN VAN OSTADE

76. *Drawing for a Group Portrait*, c. 1654
  Pen and brown ink over graphite, gray-brown wash,
  on paper
  12.2 × 23.2 cm (4¹³⁄₁₆ × 9⅛ in.)
  Fondation Custodia, Collection Frits Lugt,
  Paris, 1190

ADRIAEN VAN OSTADE

77. *Drawing for a Group Portrait*, c. 1654
  Pen and brown ink over graphite, gray-brown wash,
  on paper
  12.6 × 21.3 cm (4¹⁵⁄₁₆ × 8⅜ in.)
  Fondation Custodia, Collection Frits Lugt,
  Paris, 5037

ADRIAEN VAN OSTADE

78. *Drawing for a Group Portrait*, c. 1654
   Pen and brown ink over graphite, gray-brown wash,
   on paper
   16.2 × 20.1 cm (6⁵⁄₁₆ × 7¹⁵⁄₁₆ in.)
   Fondation Custodia, Collection Frits Lugt,
   Paris, 5096

HENDRICK CORNELISZ VAN VLIET

c. 1611–1675

The type of composition featuring imaginary architecture put together from classical elements that had been devised by Hans Vredeman de Vries in the sixteenth century evolved in the seventeenth into depictions of existing or conceivable architecture, including countless church interiors. Haarlem painters Pieter Jansz Saenredam (pp. 140–150) and Gerrit Berckheyde (pp. 260–269) were renowned for depicting church architecture (both interior and exterior) and townscapes, respectively. In Delft, Hendrick van Vliet, Gerard Houckgeest, and Emmanuel de Witte were celebrated painters of 'Perspectives,' as architectural paintings were called.

A rare, incomplete sketchbook by Hendrick van Vliet contains nineteen sheets of blue paper, with recto and verso drawings in black and red chalk (cat. 79). Van Vliet started out as a pupil of his uncle Willem van Vliet, and he then may well have trained with leading portrait painter Michiel van Miereveld. Hendrick Van Vliet began his career as a portraitist, as the many individual and group portraits in the sketchbook attest. He also sketched various figures on these sheets, several of which relate to those in his paintings. For instance his *Children Playing* turn up in an *Interior of the Oude Kerk in Delft* (fig. 1).

1. Hendrick van Vliet, *Interior of the Nieuwe Kerk*, 1655, oil on panel, Pushkin Museum, Moscow, 571.
2. Walter Liedtke, in New York/London 2001, cat. 128, 495, and n. 9.

Three drawings in the sketchbook depict church interiors, two of them—on facing pages—show the Nieuwe Kerk in Delft. On the right is the tomb of William the Silent and on the left an element that also appears in a painting of a broader view of the church's interior, 1665 (Pushkin Museum, Moscow).[1] He also drew the pulpit in the Nieuwe Kerk and one of the memorial plaques. Architectural sketches like these seem to have been exercises, and it is not clear whether Van Vliet used them as actual preliminary studies.[2]   [PS]

Fig. 1. Hendrick van Vliet, *Interior of the Oude Kerk in Delft*, c. 1660, oil on panel. Bayerische Staatgemäldesammlungen, Munich, 10361

HENDRICK CORNELISZ VAN VLIET
79. *Sketchbook*, 19 sheets, n.d.
Black, white, and red chalk on nineteen leaves
of blue paper
27.5 × 22 cm (10¹³⁄₁₆ × 8¹¹⁄₁₆ in.)
Museum Boijmans Van Beuningen, Rotterdam, HVV 1

80. *Standing Man beside a Table*, 1644–before 1646
   Black chalk, heightened with white, on blue paper
   39.2 × 24 cm (15⁷⁄₁₆ × 9⁷⁄₁₆ in.)
   Rijksprentenkabinet, Rijksmuseum, Amsterdam,
   Purchased with the support of the Vereniging
   Rembrandt, RP-T-1975-84

Govert Flinck first studied with the history painter Lambert Jacobsz in Leeuwarden, where he met Jacob Backer (see p. 178–181), then a senior pupil or assistant in Jacobsz's workshop. Around 1635–1636 Flinck completed his training with Rembrandt, learning to imitate his master's brushwork and color so skillfully that his pictures passed as originals by Rembrandt himself.[1] Eventually, wrote Arnold Houbraken, 'with great effort and difficulty he turned away from [Rembrandt's] way of painting,'[2] developing a lighter and more fluent style based on the work of Peter Paul Rubens and Anthony van Dyck. During the 1640s and 1650s, Flinck attracted prestigious commissions for portraits and history paintings, reaching the apogee of his career with the monumental canvases he produced for the Amsterdam Town Hall.[3]

Flinck's early drawings date from c. 1635–1640. Comprising ink-and-wash compositions and figure studies in red and black chalk, they closely recall Rembrandt's work of that period.[4] During the 1640s Flinck joined Backer and other Amsterdam artists who adopted the practice of drawing from nude and clothed models in black and white chalk on blue paper (see cats. 70, 71 and p. 180, fig. 1). In addition to improving their abilities to represent the human body, the artists studied figures in specific poses to prepare for the execution of paintings. Flinck's numerous works of this type are well documented; many bear his signature, and several relate directly to pictures by him.[5]

Standing Man beside a Table (cat. 80) is a preparatory study for the figure of the husband in Flinck's double portrait of an unidentified couple, dated 1646, in Karlsruhe (fig. 1).[6] The youth who posed for the drawing is clearly younger than the sitter in the portrait, and Flinck presumably dressed an apprentice or studio model in patrician clothes in order to study the costume, stance, and gesture he envisioned for the figure in the finished

Fig. 1. Govert Flinck, *Portrait of a Married Couple*, 1646, oil on canvas. Staatliche Kunsthalle, Karlsruhe, 2479

work. Apart from the face, which Flinck would have painted during a sitting with the patron, he introduced a few changes between the drawing and the canvas. In the painting, the figure is not full length, as in the drawing, but ends just below the knees, and a dog—an attribute that symbolizes marital fidelity—appears at his side. The man's hands are larger in the picture, and his left hand, which rests on the hat on the table, is more clearly articulated. The buttons and decoration of the shirt—barely suggested in the study—are rendered in detail in the painting, as are the complex folds of the red cloth on the table, details which Flinck did not elaborate in the drawing. Both the function and technique of the study relate it closely to three preparatory studies for portraits in Flinck's *Civic Guard Company of Captain Joan Huydecoper and Lieutenant Frans van Waveren* of 1648.[7] If Flinck drew a separate study for the figure of the woman in the Karlsruhe portrait, it has not come to light.   [wwr]

1. Houbraken 1718–1721, II, 20–21; London/Amsterdam 2006, 160–169.
2. Houbraken 1718–1721, II, 21.
3. Sumowski 1983, II, 999–1002.
4. On Flinck's early, Rembrandtesque drawings, see Schatborn 2010b, 4–38.
5. Sumowski 1979, IV, 1908–1909, no. 873, 1914–1927, nos. 876–882, 1930–1935, nos. 884–886, 1946–1949, nos. 892–893, 1956–1965, nos. 897–901.

6. Govert Flinck, *Portrait of a Married Couple*, 1646, oil on canvas, Staatliche Kunsthalle, Karlsruhe, 2479. Sumowski 1983, II, 1041, no. 716. Yapou 1983, 58–61, identifies the woman in the Karlsruhe portrait as Flinck's wife and, consequently, the man as Flinck. See also Lootsma 2007, 221–236, who exhaustively traces the source for the woman's pose, but does not discuss the man's pose.

7. Sumowski 1979, IV, 1914–1919, nos. 876–878. For the painting, see Sumowski 1983, II, 1041, no. 717, and 'Amsterdam Museum Collectie Online Research,' entry for *Schutters van de compagnie van kapitein Joan Huydecoper en luitenant Frans van Waveren*, inv. sa 7318, http://am.adlibhosting.com/amonline/advanced/Details/collect/38463.

AELBERT CUYP

1620–1691

84. *Three Boys in a Landscape*, early 1640s
  Black chalk, gray wash on paper
  14.7 × 19.1 cm (5¹³⁄₁₆ × 7½ in.)
  Rijksmuseum, Amsterdam, RP-T-1895-A-3057

Aelbert Cuyp received his earliest training from his father, the Dordrecht portrait painter Jacob Gerritsz Cuyp.[1] Aelbert must have subsequently apprenticed with another master, for he soon began to portray, almost exclusively, landscapes and riverscapes. This added training probably took place in Utrecht, his mother's native city and where his father had studied with Abraham Bloemaert (see pp. 76–85). In Utrecht Cuyp may have studied with Cornelis and Herman Saftleven (see pp. 175–77 and cats. 68, 69), brothers who had moved there from Rotterdam in the early 1630s.

Many similarities exist between the style and subject matter of the Saftlevens's works and Cuyp's landscape and figure drawings. For example, much like Cornelis Saftleven (see cats. 68, 69), Cuyp made bold black-chalk studies of figures posed in ways that anticipate their eventual use in paintings (see cats. 84, 85 and fig. 1).

Cuyp's connections to Utrecht artistic traditions remained strong throughout his career. The contre-jour (against daylight) effects that he introduced to his paintings around 1650 owe much to the Italianate style of Jan Both, who had returned to Utrecht in the late 1640s after having spent a number of years in Italy. Cuyp's mature paintings almost always portray a verdant, peaceful world, a sun-filled arcadia blessed with gentle breezes and billowing clouds. Shepherds tend herds of cattle and sheep in pastoral landscapes, travelers wend their way along well-beaten paths, and sailing ships

find steady winds to guide them along inland waterways.

Cuyp gained much of his inspiration by drawing after nature.[2] He not only depicted panoramic landscapes with distant towns and cities (cat. 82, 83), but also

Fig. 1. Aelbert Cuyp, *Landscape with Horseman, Herders, and Cattle*, c. 1655–1660, oil on canvas. The National Gallery, London, NG822

focused on the picturesque beauty of rugged, weatherworn trees, the broad, leafy shapes of woodland plants, or the simple dignity of a resting cow (cat. 86). His drawings provided him with a wide array of visual material from which to draw when conceiving paintings in his studio. Although Cuyp occasionally based a painting's entire composition on one drawing, he generally utilized

1. The biographical information in this
   entry is largely based on Washington/
   London/Amsterdam 2001, 15–33.

2. For an assessment of Cuyp's drawings,
   see Haverkamp-Begemann 2001. For the
   catalogue raisonné of Cuyp's paintings, see
   Chong 1992.

AELBERT CUYP

85. *Standing Herdsman with Staff*, c. 1642–1646
   Black chalk, gray wash, on two pieces of paper
   19.1 × 9.6 cm (7½ × 3¾ in.)
   Private Collection

a number of sheets when creating his works, imaginatively combining landscape studies with drawings of figures, plants, and animals.

One of the most compelling of Cuyp's mature paintings is *Landscape with Herdsmen* (cat. 81), which he executed around 1650.[3] In this work Cuyp emphasized the quiet stillness of the air warmed by the sun. Despite the evocative quality of this painting, the setting has a basis in reality: the valley of the Rhine River near the towns of Cleves and Calkar, not far from the Dutch border. Cuyp made a number of trips along inland waterways to the eastern regions of the Netherlands. He took with him sketchbooks—all of which are now unbound—and filled them with carefully rendered panoramic views of broad river valleys dotted with towns, churches, and windmills. He later referred to these drawings when making such paintings as *Landscape with Herdsmen*.

The drawing Cuyp used when executing this painting came from a large sketchbook he had with him during his first trip to the region in the early 1640s. The sheet depicts a view of Calcar with Monterberg, a hill on which stood the ruins of the castle of the dukes of Cleves (cat. 82). Cuyp subsequently worked up his black-chalk rendering of the site in his studio. He not only added green and ocher-yellow watercolor, but also created a bold chiaroscuro effect by applying gum arabic to darken the foreground plane.[4]

When Cuyp visited this region a second time in the early 1650s, he took with him a smaller sketchbook, in which he made delicate chalk and wash drawings that evoke a remarkable sense of space and atmosphere (cat. 83).[5] This drawing depicts the Monterberg from the opposite direction. The church towers of Calcar, which are also found in the earlier drawing, rise beyond the carefully delineated river valley in the middle ground.

The care with which Cuyp drew these panoramic scenes, which he later worked up in his studio, raises the question as to whether he intended to sell them on the open market as finished works. Nevertheless, this possibility seems unlikely since most of them remained in his estate. Indeed, he used both of the exhibited panoramic drawings as compositional studies for paintings that he executed years later.[6]

Neither the human figure nor animals play much of a role in Cuyp's landscape drawings. Rather, much as with the Saftlevens, Cuyp made separate figure drawings in his studio that he would then use in conjunction with landscape drawings when composing his paintings in the studio, as in *Landscape with Herdsmen* (cat. 81), and *Landscape with Horseman, Herders, and Cattle* (fig. 1), where he utilized not only the panoramic drawing of *Calcar with Monterberg in the Distance* but also two separate sheets of figure studies (including cat. 85).[7] Occasionally he combined a few figures on one sheet, providing them with a cursory landscape setting to place them into a pictorial context (cat. 84).

Drawings of animals constitute a substantial portion of Cuyp's drawn oeuvre. These careful studies of cows, sheep, horses, and a dog have great dignity and individuality. Sometimes, as with his figure drawings he focused on one animal (cat. 86), although in other instances he combined two separate studies on a single sheet (cat. 87). In most of these sheets he modeled his forms with a combination of black chalk and gray wash, and often shaded the ground near the animals to locate them in space. As with other types of drawings, Cuyp consulted these studies when composing his paintings. All three of the animals in the exhibited drawings, which he probably executed around 1650, make their appearance in one of Cuyp's most majestic late paintings, *River Landscape with Horseman and Peasants*, c. 1660 (fig. 2). As is generally the case in his work, he slightly modified the poses and coloring of the horse and cattle in his painting, but the essential connection to these drawn studies is quite evident.   [AKW]

3. For further information about this painting, see Arthur Wheelock, 'Landscape with Herdsmen,' in Washington/London/Amsterdam 2001, 142–143, cat. 25.

4. For further information about this drawing, see Wouter Kloek, 'Calcar with Monterberg in the Distance,' in Washington/London/Amsterdam 2001, 244, cat. 76.

5. For further information about this drawing, see Wouter Kloek, 'The Rhine Valley Stretching North toward the Elterberg,' in Washington/London/Amsterdam 2001, 261, cat. 93.

6. The connection between the panoramic drawing in the Lugt collection and paintings in the Metropolitan Museum of Art and Woburn Abbey is noted by Wouter Kloek in 'The Rhine Valley Stretching North toward the Elterberg,' Washington/London/Amsterdam 2001, 261, cat. 93.

7. Peter Schatborn first made this observation in Amsterdam/Washington 1981, 120–121.

AELBERT CUYP

81. *Landscape with Herdsmen*, c. 1650–1652
Oil on panel
48 × 82.5 cm (18⅞ × 32½ in.)
National Gallery of Art, Washington, Corcoran
Collection (William A. Clark Collection), 2014.79.707

AELBERT CUYP

82. *Calcar with Monterberg in the Distance*, early 1640s
Black chalk, gray wash, green and ocher yellow
watercolor, partly brushed with gum arabic, on paper
18.5 × 49.5 cm (7⁵⁄₁₆ × 19½ in.)
The Metropolitan Museum of Art, New York,
Promised Gift, 2005.330.4

AELBERT CUYP

83. *The Rhine Valley Stretching North toward the Elterberg,*
   c. 1652–1655
   Black chalk, gray wash, pencil on paper
   14.9 × 23.9 cm (5⅞ × 9⁷⁄₁₆ in.)
   Fondation Custodia, Collection Frits Lugt, Paris, 5304

AELBERT CUYP

86. *A Cow Lying Down*, c. 1650
Black chalk, gray wash, on paper
7.6 × 13.3 cm (3 × 5¼ in.)
Private Collection

AELBERT CUYP

87. *Studies of a Cow and a Horse*, c. 1650
Black chalk, brush in gray wash, traces of pencil
on paper
8.4 × 12.5 cm (3⁵⁄₁₆ × 4¹⁵⁄₁₆ in.)
Fondation Custodia, Collection Frits Lugt, Paris, 458

Fig. 2. Aelbert Cuyp, *River Landscape with Horseman and Peasants*, c. 1660, oil on canvas. The National Gallery, London. Bought with the assistance of the National Heritage Memorial Fund and The Art Fund, 1989, NG6522

KAREL DUJARDIN

1626–1678

Karel Dujardin was a versatile artist. He produced a series of etchings of landscapes and animals for which he made a number of preliminary studies. As a painter, he made southern landscapes with herdsmen and cattle, genre scenes, history works, and portraits, but no known compositional studies for these works exist.

A group of four chalk drawings of the same model—a young man with mid-length flaxen hair—were probably all made as preliminary figure studies for paintings. The model in *Walking Man Seen from Behind* (cat. 88), with his clothes hitched up, is shown standing in the water in the painting *Mountain Landscape with Shepherds and Cattle near a Bridge* of 16(?)9 (probably 1659), while on the bank a shepherdess watches over her livestock and a herdsman plays with his dog (fig. 1).[1] Dujardin drew the figure in red chalk with very fine hatching lines to create strong contrasts and to give the impression that the open areas of the figure are brightly lit. The clothes gathered

at the youth's waist indicate that Dujardin intended, from the outset, to have him wading in water. The same is true of a counterproof of a now-lost black chalk drawing of the same model, *A Shepherd with Shirt Raised*, c. 1655, in the Musées royaux des Beaux-Arts de Belgique, Jean de Grez Collection, Brussels. Although Dujardin likewise designed this figure to stand in water, no related painting has been identified.[2] This counterproof allowed the artist to create an impression of an original drawing in mirror image so that he could utilize it in different ways in his paintings. Dujardin's painting *A Woman and a Youth in a Ford*, 1657, in the National Gallery, London, shows a different model standing in water and urinating.[3]

A third drawing depicting the same model as in the Copenhagen study, *Standing Youth Seen from Behind*, 1657, is in the Musée de Grenoble. Dujardin executed this work in black and white chalk on brownish paper.[4]

---

1. Kilian 2005, no. B 16, fig. 64.
2. See Brussels/Amsterdam/Aachen 2007a and 2007b, no. 54, regarding this Brussels drawing, no. 406-0/2251.
3. Karel Dujardin, *A Woman and a Youth at a Ford*, 1657, oil on canvas, National Gallery, London, 827.

4. See Grenoble 2014, no. 85, regarding this work, no. MG G 668 at the Musée de Grenoble.
5. This painting is in the Kunstmuseum, Basel, no. 1510. See Kilian 2005, no. B 16, as 'problematic attribution, copy?'
6. In Besançon there is a not dissimilar black chalk drawing of a *Youth beside a*

Donkey, with an inscription including Dujardin's name on the verso, but the hatching is much harsher and the drawing does not have the strong shadow contrasts characteristic of Dujardin, nor is this flaxen-haired youth wearing exactly the same clothes. This casts some doubt on the attribution. See Besançon 1999, no. 9.

This figure appears in *Italian Landscape with Two Horsemen*, 1657,[5] where he stands beside a rider whom he has presumably helped into the saddle.[6] Finally, Dujardin drew this model one more time with red chalk, in strongly contrasting tones, as *Seated Man Removing his Boots*, c. 1655, in the Fogg Art Museum.[7] While the purpose for which Dujardin made these figure studies is often clear, his intent for the Fogg Art Museum drawing is unknown. The drawings of the young man in the same clothes—twice without his breeches—probably date from around the same time, which can only be approximated.

Dujardin's *Piazza Santa Maria Maggiore in Rome* of 1653 at the Fondation Custodia, Collection Frits Lugt, bears the monogram 'K.D.I.' and the date 1653,[8] which indicates the artist must have spent time in Rome that year. He is not recorded as working in Amsterdam between September 1652 and September 1655.[9] The group of four drawings can probably be dated after his travel to Italy but before 1657, because the earliest painting in which the young model appears dates from that year.

In the late 1640s Dujardin visited Lyon, where, according to Houbraken, he met his wife—probably in 1649, the year of their marriage in Paris.[10] Similar to many Netherlandish artists who went to Italy, he also would have stopped en route in Lyon. West of this city, Château de Francheville stood near a bridge over the Yzeron. This arched bridge with a small, square stone building in the middle was drawn by several Netherlandish artists. Dujardin included it in his painting *Mountain Landscape*, probably from a drawing he had done there. The rest of the landscape is imaginary.[11]

[PS]

7. This drawing is no. 2009.205 in the Fogg Art Museum, Harvard University, Maida and George Abrams Collection, Cambridge, Massachusetts. See Amsterdam/Vienna/New York/Cambridge 1991, no. 73.

8. Karel Dujardin, *The Piazza Santa Maria Maggiore in Rome*, 1653, Fondation Custodia, Collection Frits Lugt, Paris, 2778. See Amsterdam 2001, 154-155, fig. B.

9. Kilian 2005, 101-102, docs. 56, 60, 61.

10. Houbraken erroneously thought that they married in Lyon: Houbraken 1718–1721, III, 56–61, 201.

11. Paris/Amsterdam 2008, 202–203.

KAREL DUJARDIN

88. *Walking Man Seen from Behind*, c. 1655
Red chalk on paper
23.6 × 13.4 cm (9⁵⁄₁₆ × 5¼ in.)
Statens Museum for Kunst, Copenhagen, KKS 9352

[204]

Fig. 1. Karel Dujardin, *Mountain Landscape with Shepherds and Cattle near a Bridge*, 1659(?), oil on canvas. Private Collection

GERBRAND VAN DEN EECKHOUT

1621–1674

89. *David Promises Bathsheba to Designate Solomon as His Successor (David's Promise to Bathsheba)*, 1642–1643
Brown ink and brown wash, over red and black chalk on paper
18.8 × 27 cm (7½ × 10¼ in.)
The Metropolitan Museum of Art, New York,
Gift of Robert Lehman 1941, 41.187.4

Rembrandt's 'great friend and favorite pupil,'[1] Gerbrand van den Eeckhout, was the most versatile artist among the master's students and close followers. His two hundred surviving drawings, executed in a broad range of media, represent biblical compositions, genre scenes, portraits, figure studies, landscapes, and designs for prints and goldsmith work.[2] Many of his compositions and figure studies are preparatory for paintings.

Two drawings relate to Van den Eeckhout's painting of 1646, *David Promises Bathsheba to Designate Solomon as His Successor* in the Národní galerie, Prague (fig. 1), which illustrates a passage in the Book of Kings (1 Kings 1:28–33).[3] Informed that his fourth son, Adonijah, has declared himself successor to the throne of Israel, the aged King David has summoned Bathsheba, his wife, to reassure her that he intends to fulfill an earlier promise to her that Solomon, the son of her union with David, would reign after his death.

Although pictorially finished in brown ink and brown wash over red and black chalk, the composition study (cat. 89) in the Metropolitan Museum of Art, New York, differs in major and minor ways from the Prague picture.[4] For example, in the drawing, David's chair rests on crescent-shaped platform that also supports the bed, while in the painting Van den Eeckout reduced the

Fig. 1. Gerbrand van den Eeckhout, *David Promises Bathsheba to Designate Solomon as His Successor*, 1646, oil on canvas. Národní Galerie, Prague

platform so that it supports only the bed, with the chair sitting on the floor beside it. He replaced the Solomonic column in the study with a pier and inserted a decorated screen or throne behind the seated king. A female servant, who figured in the drawing as a mere shadow to the right of the column, assumes—in the painting—a prominent place between David and the bed. The elaborate canopy and curtains that Van den Eeckhout

1. Houbraken 1718–1721, I, 137, 174, II, 79.
2. Sumowski 1962, 11–39; Sumowski 1979, III, 1311, nos. 601–819xx. Bevers 2010, 39–40.

3. Gerbrand van den Eeckhout, *David Promises Bathsheba to Designate Solomon as His Successor*, 1646, oil on canvas, formerly signed and dated 'G. V. Eeckhout 1646,' Národní Galerie, Prague. See Sumowski 1983, II, 728, no. 403.

4. Haverkamp-Begemann and Logan regarded the New York drawing as an independent variant, rather than a study for the painting, and, accepting their interpretation, Sumowski dated it c. 1642–1643. Chicago/Minneapolis/Detroit 1969, 188, no. 166; Sumowski

included over the bed in the study do not appear on the canvas, where the artist painted a massive gilt relief over the headboard. Finally, in the drawing, on the table at the foot of the bed, the artist sketched David's traditional attributes of a scepter, crown, and harp, whereas Van den Eeckhout painted a still life with a cup in the auricular style which resembles a cup by master silversmith Adam van Vianen that the artist included in other works.[5]

1979, III, 1320, no. 605; Sumowski 1983, II, 728, under no. 403. In my view, the drawing was directly preparatory for the oil painting and presumably dates from the same time.
5. Sumowski 1979, III, 1320, no. 605; Sumowski 1983, II, 728, under no. 403.

After completing the composition sketch, Van den Eeckhout executed the study in the Kunsthalle Hamburg (cat. 90) from a model dressed and posed as David that would appear in the painting. He introduced a number of refinements to the figure and costume: David's beard is shorter than in the New York sketch; he holds his head erect and less inclined to the left; the subject's right hand extends over the arm of the chair, rather than resting upon it; and a prominent jeweled brooch fastens the two sides of his cloak. In the painting, the artist scrupulously reproduced these details, as well as the folds and highlights of the drapery over the king's legs, from the Hamburg study.

Two composition sketches are associated with Van den Eeckhout's painting *Jacob's Dream*, 1672, at the Agnes

GERBRAND VAN DEN EECKHOUT

90. *Seated Oriental*, before 1646
   Black and white chalk on gray paper
   38.9 × 26.2 cm (15⁵⁄₁₆ × 10⁵⁄₁₆ in.)
   Hamburger Kunsthalle, Hamburg,
   Bequest of Georg Ernst Harzen, 1863, 21944

Etherington Art Centre, Kingston, Ontario, which is the latest of his three paintings representing this subject (fig. 2).[6] Genesis 28:10–15 describes how Isaac sent his son Jacob out of Canaan to Padan-aram to find a wife among the daughters of their kinsman Laban. Overtaken by night, Jacob assembled some stones to use as pillows and went to sleep, whereupon 'he dreamed, and behold a ladder set up on the earth, and the top of it reached to heaven: and behold [he saw] the angels of God ascending and descending on it.' Van den Eeckhout did not depict a ladder or staircase, thus departing from the biblical text and iconographic tradition of the subject. The angels descend on clouds, illuminated in the darkness by a heavenly light.[7]

The red chalk study (cat. 91) in Vienna shares with the canvas both its vertical format and the location of Jacob at the lower right, but the two works have little else in common. In this sketch, Van den Eeckhout tried out a pose for the sleeping youth that differs from his figure in his other renditions of the subject in which Jacob reclines on the ground on his back. Conspicuously absent from the Vienna drawing is the large angel in the foreground that benevolently raises his hand over Jacob in the painting. In the black chalk sketch in Schwerin (cat. 92), the angel and most other major elements of the composition appear almost exactly as they do on the canvas. The two works differ only in a few details: the format of the picture is narrower at the left; Jacob's hat is larger and tipped back off his head; the angle of his staff is different; and he rests his right hand limply on his chest rather than tucking it into his cloak. A pentimento in the painting confirms the close connection between it and the Schwerin sketch. In the drawing, the wings of the angel seated on a cloud spread out horizontally, and Van den Eeckhout initially blocked them in on the canvas in that position. While working on the picture, he reduced the seated angel's wings and foreshortened them so that they appear to

stretch out behind him. The pigments have become transparent over time, and the dark shape of the laterally extended wings is now visible to the naked eye beneath the surface layer of the paint.[8]

Fig. 2. Gerbrand van den Eeckhout, *Jacob's Dream*, 1672, oil on canvas. Agnes Etherington Art Centre, Queen's University, Kingston, Ontario, 44-008

Werner Sumowski dated both drawings to the early 1650s, asserting that Van den Eeckhout reverted to a twenty-year-old design as the basis for the picture.[9] In my view, the Schwerin sketch, which corresponds closely to the finished composition, immediately preceded the work on the canvas and therefore dates from c. 1672. The connection of the Vienna drawing to the Kingston picture is less straightforward. It probably represents Van den Eeckhout's first idea for the painting, in which case it, too, must belong to the early 1670s. However, given the considerable differences between the two compositions, this is not certain. The Vienna work could be a study for a lost painting of the subject or an independent sketch. [WWR]

6. Gerbrand van den Eeckhout, *Jacob's Dream*, 1672, oil on canvas, Agnes Etherington Art Centre, Queen's University, Kingston, Ontario, Gift of Alfred and Isabel Bader, 2001, 44-008. Sumowski 1983, II, 743, no. 481; De Witt 2008, 122–123, no. 70. Also see earlier paintings of the subject by Van den Eeckhout in Sumowski 1983, II, 725, no. 395, and 741, no. 469, and a drawing in the Victoria and Albert Museum, London, in Sumowski 1979, III, 1538, no. 713; Shoaf Turner and White 2014, I, 98–99, no. 54.

7. Volker Manuth in De Witt 2008, 123, no. 70.

8. Kingston 1984, 30, no. 20. See also De Witt 2008, 123, no. 70.

9. Sumowski 1983, II, 743, under no. 481; Sumowski 1979, III, 1346, no. 618; De Witt 2008, 123, no. 70.

GERBRAND VAN DEN EECKHOUT

91. *Jacob's Dream*, [n.d.]

   Red chalk on paper

   26.2 × 20 cm (10¼ × 8 in.)

   Albertina, Vienna, 9549

GERBRAND VAN DEN EECKHOUT

92. *Jacob's Dream*, 1672

Black chalk on paper

22.4 × 19.6 cm (8¾ × 7¾ in.)

Staatliches Museum, Schwerin, Hz 4486

ISACK VAN OSTADE

1621–1649

93. *The Schoolroom*, c. 1639
   Pen and brown ink, pinkish brown and gray wash,
   over black chalk or graphite, on paper
   16.9 × 23.6 cm (6⅝ × 9⁵⁄₁₆ in.)
   Maida and George Abrams Collection, Boston

Isack van Ostade, Adriaen van Ostade's younger brother
and pupil (see pp. 182–188), died at the age of twenty-
eight but managed to create a sizeable and varied oeuvre
in his short life.[1] Isack's first paintings date from 1639.[2]
His early work shows the influence of his older brother in
both style and subjects: tavern scenes and peasant
interiors. However, Isack also depicted subjects in which
the landscape played a greater role, such as travelers
outside an inn and winter landscapes with figures.[3] Like
his brother, Isack was a talented and versatile draftsman,
and he also worked chiefly in pen-and-ink over sketches
in black chalk or graphite. Afterward, he often worked
up his pen drawings with washes, watercolor, and
colored chalk.

Surviving works by Isack include sketches and composition drawings, whereas few figure studies are extant.[4]
He rarely signed his drawings and dated only some of
them, which makes it difficult to establish a chronology
of his work.[5] The difference in the brothers' styles is not
always easy to distinguish, and for a long time many of
Isack's drawings were attributed to Adriaen.[6] In general,
however, the younger Van Ostade's drawings are livelier
and more spontaneous.

Bernhard Schnackenburg reconstructed Isack's drawn
oeuvre, in part, on the basis of drawings that can be

Fig. 1. Isack van Ostade, *Children in a Classroom*, c. 1639,
oil on panel. The Branicki Collection, formerly deposited
in the Muzeum Narodowe, Warsaw, 184855

linked to paintings.[7] Unfortunately, only a few works
exist in this category, and his figure studies often differ
from the results in oil.[8] Furthermore, it is probable that
Isack saw his drawings as finger exercises or as free
sources of inspiration.[9] Interestingly, he drew many
interior scenes, whereas his paintings are more often set
in the open air, which lends credence to this idea.[10]

A very early example of a drawing that Isack used for a

1. For a biography see Schnackenburg 1996
   and Irene van Thiel-Stroman, 'Biographies
   15th–17th Century,' in Köhler 2006,
   261–262.
2. Schnackenburg 1981, I, 33–34.
3. Philadelphia/Berlin/London 1984,
   290–291; Amsterdam/Boston/Philadel-
   phia 1987, 39, 390–394.

4. Schnackenburg 1981, I, 54–55, nos.
   475, 476, 541; Schatborn 1986, 87–88,
   ill. 14.
5. Schnackenburg 1981, I, 49, 51, nos. 477,
   510, 511, dated 1643 and 1644.
6. Another reason for this is that Adriaen and
   later Cornelis Dusart sometimes worked up
   Isack's drawings. See Trautscholdt 1959,

303–305; Trautscholdt 1967, 160–161;
   Schnackenburg 1981, I, 24–25, 60–61.
7. Schnackenburg 1981, I, 49.
8. For the few works that correspond to
   paintings, see Schnackenburg 1981, I, 51,
   55 (e.g., nos. 411, 415, 434, 447, 483);
   for figure drawings that differ from Isack's
   painted figures: Schnackenburg 1981, I,

painting is that of a class in a village school (cat. 93).[11] This composition sketch is one of the first known drawings by the young artist, and in Schnackenburg's opinion, it may have been made prior to or in 1639, while he was still an apprentice.[12] The painting (fig. 1),[13] which had long been attributed to Adriaen, is rather clumsy, but it does already have the vitality that was typical of Isack.

In the schoolroom drawing, the young artist was struggling with perspective: the walls are not convincingly depicted and the figures are placed awkwardly in space. The handling of line is indecisive, although Isack is already using the variation of straight and meandering lines that he frequently employed in later drawings. The fact that the sheet is signed may indicate that the fledgling painter was happy with the result.[14]

55, no. 432; Amsterdam/Vienna/New York/Cambridge 1991, no. 89.

9. Schnackenburg 1981, I, 55.

10. Schnackenburg 1981, I, 55; Schnackenburg 1996, 614.

11. Schnackenburg 1981, I, 47, 59.

For the theme of the school class see Philadelphia/Berlin/London 1984, no. 107; Durantini 1983, 130–136.

12. Schnackenburg 1981, I, 47, no. 406.

13. Michałkowa 1955, no. 40; Białostocki 1969, II, no. 923, as A. van Ostade;

Schnackenburg 1981, I, 34 and under no. 406; Durantini 1983, 133, ill. 67, as A. van Ostade.

14. For the signature see Schnackenburg 1981, I, 48.

Isack copied the composition into the painting almost in its entirety, although he adjusted the size of some figures (for example, in particular, the schoolmaster in the center) to improve the overall proportions of the scene. He also moved the ladder, with the little boy climbing up to the attic, to the left corner. Isack had probably taken this last motif from a drawing of a school class by Adriaen.[15] In painting, Isack made the ladder, although in mirror image, correspond more closely to his brother's original idea than to the one in his own preparatory drawing.

Isack also made drawings of houses, villages, landscapes, agricultural implements, and carts.[16] Some village views depict existing places.[17] A number of very accurately executed drawings form a stylistic group.[18] Some of these can be linked to paintings dating from the period 1646 to 1649.[19]

The drawing exhibited (cat. 94) belongs to this group. The houses and church steeple were used in a painting dating from 1649, *The Halt at the Inn* (fig. 2), one of Isack's favorite subjects.[20] The portrait format, the clarity of the composition, and a degree of monumentality are typical of his late work.[21] This is manifested here in the large tree that not only dominates the image but almost forms a single mass with the house beneath it and

Fig. 2. Isack van Ostade, *The Halt at the Inn*, 1649, oil on canvas. Private Collection

the church steeple behind it. These components are already present in the drawing, but in the painting the house became an inn: travelers and peasants relax outside the door, and the composition has been expanded at the left to accommodate chickens and other animals. Some details have also been changed. The bench or hitching post made of a tree stump in the drawing was replaced with a trough. Many such changes reinforce the picturesque character that Isack was seeking.   [RSB]

15. Schnackenburg 1981, no. 15.

16. Trautscholdt 1959, 303–305; Schnackenburg 1981, I, 52–54, and nos. 416 verso, 419 verso, 421 verso, 423, 424, 428, 429, 559–580, 627U–630U; Schatborn 1986, 85–91.

17. Schnackenburg 1981, I, 52–54, nos. 424, 429; Schatborn 1986, 85–91; Vermeeren 1986, 228–236; Schnackenburg 1996, 614; see also Wheelock 1995, 191–194.

18. Schnackenburg 1981, I, 54, nos. 560–580.

19. Schnackenburg 1981, I, 54–55.

20. Hofstede de Groot 1907–1928, III (1910), no. 24; London 1952, no. 425; Schnackenburg 1981, I, 35–36, 275, fig. 61 and under no. 580; Schnackenburg 1996, 613.

21. Schnackenburg 1981, I, 35; Schnackenburg 1996, 613.

ISACK VAN OSTADE

94. *Group of Houses with a Church Tower in the Background*, c. 1649
   Pen and brown ink, black chalk or graphite, colored chalks,
   watercolor, on paper
   29.8 × 24.3 cm (11¾ × 9⁹⁄₁₆ in.)
   Staatliche Museen, Berlin, Kupferstichkabinett, κdz 10 599

PAULUS POTTER

1625–1654

95. *A Sow and Her Farrow*, c. 1650
　　Black chalk on paper
　　10.2 × 14.9 cm (4 × 5⅞ in.)
　　Maida and George Abrams Collection, Boston

Paulus Potter was one of the first artists to depict animals, mostly cattle, as the principal subjects of his paintings, and place them in a Dutch landscape.[1] Although he died young, Potter is regarded as an innovative and influential artist in landscape art and works that feature livestock.[2] Potter is known for his meticulously designed compositions in which the placement and subtle interaction of the animals ensure that the viewer's gaze is drawn into the scene. His work is further praised for the effects of light and the expression of surface and texture in rendering the hides of animals, trees, and plants.

Potter chiefly used sketches from life and composition studies to prepare his paintings.[3] According to Arnold Houbraken, Potter often had a sketchbook in his pocket on his rambles so that he could record on the spot anything he thought he might be able to use in a painting.[4] Some sheets known to be by Paulus Potter must indeed have come from one or more sketchbooks measuring approximately 10 × 15 centimeters (4 × 6 in.).[5] These sketches were executed swiftly in black chalk; they show animals—alone or in groups—in various positions or from different viewpoints, which were clearly drawn from life.[6] Potter had an unerring ability to capture the character of animals. The sketches, rarely signed, are often hard to date.[7] They provided a wealth of subjects on which the artist could draw for his paintings, finished drawings, and prints. Potter regularly reused motifs from this repertoire; some animals feature repeatedly in his work.[8]

The drawing of a group of pigs in the Maida and George Abrams Collection (cat. 95) is a striking

1. For a biography see Amy Walsh, 'Het Leven van Paulus Potter (1625–1654),' in The Hague 1994, 10–19, and Buvelot 2015.

2. Amsterdam/Boston/Philadelphia 1987, 10, 416–422; Dordrecht/Leeuwarden 1988, 19–21, nos. 24–26; The Hague 1994; Brown 1995; Lammertse 1995; New York/London 2001, 332–483.

3. For the relatively small group of drawings where there is agreement about the attribution, see Ben Broos, 'Paulus Potter als Tekenaar en Etser,' in The Hague 1994, 38–53.

4. Houbraken 1718–1721, II, 129; Buvelot 2015, 95.

5. The Hague 1994, 45–48. The sheets range in height from 9 to 10 cm, and in width from 13.5 to 15 cm.

6. Potter also made drawings in which the outlines are strongly accentuated (Broos in The Hague 1994, 46), and more detailed sketches of animals in a landscape (see Broos and Schapelhouman 1993, nos. 102, 103; The Hague 1994, nos. 42, 43 and Turner and White 2014, no. 151).

7. Ben Broos states that after 1647 the artist started to draw more loosely and sketchily. See Broos in The Hague 1994, 172.

8. Even compositions were regularly repeated.

Fig. 1. Paulus Potter, *Cattle in a Meadow*, 1652, oil on panel.
Royal Picture Gallery Mauritshuis, The Hague, 138

example of the use of such a sketch in a painting. In the drawing Potter depicted a sow lying down, surrounded by her litter, with a few swift, skillful touches. The sheet is unusual because it depicts a group of animals as opposed to the more usual sketches of individual beasts.[9] It shows Potter's ability to render what he saw with great realism.[10]

A Sow and Her Farrow must have been made in or before 1652. In that year the group of pigs was used almost in its entirety in the painting *Cattle in a Meadow* (fig. 1).[11] In the painting Potter left out some of the piglets on the right and in the foreground that are evident in the drawing and added a standing pig. He also changed the sow's ears into lop ears, which makes her look even more good-natured. For this change he probably used a more detailed study, and turned the head slightly in the painting so that it corresponds with the direction in the Abrams sketch.[12] Potter succeeded in depicting the sow and piglets in the painting as realistically as he had on the sketchbook page.

In addition to his sketches of animals, Potter very likely also made studies of landscapes and figures. They play important roles in his paintings, but hardly any drawings by him in these other genres have survived.[13]

In setting up his paintings Potter combined different sketches in otherwise imaginary compositions. Amy Walsh has drawn attention to the fact that while working up these drawn studies, Potter sometimes failed to take into account the relative proportions; on occasion this resulted in unfortunate differences in scale between animals and people.[14] These disproportions may indicate that Potter actually put his preliminary drawings straight onto canvas or panel.[15]

Only a few drawings that can be regarded as composition sketches or designs for paintings have survived.[16] Used for studying composition and light, they were set down swiftly and sketchily in black chalk, often on colored paper. He indicated the light—a significant quality in Potter's work—with white chalk. The paintings known to be made from these composition sketches follow these designs faithfully.   [RSB]

9. A similar, closely related sheet is in Fondation Custodia, Collection Frits Lugt, Paris, 5100; see New York/Paris 1977, no. 80.

10. In 1604 Karel van Mander had recommended the careful observation of animals in nature; see Dordrecht/Leeuwarden 1988, 23–29.

11. The Hague 1994, no. 25.

12. Paulus Potter, *A Hog Lying Down*, black chalk, British Museum, 1895,0915.1247; see Hind 1931, no. 21. He probably used the more detailed drawing in the Fondation Custodia, Collection Frits Lugt, Paris, 5100, for the sitting piglet; see New York/Paris 1977, no. 80.

13. For the landscape drawings see Stefes 2011, II, nos. 820, 821; Leiden 1994, 31, no. 17; and The Hague 1994, no. 18, and 178, n. 2. For the figure studies: Broos and Schapelhouman 1993, no. 101, and Fondation Custodia, Collection Frits Lugt, Paris, 113c. Frits Lugt acquired another figure study, but the attribution of this sheet has still not been thoroughly researched; Fondation Custodia, Collection Frits Lugt, Paris, 3663.

14. Amy Walsh, 'Het Leven van Paulus Potter (1625–1654),' in The Hague 1994, 28.

15. For underdrawings in Potter's paintings see Verslype 2005, 100–101.

16. The Hague 1994, 49–51, 164, fig. 1, and nos. 9, 37. See for another composition sketch Bolten 1995 and Fondation Custodia, Collection Frits Lugt, Paris, 1695.

JAN DE BRAY

c. 1627–1697

Jan de Bray was born in Haarlem into a creative, cultured family. His father Salomon de Bray was an architect, urban planner, and painter who helped establish the town's St. Luke's Guild in the 1630s. Two of Jan's brothers, Dirck and Joseph, were painters as well. Jan de Bray had a very successful career, serving as dean of the St. Luke's Guild several times in the 1670s and 1680s. He was one of the most important Dutch artists working in the classical tradition, a style of painting that fused naturalism with ideals of beauty derived from antiquity.[1] De Bray was also an architect and inventor, but the evocative drawing and intimate portrayal of Abraham Casteleyn and his wife, Margarieta van Bancken, prove Jan's worth as a portraitist.

In 1663, Jan de Bray painted a delightfully tender double portrait of the Casteleyns relaxing on a terrace (fig. 1). Far more informal than most portraits of married couples, their clasped hands convey a loving and cheerful companionship. Margarieta's warm smile expresses more joy and intimacy than was common in seventeenth-century Dutch portraiture, which called for the depiction of solemn self-control.[2] When De Bray painted them in 1663, the couple had been married for two years. They were devout Mennonites who eschewed ostentatious living, which might explain their outmoded black outfits. This hint at a sober lifestyle is, however, subtly countered by the bright flash of red of Margarieta's underskirt.

De Bray's lovely preparatory drawing of the couple (cat. 96) displays his superb skills as draftsman. Using a fine pen to draw the forms, he rounded out the shapes with gray wash. Subtly applied geometric planes enhance the composition's harmony: Abraham's underarm runs parallel to Margarieta's arm; the placket of her black dress runs parallel to the paper edge of the large tome hidden behind the atlas; and these parallels are at a ninety-degree angle to the shadow on the wall.

Seen next to the painting, the refined drawing is nonetheless puzzling. Is it, as many art historians have assumed, the preparatory drawing? Or is it Jan de Bray's drawn copy after his own finished painting? Although the painting echoes the left two-thirds of the drawing to the letter, the drawing includes an additional section that depicts an arch through which a garden and two approaching figures are visible. Either De Bray faithfully replicated only the left portion of the preparatory drawing in paint and dropped the idea of the vista in order to keep the focus on the couple,[3] or he followed a family workshop practice and made a drawn copy of the portrait following its completion, but added the garden vista.

The refined execution of the drawing and its close replication of the painted portrait support the latter interpretation. In their article about drawn archival copies of paintings by the De Bray family, Jeroen Giltaij and Friso Lammertse identified the drawing as one

1. For the biography of De Bray, see Biesboer 2008, 18–26, as well as 'Jan de Bray,' *RKD Nederlands Instituut voor Kunstgeschiedenis Index*, https://rkd.nl/en/explore/artists/12194.
2. The informality of this double portrait echoes the double portrait of *Isaac Massa and Beatrix van der Laen*, c. 1622 (Rijksmuseum, Amsterdam, SK-A-133), painted almost forty years earlier by Frans Hals, who preceded Jan de Bray as Haarlem's foremost portraitist.
3. Haarlem/London 2008, no. 27 and fig. 27a, 88, 146 (n. 27-7). The catalog entry proposes that the drawing is 'probably the first draft for the composition.' See also Haarlem 1986, 181–183, no. 36, and Dordrecht 2012, 63, fig. 3, and 132–133, no. 28.

Fig. 1. Jan de Bray, *Abraham Casteleyn and his Wife, Margarieta van Bancken*, 1663, oil on canvas. Rijksmuseum, Amsterdam, SK-A-3280

such copy by Jan after his own work, but they did not address the addition of the arched view into the garden.[4] Technical studies on the painting confirm that the canvas was never larger than its current dimensions.[5] Thus, if the drawing indeed started off as a copy after the painting, De Bray negated the drawing's purported role as an archival record of a completed canvas by adding the arch, the garden, and the two figures as fanciful afterthoughts.[6]

Abraham Casteleyn (c. 1628–1681) was the son of Haarlem's municipal printer. In 1656, he started the *Weeckelijke Courante van Europa*, a single-sheet, two-page weekly newspaper that quickly evolved into the biweekly *Haarlemse Courant*, which included the latest news from major cities across Europe. Casteleyn became renowned as the best-informed newspaper publisher in Europe, and his network of foreign correspondents was so effective that the *Haarlemse Courant* often contained information still considered top secret by the governments that were involved.[7]

The stone bust depicts Laurens Janszoon Coster, the Haarlem native who, according to seventeenth-century Dutchmen, had invented the movable-type printing process before Gutenberg. As Haarlem's first city printer, Coster was Casteleyn's most illustrious predecessor and thus an important symbolic presence in the portrait. The globe refers to Casteleyn's far-reaching intelligence network, while the books represent publications produced in his printing house.

The Casteleyns may have commissioned their portrait to celebrate their worldly success, which, in Protestant circles, clearly indicated that God's light shone favorably on the couple: in 1658 Abraham was appointed municipal printer; he and Margarieta had married in 1661; and in the spring of 1662 Abraham had moved his printing house to a new building aptly named 'In de Blye Druck' (In the Happy Print). Margarieta van Bancken outlived her husband by at least eleven years. She was a capable businesswoman in her own right, and the city council appointed her as the municipal printer following Abraham's death in 1681 and extended Casteleyn's monopoly on the *Haarlemse Courant* to her.[8]   [HR]

4. Giltaij and Lammertse, 2001, 367–394. The drawn copies of the painted works 'served as an archive of past projects and as source material for future commissions.'

5. Haarlem/London 2008, 88. Conservation treatment by the Rijksmuseum in 1986.

6. An eighteenth-century drawn copy after the painting, in black and red chalk, with pen and black ink on vellum, was sold at Sotheby Mak van Waay, Amsterdam, on November 18, 1980; sale catalog 320, lot 181. Illustrated in Haarlem 1986, 182, fig. 36b.

7. *Nieuw Nederlandsch Biografisch Woordenboek* (*NNBW*), IX, 132–134. For the *Haarlemse Courant,* see http://noord -hollandsarchief.nl/collecties/museum -enschede (accessed on February 2, 2016).

8. Maarten Hell, *Bancken, Margaretha van,* in: *Digitaal Vrouwenlexicon van Nederland,* http://resources.huygens.knaw.nl/ vrouwenlexicon/lemmata/data/Bancken (accessed on January 13, 2014).

JAN DE BRAY

96. *Double Portrait of Abraham Casteleyn and Margarieta
van Bancken*, 1663
Pen and brown ink, gray wash, on paper
10.2 × 20.3 cm (4 × 8 in.)
Fondation Custodia, Collection Frits Lugt, Paris,
5124

BAREND GRAAT

1628–1709

97. *Seated Man*, 1659/1660
   Black and white chalk on blue paper (faded to gray),
   lined
   22.9 × 17.9 cm (9 × 7¹⁄₁₆ in.)
   Fondation Custodia, Collection Frits Lugt, Paris, 303

The earliest biography of Barend Graat describes an artist whose life was dominated by drawing.[1] As a boy he supposedly smuggled stumps of candles from church after the sermon, so that he could carry on working at home well into the night. As a young painter he continued to draw obsessively: every day in the summer he would be up before dawn to record horses, cows, and other animals on paper. Later in life, for fifteen years, he ran a drawing academy in his home, where painters could come twice a week to work from male and female nude models.[2] Graat's figure studies, or at least some of them, must have survived for some time, as groups of 'academy pictures,' 'college pictures,' and 'women and men drawn skillfully from life' feature in various eighteenth-century catalogs.[3]

   In light of this evidence and other sources, it is amazing how few of his drawings are extant. The recently published monograph on Graat describes seventeen sheets we know of today, which include preliminary studies for paintings, drawings of sculptures, and a few figure studies.[4] Of the studies of animals that Graat, according to his earliest biographer, Arnold Houbraken, often drew, no known examples exist, and only one of his nude studies drawn from life has survived.[5] Some sheets may have been attributed to other artists, as was case

Fig. 1. Barend Graat, *Portrait of a Couple Sitting in a Garden*, 1660, oil on canvas. Gemäldegalerie der Akademie der bildenden Künste, Vienna, 1398

with *Seated Man* (cat. 97), which had been linked to better known artists such as Gerard ter Borch, Bartholomeus van der Helst, and Govert Flinck.[6] With the discovery of the drawing's relationship to the man in

1. Houbraken 1718–1721, II, 201–208.
2. For a discussion of seventeenth-century drawing academies and drawing from nude models see Peter Schatborn, 'Inleiding,' in Amsterdam/Washington 1981, 20–22.
3. These works are cited as 'Academiebeelden,' 'collegiebeelden,' and 'Vrouwtjes

en Mannen, konstig na 't leven getekent.' Quoted from Hut 2015, 216–217, 219.
4. Hut 2015, 54–59, 197–209. See also the two figure studies in black and white on blue paper attributed to Barend Graat in the Print Room of the Kunsthalle

in Hamburg; Stefes 2011, I, 251–253, 388, 389, III, 143 (figs).
5. Hut 2015, 203, no. A/T9 (fig.).
6. See for these old attributions Amsterdam/Washington 1981, 137, and the RKD Netherlands Institute for Art History online database, The Hague.

Graat's signed and dated double portrait in Vienna (fig. 1), the identity of the draftsman became clear.[7]

This attractive figure study was undoubtedly drawn from life. Like many artists of the time, Graat used blue paper—now faded to gray—so that he could work with both black and white chalk.[8] He posed his model informally: seated, ankles crossed, and left hand raised. In the painting the man strikes the same pose, except he holds a carnation, which he offers to his wife. Houbraken described the ease with which the artist gave his drawings 'een natuurlyken zweem' (a natural look), but Graat was unable to recapture—in the painting—the pleasing spontaneity of the preliminary study.[9] The painted man looks stiffer, partly because of the altered position of his head and the lack of facial expression.

For practical reasons Graat drew the man separately.[10] This was common practice in the seventeenth century when making preliminary studies for figural works and group portraits.[11] Individual detailed studies could then be brought together on the canvas or panel, possibly with the aid of a compositional sketch, to create a harmonious whole.[12] One advantage of this approach was that artists were able to concentrate on depicting the individual sitters and their costume, and could then correct details without having to redo the entire composition. It is unclear whether Graat made other drawings in preparation for the double portrait in Vienna: neither a preliminary study for the woman nor a sketch for the composition is known.

The identity of the sitters is likewise unknown, but they are evidently a husband and wife from Amsterdam who were married in, or shortly before, 1660, because this painting, although somewhat unconventional, has all the hallmarks of a wedding portrait.[13] Interestingly, Graat himself married a wealthy widow in March of that year.[14] It is not out of the question that the artist portrayed himself and his new bride (he was thirty-one and she was about twenty-five) in this intimate double portrait, although no such proof exists.[15] If this work is indeed a self-portrait with his new wife, Graat must have used a mirror and/or model who resembled him for the preliminary study. This working method could also explain the differences between the drawing and the painted version   [GW]

7. Schaffran 1957. For the painting see Trnek 1992, 148–151, no. 52.

8. Schatborn in Amsterdam/Washington 1981, 24, and Peter van den Brink, 'Uitmuntend Schilder in het Groot: De Schilder en Tekenaar Jacob Adriaensz. Backer,' in Amsterdam/Aachen 2008, 71, both examine the use of blue paper.

9. Houbraken 1718–1721, II, 204.

10. See Trnek 1992, 150, where it is argued that the woman may have been portrayed posthumously.

11. A well-documented example of a group portrait that was prepared in a number of individual studies, in this case by Jacob Backer, is described by Van den Brink in Amsterdam/Aachen 2008, 72–74.

12. An example from Graat's own oeuvre is his group portrait in the Rijksmuseum, Amsterdam, for which a preliminary study for the servant on the right in the background has survived; see Hut 2015, 200, no. A-T6 (fig.).

13. The possible clients include Michiel van Santen and his wife, Aletta van Heijningen, who married in 1659 and owned a double portrait of themselves by Graat; see Hut 2015, 286, no. 24. For the genre of the marriage portrait see Smith 1982 and Haarlem 1986.

14. Hut 2015, 13.

15. We know of no other portraits of the young Graat or his wife. Shortly before his death he gave his daughter Geertruijd a significant quantity of art, including a number of unspecified portraits; see Hut 2015, 278–280.

JACOB VAN RUISDAEL

1628/29–1682

Early in the 1650s Jacob van Ruisdael made a series of swift drawings in black chalk, all more or less the same size. It is a clearly distinguishable group of some thirty sheets.[1] Of these, a sketch in the Albertina (cat. 98) is the only one that can be linked to a painting, *Landscape near Muiderberg,* c.1650–1655 (fig. 1).[2] It is also the sole surviving study for the more than 150 tree-dominated landscapes that Ruisdael would paint. Seymour Slive assumed that most of Ruisdael's canvases were based on such a sketch, when he wrote that 'we can only surmise how many similar working drawings the artist made before touching the support for a painting of one of the subjects that was closest to his heart.'[3]

Ruisdael followed the composition of the drawing relatively faithfully. The position of the group of trees in the picture plane, the buildings on the left, and the location of the tree trunk in the flowing water, as well as such details as the man with a stick over his shoulder in the distance and the remains of a split tree trunk in the left foreground, correspond very closely. The birds in the drawing are in the painting, too, although they are flying further apart in the latter work. The copse is significantly larger in the painting, which means that the tower of the ruined church seems closer. The drawing is quite heavily hatched, although no hatching was used in the zone in front of the church. In the painting Ruisdael used his familiar cool green to show that the land is bathed in bright light. The clouds, racing across the sky, give the landscape a drama that the looping and zigzagging lines of the sketch made on the spot would not lead one to expect.

Another small drawing by Ruisdael—no larger than an open hand (cat. 99)—was the basis for a painted *Pano-*

ramic View of Amsterdam, Its Harbor, and the IJ, c. 1665–1670 (cat. 100). An early inscription on the drawing's verso has led to the identification of the vantage point as the roof of the Nieuwe Kerk, which had been badly damaged by fire in January 1645. It was thought that Ruisdael made the drawing between 1647 and 1650 from scaffolding that had been erected for the rebuilding of the tower.[4] The drawing style is hard to reconcile with such an early date, however, so it has been suggested that he used the scaffolding put up for the construction of the cupola of the new town hall, which would indicate that the sheet was drawn around 1664 or 1665.[5] This hypothesis is reinforced by the drawing's atmospheric effect and the manner in which it captures a huddle of houses and the bustle of a town within a very small compass. With the drawing set up where Ruisdael could see it, he created a virtually square painting, but one with far more clouds: two-thirds of the picture is occupied by a lowering sky that casts an extraordinary light on the city, reminiscent of the effect in the *Bird's-Eye View of Amsterdam* by Jan Christiaensz Micker of around 1652, which in turn derives from a woodcut by Cornelis Anthonisz.[6] Ruisdael followed his drawing for both topographical accuracy and countless small details, such as the sail of the boat on the Damrak. He also recorded in the painting elements of the high scaffolding from which he had captured the view on paper. As in the drawing, to quote Slive, Ruisdael 'did not include a single soul in the mighty metropolis.'[7]

The close-up Ruisdael drew of a number of striking graves in the Portuguese Jewish cemetery in Ouderkerk aan de Amstel, probably around 1655 (cat. 101), is completely different in vision and detailing. It is not

1. Giltay 1980, 148–149; Slive 2001, 492.
2. Slive 2001, 102–103, no. 77.
3. Slive 2001, 581–582.
4. Regteren Altena 1942–1950, 306–307;

Giltay 1980, 161–164.
5. Slive 2001, 493.
6. Jan Christiaensz Micker, *Bird's-Eye View of Amsterdam*, c.1652, Amsterdam

Museum, SA 1531; Cornelis Anthonisz, *Bird's-Eye View of Amsterdam*, 1538, Amsterdam Museum, SA 3009.
7. Slive 2001, 18.

JACOB VAN RUISDAEL

98. *Landscape with the Ruins of the Church of Muiderberg
in the Distance*, c. 1650–1655
Black chalk on paper
15.1 × 19.3 cm (5¹⁵⁄₁₆ × 7⅝ in.)
Albertina, Vienna, 10116

Fig. 1. Jacob van Ruisdael, *Landscape near Muiderberg*,
c. 1650–1655, oil on canvas. Ashmolean Museum, Oxford,
A 875

JACOB VAN RUISDAEL

99. *View over Amsterdam and the IJ*, c. 1665
   Black chalk, gray wash, on paper
   8.6 × 15.2 cm (3⅜ × 6 in.)
   Rijksmuseum, Amsterdam, RP-T-1960-116

JACOB VAN RUISDAEL

100. *Panoramic View of Amsterdam, Its Harbor, and the IJ,*
c. 1665–1670
Oil on canvas
41.5 × 40.7 cm (16⅚₁₆ × 16 in.)
Private Collection, England, on loan to the National
Gallery, London, L1052

JACOB VAN RUISDAEL

101. *The Jewish Cemetery at Ouderkerk aan de Amstel,*
c. 1665
Black chalk, brush and black ink, gray wash, on paper
19.1 × 28.3 cm (7½ × 11⅛ in.)
Teylers Museum, Haarlem, Q 48

inconceivable that he based this sheet and a second drawing of the graves with the Church of St. Urban in the background—the same size as the first—on studies made on the spot.[8] The appearance of the graves and their position in this drawing recur in two famous paintings by Ruisdael that certainly do not offer precise depictions of the graveyard, which still exists, but that can be seen as allegories of mortality (figs. 2, 3).[9] The artist saw the visual power of the tombs and detached them from their topographical and historical reality, exploiting their associative impact in conjunction with such ingredients as dead trees, a waterfall, a stormy sky with a rainbow, and a ruin. For this ruin he used one of his own drawings of the derelict castle in Egmond aan den Hoef (fig. 4).[10] One can imagine Ruisdael working with drawings in his studio, similar to Michiel van Musscher's artist at his easel (cat. 13). These were drawings for paintings—but this series clearly shows the different ways Ruisdael achieved each transformation into paint. [GL]

8. That drawing is likewise in Teylers Museum in Haarlem, Q 49. See Giltay 1980, 151, 195, no. 56 (ill.); Plomp 1997b, 361, no. 413 (ill.); and Slive 2001, 537–538, D61.
9. For an in-depth discussion, see Slive 2001, no. 180 (ill.), for notes about the painting in Dresden, and 178 (ill.) for notes about the much larger canvas in Detroit. The burial records for the cemetery have survived, so we know the names of those buried there.
10. Giltay 1980, 150, no. 98; Slive 2001, D120.

Fig. 2. Jacob van Ruisdael, *The Jewish Cemetery*, c. 1655, oil on canvas. Gemäldegalerie Alte Meister, Staatliche Kunstsammlungen, Dresden, 1502

Fig. 3. Jacob van Ruisdael, *The Jewish Cemetery*, c. 1654–1655, oil on canvas. Detroit Institute of Arts, Detroit, 26.3

Fig. 4. Jacob van Ruisdael, *Ruins of Egmond Castle at Egmond aan den Hoef*, c. 1653–1655, black chalk, gray wash. Staatsgalerie, Stuttgart, C 64/1329

LUDOLF BACKHUYSEN

1630–1708

Ludolf Backhuysen, who was born in the German town of Emden, was the son of a scribe, Gerhard Backhaus. He initially followed in his father's footsteps, working as a clerk in the government offices at Emden, where he perfected his penmanship with calligraphic exercises. After the family moved to Amsterdam in 1649, he held a similar post with the firm of the wealthy merchant Guillelmo Bartolotti van den Heuvel, a fellow native of Emden.

From 1650 on Backhuysen was also working as a draftsman, producing grisailles and 'pen paintings' in the manner of Willem van de Velde the Elder. In 1656 he is recorded as a member of Kalligraphie, a society of those proficient in beautiful penmanship. He is referred to as a draftsman as late as 1660, even though by that time he had begun painting as well. No contemporary records of an apprenticeship survive, but Arnold Houbraken states that Backhuysen studied first with Allart van Everdingen and then with Hendrick Dubbels.[1] He did not join the painters' guild in Amsterdam until February 1663.

Backhuysen rapidly gained widespread fame and patronage, particularly after Willem van de Velde and his son Willem van de Velde the Younger immigrated to England in late 1672 or early 1673. Nevertheless, even as early as 1665, it was to Backhuysen that the burgo-masters of Amsterdam turned when commissioning a large view of the city's harbor to send as a gift to a minister of Louis XIV of France. Backhuysen's clientele included a number of other European rulers and his works continued to be extremely popular with leading collectors throughout the eighteenth and early nineteenth centuries. In addition to his seascapes, Backhuysen painted some portraits, allegorical compositions, and townscapes.[2]

Backhuysen was a prolific draftsman throughout the course of his long career, and depicted a wide range of subjects related to maritime life, from views of inland waterways to ships on the high seas. He seems to have created many of these drawings for the open market, but some also served as compositional studies for his paintings.[3]

In this luminous pen-and-wash drawing (cat. 102) Backhuysen has depicted a view in Amsterdam along the Oude Schans canal, looking north toward the docks in the distance and the River IJ beyond.[4] The small bridge at the end of the canal is the Kikkerbilsluis, which is situated on the Kalkmarkt, a dike separating this part of the city from the IJ. The large buildings at the right are the storehouses of the West India Company. The dramatic structure at the left of the sheet is the Montelbaans tower, which was built in the early sixteenth century as part of the defensive fortification system. In the early seventeenth century Hendrick de Keyser added an elegant clock tower to its solid masonry base.

This quiet, harmonious scene, with its beautiful light effects and subtle reflections of boats and buildings animating the stillness of the day, demonstrates the remarkable sensitivity of Backhuysen's use of brown pen lines and gray wash. Close observation also reveals a surprising level of activity in this scene, for amassed along the quay at the foot of the Montelbaans tower is a large group of soldiers, many with muskets resting on their shoulders. The soldiers are about to board two moored sailing vessels that will take them to large transport ships anchored in the IJ beyond the Kalkmarkt.

The scene, in fact, depicts a specific event, as is evident from its connections to a large painting by Backhuysen, dated 1685, in the Wellington Museum, Apsley House,

1. Houbraken 1718–1721, II, 237.
2. For an excellent overview of the artist's life and work, see Beer 2002.
3. For an overview of his drawings, see Amsterdam 1985.
4. For a further discussion of this drawing, see Amsterdam 2004, 82–83, cat. 28.

Fig. 2. Ludolf Backhuysen, *View of the Montelbaans Tower, Amsterdam*, c. 1685, graphite, brown pen and gray wash. Rijksmuseum, Amsterdam, RP-T-1888-A-1557

London (fig. 1). Nannen has noted that three times a year (after Christmas, Easter, and the yearly kermis) sailors and soldiers recruited by the Dutch East India Company embarked from this site. They would first be taken by small transport ships to larger vessels anchored in the IJ, and from there they would journey to Texel to board large merchantmen for their voyage to the Far East.[5]

The horizontal and vertical squaring on the drawing suggests that Backhuysen must have similarly squared the painting's canvas support to transfer the composition. Although the topographical elements remained

quite similar, he made the painting more active by adding ships, emphasizing flags and sails, and massing clouds along the horizon. Interestingly, the squaring, which he drew with black chalk, has been largely erased, presumably so that the pen and wash drawing could be sold as an independent work. Backhuysen also made another drawing of the site, now in the Rijksprenten-kabinet, Rijksmuseum, Amsterdam, that more carefully renders the architectural details of the scene (fig. 2). It is likely that he also consulted this drawing when composing his painting.[6]   [AKW]

5. Nannen 1985, 140.
6. According to Beer 2002, 114, n. 228, a third drawing of this site, dated 1683, was sold at an auction in Paris in 1996.

LUDOLF BACKHUYSEN
102. *View of the Montelbaenstoren*, c. 1685
Pen and brown ink with gray wash on paper
17 × 26.6 cm (6¹¹⁄₁₆ × 10½ in.)
Stadsarchief Amsterdam, Afbeeldingsbestand
010055000601

Fig. 1. Ludolf Backhuysen, *Soldiers of the Dutch East India Company Embarking at the Montelbaans Tower, Amsterdam*, 1685, oil on canvas. Wellington Museum, Apsley House, London, WM 1504–1948

CORNELIS BEGA

1631/32–1664

103. *Peasant Woman, Turned Three-Quarters to the Left,
Holding a Glass*, [n.d.]
Red chalk on paper
14.6 × 24.7 cm (5¾ × 9¾ in.)
The Samuel Courtauld Trust, The Courtauld Gallery,
London, D.1952.RW.2174

Two figure studies exemplify the masterful draftsmanship of Cornelis Bega, whose death at the age of thirty-two or thirty-three cut short an already prolific artistic career. Bega drew his figures with bold strokes and emphasized the modeling of drapery, resulting in depictions of strong, dignified individuals. *Peasant Woman, Turned Three-Quarters to the Left, Holding a Glass* (cat. 103) was previously attributed to Bega's contemporary Gerrit Berckheyde (see cat. 125), but this work is now considered to be an early Bega drawing after a model.[1]

More than one hundred drawings have been attributed to Bega, including at least sixteen works on paper that are now identified as figure studies for his paintings.[2] The sensitive figure study of a man leaning on his bellows (cat. 104) is the preparatory drawing for *The Alchemist*, a work he painted in 1663[3] (cat. 105). When incorporating such preliminary studies in his genre paintings, the clarity of his palette and refined brushwork allowed Bega to retain, and even strengthen, the humanity of his figures.[4]

Several aspects of this preparatory drawing demonstrate that Bega already had a well-developed plan for the painting's composition when he drew the model.

Although the hunched pose, the angular folds of the alchemist's clothing, and the highlights in white chalk precisely correspond to the painted image, Bega did not draw the lower part of the man's right leg, suggesting that he knew that—in the painting—it would be hidden behind the reddish clay receptacle for distillate. He also drew the model's upper torso and head in a relatively upright position, giving the alchemist an aura of competent anticipation.

As is evident in the crisp lines and texture of the alchemist's leather jerkin, Bega was more interested in the drape of textiles and clothing than in the careful representation of his models' features, hands, or feet. In the drawing, he merely hinted at the alchemist's left hand with a faint oval. The use of blue paper allowed him also to model his forms with white heightening, whereby he created drawn characteristics that were easily translated into paint.[5] The relationship between drawing and painting is especially close, given that Bega transferred the figure of the alchemist to the painting at the exactly the same scale as that of the drawing. The virtuoso depiction of drawn folds and ridges is

1. Robinson and Schatborn essay, p. 12. See also Schatborn 1991, 10–11, figs. 7, 8. At the time, Schatborn attributed the Fondation Custodia drawing (cat. 125) to Bega and the Courtauld Gallery's drawing (cat. 103) to Berckheyde, attributions that he recently reversed, as noted in correspondence of September 3, 2015.
2. Baukje Coenen discusses Bega's career as draftsman in 'Experimentierfreudig und

Versiert: Cornelis Bega als Zeichner und Grafiker,' in Aachen/Berlin 2012, 41–59.
3. Coenen first identified cat. 104 as the preparatory drawing for the painting of an alchemist in his workshop (cat. 105). See 'Studie eines Alchemisten' in Aachen/Berlin 2012, 239–240, no. 68. The painting is no. 147 in the catalogue raisonné of Bega's oeuvre. Scott 1984, 335, no. 147. At the time, Scott was not aware of the existence of

the preparatory drawing. In his *Dutch Figure Drawings from the Seventeenth Century*, Peter Schatborn has posited that none of Bega's preparatory studies had survived. Amsterdam/Washington 1981, 105.
4. Baukje Coenen, 'Studie eines Alchemisten' in Aachen/Berlin 2012, 239–240, no. 68.
5. For the benefits of blue paper as medium for a preparatory drawing, see Coenen 2012a, 48.

CORNELIS BEGA

104. *The Alchemist*, c. 1663

Black chalk with white heightening on blue paper

17.3 × 14.2 cm (6¹³⁄₁₆ × 5⁹⁄₁₆ in.)

Museum Mayer van den Bergh, Antwerp, MMB.1049

CORNELIS BEGA

105. *The Alchemist*, 1663

Oil on canvas mounted on panel

35 × 28.6 cm (13¾ × 11¼ in.)

National Gallery of Art, Washington, from the

Collection of Ethel and Martin Wunsch, 2013.34.1

multiplied in the painting, where the alchemist, the crumpled cloth on the hearth, and the pages of the books strewn on the workshop floor create a triangle of spectacular surfaces.

In the painting, Bega seems to allude to the chancy and experimental nature of alchemy, a proto-science that in the seventeenth century straddled the line between magic and science.[6] Alchemists studied chemistry, conducting experiments to separate out the essence of matter and to transform one or more elements into another. Nevertheless, alchemy's ambiguous status derived from its origins, which drew from the realms of natural philosophy, metaphysics, and religion. Its practitioners were, furthermore, secretive about the processes leading to transformations, and their treatises utilized a wide range of occult signs and symbols. The most sought-after transmutation was to turn a base metal—such as lead—into gold. While many alchemists made significant contributions to the scientific development of pharmaceuticals, cosmetics, pigments, and dyes, that futile quest for gold caused alchemists in general to be objects of mockery.[7] This perception, in turn, made them gratifying subjects of genre painters. Yet, while many artists portrayed alchemists as fools who squandered their increasingly meager worldly possessions, Bega's alchemist seems to be a serious— albeit only moderately successful—professional practitioner of proto-chemistry.

Bega must have been familiar with the work of alchemists, having grown up in a world where crafting fine objects from precious noble metals—those resistant to corrosion and oxidation—was a matter of daily concern. Several members of his family were gold- and silversmiths, including his father, Pieter Jansz Begijn, with whom Bega likely trained before 1648, the year he entered the workshop of the painter Adriaen van Ostade).[8] It is thus not surprising that Bega depicts his alchemist, in both the drawing and the painting, as a dignified man instead of a caricature.   [HR]

6. In 1663 Bega also painted *The Astrologer* (National Gallery, London, NG 1481), another subject that drew upon both science and magic. See Aachen/Berlin 2012, 233–236, no. 66.

7. For the history of alchemy, see Snelders 1993, 11–25, and Principe and De Witt 2002.

8. For information on Bega's family, see Biesboer, 'Cornelis Bega (Haarlem, 1631–1664): Eine Biografie,' in Aachen/Berlin 2012, 25–26. Bega's father was a gold- and silversmith; his paternal uncle was a silversmith and sculptor; the brother of his paternal grandmother was a noted silversmith; Bega's sister was married to a silversmith; and their son also followed his father in this profession.

WILLEM VAN DE VELDE
THE ELDER
1611–1693

WILLEM VAN DE VELDE
THE YOUNGER
1633–1707

The Van de Veldes, father and son, were among the most productive draftsmen of the seventeenth century. Some two thousand of their drawings exist in the superb collections of Museum Boijmans Van Beuningen in Rotterdam and the National Maritime Museum in Greenwich alone.[1] The two oeuvres are hard to differentiate. Fortunately, the son quite often added his easily recognizable initials, which give the critical art historian a good starting point. But, it must be said, the enormous number of works have hampered a serious study of the efforts of the two artists.[2]

The activities of the two Van de Veldes have been described in terms of a business that specialized in marine works.[3] It is certain that father and son fully exploited the benefits of this specialization. Recognizing that mastering the depiction of ships required in-depth knowledge, they cleverly served the market, between them taking advantage of their different talents with pen paintings (the father) and works in color (the son). That the father—who called himself a 'scheepsteyckenaer' (ship's draftsman)—wanted to make a real painter of his son is evident from the fact that he apprenticed him to Simon de Vlieger, the specialist of the 1640s.[4] Accuracy—the Van de Veldes's trademark—was essential, as potential customers knew their own ships down to the smallest detail. Both Van de Veldes sketched on the wharves and docks, and went to sea to observe events with their own eyes.

The great naval battles that the Dutch and the English fought in the third quarter of the seventeenth century—sometimes involving more than three hundred ships—still appeal strongly to the imagination. One of the famous actions was the Four Days' Battle, fought from June 1 to 4, 1666 (June 11 to 14).[5] It was clear beforehand that a great battle would take place. On May 27 (June 6), Admiral Michiel de Ruyter signed an order to the captain of a galliot—a long, narrow ship—telling him to take Willem van de Velde the Elder to record the events.[6] Although no record verifies that both father and son were on board, subsequent drawings suggest that both were present. The Van de Veldes followed the fighting and, while at sea, made swift situation sketches and impressions of particular episodes on large rolls of paper, jotting down notes as reminders. Later, in the studio, these were worked up in more detail, and new composition sketches were also made. The two artists undoubtedly produced paintings of the battle in the same year that the conflict took place. Possibly, the painting by Willem van de Velde the Younger, now in the Rijksmuseum on loan from a private collection, is one of these.[7] The artists' stock of drawings also allowed them

1. Daalder 2013, 23, estimates the total number of drawings by the Van de Veldes in public collections to be more than 2,500.
2. Michael Robinson cataloged the drawings in Greenwich and, with Weber, those in Museum Boijmans Van Beuningen. Although he made a serious attempt to separate the two oeuvres, he also hesitated many times; see Robinson 1958–1974 and Robinson and Weber 1979. Robinson also wrote a catalog of the paintings; see Robinson, M. S. 1990.
3. Daalder 2013, 20.
4. Daalder 2013, 84–85.
5. The Four Days' Battle was fought from June 1 through 4, 1666, in the Julian or Old Style calendar then used in England (which corrolates to June 11 through 14 in the New Style Calendar).
6. Voorbeijtel Cannenburg 1950, 193.
7. See Willem Van de Velde II, *The Conquest of the Royal Prince during the Four Days' Battle*, c. 1679, Rijksmuseum, Amsterdam, sk-c-1743.

WILLEM VAN DE VELDE THE YOUNGER

106. *The Surrender of the Royal Prince on the Third Day
of the Four Days' Battle, June 13, 1666*, c. 1670
Oil on canvas
35.2 × 45.3 cm (13⅞ × 17¹³⁄₁₆ in.)
Fondation Custodia, Collection Frits Lugt, Paris,
5807

WILLEM VAN DE VELDE THE YOUNGER
107. *The Surrender of the Royal Prince on the Third Day of the Four Days' Battle, June 13, 1666*, c. 1666
Pencil and gray wash on paper
21 × 43.2 cm (8¼ × 17 in.)
National Maritime Museum, Greenwich, PAH 3879

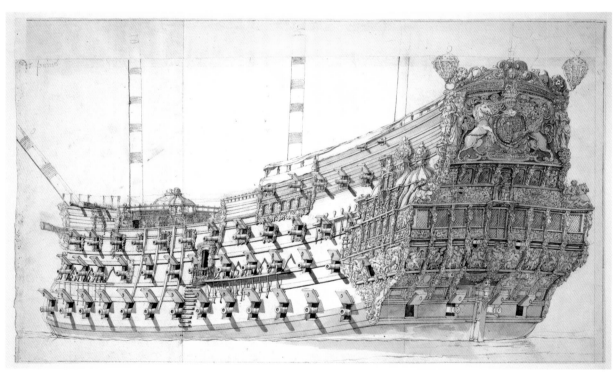

WILLEM VAN DE VELDE THE ELDER
109. *Ship's Portrait of the Royal Prince*,
counterproof, 1661
Black chalk on paper
33.4 × 45.4 cm (13⅛ × 17⅞ in.)
Museum Boijmans Van Beuningen, Rotterdam,
MB 1866 T 389

WILLEM VAN DE VELDE THE ELDER
108. *Ship's Portrait of the Royal Prince*, 1670(?)
Paris only
Pencil, pen, and wash on paper
44.9 × 73.9 cm (17¹¹⁄₁₆ × 29⅛ in.)
Museum Boijmans Van Beuningen, Rotterdam,
MB 1866 T 352

to meet later demand. For instance, when Cardinal Leopoldo de' Medici asked the elder Van de Velde for a record of the Four Days' Battle, he received a pen painting that was finished in 1672.[8] The painting (cat. 106) in the Fondation Custodia's collection was probably produced sometime between the dates for these two works. The three paintings capture the same moment.[9]

On the third day of the battle, thanks to the cunning of Lieutenant-Admiral Michiel de Ruyter, several large English warships ran aground on the Galloper sandbank in their attempt to pursue smaller Dutch vessels. The *Royal Prince*, with Vice-Admiral George Ayscue on board, was forced to surrender. The paintings show the transfer of the captive crew to the *Gouda*. The composition for the Fondation Custodia's painting was prepared in a sketch that was undoubtedly made in the workshop by the young Van de Velde but retouched by a later hand (cat. 107).[10] The *Royal Prince* was recorded by young artist's father in a meticulous ship's portrait (cat. 108). Van de Velde the Elder must have used the time after the crew evacuated the ship, and later made his escape when the vessel was set on fire at De Ruyter's order. Van de Velde the Younger used this last drawing in his painting in Paris. He must have utilized a counterproof for the painting in the Rijksmuseum, as it is a mirror image (fig. 1).[11] The same applies to the pen painting in Karlsruhe, where the elder Van de Velde chose a different view of the ship, but worked out the stern accordingly. A counterproof in Rotterdam of the same *Royal Prince* (cat. 109), which shows the ship with slightly different details, was evidently traced from another ship's

Fig. 1. Willem van de Velde the Younger, *Captured English Ships after the Four Days' Battle*, c. 1666, oil on canvas. Rijksmuseum, Amsterdam, SK-A-439

portrait.[12] The drawings form part of a long series of ships' portraits, seen obliquely from the stern, with good views of this part of the ship and also its beam, making it easy to see the firepower from numerous gun ports.

The Van de Veldes were also at sea on May 28 (June 7), 1672, during the Battle of Solebay.[13] It was the first naval battle of the 'disaster year,' when the Republic of the Seven United Provinces was being attacked on all sides. In a last desperate effort the Dutch coast was defended against English and French attacks by the navy under the command of De Ruyter. The Duke of York, later King James II, was the commander in chief of the combined English and French fleet. Although one might wonder what the draftsmen were actually able to see— given little wind and the smoke that masked the ships— the young Van de Velde was able to make a superb drawing of the burning *Royal James* (cat. 110), which had been set ablaze by the fire ship *Vrede*. (Fire ships were laden with waste wood and were used to set fire to enemy boats.) Van de Velde the Younger relied upon this draw-

8. The work is in the Staatliche Kunsthalle, Karlsruhe; see Vey 1986, 153–160. Robinson, M. S. 1990, I, 34–38, no. 431.
9. For a list of the reproductions of this incident by the Van de Veldes, see Paris 1989, 14–15.
10. Robinson 1958–1974, I, 67, 131, pointed out that the drawing had been

greatly worked up, probably by Charles Gore. The jack (the main flag) and the vanes of the *Royal Prince* are incorrect additions.
11. It is notable that the details of the stern do not correspond exactly to the *Royal Prince*.
12. Such information was probably taken from a drawing in the Victoria and Albert

Museum, London. See Robinson and Weber 1979, I, 120.
13. The Battle of Solebay, the first naval engagement of the Third Anglo-Dutch War, took place on May 28, 1672 (Old Style Calendar), or June 7, 1672 (New Style Calendar).

WILLEM VAN DE VELDE THE YOUNGER

110. *Burning of the Royal James at the Battle of Solebay,*
    June 7, 1672, 1673(?)
    Gray wash, graphite on paper
    44.3 × 63.4 cm (17 7/16 × 24 15/16 in.)
    National Maritime Museum, Greenwich, PAI 7272

Fig. 2. Willem van de Velde the Younger and studio, *The Battle of Solebay, June 7, 1672,* 1675, oil on canvas. Nederlands Scheepvaartmuseum, Amsterdam, A.0004

ing in a composition known from a few paintings, including one in the Scheepvaartmuseum, Amsterdam (fig. 2).[14] The enormous *Royal James,* with one hundred guns and a crew of seven hundred, was the flagship of Edward Montague, Earl of Sandwich, who lost his life in this battle. The fierceness of the engagements on that day in June was pithily summed up by an English prisoner, who, according to De Ruyter's biographer Gerard Brandt, said to the admiral, 'My Lord, that is fighting! It is not yet noon and already more has been done than in all four days in the year MDCLXVI' (the Four Days' Battle of 1666).[15] Given that the painting must have been made some years later, it seems likely that the commissioning client was English. It is also possible that paintings such as this were made in memory of dead naval heroes.[16]

In the winter of 1672, the 'disaster year,' the Van de Veldes cut their losses and moved to England, where, in the Queen's House in Greenwich, King Charles II placed a studio at their disposal. This move, which was not popular with all patriotic Dutchmen, was in itself understandable: the Republic was threatened with division, and before this, the First Anglo-Dutch War

(1652–1654) had brought about the collapse of the market for luxury goods. It goes without saying that the Van de Veldes would have feared a similar collapse. King Charles II's generous offer would certainly have been very attractive. Furthermore, they were not the only ones who sought safety in England.

In the service of their new royal master, the Van de Veldes no longer went to sea as 'reporters.' In these years Willem van de Velde the Younger slowly but surely abandoned his precise manner of working. He eventually evolved into an artist with an eye for weather conditions, for the atmosphere of a violent engagement or a fierce squall. His sense of drama is manifest in the painting in the Scheepvaartmuseum (see fig. 2). In his later work his imaginative talent increasingly emerged—an aspect that was lacking in his father's work. [WK]

14. Robinson, M.S. 1990, 177, no. 427 [2]; see also Daalder in Spits 2013, 12–13. For another, probably better version, see Robinson, M.S. 1990, 177, no. 427 [1] (sale Amsterdam March 14–15, 1983, no. 33).

15. 'Myn Heer, is dat vechten!' T en is noch geen middagh, en daar is alreeds meer gedaan dan in den jaare MDCLXVI in alle vier de daegen.' Brandt 1687, 671.
16. This, for example, is certainly true in the case of the *Battle of Ter Heide* in the

Rijksmuseum, Amsterdam, SK-A-1365, which was made in memory of the deceased admiral Maerten Harpertsz Tromp by Willem van de Velde the Elder. See also Sigmond and Kloek 2014, 82–83, 116–117, fig. 059.

NICOLAES MAES

1634–1693

Nicolaes Maes studied with Rembrandt in Amsterdam during the late 1640s and early 1650s. He returned by 1653 to his native Dordrecht and began his career as an independent painter specializing in scenes of everyday life, biblical subjects, and portraits. From the early 1660s until the end of his life, Maes devoted himself exclusively to portraiture. In 1673 he left Dordrecht and settled permanently in Amsterdam, where, to judge from archival documents and the large number of surviving portraits dating from the middle of the 1670s to the early 1690s, he enjoyed a steady stream of commissions and a substantial income.[1]

Many of Maes's surviving drawings relate to the few paintings of biblical subjects and approximately three dozen oils of women performing everyday tasks in domestic settings, including *The Lacemaker* (cat. 111), which he produced in Dordrecht during the 1650s.[2] His studies for these works fall into two groups. The ink-and-wash sketch for *The Lacemaker* (cat. 112) is typical of his compositional projects, most of which are small, summarily handled with loosely drawn contours and broadly washed shadows, and concerned with only the essential elements—particularly the poses and gestures of the figures—of the design that he had in mind. In some composition studies Maes combined ink and/or wash with red chalk and/or white opaque watercolor, while a few are rendered entirely in red chalk.[3] In addition to compositional projects, several detailed studies for the principal figures in Maes's paintings have survived. Here, too, he was inconsistent in his choice of media. He used red chalk for *Seated Woman Making Lace* (cat. 113) and a few other studies, but he also drew figures in ink and wash and in combinations of ink, wash, chalk, and white opaque watercolor.[4]

The diminutive composition sketch for *The Lacemaker*

shows the two main components of the painting: the woman, facing the viewer, hunches over her work behind a counter or credenza set parallel to the picture plane. In the drawing she sits before a doorway, whose shape repeats the arched framing line Maes drew at the top of the sheet. To the right of the doorway a chair stands in front of the back wall—the only furnishing, apart from the counter, indicated in the sketch. Two horizontal pen lines behind the woman's head suggest that Maes already considered replacing the doorway with a wall embellished with a molding above the wainscoting. Other decorative elements introduced in the painting include a framed picture with a curtain, a portrait print suspended on rollers, and a calendar showing the date, '1655/Martius/9.' The inkwell, ledger books, black-and-white tiled floor, and disciplined concentration of the lacemaker herself contribute to the impression of an industrious, prosperous, orderly household.

In the red chalk drawing in Rotterdam (cat. 113), Maes executed a detailed study of the lacemaker absorbed in her work—her frontal pose, costume, and the position of the fingers as they manipulate the bobbins. He generally followed the study during his work on the panel, but made several adjustments. As in the drawing, the light in the painting falls from the upper left. The woman's face is narrower in the picture; Maes revised the shape and decoration of the headpiece; and he eliminated the cuff on the sleeve of her right arm. In the painting, the lacemaking cushion rests higher on her lap and is foreshortened accordingly. The two middle fingers of the woman's left hand are extended in the painting, rather than bent as they are in the drawing, and he elaborated the crisp folds of the white collar, which he had only suggested with a few lines and hatchings in the study.   [WWR]

1. Krempel 2000, 42–109.

2. Sumowski 1979, VIII, 3954–4023, nos. 1759–1788; Robinson 1989, 146–154.

3. Sumowski 1979, VIII, 3964–3965, no. 1764, 4018–4019, no. 1786, 4022–4023, no. 1788, 4034–4035, no. 1793ax; Robinson 1989, 147–151, figs. 6, 7, 9, 11.

4. Sumowski 1979, VIII, 3790–3791, no. 1765b, 3988–3991, nos. 1771, 1772, 3998–4007, nos. 1776–1780; Robinson 1989, 148, fig. 3, 150–155, figs. 17–23.

NICOLAES MAES

111. *The Lacemaker*, 1655
   Oil on panel
   57.1 × 43.8 cm (22½ × 17¼ in.)
   National Gallery of Canada, Ottawa, 6189
   Washington only

FRANS VAN MIERIS
THE ELDER

1635–1681

Fig. 1. Frans van Mieris, *Willem Paedts in the Cradle*, 1665, black chalk. Fondation Custodia, Collection Frits Lugt, Paris, 1970-T.33

Frans van Mieris was the most talented student of Gerrit Dou and became the leading *fijnschilder* (fine painter) of the second generation. With great wit and virtuosity he primarily painted small genre scenes and a few portraits. Unlike Dou's depictions of the working class ensconced in daily duties, Van Mieris's paintings mostly feature the pastimes of the wealthy. Already during his lifetime, he was known for his exquisite rendering of different fabrics and textures.

When it came to drawing, Van Mieris was something of a child prodigy. Arnold Houbraken's colorful account of the artist's life describes the youthful artist covering the walls of his father's goldsmith workshop with charcoal drawings, instead of mastering his father's profession. The boy's high-quality creations eventually led his father to send the boy to Abraham Toorenvliet, a draftsman and glass painter, and then to Dou shortly thereafter.[1]

Around thirty-five drawings by Van Mieris have come down to us, though records show that there must have been more.[2] For an artist with an apparently incessant urge to draw, this number perhaps seems small, but it is rather high in comparison to Dou and the other *fijnschilders,* from whom hardly any drawings survive.[3] Virtually all of Van Mieris's drawings are executed in black chalk,

no doubt the artist's preferred medium and similar in handling to the charcoal that he used as a child.[4] Most of them are highly finished, signed drawings on vellum that were intended for sale. It is in these exquisite works that we catch a glimpse of Houbraken's words and witness the artist's virtuosity and lifelong passion for drawing.[5] For one of these finished drawings on vellum, *Willem Paedts as an Infant*, there even exists a preparatory study on paper (fig. 1).[6]

A small number of Van Mieris's drawings relates to his paintings. A few designs are known for entire compositions, which all depart significantly from the finished

1. Houbraken 1718–1721, III, 2. Unfortunately, very few works by Toorenvliet are known today.

2. Naumann 1978, 23–32, cataloged thirty drawings. See The Hague/Washington 2005, 240–241, for two de-attributions and four additions, and Wuestman 2015 for a newly discovered drawing. Otto Naumann is currently preparing an addendum to his 1978 catalogue raisonné, which will include recent findings. For unidentified drawings and sketchbooks by Frans van Mieris mentioned in eighteenth- and nineteenth-century sources, see Naumann 1978, especially 22, n. 41.

3. For Dou's few extant drawings, none of which are preparatory, see Baer 2000, 40; for a discussion of Van Mieris's drawings in the context of Dou and the *fijnschilders*, see Naumann 1978. Also see Naumann 2005, 32, for the observation that Van Mieris's superb drawing skills set him apart from other genre painters.

4. For a drawing in graphite, *Two Studies of a Spaniel* at the Fondation Custodia in Paris, see Quinten Buvelot, 'Two Studies of a Spaniel,' in The Hague/Washington 2005,

142–143, no. 24. In a few instances, Van Mieris added washes to the black chalk; see the catalog of drawings in Naumann 1978.

5. See, for instance, the marvelous *Sad News* on vellum, dated 1660, which was auctioned at Christie's New York, January 29, 2015, no. 57. Naumann 1978, 7, rightly notes that these drawings were 'meant as the visual equivalent to his paintings.'

6. See Naumann 1978, no. 17, for the finished drawing in the British Museum, and no. 12 for the study at the Fondation Custodia (fig. 1 in this entry).

FRANS VAN MIERIS THE ELDER
114. *Sleeping Spaniel*, c. 1665–1670
Black chalk on paper
7.1 × 9.3 cm (2.8 × 3.7 in.)
Private Collection
(*Real size*)

paintings.[7] The reason for this discrepancy is that, much like his master Dou, Van Mieris generally prepared his paintings with underdrawings and brush sketches straight on the panel, adjusting the design during various phases of the preparation process and sometimes even in the painting stage.[8] In addition to the composition drawings, a handful of drawings with separate studies of details and figures that relate to Van Mieris's paintings are known. In these cases, Van Mieris seems to have been carefully trying to capture a particular position or expression, for which he turned to his preferred black chalk and paper.[9]

The little *Sleeping Spaniel* (cat. 114) is featured in Van Mieris's *The Song Interrupted*, 1671 (fig. 2) as an oblivious witness to a courting scene.[10] Spaniels were popular with upper-class women and were frequently incorporated as staffage (secondary subjects) in the repertoire of

Fig. 2. Frans van Mieris the Elder, *The Song Interrupted*, 1671, oil on panel. Musée du Petit Palais, Paris, Dutuit Collection, PDUT00915

genre painters, including in several drawings and paintings by Van Mieris.[11] Sleeping dogs were also part of a broader pictorial tradition and were depicted on several occasions by artists such as Rembrandt and Hendrick Goltzius.[12] Van Mieris probably did not make this drawing with a specific painting in mind. Instead, its spontaneous character suggests that Van Mieris drew the lapdog, possibly a pet in his own household, from life at the spur of the moment.[13] With just a few lines, Van Mieris skillfully explored the chalk's full potential by using its sharp tip to indicate the spaniel's longer hairs, and the blunt edge to render its soft fur.

The execution of the drawing, especially the strong, dark lines in the shaded areas, is reminiscent of *Willem Paedts in the Cradle*, which is dated 1665 (fig. 1).[14] Van Mieris probably drew the *Sleeping Spaniel* at approximately the same time, but definitely before 1671, when he painted *The Song Interrupted*. Van Mieris was clearly satisfied with the drawing, for he used the dog in several other paintings about ten years later, near the end of his life, during a period in which his inventiveness dwindled and he often repeated old motifs.[15]   [IVT]

7. See Buvelot, 'Old Man Sharpening His Pen,' in The Hague/Washington 2005, 72–75, no. 1, which dates from around 1650–1655; Naumann 1978, no. 26, for two sketches for *Doctor's Visit*, 1657, Vienna, on the verso of a more worked-out drawing of a *Hermit Praying*; and Wuestman 2015 for a rudimentary design on the back of a family document for *Double Portrait of an Unknown Couple*, 1675, in Philadelphia.

8. For Van Mieris's painting preparation and technique, see Pottash 2005. For a recent study of Dou's working process, see Surh, Van Tuinen, and Twilley 2014.

9. For a study of an *Old Woman* at the Morgan Library & Museum, which Van Mieris incorporated into his painting of *The Quack* in the Uffizi, see Buvelot in The Hague/Washington 2005, 79–81, no. 4. For a discussion of other partial studies, see Naumann 2005.

10. For the painting, see Naumann 1981, II, 100, no. 88.

11. See Buvelot in The Hague/Washington 2005, 142–143, no. 24, for references to the drawings and for the etching of 1656 that has traditionally been attributed to him.

12. For a concise discussion of sleeping dogs in Dutch art, see Ger Luijten, 'Sleeping Dog,' in Amsterdam/London 2000, 179–181, no. 37.

13. For the instances in which Van Mieris depicted a spaniel in a painting featuring a couple who look like Van Mieris and his wife, making it probable that they had such a dog at home, see Buvelot in The Hague/Washington 2005, 142–143, no. 24.

14. Naumann 1978, no. 17: the inscription was added by a member of the Paedts family shortly after the drawing was made.

15. See Naumann 1981, II, for all of the following: 113, no. 103 (*A Concert of Six Figures*, c. 1675, whereabouts unknown), dog mirrored; 123, no. 118 (*Woman Writing a Letter*, 1680, Rijksmuseum, Amsterdam); and 125, no. 121 (*Holy Family*, 1681, whereabouts unknown), dog mirrored.

ADRIAEN VAN DE VELDE

1636–1672

---

115. *Study after a Male Model*, [n.d.]
Red chalk on paper
34.9 × 22.9 cm (13¾ × 9 in.)
Private Collection

The extensive oeuvre of drawings by Adriaen van de Velde, who specialized in paintings and etchings of pastoral scenes with herders and cattle, includes composition sketches and detailed studies of figures and animals for his paintings.[1]

Arnold Houbraken wrote that Van de Velde went once a week into the countryside to paint and sketch landscapes and cattle,[2] and *Landscape with Trees* (cat. 116) probably originated on one of those excursions. The artist initially recorded the view in pen-and-ink, using diagonal and zigzag hatchings to describe foliage and shadows. Later he added brown and gray-brown washes to deepen selected areas of shadow, especially in the right and center foreground. He adapted this *naer 't leven* (from life) study for the composition of a painting, *The Farm*, 1666 (fig. 1).[3] In contrast to the oblong shape of the drawing, the Berlin canvas is nearly square. Van de Velde accommodated the motif recorded in the drawn study to the format of the painting by narrowing the space between the groups of large trees that dominate the left and right sides of the composition. He extended the foreground and heightened the sky in the painting, raising and enlarging the crown of the tree at the right so

1. Robinson 1979, 4–16, 18–23, nos. A-1 to B-17, and D-1 to D-26. As noted by Angelique van den Eerenbeemd, the drawings described as *modelli*, or finished compositional studies, in Robinson 1979, 20, nos. C-1 to C-6, were not preparatory to paintings but instead copies by the artist after completed paintings, which he presumably made as independent drawings for sale. See Eerenbeemd 2006, 14–16. It is also possible that they were *ricordi*, that is, records of pictures that were leaving the workshop upon sale.

2. Houbraken 1718–1721, III, 90.

3. Adriaen van de Velde, *The Farm*, 1666, oil on canvas, Staatliche Museen, Berlin, Gemäldegalerie, 922C. See Bock 1996, 123, 392, pl. 1640; Robinson 1979, 4–5, fig. 1, 18, under no. A-1.

4. On Van de Velde's use of figure studies, see Schatborn 1975, 159–165; Robinson 1979, 10–13; and Amsterdam/Washington 1981, 116–119.

5. Robels 1983, 248, no. 613. On Van de Velde's use of counterproofs, see Robinson 1979, 10; Amsterdam/Washington 1981,

28–29, 116; and Robinson 1993, 54–56.

6. The kneeling woman in the drawing shows up in what appears to be a crude copy after Van de Velde, *A Farmyard with Animals*, Collection Thomas Dormer, Rousham House, photo Courtauld Institute neg. no. B 72/1450. A similar figure of a woman milking a goat—in which she looks up at another woman, but otherwise corresponds closely to the Abrams study—appears in a pastoral landscape dated 1662 in the Pushkin Museum of Fine Arts, Moscow; Kuznetsov

that it reaches the top of the support. Both revisions enhanced the illusion of space and depth in the painting. Finally, Van de Velde animated the scene by adding resting and grazing farm animals and the figures of a man and a woman who have come out to the pasture to milk the cows.

The drawing for *The Farm* is a rare survivor in the artist's oeuvre of a landscape study from nature that he adapted for a painting. Most of the working drawings related to Van de Velde's pictures are ink-and-wash composition studies—which he sketched in the studio from the imagination—and studies of figures and animals. He drew most of his figure studies in red chalk on cream paper, but for several he used black chalk, or black and white chalk, on gray or gray-brown prepared paper. While Van de Velde executed some figure studies with a particular composition in mind, other works by the artist served to build up a stock of motifs for him to use when the need arose.[4] He posed his models in characteristic attitudes of the working and relaxing herdsmen who grace his pastoral landscapes. *Kneeling Woman* (cat. 117) represents a model in the costume and pose of a woman milking a goat. As in many of his model studies, Van de Velde quickly sketched the outlines of the figure in black chalk, and then he worked painstakingly with red chalk, often ignoring the initial contours. In order to double the practical value of his studies, he routinely took counterproofs of them, producing a second image in the reverse of the first. The counterproof of *Kneeling Woman* has survived.[5] Although neither the original nor the counterproof was reproduced exactly in any known painting by Van de Velde, a very similar figure, perhaps based on this drawing or a variant study of the model, occurs in a work

of 1662.[6] After the artist's death in January 1672, his pupil Dirck van Bergen acquired his master's studio estate, and during the 1670s and 1680s Van Bergen made a career of painting variants and pastiches of Van de Velde's compositions, many of which incorporate the master's figure and animal studies. Van Bergen adapted *Kneeling Woman* for an Italianate pastoral scene with a woman milking a goat near the ruin of a Roman mausoleum (fig. 2).[7] In the painting, her left arm is obscured by the goat and her right arm is lower than it is in the drawing, but Van Bergen reproduced the rest of the study exactly, including details of the dress and hair.

In addition to studies of herdsmen in rustic attire, Van de Velde also drew in the workshop from nude models. A few of his life drawings were preparatory to paintings. In two instances, nude and clothed studies for a figure in a picture survive, and he probably followed this practice for other paintings that called for figures on a scale larger than that of mere staffage.[8] However, he evidently produced most of his drawings from the nude solely to improve his ability to represent the human body.[9] *Study after a Male Model* (cat. 115) exemplifies the type of life study he made for practice and discipline.[10] Dressed only in a loincloth, the model uses a staff to hold the pose long enough for the draftsman to complete his work. Van de Velde took considerable care over the drawing, wetting the red chalk for the darkest accents and extensively stumping—rubbing the lines with a cloth or rolled paper to blend them into areas of tone—to achieve nuanced effects of modeling. [WWR]

and Linnik 1982, no. 202, where the date is given incorrectly as 1652. Composition studies for this painting are Robinson 1979, 18, nos. B-1, B-2.

7. Dirck van Bergen, *Landscape with Herdsmen and Cattle near a Tomb*, 1660–1690, oil on canvas, Rijksmuseum, Amsterdam, on loan from the City of Amsterdam (A. van der Hoop Bequest), SK-C-105. See Thiel et al. 1976, 114.

8. Robinson 1979, 11–13, fig. 8, 22, cat. nos. D-14, D-15, pls. 10, 11; Robinson 1993, 54–59, figs. 1–7.

9. Robinson 1993, 59–63, figs. 9–15.

10. The pose in *Study after a Male Model* shares elements with the figure of the angel in Van de Velde's *Annunciation* of 1667 in the Rijksmuseum, Amsterdam (Robinson 1979, 21, cat. no. D-11), and with the figure in the bow of the boat in *The Ferry*, dated 16(5?)9 in Schwerin and the study for it in the Louvre (Eerenbeemd 2006, 39, under no. 43), but the drawing cannot be considered directly preparatory for either picture.

ADRIAEN VAN DE VELDE

116. *Landscape with Trees*, 1660–1669
  Pen and brown ink, brown and gray-brown wash
  on two pieces of paper joined vertically at left
  28.5 × 45.6 cm (11¼ × 17¹⁵⁄₁₆ in.)
  Amsterdam Museum, bequest of C.J. Fodor
  A 10348

Fig. 1. Adriaen van de Velde, *The Farm*, 1666, oil on canvas.
Staatliche Museen, Berlin, Gemäldegalerie, 922C

ADRIAEN VAN DE VELDE

117. *Kneeling Woman*, c. 1660(?)
Red chalk over black chalk on paper
23.2 × 19 cm (9⅛ × 7½ in.)
Maida and George Abrams Collection, Boston

Fig. 2. Dirck van Bergen, *Landscape with Herdsmen and Cattle near a Tomb*, 1660–1690, oil on canvas. Rijksmuseum, Amsterdam, on loan from the City of Amsterdam (A. van der Hoop Bequest), SK-C-105

GERRIT BERCKHEYDE

1638–1698

---

118. *The Grote or St. Bavokerk in Haarlem*, 1666
Oil on panel
60.3 × 84.5 cm (23¾ × 33¼ in.)
Otto Naumann Ltd., New York
Washington only

Gerrit Berckheyde probably received his artistic training from his older brother Job, with whom he also traveled to Germany prior to joining the Haarlem St. Luke's Guild in 1660, but it is not certain that Job inspired him to become a specialist in architectural painting.[1] On that trip to Germany, however, he was already drawing views of German cities—particularly in Cologne, where he and his brother stayed for an extended period of time—which he would continue to consult later in his career when painting views of cities situated along the Rhine (fig. 1). For the most part, however, he devoted his career to painting views of his native Haarlem, and also Amsterdam and The Hague, capturing in these works the enormous sense of civic pride associated with these urban centers.

In his paintings of Haarlem and Amsterdam, one encounters time and again the dominating structures that defined their civic cores, the great church of St. Bavo in Haarlem (cat. 118), and the new Town Hall in Amsterdam (cats. 120, 121). His viewpoints were often unusual, as though he had come across these hallmarks unexpectedly while turning a corner. In his paintings one sees new buildings rising near old, feels the weight of stone and the roughness of brick, and senses the energy of the marketplace, while reveling in the quiet reflections of buildings, boats, and figures in tree-lined canals. He often accented contrasts of light and shade to emphasize the three-dimensional character of the space and the physical substance of the buildings. His city views inevitably show places that are clean and well kept, with nary a dilapidated building nor a piece of trash disturbing the sense of a prosperous urban environment.

These qualities are particularly evident in two views he painted in the early 1670s of the Town Hall in Amsterdam, as seen from the Nieuwezijds Voorburgwal canal: one in the Los Angeles County Museum of Art (cat. 120) and the other in the Amsterdam Museum (cat. 121). In each of these virtually identical paintings Berckheyde rendered morning light articulating the architectural character of the town hall—crisp edges of engaged pilasters separate the windows and the circular dome of the cupola is marked by modulated shadows. He contrasted the brilliant color of light of this massive classical structure with the rhythmic patterns of stepped gables and peaked salmon-colored tile roofs of the private dwellings lining the canal. Along the broad quays on either side of the Nieuwezijds Voorburgwal are open-air markets, whose products would have been frequently transported by flat-bottomed boats. At the left of the canal is a flower market, with pots of flowering plants placed at regular intervals for the inspection of potential customers. Beyond this market are barrels of beer brought by the barge moored along the quay, their presence almost certainly connected to a pub or brewery situated in the brick building at the left. Horse-drawn sleighs, such as the one crossing the bridge over the canal or on the quay at the right of the canal, also would have brought goods to these markets.

Although these two paintings seem virtually identical, one striking difference exists between them: the Los Angeles County Museum of Art work includes a dwelling with a curved-neck gable to the right of the tall twin-gabled dwellings, whereas the Amsterdam painting has no such building. Instead, a smaller, older style

house is depicted. This addition indicates how con-cerned Berckheyde was with topographical accuracy and documenting urban change. In fact, five paintings are known of this site, ranging from around 1670 to 1686, each with slight differences that reflect the construction of new buildings along this stretch of the Nieuwezijds Voorburgwal.[2]

Berckheyde based each of these paintings on a prelimi-nary drawing that contained all of the essential pictorial elements, even the boats and the horse on the quay (cat. 119). The architectural elements along the quay in this drawing relate most closely to the painting in Los Angeles. Nevertheless, the preliminary drawing also was used for the Amsterdam painting, as Berckheyde clearly inserted this new building into his previously drawn composition: the gable of the old house overlaps the gutter of the building behind it.[3] Berckheyde contoured the buildings in his drawing, but he did not introduce contrasts of light and dark, presumably to give himself more flexibility when making paintings of this scene. By controlling the direction of the light in his paintings, Berckeyde could adapt the scene to reflect different times of the day.

1. For Berckheyde's biography, see Lawrence 1991, 17–27.
2. For a discussion of the topographical differences in these versions, see Los Angeles/Boston/New York 1981, 8–11.
3. See Jan Peeters's entry on this drawing in Amsterdam 1997b, 97–98, cat. 4.

Fig. 1. Gerrit Berckheyde, *The Nieuwezijds Voorburgwal with Flower Market, Amsterdam*, 1686, oil on canvas. Museo Thyssen-Bornemisza, Madrid, 42 (1959.3)

GERRIT BERCKHEYDE

119. *View of the Nieuwezijds Voorburgwal in Amsterdam,* [n.d.]
Graphite, pen, and brown ink on paper
16.9 × 27.6 cm (6⅝ × 10⅞ in.)
Koninklijk Oudheidkundig Genootschap,
Amsterdam, KOG-AA-2-13-261

GERRIT BERCKHEYDE

120. *The Nieuwezijds Voorburgwal with the Flower and Tree Market in Amsterdam*, c. 1675
Oil on wood
36.8 × 47.6 cm (14½ × 18¾ in.)
Los Angeles County Museum of Art, Gift of Mr. and Mrs. Edward William Carter, M.2009.106.1
Washington only

GERRIT BERCKHEYDE

121. *The Nieuwezijds Voorburgwal with the Flower Market in Amsterdam*, c. 1668–1670
Oil on canvas
45 × 61 cm (17¹¹⁄₁₆ × 24 in.)
Amsterdam Museum, SA7455
Paris only

GERRIT BERCKHEYDE
122. *View on the Herengracht from the Vijzelstraat
in Amsterdam*, c. 1671–1672
Graphite, gray wash on paper
20.8 × 39.5 cm (8³⁄₁₆ × 15⁹⁄₁₆ in.)
Stadsarchief, Amsterdam, Afbeeldingsbestand
010001000009

Fig. 2. Gerrit Berckheyde, *View of the Golden Bend in the Herengracht*, 1671–1672, oil on panel. Rijksmuseum, Amsterdam, SK-A-5003

For example, while the Los Angeles and Amsterdam paintings depict a morning light, a late afternoon sun shines on the facades of the buildings lining the canal in the version of this composition in the Thyssen-Bornemisza Collection, dated 1686 (fig. 1). Just how Berckheyde transferred this image to the canvas supports of his paintings is not known. The scale of this drawing is smaller than that of the paintings, and yet no trace of a grid is evident, nor is there scoring along the any of the lines. Perhaps he made a carefully ruled construction drawing in the manner of Pieter Jansz Saenredam after tracing this image onto another sheet, but such a drawing would presumably have been damaged through multiple uses and thus lost to posterity.

The growth in Amsterdam's stature and power symbolized by the construction of the new Town Hall was further realized by an ambitious plan in the early 1660s to extend the imposing ring of canals surrounding the city core—the Herengracht, the Keizersgracht, and the Prinsengracht—around the eastern portions of the city.

Wealthy regents and merchants took pride in constructing finely appointed dwellings and gardens along these canals, along which were planted trees and which, after 1669, were illuminated with oil-burning lanterns designed by the successful artist-inventor Jan van der Heyden. Around 1672 Berckheyde painted two remarkable views of the most luxurious of these canals, the Herengracht, one looking west from the Vijzelstraat (fig. 2) and the other looking east from the Leidsestraat.[4] The housing lots along bend in the canal that he depicted—later nicknamed the Golden Bend—had not all been filled in by 1672, and hence his paintings provide a remarkable documentary record of the construction of this monument to civic pride. The accuracy of his view from the Vijzelstraat can be confirmed by extensive building documents that not only date the construction of homes but also name their architects.

Connected to this remarkable painting is a carefully rendered drawing that has all the characteristics of a construction drawing. It not only accurately describes all

4. For a discussion of these paintings and related drawings, with a full discussion of the architectural setting, see The Hague/Washington 2008, 86–89, cat. 10.

GERRIT BERCKHEYDE
123. *Walking Boy with a Basket*, 1670s
   Black chalk on paper
   19 × 10.9 cm (7½ × 4⁵⁄₁₆ in.)
   Rijksmuseum, Amsterdam, purchased with the support
   of the Vereniging Rembrandt, RP-T-1883-A-264

Fig. 3. Gerrit Berckheyde, *View of the Bank of the Rhine near Cologne*, c. 1670, oil on panel.
Museum Boijmans Van Beuningen, Rotterdam, 1042 (OK)

GERRIT BERCKHEYDE

124. *Seated Man, Drinking*, [n.d.]

Red chalk on paper

13.3 × 16.8 cm (5¼ × 6⅝ in.)

Rijksmuseum, Amsterdam, purchased with the support of the Vereniging Rembrandt,
with additional funding from the Prins Bernhard Fonds, the Rijksmuseum-Stichting
and the Ster Holding BV, RP-T-1989-106

GERRIT BERCKHEYDE

125. *Standing Woman*, [n.d.]

Red chalk on paper

27.1 × 14.4 cm (10¹¹⁄₁₆ × 5¹¹⁄₁₆ in.)

Fondation Custodia, Collection Frits Lugt, Paris,

5112

of the buildings in the painting, but also captures the significant areas of light and dark that help locate the empty lots (cat. 122). Here Berckheyde has directed his full attention to describing the city's architecture, even adding color notations on the sheet, while leaving the scene devoid of human activity. The apparently straightforward connection between this drawing and the painting, however, is not as simple as it first seems to be. A number of houses depicted in the drawing had not yet been built when the painting was made around 1672. Two of them flanking the Spiegelgracht (the second open area from the left) were not built until the late 1680s. The question then arises whether this drawing is indeed the preliminary drawing that he made for the painting around 1672, or a revised drawing, based on the first, which he made to record changes in the site's topography. A date from the 1680s for this drawing seems appropriate when one considers the style of dress of the staffage figures in a comparable drawing Berckheyde made of the Herengracht as seen from the Leidsestraat.[5] Such an explanation is in accord with Berckheyde's commitment to topographical accuracy, as evident in the revisions he made to his drawing of the Town Hall from the Nieuwezijds Voorburgwal (see cat. 119). In this respect his approach differs markedly from that of the two other major Dutch architectural painters: Pieter Jansz Saenredam and Jan van der Heyden, both of whom freely altered the buildings and sites they depicted for compositional and thematic purposes.

Berckheyde generally enlivened his city views by including an array of human activities within his scenes. He had a keen sense of how to portray figures so that they would give a context for the buildings and public spaces surrounding them. As with many artists, Berckheyde drew upon a repertoire of large-scale black or red chalk drawings that he made in his studio when painting these figures. His style is extremely close to that of his slightly older Haarlem colleague Cornelis Bega, and it is likely that these two artists drew together from models in the early 1660s, after Berckheyde joined the guild and before Bega's premature death in 1664. Indeed, the attributions of their figure drawings have been a source of confusion over the years, and they are still being assessed. At this point in time, only a handful of his figure drawings are known.

Fortunately, Berckheyde signed a few of his figure drawings, such as a red chalk depiction of a seated man drinking from a round cup (cat. 124), where firm strokes create contours of the man's form and nuanced diagonal parallel hatchings model his body. Broader parallel hatchings around the figure suggest a spatial context for his form. Exactly the same qualities are evident in a black chalk study of a young boy holding a basket and wearing an oversized hat in the Rijksmuseum (cat. 123) and in a study of a standing woman in the Lugt Collection (cat. 125).

Aside from such stylistic comparisons, the artist's use of a figure study in one of his paintings is another means of determining attribution. The boy in the black chalk drawing shown here, for example, appears in several of the artist's paintings, sometimes facing right and sometimes facing left, as is the case in his imposing depiction of Cologne, which he probably executed in the 1670s (fig. 3). The reversed position of the boy indicates that Berckheyde based his figure on a counterproof of the original drawing, an approach that many artists used to expand upon the compositional possibilities in painting. Berckheyde also used the red chalk drawing of the seated man seen here in composing the group of figures who are situated along the Rhine, outside the city walls. [AKW]

5. See The Hague/Washington 2008, 89, fig. 10.3.

PIETER CORNELISZ VAN SLINGELANDT

1640–1691

From the seventeenth century on, Pieter Cornelisz van Slingelandt was thought of as possibly the best pupil trained by Gerard Dou after Frans van Mieris, who was five years his senior.[1] Arnold Houbraken in 1718 noted that the artist 'not only followed his master Gerard Dou in his choice of similar subjects, he also equaled him in his attention to detail.'[2]

Van Slingelandt follows a rich iconographic tradition in presenting a peaceful interior, where a young woman sits, sewing beside a cradle (cat. 127). Dutch painters of the Golden Age were particularly fond of this setting, which allowed them to depict many of the domestic duties in which women engaged. Those who painted scenes of this type included Jan Miense Molenaer in Haarlem, Pieter de Hooch in Delft, Samuel van Hoogstraten and, more notably, Nicolaes Maes—the latter two of whom were Rembrandt's pupils.[3] Above all, in Leiden, Gerard Dou and subsequently his many followers produced the majority of such interiors. Dou's famous *Young Mother* (Mauritshuis)—part of the 'Dutch Gift' from the United Provinces to Charles II of England—certainly played an important role in the popularity of the iconography that was centered on the cradle.[4] In the many works with this theme, nearly all of the bassinets are of a 'Moses' design and look like the one in Van Slingelandt's painting: a woven wicker holder that rests on two rockers and has a blue striped blanket covering the little bed. Most of these cradles have an exterior handle at the foot—missing here—used for moving them around easily and also for rocking the child.

The Fondation Custodia's *Study of a Cradle* (cat. 126) has long been regarded as preparation for the Munich painting,[5] but this suggestion requires qualification. Apart from painters in the Van Mieris family, there is little information about the way the Leiden *fijnschilders* (fine painters) used—or did not use—drawings to prepare their precious paintings.[6] The same is true of Van Slingelandt's working methods. It is known that he was a fine draftsman, given the abundance of his portraits in pen and brush on vellum, usually only in black ink, although some occasionally included watercolor.[7] These drawings were highly finished commissioned works, however, and certainly not preparatory sketches for painting.

1. Peter Hecht in Amsterdam 1989a, 218.
2. Houbraken 1718–1721, III, 161; 'Deze volgde zyn Leermeester Ger. Dou niet alleen omtrent gelyke verkiezingen, maar evenaarde hem ook in netheid.'
3. Regarding Pieter de Hooch, see London/ Hartford 1998, nos. 28, 54, 66, 74, 75, 77, 100, 103, 104, 115, 116, 128, 135; regarding Rembrandt's pupils, see, for example, Sumowski 1979, III, nos. 1334–1336, 1346, 1348; and Robinson 1996, nos. A-8, A-10, A-11, A-32.
4. See Aono 2015, 132, no. 44. Gerard Dou may have taken this iconography from some of his fellow artists, notably from Adriaen van Gaesbeeck, to whom Fred G. Meijer

henceforth attributes the painting given to Van Slingelandt in Leiden 1988 (no. 66). See 'Adriaen van Gaesbeeck,' in RKD Netherlands Institute for Art History: https://rkd.nl/explore/images/1381 (last modified August 15, 2015). The author of the entry already commented that Dou started to paint interiors with a cradle only from the end of the 1650s, whereas Maes and De Hoogh appear to have used this theme from 1650 on. See Leiden 1988, no. 66, n. 10.
5. See Rotterdam/Paris/Brussels 1977, no. 124, and the entry in the catalog, sale London, Christie's, July 10, 2014, lot 68, which records the painting as

having disappeared during World War II.
6. On this point, see Ilona van Tuinen's entry on Frans van Mieris in this catalog (cat. 114), particularly n. 3.
7. Regarding drawings only in ink, see, for example, the pairs of portraits in the Stichting P. & N. de Boer's collection (published in Paris 2014, nos. 98a, 98b) and in the Rijksmuseum in Amsterdam (*Portrait of a Woman* and *Portrait of a Man*, nos. RP-T-1903-A-4763/4). For those that include watercolor, see the *Portrait Presumed to Be Johanna de la Court (1622–1678)* in Fock and Ekkart 1981, 197, no. 12, fig. 11.

Works of another kind are also often attributed to him. These are full compositions in black chalk, with some red and white chalk highlights, and sometimes with ink wash, on blue paper.[8] The technical consistency of these drawings, the similarity of the figures' physiognomies, and the general themes to those in Van Slingelandt's painted works justify attribution to him. From the eighteenth century onward, moreover, his name is often associated with these works.[9] The purpose of these drawings, however, is not yet clear. They could have served as preparatory sheets for compositions, or as *ricordi* of the artist's paintings—like those by Salomon and Jan de Bray (see cats. 47, 48, 49). They might also have been intended as finished drawings produced for the art market.

Study of a Cradle is quite different because it is a study, clearly from life, of an object that is one of the key elements of a painted composition. Many differences are apparent between the little bed in the drawing and that in the painting: the angle of the rockers in relation to the bassinet, the detail of the woven wicker, and the arrangement of bedclothes. Given the mimetic precision that the fine painters sought to achieve in their paintings,[10] it is possible that Van Slingelandt may have needed a very detailed sketch for his painting, and may therefore have used another drawing—probably also in chalk and on blue paper—to show the exact same crib. This method, at least, was the way that Frans van Mieris worked with his studies of details.[11]

Fig. 1. Pieter Cornelisz van Slingelandt, *Study of a Young Woman Sewing*, black chalk, red chalk, and white chalk highlights on blue-green paper. Hessisches Landesmuseum, Darmstadt, AE 811

A second drawing attributed to Van Slingelandt, *Study of a Young Woman Sewing* in Darmstadt (fig. 1), has many points in common with the Munich painting. However, some details, such as the woman's physiognomy, are quite unlike that in the painted version, suggesting that it was more likely a different but closely related sketch that the painter used to depict the woman in the Munich painting. [CT]

8. Two of these sheets are in Frankfurt's Graphische Sammlung im Städelschen Kunstinstitut: *Boy Writing by Candlelight* and *Young Woman Sitting by the Fire*, inv. nos. 933, 934.
9. The sheet put up for sale in Amsterdam in 1980 already had this attribution when it was part of the collection of Cornelis Ploos van Amstel (1726–1798) (Sotheby's, November 18, 1980, no. 84). Another such attributed sheet, which had been owned by Johann van der Marck (1707–1772), was sold in 1999 (Amsterdam sale, Sotheby's, November 9, 1999, no. 22).
10. See Sluijter 1988, 19–23.
11. See Frans van Mieris entry, cat. 114.

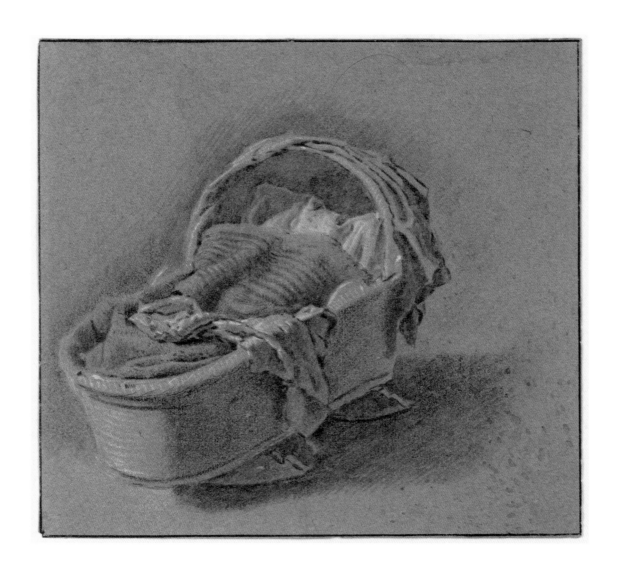

PIETER CORNELISZ VAN SLINGELANDT

126. *Study of a Cradle*

Black and white chalk on blue paper

18.3 × 19.1 cm (7³⁄₁₆ × 7½ in.)

Fondation Custodia, Collection Frits Lugt, Paris,

2015-T.1

PIETER CORNELISZ VAN SLINGELANDT

127. *Interior with a Woman by a Cradle*, c. 1670

Oil on panel

45.6 × 38.6 cm (17¹⁵⁄₁₆ × 15³⁄₁₆ in.)

Bayerische Staatsgemäldesammlungen,

Alte Pinakothek, Munich, 1064

BALTHASAR VAN DER AST
(1593/94–1657)

CAT. 38
Study of a Tulip (Admirael Pottebacker) and a Fly, 1620–1630
Gouache, watercolor, and tempera on paper
31.3 × 20.2 cm (12⁵⁄₁₆ × 7¹⁵⁄₁₆ in.)
Signature: '.BA.' (brown ink)
Inscriptions: '162' (brownish gray ink),
'Admirael Pottebacker' (brown ink)
Fondation Custodia, Collection Frits Lugt, Paris, 6534/42
SELECTED BIBLIOGRAPHY:
Michiel C. Plomp in New York/London 2001, 445–447,
under nos. 96–98

CAT. 39
Flower Still Life, c. 1630
Oil on panel
37.2 × 24.5 cm (14⁵⁄₈ × 9⁵⁄₈ in.)
Signature: 'B. vander.ast.'
Rose-Marie and Eijk van Otterloo Collection
EXHIBITIONS:
The Hague 2010, 57, 59, 95 (ill.), 140, no. 2
Salem/San Francisco/Houston 2011, 60–63, no. 3 (ill.)

CAT. 40
Two Shells, 1620–1630
Gouache, watercolor, and tempera on paper
31.4 × 20.2 cm (12³⁄₈ × 7¹⁵⁄₁₆ in.)
Signature, lower right: '.BA.' (black ink)
Inscriptions: '189,' 'Swart Lobhoren,' 'En Castaenije Bont'
(brown ink)
Fondation Custodia, Collection Frits Lugt, Paris, 6534/49
EXHIBITION:
Paris 1984, 51, no. 55 (ill., as Bartholomeus Assteyn)
SELECTED BIBLIOGRAPHY:
Michiel C. Plomp in New York/London 2001, 445–447,
under nos. 96–98

HENDRICK AVERCAMP
(1585–1634)

CAT. 27
A Standing Girl with Her Hands under Her Apron, c. 1620
Black and red chalk on paper
26 × 13.2 cm (10¼ × 5¹³⁄₁₆ in.)
The Royal Collection / HM Queen Elizabeth II, 906506
EXHIBITION:
Amsterdam/Washington 2009, fig. 131

CAT. 28
An Elegantly Dressed Youth Skating, c. 1620
Pen and brown ink over graphite, shaded with graphite on paper
17.1 × 11.5 cm (6¾ × 4½ in.)
The Royal Collection / HM Queen Elizabeth II, 906477

CAT. 29
A Scene on the Ice, c. 1625
Oil on panel
39.2 × 77 cm (15⁷⁄₁₆ × 30⁵⁄₁₆ in.)
National Gallery of Art, Washington, Ailsa Mellon Bruce Fund,
1967.3.1

CAT. 30
A View of Kampen from outside the Walls, c. 1620
Pen and brown ink with watercolor over graphite on paper
12.2 × 31 cm (4¹³⁄₁₆ × 12³⁄₁₆ in.)
The Royal Collection / HM Queen Elizabeth II, 906507
EXHIBITION:
Amsterdam/Washington 2009, 116, fig. 143

CAT. 31
Winter Scene outside the Walls of Kampen, c. 1613–1615
Oil on panel
44.5 × 72.5 cm (17½ × 28⁹⁄₁₆ in.)
Private Collection, The Netherlands
EXHIBITION:
Amsterdam/Washington 2009, figs. 41, 49

JACOB ANDRIAENSZ BACKER
(1608–1651)

CAT. 70
Seated Female Nude (Study for Venus), c. 1650
Black and white chalk on blue laid paper, double framing
line in brown ink on paper
32.3 × 23.2 cm (12¹¹⁄₁₆ × 9⅛ in.)
The Maida and George Abrams Collection, Fogg Art Museum,
Harvard University, Cambridge, Massachusetts, Gift of George
S. Abrams in appreciation of William Robinson's services
as Curator of Drawings, 1988–2013, 2013.170
EXHIBITIONS:
London/Birmingham/Leeds 1962, 18, no. 80, pl. 13
Amsterdam/Aachen 2008, 71–72, 168, under no. 37, 195,
under no. 54, 198–199, no. 55
Greenwich/Houston 2011, 72–73, no. 18
SELECTED BIBLIOGRAPHY:
Sumowski 1979, I, 38–39, no. 12, 122, under no. 54x
Sumowski 1983, I, 195, under no. 14
London/Cambridge/Paris 2002, 124, under no. 49, fig. 1

Robinson 2010, 57–58
Schatborn 2010a, I, 104, under no. 32
Robinson and Anderson 2016, no. 2

CAT. 71
Seated Female Nude, 1648
Black and white chalk on blue paper
28.8 × 22.8 cm (11 5/16 × 9 in.)
Maida and George Abrams Collection, Boston
EXHIBITIONS:
London/Birmingham/Leeds 1962, 18, no. 81
Amsterdam/Washington 1981, 90–91, fig. 4, 129, no. 5
Amsterdam/Vienna/New York/Cambridge 1991, 118–119, no. 50
London/Paris/Cambridge 2002, 124–25, no. 49
Amsterdam/Aachen 2008, 71–72, fig. 81, 194–195, no. 54A
Greenwich/Houston 2011, 70–71, no. 17
SELECTED BIBLIOGRAPHY:
Sumowski 1979, I, 122–123, no. 54x
Edinburgh/London 2001, 52–53, fig. 57

LUDOLF BACKHUYSEN (1630–1708)

CAT. 102
View of the Montelbaenstoren, c. 1685
Pen and brown ink with gray wash on paper
17 × 26.6 cm (6 11/16 × 10 1/2 in.)
Stadsarchief Amsterdam, Afbeeldingsbestand 010055000601
SELECTED BIBLIOGRAPHY:
Beer 2002, 114, fig. 123

CORNELIS BEGA (1631/32–1664)

CAT. 103
Peasant Woman, Turned Three-Quarters to the Left, Holding a Glass,
[n.d.]
Red chalk on paper
14.6 × 24.7 cm (5 3/4 × 9 3/4 in.)
The Samuel Courtauld Trust, The Courtauld Gallery, London,
D.1952.RW.2174

CAT. 104
The Alchemist, c. 1663
Black chalk with white heightening on blue paper
17.3 × 14.2 cm (6 13/16 × 5 9/16 in.)
Museum Mayer van den Bergh, Antwerp, MMB.1049
EXHIBITION:
Aachen/Berlin 2012, no. 68, repro.

CAT. 105
The Alchemist, 1663
Oil on canvas mounted on panel
35 × 28.6 cm (13 3/4 × 11 1/4 in.)
National Gallery of Art, Washington, From the Collection
of Ethel and Martin Wunsch, 2013.34.1
EXHIBITION:
Aachen/Berlin 2012, no. 69, repro.
SELECTED BIBLIOGRAPHY:
Scott 1984, 335, no. 147
Peter Sutton in The Hague/San Francisco 1990, 113
Franits 2004, 282, no. 36

NICOLAES PIETERSZ BERCHEM (1620–1683)

CAT. 4
Four Sheep and a Cow, c. 1652
Red chalk on laid paper with counterproof
13 × 19.5 cm (5 1/8 × 7 11/16 in.)
National Gallery of Art, Ailsa Mellon Bruce Fund, 2002.141.1

GERRIT BERCKHEYDE (1638–1698)

CAT. 118
The Grote or St. Bavokerk in Haarlem, 1666
Oil on panel
60.3 × 84.5 cm (23 3/4 × 33 1/4 in.)
Otto Naumann Ltd., New York
EXHIBITION:
The Hague/Washington 2008, cat. 3

CAT. 119
View of the Nieuwezijds Voorburgwal in Amsterdam, [n.d.]
Graphite, pen, and brown ink on paper
16.9 × 27.6 cm (6 5/8 × 10 7/8 in.)
Koninklijk Oudheidkundig Genootschap, Amsterdam,
KOG-AA-2-13-261

CAT. 120
*The Nieuwezijds Voorburgwal with the Flower and Tree Market
in Amsterdam*, c. 1675
Oil on wood
36.8 × 47.6 cm (14 1/2 × 18 3/4 in.)
Los Angeles County Museum of Art, Gift of Mr. and Mrs. Edward
William Carter, M.2009.106.1

EXHIBITION:

The Hague/Washington 2008, cat. 11

SELECTED BIBLIOGRAPHY:

J.P. Walsh and C.P. Schneider in Los Angeles/Boston/New York
1981, no. 2

Gaskell 1989, 294

Peeters 1990, 82–89

Amsterdam 1997b, 46–47, 97–98

CAT. 121

The Nieuwezijds Voorburgwal with the Flower Market in Amsterdam,
c. 1668–1670
Oil on canvas
45 × 61 cm (17¹¹⁄₁₆ × 24 in.)
Amsterdam Museum, SA7455

CAT. 122

View on the Herengracht from the Vijzelstraat in Amsterdam,
c. 1671–1672
Graphite, gray wash on paper
20.8 × 39.5 cm (8³⁄₁₆ × 15⁹⁄₁₆ in.)
Stadsarchief Amsterdam, Afbeeldingsbestand 010001000009

CAT. 123

Walking Boy with a Basket, 1670s
Black chalk on paper
19 × 10.9 cm (7½ × 4⁵⁄₁₆ in.)
Rijksmuseum, Amsterdam, purchased with the support
of the Vereniging Rembrandt, RP-T-1883-A-264

SELECTED BIBLIOGRAPHY:

Amsterdam 1973, cat. 8

Amsterdam/Washington 1981, 108, cat. 15

CAT. 124

Seated Man, Drinking, [n.d.]
Red chalk on paper
13.3 × 16.8 cm (5¼ × 6⅝ in.)
Rijksmuseum, Amsterdam, purchased with the support
of the Vereniging Rembrandt, with additional funding
from the Prins Bernhard Fonds, the Rijksmuseum-Stichting
and the Ster Holding BV, RP-T-1989-106

SELECTED BIBLIOGRAPHY:

Amsterdam 1989c, 70, no. 25

CAT. 125

Standing Woman, [n.d.]
Red chalk on paper
27.1 × 14.4 cm (10¹¹⁄₁₆ × 5¹¹⁄₁₆ in.)
Fondation Custodia, Collection Frits Lugt, Paris, 5112

ABRAHAM BLOEMAERT (1566–1651)

CAT. 16

Landscape with Dilapidated Buildings and Figures, 1629
Oil on canvas
91.5 × 135.5 cm (36 × 53⅜ in.).
Signed and dated at bottom left: 'A.Bloemaert.fe. 1629'
Hamburger Kunsthalle, Hamburg, 732

EXHIBITION:

Hamburg 1952, no. 21

SELECTED BIBLIOGRAPHY:

Delbanco 1928, 76, no. 34

Amsterdam 1991a, 114–115, fig. 80

Roethlisberger and Bok 1993, 310–311, no. 482, fig. 664

CAT. 17

Ruins of a Farmhouse, c. 1571–1629
Black chalk, brushed in red and light green, on paper
15.2 × 20.8 cm (6 × 8³⁄₁₆ in.)
Rijksmuseum, Amsterdam, purchased with the support
of the Vereniging Rembrandt, RP-T-1886-A-1159

SELECTED BIBLIOGRAPHY:

Boon 1978, I, 26, no. 70, II, 26 (ill.)

Kettering 1988, II, 72, no. 5

Bolten 2007, I, 426–427, no. 1444, II, 434 (ill.)

Bok 2011, 31–32, fig. 42

CAT. 18

Two Seated Boys with Studies for Hands and Feet, c. 1620–1629
Pen and brown ink, red chalk, heightened with white gouache
on beige paper
14 × 18 cm (5½ × 7¹⁄₁₆ in.)
Musée du Louvre, Paris (on long-term loan to Musée Bonnat-
Helleu, Bayonne), RF 50861

SELECTED BIBLIOGRAPHY:

Bolten 2007, I, 314–315, no. 957, II. 359 (ill.)

CAT. 19

Study of Trees (Studies of Two Pollard Willows), [n.d.]
Pen and brown ink, watercolor, traces of black chalk, on paper
21 × 31 cm (8¼ × 12³⁄₁₆ in.)
Metropolitan Museum of Art, New York, Rogers Fund, 1970,
1970.242.3

EXHIBITIONS:

New York 1973, no. 29

Poughkeepsie 1976, 26, no. 4 (ill.)

Cambridge/Montreal 1988, 70, no. 11 (ill.)

Utrecht/Schwerin 2011, 164–165, under no. 65

SELECTED BIBLIOGRAPHY:
Mules 1985, 28–29 (ill.)
Bolten 2007, I, 439, no. 1492, II, 446 (ill.)
Bok 2011, 31–32, fig. 43

CAT. 20
Studies of Arms, Legs, and Heads, [n.d.]
Red and white chalk, some pen in brown ink, on paper
25.7 × 16.7 cm (10⅛ × 6⁹⁄₁₆ in.)
Rijksmuseum, Amsterdam, RP-T-1886-A-686 (verso)

CAT. 21
Head of an Old Man Turned and Looking to Right, 1625–1635
Black chalk, with gray wash, white body color, heightened
with white (partly oxidized), on gray prepared paper
41.5 × 29.7 cm (16⁵⁄₁₆ × 11¹¹⁄₁₆ in.)
The British Museum, London, PD A, 17.65
SELECTED BIBLIOGRAPHY:
Hind and Popham 1915–1932, V, 92, no. 9
Bolten 2007, I, 277, no. 816, II, 326 (ill.)

CAT. 22
Head of an Old Man, 1630–1640
Oil on panel
48.3 × 36.3 cm (19 × 14⁵⁄₁₆ in.)
National Gallery of Art, Washington, Joseph F. McCrindle
Collection, 2010.93.41
SELECTED BIBLIOGRAPHY:
Roethlisberger and Bok 1993, I, 333, no. 528, II, fig. 712

AMBROSIUS BOSSCHAERT
(1573–1621)

CAT. 12
Bouquet of Flowers in a Glass Vase, 1621
oil on copper
31.6 × 21.6 cm (12⁷⁄₁₆ × 8½ in.)
National Gallery of Art, Washington, Patrons' Permanent Fund
and New Century Fund, 1996.35.1
Inscriptions: lower right in monogram: '.AB.1621'; across bottom
in blue field: 'C'est l'Angelicq[ue] main du gra[n]d Peinctre de
Flore/AMBROISE, renommé jusqu' au Rivage Moré.' (This is the
angelic hand of the great painter of Flora, Ambrosius, renowned
even to the banks of the Moré); verso: 'Jonckheere . . .'
EXHIBITION:
Washington 1999, no. 11, fig. 32
SELECTED BIBLIOGRAPHY:
Washington 1999, 42–43, 83, no. 11, fig. 32
Washington 2002, 81–82, fig. 4

JAN DE BRAY (c. 1627–1697)

CAT. 96
Double Portrait of Abraham Casteleyn and Margarieta van Bancken,
1663
Pen and brown ink, gray wash, on paper
10.2 × 20.3 cm (4 × 8 in.)
Fondation Custodia, Collection Frits Lugt, Paris, 5124
EXHIBITION:
Haarlem 1986, 181
SELECTED BIBLIOGRAPHY:
Haarlem/London 2008, 88, fig. 27a

SALOMON DE BRAY (1597–1664)

CAT. 47
The Twins Clara and Albert de Bray, August 12, 1646
Red chalk, over faint indications in black chalk, on paper
16 × 15.2 cm (6⁵⁄₁₆ × 6 in.)
The Morgan Library & Museum, New York, Purchased in 1909,
acc. no. III, 176
Dated and inscribed at lower right in red chalk: '1646 8/12 |
Neef Simon de Braÿ Symons[zoon] | 2 lingen {Clara | Alberty.'
EXHIBITIONS:
Washington/Denver/Fort Worth 1977, no. 25
Paris/Antwerp/London/New York 1979, no. 61
New York 1996 (no catalog)
SELECTED BIBLIOGRAPHY:
Moltke 1938, no. Z 104
Felice Stampfle in Shoaf Turner 2006, no. 44
Ariane van Suchtelen in London/The Hague 2007, under no. 7,
fig. 7a
Haarlem/London 2008, under no. 6, fig. 6a.

CAT. 48
The Twins Clara and Albert de Bray, 1646 or after
Oil on canvas
82.6 × 64.8 cm (32½ × 25½ in.)
Private Collection, on loan to the National Gallery of Scotland,
Edinburgh, NGL 002.95
EXHIBITIONS:
Edinburgh 1992, no. 10
Amsterdam 2000, 351, no. 73
London/The Hague 2007, no. 7
Haarlem/London 2008, no. 6.
SELECTED BIBLIOGRAPHY:
Moltke 1938, nos. 95, 95a
Franklin W. Robinson in Washington/Denver/Fort Worth 1977,
under no. 25

Felice Stampfle in Paris/Antwerp/London/New York 1979,
under no. 61
Felice Stampfle in Shoaf Turner 2006, under no. 44.

BARTHOLOMEUS BREENBERGH
(1598–1657)

CAT. 56
Reclining Male Nude (Study for Venus Mourning the Death of Adonis),
1646
Oiled charcoal and white chalk on blue laid paper
24.8 × 35.7 cm (9¾ × 14¹⁄₁₆ in.)
Inscriptions: (by later hands) lower left, brown ink, 'bordone';
lower left, brown ink, '39'
Harvard Art Museums/Fogg Museum, Cambridge, Anonymous
fund in honor of John and Anne Straus, and through the generosity
of the Fifth Floor Foundation, Howard and Sally Lepow, Leena
and Sheldon Peck, Maida and George Abrams and Kathryn
and William W. Robinson, 1996.303
EXHIBITION:
Cambridge 1998, 31, no. 7
SELECTED BIBLIOGRAPHY:
Haboldt 1989, 21
Amsterdam/Aachen 2008, 71, n. 206, 80–81, fig. 95
Stefes 2011, I, 82, n. 13
Haboldt 2012, 10, 199
Robinson and Anderson 2016, 64–66, no. 13

CAT. 57
Venus Mourning the Death of Adonis, 1646
Oil on panel
38.7 × 49.5 cm (15¼ × 19½ in.)
Signed and dated: 'BB f. 1646'
Harvard Art Museum/Fogg Museum, Cambridge, Kate, Maurice
R., and Melvin R. Seiden Special Purchase Fund, Janine Luke,
The Louis Agassiz Shaw Bequest, and William and Ami Danoff
in honor of Seymour Slive, 1997.5
SELECTED BIBLIOGRAPHY:
Roethlisberger 1981, 86, no. 219

LEENDERT VAN DER COOGHEN
(1632–1681)

CAT. 6
Study of a Nude Man, Seated Three-Quarters Length on a Cushion,
[n.d.]
Black chalk on paper
39.1 × 26 cm (15⅜ × 10¼ in.)

[279]

Dated and inscribed at lower right, in black chalk: '1660 12/14 |
het eerste vande winter | 14'
Fondation Custodia, Collection Frits Lugt, Paris, 6634
SELECTED BIBLIOGRAPHY:
Amsterdam/Washington 1981, 131 and 134, under cat. no. 34
Coenen 2005, 36–38, fig. 41, cat. no. A53

GONZALES COQUES
(1614/18–1684) (attributed)

CAT. 9
Portrait of a Man Receiving a Letter from a Boy, c. 1660
Oil on panel
55.9 × 44.2 cm (22 × 17⅜ in.)
The Orsay Collection, London, Paris
EXHIBITION:
New York 2016
SELECTED BIBLIOGRAPHY:
Washington/Detroit 2004, 12–13, fig. 10
Christie's 2012, lot 16

AELBERT CUYP (1620–1691)

CAT. 81
Landscape with Herdsmen, c. 1650–1652
Oil on panel
48 × 82.5 cm (18⅞ × 32½ in.)
National Gallery of Art, Washington, Corcoran Collection
(William A. Clark Collection), 2014.79.707
EXHIBITION:
Washington/London/Amsterdam 2001, 142–143, 195–196, no. 25

CAT. 82
Calcar with Monterberg in the Distance, early 1640s
Black chalk, gray wash, green and ocher yellow watercolor, partly
brushed with gum arabic, on paper
18.5 × 49.5 cm (7⁵⁄₁₆ × 19½ in.)
The Metropolitan Museum of Art, New York, From the Collection
of Rita and Frits Markus, Bequest of Rita Markus, 2005,
2005.330.4
EXHIBITION:
Washington/London/Amsterdam 2001, 244, 284, no. 76

CAT. 83
The Rhine Valley Stretching North toward the Elterberg, c. 1652–1655
Black chalk, gray wash, pencil on paper
14.9 × 23.9 cm (5⅞ × 9⁷⁄₁₆ in.)
Fondation Custodia, Collection Frits Lugt, Paris, 5304

EXHIBITION:

Washington/London/Amsterdam 2001, 261, 288, no. 193

CAT. 84

Three Boys in a Landscape, early 1640s

Black chalk, gray wash on paper

14.7 × 19.1 cm ($5^{13}/_{16}$ × $7^{1}/_2$ in.)

Rijksmuseum, Amsterdam, RP-T-1895-A-3057

EXHIBITION:

Amsterdam/Washington 1981, 120–121, fig. 2, no. 35

CAT. 85

Standing Herdsman with Staff, c. 1642–1646

Black chalk, gray wash, on two pieces of paper

19.1 × 9.6 cm ($7^{1}/_2$ × $3^{3}/_4$ in.)

Private Collection

EXHIBITION:

Amsterdam/Washington 1981, 120–121, fig. 3

CAT. 86

A Cow Lying Down, c. 1650

Black chalk, gray wash, on paper

7.6 × 13.3 cm (3 × $5^{1}/_4$ in.)

Private Collection

EXHIBITION:

Washington/London/Amsterdam 2001, 271, 290, no. 103

CAT. 87

Studies of a Cow and a Horse, c. 1650

Black chalk, brush in gray wash, traces of pencil on paper

8.4 × 12.5 cm ($3^{5}/_{16}$ × $4^{15}/_{16}$ in.)

Fondation Custodia, Collection Frits Lugt, Paris, 458

EXHIBITION:

Washington/London/Amsterdam 2001, 268, 289, no. 100

KAREL DUJARDIN (1626–1678)

CAT. 88

Walking Man Seen from Behind, c. 1655

Red chalk on paper

23.6 × 13.4 cm ($9^{5}/_{16}$ × $5^{1}/_4$ in.)

Statens Museum for Kunst, Copenhagen, KKS9352

SELECTED BIBLIOGRAPHY:

Amsterdam/Washington 1981, under no. 38

Amsterdam/Vienna/New York/Cambridge 1991, under no. 73, fig. 1

Gruijs 2003, no. II-7

Kilian 2005, under B 10, fig. 63

Brussels/Amsterdam/Aachen 2007, under no. 54; fig. 1

Grenoble 2014, under no. 85

GERBRAND VAN DEN EECKHOUT
(1621–1674)

CAT. 89

David Promises Bathsheba to Designate Solomon as His Successor (David's Promise to Bathsheba), 1642–1643

Brown ink and brown wash, over red and black chalk on paper

18.8 × 27 cm ($7^{1}/_4$ × $10^{1}/_2$ in.)

Inscriptions: verso, upper left, graphite, 'David en Abiraz/dich: 1 cap. 1,2,3:4'; verso, lower left, graphite, 'Eckout'

The Metropolitan Museum of Art, New York, Gift of Robert Lehman 1941, 41.187.4

EXHIBITION:

Chicago/Minneapolis/Detroit 1969, 188, no. 166

SELECTED BIBLIOGRAPHY:

Sumowski 1979, III, 1320–22, no. 605

Sumowski 1983, II, 728, under no. 403

Plomp 2006, 38, fig. 46

Stefes 2011, 204, under no. 285

CAT. 90

Seated Oriental, before 1646

Black and white chalk on gray paper

38.9 × 26.2 cm ($15^{5}/_{16}$ × $10^{5}/_{16}$ in.)

Inscriptions: verso, center, graphite, 'G. Flinck,' lower left, 'by Georg Ernst Harzen,' graphite, '9.8 /14.5,' lower left, graphite, 'No 23.1,' lower left, graphite, 'fm-ooc-'

Hamburger Kunsthalle, Kupferstichkabinett, Hamburg, 21944

EXHIBITIONS:

Hamburg 1994, 144, no. 39

Bremen/Hamburg 2000, 50–51, no. 14

SELECTED BIBLIOGRAPHY:

Henkel 1943, 76, under no. 8

Sumowski 1962, 17

Moltke 1965, 265, no. 189

Sumowski 1979, III, 1334, no. 612

Sumowski 1983, II, 728, under no. 403

Stefes 2011, I, 204, no. 285

CAT. 91

Jacob's Dream, [n.d.]

Red chalk on paper

26.2 × 20 cm ($10^{1}/_4$ × 8 in.)

Inscribed, upper left, graphite, '54'

Albertina, Vienna, 9549

SELECTED BIBLIOGRAPHY:

Sumowski 1979, III, 1348, no. 619

Sumowski 1983, II, 743, under no. 481

DeWitt 2008, 123, under no. 70, n. 6

CAT. 92
Jacob's Dream, 1672
Black chalk on paper
22.4 × 19.6 cm (8¾ × 7¾ in.)
Staatliches Museum Schwerin, HZ 4486
EXHIBITION:
Berlin 1992, 54–55, no. 28, repro.

SELECTED BIBLIOGRAPHY:
Sumowski 1979, III, 1346–1347, no. 618
Sumowski 1983, II, 742, under no. 481
Kingston 1984, 30, under no. 20
DeWitt 2008, 123, under no. 70, fig. 70b

GOVERT FLINCK (1615–1660)

CAT. 80
Standing Man beside a Table, 1644–before 1646
Black chalk, heightened with white, on blue paper
39.2 × 24 cm (15⁷⁄₁₆ × 9⁷⁄₁₆ in.)
Rijksmuseum, Amsterdam, purchased with the support
of the Vereniging Rembrandt, RP-T-1975-84
EXHIBITIONS:
Chicago/Minneapolis/Detroit 1969, 191, no. 174
Amsterdam/Washington 1981, 88–89, fig. 1, 136, no. 50
SELECTED BIBLIOGRAPHY:
Moltke 1965, 50, 202, no. D 153, pl. 63
Sumowski 1979, IV, 1208–1209, no. 873
Sumowski 1983, II, 1041, under no. 716

JACQUES DE GHEYN II (1565–1629)

CAT. 14
*Three Flowers: A Double Carnation, a Tulip, and a Liverwort
or Liverleaf*, 1601
Gouache and tempera on vellum, probably over a sketch
in metalpoint (silverpoint?)
(fol. 6 from an album)
22.8 × 17.6 cm (9 × 6¹⁵⁄₁₆ in.)
Signature: 'IDGheijn . Fe . 1601.'
Inscription: 'N.o 6' (nineteenth century)
Fondation Custodia, Collection Frits Lugt, Paris, 5655-6
EXHIBITION:
Paris 1985, 21, under no. 9 (fol. 6)
SELECTED BIBLIOGRAPHY:
Regteren Altena 1983, I, 70, II, 142, no. 914, III, 201, fig. 177
Boon 1992, I, 136, no. 80, fol. 6, III, pl. 167

CAT. 15
Democritus and Heraclitus, 1602/1603
Black and white chalk on light brown paper
23.7 × 28 cm (9¹⁵⁄₁₆ × 11 in.)
P. & N. de Boer Foundation, Amsterdam, B 509
EXHIBITIONS:
Laren 1966, 16, no. 86, fig. 22
Rotterdam/Washington 1985, 56, no. 38 (ill.)
Paris 2014, 126–127, no. 56 (ill.)
SELECTED BIBLIOGRAPHY:
Regteren Altena 1983, I, 84–85, II, p. 38, no. 136, III, 137,
fig. 264
Ger Luijten in Paris 2014, 126–127 (ill.)

JAN VAN GOYEN (1596–1656)

CAT. 42
The 'Haringpakkerstoren' in Amsterdam, c. 1651
Black chalk, gray wash, on paper
9.9 × 15.7 cm (3⅞ × 6³⁄₁₆ in.)
Fondation Custodia, Collection Frits Lugt, Paris, 2997G
SELECTED BIBLIOGRAPHY:
Beck 1957, 246, 248, fig. 18
Beck 1972–1991, I, 306, no. 847/155

CAT. 43
Sailing Ships, 1653
Black chalk, gray wash, on paper
11.4 × 19.5 cm (4½ × 7¹¹⁄₁₆ in.)
Musées royaux des Beaux-Arts de Belgique, Brussels, 4060/1407
EXHIBITION:
Brussels/Amsterdam/Aachen 2007, no. 35
SELECTED BIBLIOGRAPHY:
Beck 1972–1991, I, 157, no. 462
Vogt in Brussels/Amsterdam/Aachen 2007, 113–114, no. 35

CAT. 44
Ships under a Cloudy Sky, 1655
Oil on panel
32.5 × 32 cm (12¹³⁄₁₆ × 12⅝ in.)
Musée des Beaux-Arts, Rouen, 1811.35
EXHIBITION:
Paris 2009b, no. 17
SELECTED BIBLIOGRAPHY:
Beck 1972–1991, II, 399, no. 886
Vogt in Brussels/Amsterdam/Aachen 2007, 113–114, under no. 35
Bakhuÿs in Paris 2009b, 67–70, no. 17

BAREND GRAAT (1628–1709)

CAT. 97
Seated Man, 1659/1660
Black and white chalk on blue paper (faded to gray), lined
22.9 × 17.9 cm (9 × 7¹⁄₁₆ in.)
Fondation Custodia, Collection Frits Lugt, Paris, 303
EXHIBITION:
Amsterdam/Washington 1981, no. 55
SELECTED BIBLIOGRAPHY:
Schaffran 1957, 47–48, fig. 11
Schatborn in Amsterdam/Washington 1981, 96, 137, no. 55 (ill.)
Trnek 1992, 150 (ill.)
Hut 2015, 198, no. A-T5 (ill.)

JORIS VAN DER HAAGEN
(c. 1615–1660)

CAT. 1
View in the Vicinity of Doorwerth, 1650
Black chalk and gray wash, pen and brown ink, on paper
19.5 × 25.9 cm (7¹¹⁄₁₆ × 10³⁄₁₆ in.)
Inscriptions: top center, inscribed, signed, and dated:
'dit gesicht is de doorewaertsen berg wt de weijen te syen
JVHagen 1650'
Rijksmuseum, Amsterdam, purchased with the support
of the Vereniging Rembrandt, RP-T-1884-A-342
EXHIBITION:
Amsterdam 1987, 72–73
SELECTED BIBLIOGRAPHY:
Haagen 1932, 33
Eeghen 2015, no. 91

DIRCK HALS (1591–1656)

CAT. 34
Sitting Pipe Smoker, 1622–1627
Brush and brown ink with oil containing paint, heightened
with white, over a sketch in black chalk on paper
27.7 × 17.8 cm (10⅞ × 7 in.)
Rijksmuseum, Amsterdam, RP-T-1965-180
EXHIBITIONS:
Düsseldorf 1964, cat. 54, fig. 18 (as Willem Cornelisz Duyster)
New York/Boston/Chicago 1972, no. 45
Amsterdam 1973, no. 45
Amsterdam/Washington 1981, no. 56

Vancouver 2009 (without numbers), 216–217
Paris 2009a, no. 114
SELECTED BIBLIOGRAPHY:
Schatborn 1973, 110–112, 114–115, no. 1, fig. 9
Schapelhouman and Schatborn 1998, no. 207
Nehlsen-Marten 2003, 225, 319, no. 396 (with wrong location),
415, fig. 250
Kolfin 2005, 146–147, fig. 117
Marijn Schapelhouman in Paris 2009a, 280

CAT. 35
Seated Man, Leaning Backwards, [n.d.]
Brush in brown and gray oil containing paint on paper
22.6 × 19.4 cm (8⅞ × 7⅝ in.)
Fondation Custodia, Collection Frits Lugt, Paris, 1796
EXHIBITIONS:
Paris 1965, no. 75
New York/Paris 1977, no. 57
Amsterdam/Washington 1981, no. 57
SELECTED BIBLIOGRAPHY:
Schatborn 1973, 109, 116, no. 9, fig. 7
Nehlsen-Marten 2003, 225, 319, no. 396 (with wrong title),
415, fig. 249

JAN VAN DER HEYDEN (1637–1712)

CAT. 11
View Down a Dutch Canal, c. 1670
Oil on panel
32.5 × 39 cm (12¹³⁄₁₆ × 15⅜ in.)
Inscription: lower right on the boat, in ligature, 'IVH'
National Gallery of Art, Washington, Gift of George M. and Linda
H. Kaufman, 2012.73.2
EXHIBITIONS:
The Hague/San Francisco 1990, no. 31
Greenwich/Amsterdam 2006, no. 16
The Hague/Washington 2008, no. 25
SELECTED BIBLIOGRAPHY:
Wagner 1971, 83, 87–88, no. 91
The Hague/San Francisco 1990, 280–284, no. 31

GERARD VAN HONTHORST (1592–1656)

CAT. 33
Merry Company, 1621/1622
Pen and black-brown ink, white chalk highlights,
over a preliminary sketch in black chalk, on paper
18.3 × 27.1 cm (7³⁄₁₆ × 10¹¹⁄₁₆ in.)

Inscription: 'N.06' (nineteenth century)

Albertina, Vienna, 8437

EXHIBITION:

Utrecht/Antwerp 1952 (section drawings, supplement), 4, no. 10

SELECTED BIBLIOGRAPHY:

Utrecht/Braunschweig 1986, 288, 290, fig. 28

Judson and Ekkart 1999, 9, 220, 346, no. D55, pl. 167

Gert Jan van der Sman, 'I disegni di Gerrit van Honthorst,' in Florence 2015, 111–112, fig. 13

CORNELIS JONSON VAN CEULEN (1593–1661)

CAT. 7

Study of a Woman's Hands, c. 1652

Black chalk, heightened with white on blue paper

23 × 38.8 cm (9¹/₁₆ × 15¼ in.)

Inscription: verso, in pen and brown ink, in the hand of the artist, 'jouvrouw Hinloopen'

Musée de Grenoble, MG D 230

EXHIBITION:

Grenoble 2014, 172–173, no. 81

SELECTED BIBLIOGRAPHY:

Amsterdam 2014a, 86–87, n. 5

JAN VAN KESSEL (1626–1679)

CAT. 3

Sketchbook, 146 pages, 1659–1660

Black chalk and gray or brown wash on paper

(closed): 9.9 × 16 cm (3⅞ × 6⁵/₁₆ in.)

Fondation Custodia, Collection Frits Lugt, Paris, 2006-T.30

SELECTED BIBLIOGRAPHY:

Giltaij 2007, 51–93

Buvelot 2010, 33–34

THOMAS DE KEYSER (1596–1667)

CAT. 45

Company of Allaert Cloeck, 1630

Pen and brown ink, violet wash, over black chalk, squared, on paper

20.4 × 40.9 cm (8¹/₁₆ × 16¹/₁₆ in.)

Albertina, Vienna, 9246

EXHIBITION:

Haarlem 1988, 377–378, no. 182

CAT. 46

Officers and Other Civic Guardsmen of the IIIrd District of Amsterdam, under the Command of Captain Allaert Cloeck and Lieutenant Lucas Jacobsz Rotgans, c. 1630

Pen and deep brown ink, grey brown wash over black chalk, squared, on paper

20.2 × 40.8 cm (8¹/₁₆ × 16¹/₁₆ in.)

Statens Museum for Kunst, Copenhagen, KKSgb7824

PIETER VAN LAER (1599–after 1641)

CAT. 37

Two Studies of a Seated Shepherd, c. 1630–1637(?)

Black and white chalk on blue paper

18.6 × 26.2 cm (7⁵/₁₆ × 10⁵/₁₆ in.)

Inscription: by Jan Pietersz Zomer, below left, with black chalk, 'Bamboots'

Musée des Beaux-Arts et d'Archéologie, Besançon, D 805

EXHIBITIONS:

Besançon 1999, no. 19

Grenoble 2006, no. 55

SELECTED BIBLIOGRAPHY:

Schatborn 1974, 4–5, fig. 3

Amsterdam/Washington 1981, 62–63, fig. 1

Duparc 1993, 264

PIETER LASTMAN (1583–1633)

CAT. 24

Reclining Woman, as Rachel, 1622

Red and some black chalk, heightened with white, on orange prepared paper

22.9 × 20.2 cm (9 × 7¹⁵/₁₆ in.)

The Ashmolean Museum, Oxford, WA1953.114

EXHIBITIONS:

Amsterdam/Washington 1981, 48–49, fig. 3, 138, no. 63

Amsterdam 1991b, 135, no. 30

Hamburg 2006, under no. 27, fig. 1

SELECTED BIBLIOGRAPHY:

Bauch 1960, 107, fig. 70

Sacramento 1974, 20, fig. 14

Sumowski 1975, 177, note 5 a

Royalton-Kisch 1989, 129, fig. 1

Schatborn 2010a, under no. 110

Seifert 2011, 204–207, fig. 222

CAT. 25

Laban Seeking the Idols, 1622

Oil on panel

110 × 152 cm (43⅝16 × 59¹³⁄16 in.)

Signed 'PLastman fecit 1622'

Musée municipal, Boulogne-sur-Mer, 147/13

EXHIBITIONS:

Paris 1970, no. 133

Hamburg 2006, no. 27

SELECTED BIBLIOGRAPHY:

Freise 1911, no. 17, afb. 23

Bauch 1960, 54, fig. 32

Amsterdam 1991b, under no. 30, fig. 30a

Seifert 2011, 204, figs. 223, 209

CAT. 26

David Gives Uriah a Letter for Joab, 1619

Oil on panel

42.8 × 63.3 cm (16⅞ × 24¹⁵⁄16 in.)

Signed and dated in light paint along lower right corner:

PLastman fecit 1619

The Leiden Collection, New York, PL-100

EXHIBITION:

Detroit 1923, no. 35

Washington/Detroit/Amsterdam 1980, no. 22

Greenwich/New York/San Antonio 2008, no. 12

Kyoto/Sendai/Tokyo 2011, no. 26

SELECTED BIBLIOGRAPHY:

Freise 1911, 43, no. 32

Washington/Detroit/Amsterdam 1980, 130–131, no. 22, 184

Buvelot 2004, 182–183, no. 1074

Neumeister and Krempel 2005, I, 374, no. 355

Greenwich/New York/San Antonio 2008, 124–129, no. 12

Yeide 2009, 275, no. A339

JAN LIEVENS (1607–1674)

CAT. 2

Forest Interior with a Draftsman, 1660s

Pen and brown ink and brown wash on paper

24 × 36.2 cm (9⁷⁄16 × 14¼ in.)

Maida and George Abrams Collection, Boston

EXHIBITION:

Washington/Milwaukee/Amsterdam 2008, no. 132

SELECTED BIBLIOGRAPHY:

Schneider and Ekkart 1973, 235, 372, no. Z313

Sumowski 1979, VII, 3732, no. 1675a

Paris/Haarlem 1997, 196, under no. 87

London/Paris/Cambridge 2002, no. 60

NICOLAES MAES (1634–1693)

CAT. 111

The Lacemaker, 1655

Oil on panel

57.1 × 43.8 cm (22½ × 17¼ in.)

Purchased 1954

National Gallery of Canada, Ottawa, 6189

SELECTED BIBLIOGRAPHY:

Sumowski 1979, VIII, 3396, 3998, under nos. 1775, 1776

Amsterdam/Washington 1981, 84, fig. 2

Sumowski 1983, III, 2014, no. 1342

Giltaij 1988, 225, under no. 114

Robinson 1989, 151, 153, fig. 18

Krempel 2000, 282, no. A10, pl. 20

CAT. 112

Interior with Young Woman Making Lace, 1650s

Pen and brown ink, brown wash, on paper

8 × 6.3 cm (3⅛ × 2½ in.)

Staatliche Museen, Berlin, Kupferstichkabinett,

KDZ 16523

SELECTED BIBLIOGRAPHY:

Sumowski 1979, VIII, 3996, no. 1775

Sumowski 1983, III, 2014, under no. 1342

Giltaij 1988, 225, under no. 114

Krempel 2000, 282, under no. A10

CAT. 113

Seated Woman Making Lace, c. 1654–1655

Red chalk on paper

14.1 × 11.9 cm (5⁹⁄16 × 4¹¹⁄16 in.)

Inscriptions: signed or inscribed, lower right, red chalk, 'Maes(?)';

verso, graphite, '11xyz/21'

Museum Boijmans Van Beuningen, Rotterdam,

Bequest F.J.O. Boijmans 1847, MB 199 (PK)

EXHIBITION:

Rotterdam 2005, no. 81

SELECTED BIBLIOGRAPHY:

Sumowski 1979, VIII, 3998, no. 1776

Amsterdam/Washington 1981, 84, fig. 1, 140, under no. 69

Sumowski 1983, III, 2014, under no. 1342

Giltaij 1988, 225, no. 114

Robinson 1989, 151–152, fig. 17

Krempel 2000, 282, under no. A10

FRANS VAN MIERIS THE ELDER
(1635–1681)

CAT. 114
Sleeping Spaniel, c. 1665–1670
Black chalk on paper
7.1 × 9.3 cm (2.8 × 3.7 in.)
Private Collection
SELECTED BIBLIOGRAPHY:
Naumann 1978, 13, 31, no. 26
Naumann 1981, I, 82
Buvelot in The Hague/Washington 2005, 142, fig. 24a, 240, no. 26

CLAES CORNELISZ MOEYAERT
(1591–1655)

CAT. 36
Cloelia's Escape from Porsena's Camp, 1640
Black and white chalk, on brownish cartridge paper
23.1 × 38.4 cm (9¹⁄₁₆ × 15⅛ in.)
Fondation Custodia, Collection Frits Lugt, Paris, 1994-T.9
EXHIBITION:
Paris 1994, no. 25
SELECTED BIBLIOGRAPHY:
Tümpel 1974, 267, under no. 184
Starcky 1994, no. 25
Gerszi 2005, under no. 165
Schatborn 2010a, no. 34

PIETER MOLIJN (1595–1661)

CAT. 10
Landscape with Open Gate, c. 1630–1635
Oil on panel
33.6 × 47.9 cm (13¼ × 18⅞ in.)
National Gallery of Art, Washington, Ailsa Mellon Bruce Fund
and Gift of Arthur K. and Susan H. Wheelock, 1986.10.1
EXHIBITIONS:
Washington 1998, no. 39
Grand Rapids 1999, no. 17
SELECTED BIBLIOGRAPHY:
Washington 1998, 67, no. 39

MICHIEL VAN MUSSCHER (1645–1705)

CAT. 13
An Artist in His Studio with His Drawings, mid–1660s
Oil on panel
47 × 36 cm (18½ × 14³⁄₁₆ in.)
Collections of the Prince of Liechtenstein, Vaduz-Vienna, GE 23 97

CASPAR NETSCHER (1639–1684)

CAT. 8
Studies of Two Female Arms, 1675
Black and white chalk, some brush in black on blue paper
24.2 × 22.4 cm (9½ × 8¹³⁄₁₆ in.)
Inscription lower right: 'Casper Netscher/1675'
Rijksmuseum, Amsterdam, RP-T-1890-A-2375
EXHIBITION:
Amsterdam/Washington 1981, no. 71
SELECTED BIBLIOGRAPHY:
Wieseman 2002, 113, fig. 57

ADRIAEN VAN OSTADE (1610–1685)

CAT. 72
Dancing Man, c. 1659
Black and white chalk on light brown paper
14.4 × 7.5 cm (5¹¹⁄₁₆ × 2¹⁵⁄₁₆ in.)
Rijksmuseum, Amsterdam, purchased with the support
of the F.G. Waller-Fonds, the Belport Familienstiftung
and a contribution from the J.A.Z. Count van Regteren Limpurg
Bequest, RP-T-1981-237
SELECTED BIBLIOGRAPHY:
Schatborn 1986, 84–85, ill. 8

CAT. 73
Peasants Dancing in a Tavern, 1659
Oil on panel
44.1 × 60.3 cm (17⅞ × 23¾ in.)
Signed and dated, lower left, on bench: 'A Ostade/1659'
Saint Louis Art Museum, Friends Fund, 147:1966
EXHIBITION:
Paris 1965, no. 42
SELECTED BIBLIOGRAPHY:
Hofstede de Groot 1907–1928, III, no. 549
Burke 1980, 5
Schnackenburg 1981, I, 32, 43, 105, 264, fig. 36
Steiner 2004, 179

CAT. 74
Dancing Figures, c. 1659
Black chalk, pen and brown ink, on paper
13.2 × 26.7 cm (5³⁄₁₆ × 10½ in.)
Watermark: letters 'CC'
Hamburger Kunsthalle, Hamburg, 22304
SELECTED BIBLIOGRAPHY:
Schnackenburg 1981, I, 32, 40, 41, 43, 63, no. 123
Stefes 2011, II, no. 764

CAT. 75
Seated Man from Behind, c. 1659
Black chalk, heightened with white, on light brown paper
20 × 19.2 cm (7⅞ × 7⁹⁄₁₆ in.)
Rijksmuseum, Amsterdam, RP-T-00-209
SELECTED BIBLIOGRAPHY:
Schnackenburg 1981, I, no. 124

CAT. 76
Drawing for a Group Portrait, c. 1654
Pen and brown ink over graphite, gray-brown wash, on paper
12.2 × 23.2 cm (4¹³⁄₁₆ × 9⅛ in.)
Watermark: Strasbourg lily with crown (fragment of the upper part)
Fondation Custodia, Collection Frits Lugt, Paris, 1190
EXHIBITIONS:
Rotterdam 1938, no. 425C
Paris 1965, no. 83
New York/Boston/Chicago 1972, no. 72
Amsterdam 1973, no. 72
Paris 1981, no. 4
SELECTED BIBLIOGRAPHY:
Paris 1970–1971, under no. 153
Schnackenburg 1981, no. 83

CAT. 77
Drawing for a Group Portrait, c. 1654
Pen and brown ink over graphite, gray-brown wash, on paper
12.6 × 21.3 cm (4¹⁵⁄₁₆ × 8⅜ in.) Inscription recto: initials 'E.P.' written in pen and brown ink lower left corner (collector's mark of Edward Peart, L.891)
Fondation Custodia, Collection Frits Lugt, Paris, 5037
EXHIBITIONS:
Rotterdam 1938, no. 425B
Paris 1965, no. 82
Paris 1981, no. 6
SELECTED BIBLIOGRAPHY:
Moskowitz 1962, no. 608
Paris 1970, under no. 153
Schnackenburg 1981, no. 85

CAT. 78
Drawing for a Group Portrait, c. 1654
Pen and brown ink over graphite, gray-brown wash, on paper
16.2 × 20.1 cm (6⁵⁄₁₆ × 7¹⁵⁄₁₆ in.)
Inscription recto: initials 'JCR' written in pen and brown ink lower right corner (collector's mark of John Charles Robinson, L.1433)
Fondation Custodia, Collection Frits Lugt, Paris, 5096
EXHIBITIONS:
London 1929, no. 676
Rotterdam 1938, no. 425A
Paris 1965, no. 81
Paris 1974, no. 69
Paris 1981, no. 5
SELECTED BIBLIOGRAPHY:
Paris 1970, under no. 153
Haverkamp-Begemann 1976, 357, fig. 4
Schnackenburg 1981, no. 84

─────────────

ISACK VAN OSTADE (1621–1649)

CAT. 93
The Schoolroom, c. 1639
Pen and brown ink, pinkish brown and gray wash, over black chalk or graphite, on paper
16.9 × 23.6 cm (6⅝ × 9⁵⁄₁₆ in.)
Inscriptions: signed, lower left, in pen and brown ink: 'Is: v. Ostade f'
Maida and George Abrams Collection, Boston
EXHIBITIONS:
London 1929, no. 687
Amsterdam/Vienna/New York/Cambridge 1991, no. 87
London/Paris/Cambridge 2002, no. 84
SELECTED BIBLIOGRAPHY:
Schnackenburg 1981, I, 25, 34, 47, 48, 55, 59, no. 406

CAT. 94
Group of Houses with a Church Tower in the Background, c. 1649
Pen and brown ink, black chalk or graphite, colored chalks, watercolor, on paper
29.8 × 24.3 cm (11¾ × 9⁹⁄₁₆ in.)
Inscriptions: in a later hand, in pen and brown ink, lower right: 'Adn: van Ostade f.'
Staatliche Museen, Berlin, Kupferstichkabinett, KDZ 10 599
EXHIBITION:
Berlin 1974, no. 134 (as I. van Ostade)
SELECTED BIBLIOGRAPHY:
Bock and Rosenberg 1930, I, 204, II, 133 (as A. van Ostade)
Bernt 1957, II, ill. 457 (as A. van Ostade)
Schnackenburg 1981, I, 35, 54, no. 580

ANTHONIE PALAMEDESZ (1601–1673)

CAT. 58
Seated Officer Holding a Glass, c. 1635
brush and brown ink and darker brown oil paint, slightly
heightened with white gouache, on paper
20.5 × 15.5 cm (8¹⁄₁₆ × 6⅛ in.)
Leiden University Library, PK-T-AW-1102

EXHIBITIONS:
Amsterdam/Washington 1981, no. 76
New York/London 2001, no. 119
Amsterdam 2014a, no. 20
Amsterdam 2014b, 149, under no. 51

SELECTED BIBLIOGRAPHY:
Schatborn 1975b, 84
Kolfin 2005, 147–148, fig. 116
Michiel Plomp in New York/London 2001, 180, 477–478,
under nos. 119–120

CRISPIJN VAN DE PASSE II
(1594/95–1670)

CAT. 5
*A Drawing School in the Evening (or 'Roman Academy or Drawing
School')* in *Van 't Light der Teken en Schilder Konst*, I, fols. 10–11
(Amsterdam, 1643)
Engraving
33 × 39.8 cm (13 × 15¹¹⁄₁₆ in.)
National Gallery of Art Library, Washington (cat. 5a)
Fondation Custodia, Collection Frits Lugt, Paris (cat. 5b)

EXHIBITIONS:
Amsterdam/Washington 1981, 15–16, fig. 10
Utrecht/Schwerin 2011, 27–28, figs. 9, 10

SELECTED BIBLIOGRAPHY:
Passe 1643
Bolten 1979, 16–25
Veldman 2001, 337–340

CORNELIS VAN POELENBURCH
(1594/95–1667)

CAT. 41
Houses in Italy (recto), c. 1620–1625
Pen and brown ink and wash over black chalk on paper
18.7 × 23.2 cm (7⅜ × 9⅛ in.)
Signature (signed with monogram): 'C.P.'
Putto Carrying an Urn (verso)

counterproof in red chalk
Private Collection

SELECTED BIBLIOGRAPHY:
Le Claire 1998, n.p., no. 11
Shawe-Taylor 2010, 132–133, no. 28
White 2015, 276–278, no. 141
Sluijter-Seijffert 2016, 361, no. 214

PAULUS POTTER (1625–1654)

CAT. 95
A Sow and Her Farrow, c. 1650
Black chalk on paper
10.2 × 14.9 cm (4 × 5⅞ in.)
Maida and George Abrams Collection, Boston

EXHIBITIONS:
Amsterdam/Vienna/New York/Cambridge 1991, no. 72
The Hague 1994, no. 44
London/Paris/Cambridge 2002, no. 100

SELECTED BIBLIOGRAPHY:
New York/Paris, 1977, under no. 80

JAN VAN RAVESTEYN (1572–1657)

CAT. 23
The Hague Magistrate Receiving the Officers of the St. Sebastiaansdoelen,
1618
Pen and black ink, brown wash, heightened with white gouache,
on paper
24.8 × 51.7 cm (9¾ × 20⅜ in.)
Fondation Custodia, Collection Frits Lugt, Paris, 3845

SELECTED BIBLIOGRAPHY:
Servaas van Rooijen 1881, 334–335
Bredius and Moes 1892, 41–52
Martin 1923, 193–198
The Hague 1998, 233
Domela Nieuwenhuis 2012, 102–106

REMBRANDT HARMENSZ VAN RIJN
(1606–1669)

CAT. 59
Old Man Seated, 1631
Red and some black chalk on pale yellowish prepared paper
22.9 × 15.9 cm (9 × 6¼ in.)

Signed with monogram and dated in red chalk at the bottom
'RHL 1631'
Private Collection

EXHIBITIONS:
Berlin/Amsterdam/London 1991b, no. 2
Amsterdam/London 2000, under no. 41, fig. a
Boston/Chicago 2003, no. 50
Los Angeles 2009, no. 2.3

SELECTED BIBLIOGRAPHY:
Benesch 1973, no. 20, fig. 20
Rembrandt Corpus II 1986, under no. A 66, 295, fig. 5, V 2011,
211, fig. 146
Straten 2005a, 176, fig. 292
Bevers 2006, under no. 4
Slive 2009, 55, fig. 5.5
Royalton-Kisch and Schatborn 2011, 327, no. 10
Schatborn 2011, 294–295, fig. 4
Royalton-Kisch 2012, www.rembrandtcatalogue.net, no. 20

CAT. 60
Joseph Telling His Dreams, 1633
Grisaille on paper
55.8 × 38.7 cm (22 × 15⅝ in.)
Signed and dated: 'Rembrandt f 1633'
Rijksmuseum, Amsterdam, purchased with the support
of the Vereniging Rembrandt and the Stichting tot Bevordering
van de Belangen van het Rijksmuseum, SK-A-3477

SELECTED BIBLIOGRAPHY:
Amsterdam 2008, 92
Jansen 2010, 138–143

CAT. 61
St. John the Baptist Preaching, 1634/1635
Oil on canvas, attached to panel
63 × 81.3 cm (24¹³⁄₁₆ × 32 in.)
Staatliche Museen, Berlin, Gemäldegalerie, 828 K

EXHIBITION:
Berlin/Amsterdam/London 1991a, no. 20

SELECTED BIBLIOGRAPHY:
Gerson 1968, no. 71
Bredius and Gerson 1969, no. 555
Rembrandt Corpus III 1989, no. A 106, V 2011, chap. 2, 179,
figs. 78, 79, VI 2014, no. 110

CAT. 62
*Two Studies of St. John for the Painting "St. John the Baptist
Preaching,"* 1634/1635
Verso: *Small Head of a Girl*
Red chalk on paper
17.6 × 18.6 cm (6¹⁵⁄₁₆ × 7⁵⁄₁₆ in.)
Courtauld Gallery, Seilern Collection, London, D 1978PG.182

EXHIBITION:
Berlin/Amsterdam/London 1991b, under cat. 7, fig.7f

SELECTED BIBLIOGRAPHY:
Bredius and Gerson 1969, 606, under no. 555
Benesch 1973, no.142a, fig. 171
Rembrandt Corpus III 1989, no. 83, fig. 13
Royalton-Kisch 1991, 278
Royalton-Kisch and Schatborn 2011, no. 26, figs. 101, 102
Royalton-Kisch 2012, www.rembrandtcatalogue.net, no. 142a

CAT. 63
*Studies of Standing Scribes for the Painting "St. John the Baptist
Preaching,"* 1634/1635
Pen and brown ink on paper
16.7 × 19.5 cm (6⁹⁄₁₆ × 7¹¹⁄₁₆ in.)
Staatliche Museen, Berlin, Kupferstichkabinett, KDZ 3773

EXHIBITIONS:
Berlin/Amsterdam/London 1991b, no. 7
Paris 2007, no. 11

SELECTED BIBLIOGRAPHY:
Tümpel 1970, no. 71
Benesch 1973, no. 141, fig. 168
Bevers 2006, no. 11
Royalton-Kisch and Schatborn 2011, 330, no. 23
Royalton-Kisch 2012, www.rembrandtcatalogue.net, no. 141

CAT. 64
Listeners for the Painting "St. John the Baptist Preaching," 1634/1635
Pen and brown ink, brown wash, and some opaque white, on paper
18.9 × 12.5 cm (7⁷⁄₁₆ × 4¹⁵⁄₁₆ in.)
Staatliche Museen, Berlin, Kupferstichkabinett, KDZ 5243

EXHIBITIONS:
Paris 2007, no. 12
Los Angeles 2009, no. 14.1

SELECTED BIBLIOGRAPHY:
Tümpel 1970, no. 70
Benesch 1973, no. 140, fig. 167
Bevers 2006, no. 12
Royalton-Kisch and Schatborn, 2011, 330, no. 22
Royalton-Kisch 2012, www.rembrandtcatalogue.net, no. 140

CAT. 65
Studies of Mary, the Mother of Christ, and Mary Magdalene,
1635/1636
Pen and brown ink, red chalk, on paper
20.1 × 14.3 cm (7¹⁵⁄₁₆ × 5⅝ in.)
Autograph inscription upper center: 'Een dijvoot tgheesoor dat
in een/fijn harte bewaert weert/tot troost haerer/beleevende siel'
(A devout treasure held in a fine heart to the comfort of her
compassionate soul)
Rijksmuseum, Amsterdam, RP-T-1947-213

EXHIBITION:

Amsterdam/Washington 1981, 54–55, no. 82

SELECTED BIBLIOGRAPHY:

Benesch 1973, no. 152, fig. 183

Schatborn 1985, no. 7

Schapelhouman 2006, 77, fig. 71

Royalton-Kisch and Schatborn 2011, no. 33

Royalton-Kisch 2012, www.rembrandtcatalogue.net, no. 152

CAT. 66

The Rape of Ganymede, 1635

Pen and brown ink, brown wash, on paper

18.3 × 16 cm (7⁵⁄₁₆ × 6⁵⁄₁₆ in.)

Kupferstich-Kabinett, Staatliche Kunstsammlungen Dresden,
C 1357

EXHIBITIONS:

Washington/New York/San Francisco 1978, no. 592

Dresden/Vienna 1997, no. 81

Berlin/Amsterdam/London 1991b, no. 10

Dresden 2004, no. 102

Dresden 2006, 20–32, fig. 1

Paris 2006b, no. 65

SELECTED BIBLIOGRAPHY:

Benesch 1973, no. 92, fig. 106

Rembrandt Corpus III 1989, under no. A 113, 167, fig. 5, V,
2011, 186, fig. 96

Bevers 2000, 70–73

Slive 2009, 185, fig. 14.8

Royalton-Kisch and Schatborn, 2011, no. 29, fig. 105

Royalton-Kisch, 2012, www.rembrandtcatalogue.net, no. 92

CAT. 67

Johannes Cornelisz Sylvius, the Preacher, 1644

Verso: *Small Head of a Horse*, illegible inscription

Pen and brown ink on laid paper

13.3 × 12.2 cm (5¼ × 4¹³⁄₁₆ in.)

National Gallery of Art, Washington, Rosenwald Collection,
1959.16.12

EXHIBITION:

New York/Cambridge 1960, no. 42

SELECTED BIBLIOGRAPHY:

Benesch 1973, no. 762, fig. 960

Royalton-Kisch 2009, under no. 37

JACOB VAN RUISDAEL
(1628/29–1682)

CAT. 98

Landscape with the Ruins of the Church of Muiderberg in the Distance,
c. 1650–1655

Black chalk on paper

15.1 × 19.3 cm (5¹⁵⁄₁₆ × 7⅝ in.)

Inscription by a later hand, lower right: 'J. Ruijsdael'
(vigorous scratching has virtually obliterated the inscription)

Albertina, Vienna, 10116

EXHIBITIONS:

Vienna 1993, no. 58 (ill.)

New York/Fort Worth 1995, no. 50 (ill.)

Los Angeles/Philadelphia/London 2005, no. 68 (ill.)

SELECTED BIBLIOGRAPHY:

Slive 1991, 602–604 (ill.)

White 1999, 135–137, under no. A875, ill. 207, fig. 19

Slive 2001, no. D122, (ill.)

The Hague/Washington 2008, 160, fig. 36.1

CAT. 99

View over Amsterdam and the IJ, c. 1665

Black chalk, gray wash, on paper

8.6 × 15.2 cm (3⅜ × 6 in.)

Inscription: verso, in pencil in a seventeenth-century(?) hand:
'Getekend van t dack der verbrande Niwe Kerk tot Amsterdam
(near 't Y).'

Rijksmuseum, Amsterdam, RP-T-1960-116

EXHIBITIONS:

Amsterdam 1932, no. 35

Washington/New York/Minneapolis/Boston/Cleveland/Chicago
1958, no. 101a

Amsterdam/Toronto 1977, no. 77

The Hague/Cambridge 1981, no. 87 (ill.)

Amsterdam 1997b, 86–87 (ill.)

Amsterdam 1998a, 66 (ill.)

Los Angeles/Philadelphia/London 2005, no. 94 (ill.)

SELECTED BIBLIOGRAPHY:

Regteren Altena n.d., 306–307 (ill.)

Stechow 1966, 128

Slive 1973, 275

Giltay 1980, 161–164, no. 3

Slive 2001, no. D1 (ill.)

CAT. 100

Panoramic View of Amsterdam, Its Harbor, and the IJ,
c. 1665–1670

Oil on canvas

41.5 × 40.7 cm (16⁵⁄₁₆ × 16 in.)

Inscription: signed on a beam of the scaffolding, lower right

Private Collection, England (on loan to the National Gallery,
London), L1052

EXHIBITIONS:

The Hague/Cambridge 1981, no. 46 (ill.)

Amsterdam 1997b, no. 23 (ill.)

The Hague/Washington 2008, no. 36

SELECTED BIBLIOGRAPHY:
Stechow 1966, 128
Walford 1991, 163–165 (ill.)
Slive 2001, no. 5 (ill.)

CAT. 101
The Jewish Cemetery at Ouderkerk aan de Amstel
Black chalk, brush and black ink, gray wash, on paper
19.1 × 28.3 cm (7½ × 11⅛ in.)
Indented and rubbed with red chalk on the verso for transfer
Teylers Museum, Haarlem, Q 48
EXHIBITIONS:
Paris 1950, no. 159;
London 1970, no. 43 (ill.)
The Hague/Cambridge 1981, no. 76 (ill.)
Cambridge/Montreal 1988, no. 81
Los Angeles/Philadelphia/London 2005, no. 80 (ill.)
SELECTED BIBLIOGRAPHY:
Vega 1975
Scheyer 1977, 133–134
Giltay 1980, 151, no. 55 (ill.)
Walford 1991, 99 (ill.)
Plomp 1997b, 360–361, no. 412 (ill.)
Slive 2001, no. D60 (ill.)

PIETER JANSZ SAENREDAM
(1597–1665)

CAT. 49
Choir and High Altar of Sint-Janskerk at 's-Hertogenbosch, 1632
Pen and brown ink with gray wash and watercolor, over black chalk on paper
40.7 × 32 cm (16 × 12⅝ in.)
Inscription: 'de St. Jans, ofte grote, kerck, in s'Hartogenbosch, in brabant, van mij Pr. Saenredam 1632 den 1 Julij aldus naer tleeven geteeckent.'
The British Museum, London, PD 1895,0915.1300
EXHIBITIONS:
Edinburgh 1984, no. 25
's-Hertogenbosch 1990, no. 8
London 1996, no. 83
's-Hertogenbosch 2013, no. 4
SELECTED BIBLIOGRAPHY:
Robinson 1876, 825
Hind and Popham 1915, I, 31

CAT. 50
The Choir of the St. Bavo in Haarlem, 1636
Oil on panel
49 × 36.6 cm (19⁵⁄₁₆ × 14⁷⁄₁₆ in.)

Signed and dated
Fondation Custodia, Collection Frits Lugt, Paris, 396
EXHIBITIONS:
Paris 1983, no. 72
Rotterdam 1991, no. 15
The Hague 2002, no. 28
SELECTED BIBLIOGRAPHY:
Schwartz and Bok 1989, no. 41

CAT. 51
St. Bavo, Haarlem, View in the Choir, 1636
Pen and gray wash on paper
48 × 37 cm (18⅞ × 14⁹⁄₁₆ in.)
Noord-Hollands Archief, Kennemer Atlas, Haarlem, 53-001702 G
EXHIBITION:
Utrecht 1961, no. 42
SELECTED BIBLIOGRAPHY:
Swillens 1935, no. 94

CAT. 52
St. Bavo, Haarlem, Part of the Nave, 1635
Pen and chalk on blue paper
54.5 × 39 cm (21⁷⁄₁₆ × 15⅜ in.)
Noord-Hollands Archief, Kennemer Atlas, Haarlem, 53-000435 G

CAT. 53
South Transept of St. Bavo in Haarlem, 1635
Pen and brush, gray wash, squared in red chalk, on paper
49 × 35.5 cm (19⁵⁄₁₆ × 14 in.)
Noord-Hollands Archief, Kennemer Atlas, Haarlem, 53-001726 G
EXHIBITION:
Utrecht 1961, no. 460
SELECTED BIBLIOGRAPHY:
Swillens 1935, no. 87

CAT. 54
Interior of Saint Bavo's Church, Haarlem, 1635
Pen and brown ink with gray wash and touches of red chalk over graphite, squared in red chalk, on paper
49.1 × 35.8 cm (19⁵⁄₁₆ × 14⅛ in.)
National Gallery of Art, Washington, Gift of Dian Woodner, 2015.149.1
EXHIBITIONS:
Utrecht 1961, no. 61
Edinburgh 1984, no. 20
Madrid 1986, no. 73
Washington 1995, no. 68
Washington 2006 (without catalog)
SELECTED BIBLIOGRAPHY:
Swillens 1935, 39, 60–61, 94–95, no. 86
Matteson 1983, 386–387

CAT. 55
Organ of the St. Bavo, Haarlem, [n.d.]
Pen and brown ink, pencil and watercolor, on paper
30.9 × 17.3 cm (12³⁄₁₆ × 6¹³⁄₁₆ in.)
Fondation Custodia, Collection Frits Lugt, Paris, 2218

CORNELIS SAFTLEVEN (1607–1681)

CAT. 68
Sleeping Hunter, 1642
Black chalk and gray wash on paper
16.9 × 23.8 cm (6⁵⁄₈ × 9³⁄₈ in.)
Inscription: signed and dated, black chalk, lower right, 'GSL/1642'
Maida and George Abrams Collection, Boston
EXHIBITION:
Amsterdam/Vienna/New York/Cambridge 1991, 158–159, no. 70
SELECTED BIBLIOGRAPHY:
Schulz 1978, 63, 85, no. 56, 228, under no. 646
Philadelphia/Berlin/London 1984, 298, under no. 97
Amsterdam/Boston/Philadelphia 1987, 476, under no. 96

CORNELIS SAFTLEVEN (1607–1681)
HERMAN SAFTLEVEN (c. 1609–1685)

CAT. 69
Sleeping Hunter in a Landscape, 1642 or later
Oil on panel
36.8 × 52 cm (14½ × 20½ in.)
Inscription: signed and dated, lower right, 'Saft-Levens 164(?)'
Maida and George Abrams Collection, Boston
EXHIBITIONS:
Philadelphia/Berlin/London 1984, l, 297–298, no. 97, pl. 91
Amsterdam/Boston/Philadelphia 1987, 476–478, no. 96, pl. 76
SELECTED BIBLIOGRAPHY:
Schulz 1978, 28, 63, 85, under no. 56, 228, no. 646
Schulz 1982, 43, 132, no. 28, pl. 10

PIETER CORNELISZ
VAN SLINGELANDT (1640–1691)

CAT. 126
Study of a Cradle, [n.d.]
Black and white chalk on blue paper
18.3 × 19.1 cm (7³⁄₁₆ × 7½ in.)
Fondation Custodia, Collection Frits Lugt, Paris, 2015-T.1

EXHIBITION:
Rotterdam/Paris/Brussels 1977, no. 124, pl. 86

CAT. 127
Interior with a Woman by a Cradle, c. 1670
Oil on panel
45.6 × 38.6 cm (17¹⁵⁄₁₆ × 15³⁄₁₆ in.)
Bayerische Staatsgemäldesammlungen, Alte Pinakothek, Munich, 1064
EXHIBITION:
Munich 2014 (without catalog)
SELECTED BIBLIOGRAPHY:
Smith 1829, I, 51, no. 5
Reber 1904, no. 427

ADRIAEN VAN DE VELDE (1636–1672)

CAT. 115
Study after a Male Model, [n.d.]
Red chalk on paper
34.9 × 22.9 cm (13¾ × 9 in.)
Inscription: lower right, brown ink, 'L. Da Vinci.'
Private Collection
EXHIBITION:
Amsterdam 1993b, 138–139, no. 64
SELECTED BIBLIOGRAPHY:
Robinson 1979, 12, 21–22, no. D11
Robinson 1993, 58

CAT. 116
Landscape with Trees, 1660–1669
Pen and brown ink, brown and gray-brown wash, on two sheets of paper joined vertically at left
28.5 × 45.6 cm (11¼ × 17¹⁵⁄₁₆ in.)
Inscriptions: lower right, brown ink, 'A v. velde f.,' verso, lower left, graphite, 'ab,' right center, graphite, '140,' lower right, graphite, '231'
Amsterdam Museum, bequest of C.J. Fodor, TA 10348
EXHIBITION:
Cambridge/Montreal 1988, 217, no. 94
SELECTED BIBLIOGRAPHY:
Robinson 1979, 4–5, 18, no. A1, pl. 1
Broos and Schapelhouman 1993, 180, no. 137

CAT. 117
Kneeling Woman, c. 1660(?)
Red chalk over black chalk on paper
23.2 × 19 cm (9⅛ × 7½ in.)
Inscription: signed or inscribed, lower left, red chalk, 'A.V.V.'
Maida and George Abrams Collection, Boston

EXHIBITIONS:
Amsterdam/Vienna/New York/Cambridge 1991, 168–169, no. 75
London/Paris/Cambridge 2002, 214–215, no. 94
SELECTED BIBLIOGRAPHY:
Robels 1983, 248

ESAIAS VAN DE VELDE (1587–1630)

CAT. 32
Standing Couple Seen from the Side, c. 1617
Black chalk with gouache highlights on blue paper
23.5 × 16.5 cm (9¼ × 6½ in.)
Rijksmuseum, Amsterdam, RP-T-1886-A-569

EXHIBITION:
Amsterdam/Washington 1981, no. 96
SELECTED BIBLIOGRAPHY:
Amsterdam/Washington 1981, 43, 144, no. 96
Keyes and Briels 1984, 228, no. D 52, pl. 126
Schapelhouman and Schatborn 1998, I, 48, no. 313, II, 167

WILLEM VAN DE VELDE THE ELDER (1611–1693)

CAT. 108
Ship's Portrait of The Royal Prince, 1670(?)
Pencil, pen, and wash on paper
44.9 × 73.9 cm (17¹¹⁄₁₆ × 29⅛ in.)
Museum Boijmans Van Beuningen, Rotterdam, MB 1866 T 352

SELECTED BIBLIOGRAPHY:
Robinson and Weber 1979, I, 119, III, 257 pl.

CAT. 109
Ship's Portrait of The Royal Prince, counterproof, 1661
Black chalk on paper
33.4 × 45.4 cm (13⅛ × 17⅞ in.)
Museum Boijmans Van Beuningen, Rotterdam, MB 1866 T 389

SELECTED BIBLIOGRAPHY:
Robinson and Weber 1979, I, 120, III, 258 pl.

WILLEM VAN DE VELDE THE YOUNGER (1633–1707)

CAT. 106
The Surrender of The Royal Prince on the Third Day of the Four Days' Battle, June 13, 1666, c. 1670
Oil on canvas

35.2 × 45.3 cm (13⅞ × 17¹³⁄₁₆ in.)
Fondation Custodia, Collection Frits Lugt, Paris, 5807

EXHIBITIONS:
Paris 1983, no. 87, pl. 52
Paris 1989, no. 10, pls. 8, 9
SELECTED BIBLIOGRAPHY:
Robinson, M.S. 1990, I, 146–148, no. 161

CAT. 107
The Surrender of The Royal Prince on the Third Day of the Four Days' Battle, June 13, 1666, c. 1666(?)
Pencil and gray wash on paper
21 × 43.2 cm (8¼ × 17 in.)
National Maritime Museum, Greenwich, PAH3879

SELECTED BIBLIOGRAPHY:
Robinson 1958–1974, I, 66, 131, no. 288, pl. 59

CAT. 110
Burning of The Royal James at the Battle of Solebay, June 7, 1672, 1673(?)
Gray wash, graphite, on paper
44.3 × 63.4 cm (17⁷⁄₁₆ × 24¹⁵⁄₁₆ in.)
National Maritime Museum, Greenwich, PAI7272

SELECTED BIBLIOGRAPHY:
Robinson 1958–1974, I, 83, 134, no. 435, pl. 98

HENDRICK CORNELISZ VAN VLIET (c. 1611–1675)

CAT. 79
Sketchbook, 19 sheets, [n.d.]
Black, white, and red chalk on nineteen leaves of blue paper
27.5 × 22 cm (10¹³⁄₁₆ × 8¹¹⁄₁₆ in.) (sheets)
Museum Boijmans Van Beuningen, Rotterdam, HVV 1

EXHIBITIONS:
Rotterdam 1991, no. 73
Delft 1996a, 69–70, fig. 54
Osaka 2000, 74–75, fig. 1
New York/London 2001, no. 128
SELECTED BIBLIOGRAPHY:
Liedtke 1982, 60, n. 4

BIBLIOGRAPHY
EXHIBITION CATALOGS

AACHEN/BERLIN 2012
Brink, Peter van den, and Bernd Wolfgang Lindemann. *Cornelis Bega: Eleganz und Raue Sitten*. Suermondt-Ludwig-Museum, Aachen; Gemäldegalerie Staatliche Museen zu Berlin. Stuttgart, 2012.

AACHEN/GOTHA 2016
Ayooghi, Sarvenaz, Sylvia Böhmer, Timo Trümper, et al. *Die Stillleben des Balthasar van der Ast (1593/94–1657)*. Suermondt-Ludwig-Museum, Aachen; Herzoglichen Museum, Gotha. Petersberg, 2016.

AMSTERDAM 1932
Regteren Altena, J. Q. van. *Kaarten, Profielen en Panorama's van Amsterdam*. Museum Fodor, Amsterdam. Amsterdam, 1932.

AMSTERDAM 1967
Houthakker, Bernard. *Master Drawings*. Bernard Houthakker Gallery, Amsterdam. Amsterdam, 1967.

AMSTERDAM 1973
Schatborn, Peter. *Hollandse Genre-Tekeningen uit de Zeventiende Eeuw*. Rijksprentenkabinet, Rijksmuseum, Amsterdam. Amsterdam, 1973.

AMSTERDAM 1984
Bakker, Noortje, Ingvar Berström, Guido Jansen, et al. *Masters of Middelburg: Exhibition in the Honour of Laurens J. Bol*. Waterman Gallery, Amsterdam. Amsterdam, 1984.

AMSTERDAM 1985
Broos, Ben P. J., Robert Vorstman, and Willem L. van de Watering. *Ludolf Bakhuizen, 1631–1708: Schryfmeester—Teyckenaer—Schilder*. Rijksmuseum, Amsterdam; Nederlands Scheepvaartmuseum, Amsterdam. Amsterdam, 1985.

AMSTERDAM 1986
Filedt Kok, J. P., W. Halsema-Kubes, and W. Th. Kloek. *Kunst voor de Beeldenstorm: Noordnederlandse Kunst, 1525–1580*. Rijksmuseum, Amsterdam. The Hague, 1986.

AMSTERDAM 1987
Schapelhouman, Marijn, and Peter Schatborn. *Land en Water: Hollandse Tekeningen uit de 17de Eeuw in het Rijksprentenkabinet*. Rijksprentenkabinet, Rijksmuseum, Amsterdam. Amsterdam, 1987.

AMSTERDAM 1988
Schatborn, Peter, and Eva Ornstein-van Slooten. *Jan Lievens, 1607–1674: Prenten en Tekeningen*. Museum het Rembrandthuis, Amsterdam. Amsterdam, 1988.

AMSTERDAM 1989a
Hecht, Peter. *De Hollandse Fijn Schilders: Van Gerard Dou tot Adriaen van der Werff*. Rijksmuseum, Amsterdam. Amsterdam, 1989.

AMSTERDAM 1989b
Heijbroek, Jan F., and Marijn Schapelhouman. *Kunst in Kaart: Decoratieve Aspecten van de Cartografie*. Rijksprentenkabinet, Rijksmuseum, Amsterdam. Utrecht, 1989.

AMSTERDAM 1989c
Bastet, Frédéric Louis. *De Verzameling van Mr. Carel Vosmaer, 1826–1888*. Rijksprentenkabinet, Rijksmuseum, Amsterdam. The Hague, 1989.

AMSTERDAM 1991a
Tümpel, Christian. *Het Oude Testament in de Schilderkunst van de Gouden Eeuw*. Joods Historisch Museum, Amsterdam. Zwolle, 1991.

AMSTERDAM 1991b
Tümpel, Astrid, and Peter Schatborn. *Pieter Lastman, the Man Who Taught Rembrandt*. Museum het Rembrandthuis, Amsterdam. Zwolle, 1991.

AMSTERDAM 1992
Bergvelt, Ellinoor, and Renée Kistemaker. *De Wereld Binnen Handbereik: Nederlandse Kunst- en Rariteitenverzamelingen, 1585–1735*. 2 vols. Amsterdams Historisch Museum. Zwolle, 1992.

AMSTERDAM 1993a
Luijten, Ger, and Ariane van Suchtelen, eds. *Dawn of the Golden Age: Northern Netherlandish Art, 1580–1620*. Rijksmuseum, Amsterdam. Zwolle, 1993.

AMSTERDAM 1993b
Schapelhouman, Marijn, and Peter Schatborn. *Tekeningen van Oude Meesters: De Verzameling Jacobus A. Klaver*. Rijksprentenkabinet, Rijksmuseum, Amsterdam. Zwolle, 1993.

AMSTERDAM 1994
Segal, Sam, and Michiel Roding. *De Tulp en de Kunst*. Nieuwe Kerk, Amsterdam. Zwolle, 1994.

AMSTERDAM 1996
Schuckman, Christiaan, Martin Royalton-Kisch, and Erik Hinterding. *Rembrandt and Van Vliet: A Collaboration on Copper*. Museum het Rembrandthuis, Amsterdam. Amsterdam, 1996.

AMSTERDAM 1997a
Jongh, Eddy de, and Ger Luijten. *Mirror of Everyday Life: Genreprints in the Netherlands, 1550–1700*. Rijksprentenkabinet, Rijksmuseum, Amsterdam. Ghent, 1997.

AMSTERDAM 1997b
Peeters, Jan. *The Royal Palace of Amsterdam in Paintings of the Golden Age*. Royal Palace of Amsterdam. Zwolle, 1997.

AMSTERDAM 1998a
Boogert, Bob van den. *Buiten Tekenen in Rembrandts Tijd*. Studies from the Rembrandt Information Centre, 2. Museum het Rembrandthuis, Amsterdam. Amsterdam, 1998.

AMSTERDAM 1998b
Coelen, Peter van der. *Everyday Life in Holland's Golden Age: The Complete Etchings of Adriaen van Ostade*. Studies in Dutch Graphic Art, 3. Museum het Rembrandthuis, Amsterdam. Amsterdam, 1998.

AMSTERDAM 1999
Wallert, Arie. *Still Lifes: Techniques and Style.* Rijksmuseum, Amsterdam. Zwolle, 1999.

AMSTERDAM 2000
Kiers, Judiekje, and Fieke Tissink. *The Glory of the Golden Age: Dutch Art of the 17th Century.* Vol.1: *Painting, Sculpture and Decorative Art,* edited by Bart Cornelis and Jan Piet Filedt Kok. Rijksmuseum, Amsterdam. Zwolle, 2000.

AMSTERDAM 2001
Schatborn, Peter. *Drawn to Warmth: 17th-Century Dutch Artists in Italy.* With a contribution by Judith Verberne. Rijksmuseum, Amsterdam. Zwolle, 2001.

AMSTERDAM 2004
Beer, Gerlinde de, Eymert-Jan Goossens, and Bert van de Roemer. *Backhuysen aan het Roer! Zeeschilder, 1630–1708.* Royal Palace, Amsterdam. Amsterdam, 2004.

AMSTERDAM 2008
Hecht, Peter. *125 Jaar Openbaar Kunstbezit: Met Steun van de Vereniging Rembrandt.* Van Gogh Museum, Amsterdam. Zwolle, 2008.

AMSTERDAM 2014a
Schaeps, Jef, et al. *Leiden Viert Feest! Hoogtepunten uit een Academische Collectie.* Museum het Rembrandthuis, Amsterdam. Amsterdam, 2014.

AMSTERDAM 2014b
Schatborn, Peter, and Leonore van Sloten. *Old Drawings, New Names: Rembrandt and His Contemporaries.* Museum het Rembrandthuis, Amsterdam. Varik, 2014.

AMSTERDAM/AACHEN 2008
Brink, Peter van den, and Jaap van der Veen. *Jacob Backer (1608/9–1651).* Museum het Rembrandthuis, Amsterdam; Suermondt-Ludwig-Museum, Aachen. Amsterdam, 2008.

AMSTERDAM/BERLIN 2006
Wetering, Ernst van de. *Rembrandt: Quest of a Genius.* Edited by Bob van den Boogert. Museum het Rembrandthuis, Amsterdam; Gemäldegalerie, Staatliche Museen zu Berlin. Zwolle, 2006.

AMSTERDAM/BOSTON/
PHILADELPHIA 1987
Sutton, Peter C., and P. J. J. van Thiel. *Masters of Seventeenth-Century Dutch Landscape Painting.* Rijksmuseum, Amsterdam; Museum of Fine Arts, Boston; Philadelphia Museum of Art. Amsterdam, 1987.

AMSTERDAM/CLEVELAND 1999
Chong, Alan, and Wouter Th. Kloek. *Still-Life Paintings from the Netherlands, 1550–1720.* Rijksmuseum, Amsterdam; Cleveland Museum of Art. Zwolle, 1999.

AMSTERDAM/LONDON 2000
Hinterding, Erik, Ger Luyten, and Martin Royalton-Kisch. *Rembrandt the Printmaker.* Rijksmuseum, Amsterdam; British Museum, London. London, 2000.

AMSTERDAM/PARIS 2015
Shoaf Turner, Jane, and Robert Jan te Rijdt. *Home and Abroad: Dutch and Flemish Landscape Drawings from the John and Marine van Vlissingen Art Foundation.* Rijksmuseum, Amsterdam; Fondation Custodia, Collection Frits Lugt, Paris. Amsterdam, 2015.

AMSTERDAM/STOCKHOLM/
LOS ANGELES 1999
Scholten, Frits, and Rosemarie Mulcahy. *Adriaen de Vries (1556–1626), Imperial Sculptor.* Rijksmuseum, Amsterdam; Nationalmuseum Stockholm; J. Paul Getty Museum, Los Angeles. Zwolle, 1998.

AMSTERDAM/TORONTO 1977
Lakerveld, Carry van. *Opkomst en Bloei van het Noordnederlandse Stadsgezicht in de 17de Eeuw / The Dutch Cityscape in the 17th Century and Its Sources.* Amsterdams Historisch Museum; Art Gallery of Ontario, Toronto. Amsterdam, 1977.

AMSTERDAM/VIENNA/
NEW YORK/CAMBRIDGE 1991
Robinson, William W. *Seventeenth-Century Dutch Drawings: A Selection from the Maida and George Abrams Collection.* Rijksmuseum, Amsterdam; Albertina, Vienna; Pierpont Morgan Library and Museum, New York; Fogg Art Museum, Cambridge. New York, 1991.

AMSTERDAM/WASHINGTON 1981
Schatborn, Peter. *Dutch Figure Drawings from the Seventeenth Century.* Rijksprentenkabinet, Rijksmuseum, Amsterdam; National Gallery of Art, Washington. Amsterdam, 1981.

AMSTERDAM/WASHINGTON 2009
Roelofs, Pieter. *Hendrick Avercamp: Master of the Ice Scene.* Rijksmuseum, Amsterdam; National Gallery of Art, Washington. Amsterdam, 2009.

ANTWERP/LONDON 1999
Royalton-Kisch, Martin. *The Light of Nature: Landscape Drawings and Watercolours by Van Dyck and His Contemporaries.* Rubenshuis, Antwerp; British Museum, London. London, 1999.

ATHENS/LAWRENCE/ANN ARBOR 1994
Pelletier, S. William, Leonard J. Slatkes, and Linda Stone-Ferrier. *Adriaen van Ostade: Etchings of Peasant Life in Holland's Golden Age.* Edited by Patricia Phagan. Georgia Museum of Art, Athens; Spencer Museum of Art, Lawrence; University of Michigan Museum of Art, Ann Arbor. Athens, 1994.

BERLIN 1974
Schulz, Wolfgang. *Die holländische Landschaftszeichnung, 1600–1740: Hauptwerke aus dem Berliner Kupferstichkabinett.* Kupferstichkabinett, Staatliche Museen Preussischer Kulturbesitz, Berlin. Berlin, 1974.

BERLIN 1992
Baudis, Hela, Kristina Hegner, and Kornelia Röder. *120 Handzeichnungen aus Fünf Jahrhunderten: Ausgewählt aus dem Kupferstichkabinett des Staatlichen Museums Schwerin, Kunstsammlungen, Schlösser und Gärten.* GrundkreditBank. Berlin, 1992.

BERLIN 2011
Bevers, Holm. *Aus Rembrandts Zeit: Zeichenkunst in Hollands 'Goldenem

Jahrhundert.' Kupferstichkabinett, Staatliche Museen zu Berlin. Leipzig, 2011.

BERLIN/AMSTERDAM/LONDON 1991a
Brown, Christopher, Jan Kelch, and P. J. J. van Thiel. *Rembrandt: The Master and His Workshop.* 2 vols. Vol. 1: *Paintings.* Gemäldegalerie Staatliche Museen Preussischer Kulturbesitz, Berlin; Rijksmuseum, Amsterdam; National Gallery, London. New Haven and London, 1991.

BERLIN/AMSTERDAM/LONDON 1991b
Bevers, Holm, Peter Schatborn, and Barbara Welzel. *Rembrandt: The Master and His Workshop.* 2 vols. Vol. 2: *Drawings and Etchings.* Gemäldegalerie Staatliche Museen Preussischer Kulturbesitz, Berlin; Rijksmuseum, Amsterdam; National Gallery, London. New Haven and London, 1991.

BESANÇON 1999
Soulier-François, Françoise. *Rubens, Rembrandt: Quelques Dessins Flamands et Hollandais.* Musée des Beaux-Arts et d'Archéologie, Cabinet des Dessins, Besançon. Besançon, 1999.

BOSTON 2014
Cole, Michael Wayne. *Donatello, Michelangelo, Cellini: Sculptors' Drawings from Renaissance Italy.* Isabella Stewart Gardner Museum, Boston. London, 2014.

BOSTON/CHICAGO 2003
Ackley, Clifford S., Ronni Baer, Tom Rassieur, et al. *Rembrandt's Journey: Painter, Draughtsman, Etcher.* Museum of Fine Arts, Boston; Art Institute of Chicago. Boston, 2003.

BREMEN/HAMBURG 2000
Röver-Kann, Anne. *Rembrandt, Oder Nicht? Zeichnungen von Rembrandt und Seinem Kreis aus den Hamburger und Bremer Kupferstichkabinetten.* Kunsthalle Bremen, Bremen; Hamburger Kunsthalle, Hamburg. Ostfildern-Ruit, 2000.

BRUSSELS/AMSTERDAM/AACHEN 2007a
Hautekeete, Stefaan. *Dessins du Siècle d'Or Hollandais: La Collection Jean de Grez.*

Musées Royaux des Beaux-Arts de Belgique, Brussels; Museum het Rembrandthuis, Amsterdam; Suermondt-Ludwig Museum, Aachen. Ghent, 2007.

BRUSSELS/AMSTERDAM/
AACHEN 2007b
Hautekeete, Stefaan. *Tekeningen uit Nederlands Gouden Eeuw in de Verzameling van Jean de Grez.* Koninklijke Musea voor Schone Kunsten van België, Brussels; Museum het Rembrandthuis, Amsterdam; Suermondt-Ludwig Museum, Aachen. Ghent, 2007.

BRUSSELS/ROTTERDAM/PARIS/
BERN 1968
Hasselt, Carlos van. *Landschaptekeningen van Hollandse Meesters uit de XVIIe Eeuw: Uit de Particuliere Verzameling Bewaard in het Institut Néerlandais te Parijs.* 2 vols. Albert I-Bibliotheek, Brussels; Museum Boymans-van Beuningen, Rotterdam; Institut Néerlandais/Fondation Custodia, Collection Frits Lugt, Paris; Kunstmuseum, Bern. Brussels, 1968.

CAMBRIDGE 1998
Saywell, Edward. *Behind the Line: The Materials and Techniques of Old Master Drawings.* Fogg Art Museum, Harvard University, Cambridge. Cambridge, 1998.

CAMBRIDGE/MONTREAL 1988
Duparc, Frederik J. *Landscape in Perspective: Drawings by Rembrandt and His Contemporaries.* Arthur M. Sackler Museum, Harvard University, Cambridge; Museum of Fine Arts, Montreal, 1988.

CHICAGO/MINNEAPOLIS/
DETROIT 1969
Judson, J. Richard, Egbert Haverkamp-Begemann, and Anne-Marie Logan. *Rembrandt after 300 Years: An Exhibition of Rembrandt and His Followers.* Art Institute of Chicago; Minneapolis Institute of Arts; Detroit Institute of Arts. Chicago, 1969.

DELFT 1996a
Kersten, Michiel C.C., and Daniëlle H.A.C. Lokin. *Delft Masters, Vermeer's Contemporaries:*

Illusionism through the Conquest of Light and Space. Stedelijk Museum het Prinsenhof, Delft. Zwolle, 1996.

DELFT 1996b
Kersten, Michiel, Daniëlle Lokin, and Michiel Plomp. *Delftse Meesters, Tijdgenoten van Vermeer: Een Andere Kijk op Perspectief, Licht en Ruimte.* Stedelijk Museum het Prinsenhof, Delft. Zwolle, 1996.

DELFT/HOUSTON 2007
Segal, Sam. *The Temptations of Flora: Jan Van Huysum, 1682–1749.* Museum het Prinsenhof, Delft; Museum of Fine Arts, Houston. Zwolle, 2007.

DETROIT 1923
Exhibition of a Selected Group of Dutch and Flemish Pictures, XV to XVII Century, from the Goudstikker Collection of Amsterdam. Detroit, 1923.

DORDRECHT 2012
Craft-Giepmans, Sabine, and Annette de Vries. *Portret in Portret in de Nederlandse Kunst, 1550–2012.* Dordrechts Museum, Dordrecht. Bussum, 2012.

DORDRECHT/LEEUWARDEN 1988
Boschma, C. *Meesterlijk Vee: Nederlandse Veeschilders, 1600–1900.* Dordrechts Museum; Fries Museum, Leeuwarden. Zwolle, 1988.

DRESDEN 2004
Dittrich, Christian, and Thomas Ketelsen. *Rembrandt: Die Dresdener Zeichnungen.* Staatliche Kunstsammlungen, Dresden. Cologne, 2004.

DRESDEN 2006
Ketelsen, Thomas, and Uta Neidhardt. *Rembrandt van Rijn: Die Entführung des Ganymed. Das restaurierte Meisterwerk, 4.* Kupferstich-Kabinett, Gemäldegalerie Alte Meister, Dresden. Dresden, 2006.

DRESDEN/VIENNA 1997
Dittrich, Christian. *Van Eyck, Bruegel, Rembrandt: Niederländische Zeichnungen des 15. bis 17. Jahrhunderts aus dem*

Kupferstich-Kabinett Dresden. Albertinum, Dresden; Kunstforum, Vienna. Eurasburg, 1997.

DÜSSELDORF 1964
Gallery C.G. Boerner. *Ausgewählte Hand-zeichnungen aus Vier Jahrhunderten*. Neue Lagerliste, 38. Düsseldorf, 1964.

EDINBURGH 1984
MacAndrew, Hugh. *Dutch Church Painters: Saenredam's 'Great Church at Haarlem' in Context*. National Gallery of Scotland, Edinburgh. Edinburgh, 1984.

EDINBURGH 1992
Lloyd Williams, Julia. *Dutch Art and Scotland: A Reflection of Taste*. National Gallery of Scotland, Edinburgh. Edinburgh, 1992.

EDINBURGH/LONDON 2001
Lloyd Williams, Julia. *Rembrandt's Women*. National Gallery of Scotland, Edinburgh; Royal Academy of Arts, London. London and New York, 2001.

FLORENCE 2015
Papi, Gianni. *Gherardo delle Notti: Quadri Bizzarrissimi e Cene Allegre*. Galleria degli Uffizi, Florence. Florence, 2015.

FRANKFURT 2000
Strech, Annette. *Nach dem Leben und aus der Phantasie: Niederländische Zeichnungen vom 15. bis 18. Jahrhundert aus dem Städelschen Kunstinstitut*. Städelsches Kunstinstitut und Städtische Galerie, Graphische Sammlung, Frankfurt. Frankfurt, 2000.

GRAND RAPIDS 1999
Wheelock, Arthur K., Jr. *A Moral Compass: Seventeenth and Eighteenth Century Painting in the Netherlands*. Grand Rapids Art Museum. New York, 1999.

GREENWICH/AMSTERDAM 2006
Sutton, Peter C. *Jan van der Heyden (1637–1712)*. Bruce Museum, Greenwich; Rijks-museum, Amsterdam. New Haven, 2006.

GREENWICH/HOUSTON 2011
Sutton, Peter, and William W. Robinson. *Drawings by Rembrandt, His Students and Circle from the Maida and George Abrams Collection*. Bruce Museum, Greenwich; Museum of Fine Arts, Houston. New Haven, 2011.

GREENWICH/NEW YORK/
SAN ANTONIO 2008
Sutton, Peter C. *Reclaimed: Paintings from the Collection of Jacques Goudstikker*. Bruce Museum, Greenwich; Jewish Museum, New York; McNay Museum of Art, San Antonio. Greenwich, 2008.

GRENOBLE 2006
Loisel, Catherine, and Jean-Claude Boyer. *L'appel de l'Italie: Artistes Français et Nordiques dans la Péninsule: Dessins des XVIIe et XVIIIe Siècles*. Musée de Grenoble. Montreuil, 2006.

GRENOBLE 2014
Mandrella, David. *La Pointe et l'Ombre: Dessins Nordiques de Musée de Grenoble XVIe–XVIIIe Siècle*. Musée de Grenoble. Paris, 2014.

HAARLEM 1986
Jongh, Eddy de. *Portretten van Echt en Trouw: Huwelijk en Gezin in de Nederlandse Kunst van de Zeventiende Eeuw*. Frans Hals Museum, Haarlem. Zwolle, 1986.

HAARLEM 1988
Carasso-Kok, M., and J. Levy-van Halm. *Schutters in Holland: Kracht en Zenuwen van de Stad*. Frans Hals Museum, Haarlem. Zwolle, 1988.

HAARLEM/LONDON 2008
Biesboer, Pieter, Friso Lammertse, and Fred G. Meijer. *Painting Family: The De Brays: Master Painters of 17th Century Holland*. Edited by Pieter Biesboer. Frans Hals Museum, Haarlem; Dulwich Picture Gallery, London. Zwolle, 2008.

HAARLEM/PARIS 2001a
Berge-Gerbaud, Mària van, and Michiel Plomp. *Collectionner, Passionnément: Les Collectionneurs Hollandais de Dessins au XVIIIe Siècle*. Teylers Museum, Haarlem; Institut Néerlandais/Fondation Custodia, Collection Frits Lugt, Paris. Paris, 2001.

HAARLEM/PARIS 2001b
Plomp, Michiel. *Hartstochtelijk Verzameld: 18de-Eeuwse Hollandse Verzamelaars van Tekeningen en Hun Collecties*. Teylers Museum, Haarlem; Institut Néerlandais/Fondation Custodia, Collection Frits Lugt, Paris. Bussum, 2001.

THE HAGUE 1994
Walsh, Amy L., Edwin Buijsen, and Ben P.J. Broos. *Paulus Potter: Paintings, Drawings, and Etchings*. Royal Picture Gallery Mauritshuis, The Hague. Zwolle, 1994.

THE HAGUE 1998
Buijsen, Edwin, Charles Dumas, and Kunsthandel Hoogsteder & Hoogsteder. *Haagse Schilders in de Gouden Eeuw: Het Hoogsteder Lexicon van Alle Schilders Werkzaam in Den Haag, 1600–1700*. Haags Historisch Museum, The Hague. Zwolle, 1998.

THE HAGUE 2002
Buvelot, Quentin, and Hans Buijs. *A Choice Collection: Seventeenth-Century Dutch Paintings from the Frits Lugt Collection*. Royal Picture Gallery Mauritshuis, The Hague. Zwolle, 2002.

THE HAGUE 2010
Buvelot, Quentin. *Made in Holland: Highlights from the Collection of Eijk and Rose-Marie de Mol van Otterloo*. Royal Picture Gallery Mauritshuis, The Hague. Zwolle, 2010.

THE HAGUE/CAMBRIDGE 1981
Slive, Seymour, and Hans Hoetink. *Jacob van Ruisdael*. Royal Cabinet of Paintings Mauritshuis, The Hague; Fogg Art Museum, Harvard University, Cambridge. New York, 1981.

THE HAGUE/SAN FRANCISCO 1990
Broos, Ben P. J. *Great Dutch Paintings from America*. Royal Cabinet of Paintings Mauritshuis, The Hague; Fine Arts Museums of San Francisco, M.H. de Young Memorial Museum. Zwolle, 1990.

THE HAGUE/SCHWERIN 2004
Duparc, Frederik J. *Carel Fabritius:*

1622–1654. Royal Picture Gallery Mauritshuis, The Hague; Staatliches Museum, Schwerin. Zwolle, 2004.

THE HAGUE/WASHINGTON 2005
Buvelot, Quentin. *Frans van Mieris, 1635–1681*. Royal Picture Gallery Mauritshuis, The Hague; National Gallery of Art, Washington. Zwolle, 2005.

THE HAGUE/WASHINGTON 2008
Suchtelen, Ariane van, and Arthur K. Wheelock, Jr. *Pride of Place: Dutch Cityscapes of the Golden Age*. Royal Picture Gallery Mauritshuis, The Hague; National Gallery of Art, Washington. Zwolle, 2008.

HAMBURG 1952
Rathe, Ewald. *Die Industrie als Kunstmäzen: Gemälde, Plastik, Kunstgewerbe gestiftet in die deutschen Museen*. Hamburger Kunsthalle, Hamburg. Hamburg, 1952.

HAMBURG 1994
Schaar, Eckhard. *Rembrandt und Sein Jahrhundert: Niederländische Zeichnungen in der Hamburger Kunsthalle*. Hamburger Kunsthalle, Hamburg. Heidelberg, 1994.

HAMBURG 2006
Sitt, Martina, Christian Tico Seifert, and Adriaan Waiboer. *Pieter Lastman: In Rembrandts Schatten?* Hamburger Kunsthalle, Hamburg. Hamburg, 2006.

'S-HERTOGENBOSCH 1990
Koldeweij, Adrianus M. *In Buscoducis, 1450–1629: Kunst uit de Bourgondische Tijd te 's-Hertogenbosch, de Cultuur van Late Middeleeuwen en Renaissance*. Noordbrabants Museum, 's-Hertogenbosch. Maarssen, 1990.

'S-HERTOGENBOSCH 2013
Hond, Jan de, and Paul Huys Janssen. *Pieter Saenredam in den Bosch*. Noordbrabants Museum, 's-Hertogenbosch. 's-Hertogenbosch, 2013.

KASSEL 2006
Weber, Gregor J. H. *Rembrandt-Bilder: Die Historische Sammlung der Kasseler Gemäldegalerie*. Gemäldegalerie Alte Meister, Kassel. Munich, 2006.

KINGSTON 1984
McTavish, David, Alfred Bader, Isabel Bader, et al. *Pictures from the Age of Rembrandt: Selections from the Personal Collection of Dr. and Mrs. Alfred Bader*. Agnes Etherington Art Centre, Queen's University, Kingston, Ontario. Kingston, 1984.

KONSTANZ/HEIDELBERG 2000
Bringmann, Michael. *Von Rembrandt bis Menzel: Meisterwerke der Zeichenkunst aus der Sammlung Brandes*. Städtische Wessenberg-Gemäldegalerie, Konstanz; Kurpfälzisches Museum, Heidelberg. Heidelberg, 2000.

KYOTO/SENDAI/TOKYO 2011
Wheelock, Arthur K., Jr., and Daniëlle H.A.C. Lokin. *Human Connections in the Age of Vermeer*. Municipal Museum of Art, Kyoto; Miyagi Museum of Art, Sendai; Bunkamura Museum of Art, Tokyo. London, 2011.

LAREN 1966
Oude Tekeningen: Een Keuze uit de Verzameling P. en N. de Boer. Singer Museum, Laren. Laren, 1966.

LEIDEN 1970
Bergström, Ingvar. *IJdelheid der IJdelheden: Hollandse Vanitasvoorstellingen uit de Zeventiende Eeuw*. Stedelijk Museum de Lakenhal, Leiden. Leiden, 1970.

LEIDEN 1988
Sluijter, Eric Jan, Marlies Enklaar, and Paul Nieuwenhuizen. *Leidse Fijnschilders: Van Gerrit Dou tot Frans van Mieris de Jonge, 1630–1760*. Stedelijk Museum de Lakenhal, Leiden. Zwolle, 1988.

LEIDEN 1994
Bolten, Jaap, Geraldine Hoekstra-van Riemsdijk, Alexander Polman, et al. *De Ruïne van Rijnsburg in Prent en Tekening, 1600–1812*. Delineavit et Sculpsit, 13. Stedelijk Museum de Lakenhal, Leiden. Leiden, 1994.

LEIDEN 1996
Vogelaar, Christiaan. *Jan van Goyen*. Stedelijk Museum de Lakenhal, Leiden. Zwolle, 1996.

LEUVEN/PARIS 2013
Van Grieken, Joris, Ger Luijten, and Jan van der Stock. *Hieronymus Cock: De Renaissance in Prent*. Museum M, Leuven; Institut Néerlandais/Fondation Custodia, Collection Frits Lugt, Paris. Brussels, 2013.

LONDON 1929
Exhibition of Dutch Art, 1450–1900. Royal Academy of Arts, London. London, 1929.

LONDON 1952
Dutch Pictures, 1450–1750. 2 vols. Royal Academy of Arts, London. London, 1952.

LONDON 1970
Regteren Altena, I. Q. van, and P.W. Ward-Jackson. *Drawings from the Teyler Museum, Haarlem*. Victoria and Albert Museum, London. London, 1970.

LONDON 1996
Royalton-Kisch, Martin, Hugo Chapman, and Stephen Coppel. *Old Master Drawings from the Malcolm Collection*. British Museum, London. London, 1996.

LONDON/AMSTERDAM 2006a
Lammertse, Friso, and Jaap van der Veen. *Uylenburgh and Son: Art and Commerce from Rembrandt to De Lairesse, 1625–1675*. Dulwich Picture Gallery, London; Museum het Rembrandthuis, Amsterdam. Zwolle, 2006.

LONDON/AMSTERDAM 2006b
Lammertse, Friso, and Jaap van der Veen. *Uylenburgh en Zoon: Kunst en Commercie van Rembrandt tot De Lairesse, 1625–1675*. Dulwich Picture Gallery, London; Museum het Rembrandthuis, Amsterdam. Zwolle, 2006.

LONDON/BIRMINGHAM/LEEDS 1962
Pouncey, Philip, Gemma Donati, and Christopher White. *Old Master Drawings from the Collection of Mr. C. R. Rudolf*. Arts

Council Gallery, London; City Museum and Art Gallery, Birmingham; Leeds City Art Gallery. London, 1962.

LONDON/HARTFORD 1998
Sutton, Peter C. *Pieter de Hooch, 1629–1684*. Dulwich Picture Gallery, London; Wadsworth Atheneum, Hartford. New Haven, 1998.

LONDON/PARIS/CAMBRIDGE 2002
Robinson, William W., and Martin Royalton-Kisch. *Bruegel to Rembrandt: Dutch and Flemish Drawings from the Maida and George Abrams Collection*. British Museum, London; Institut Néerlandais, Paris; Fogg Art Museum, Harvard University, Cambridge. New Haven, 2002.

LONDON/THE HAGUE 2007
Ekkart, Rudolf E.O., and Quentin Buvelot. *Dutch Portraits: The Age of Rembrandt and Frans Hals*. National Gallery, London; Royal Picture Gallery Mauritshuis, The Hague. London, 2007.

LOS ANGELES 2009
Bevers, Holm, Peter Schatborn, and William W. Robinson. *Drawings by Rembrandt and His Pupils: Telling the Difference*. J. Paul Getty Museum, Los Angeles. Los Angeles, 2009.

LOS ANGELES/BOSTON/NEW YORK 1981
Walsh, John, Jr., and Cynthia P. Schneider. *A Mirror of Nature: Dutch Paintings from the Collection of Mr. and Mrs. Edward William Carter*. Los Angeles County Museum of Art; Museum of Fine Arts, Boston; Metropolitan Museum of Art, New York. New York, 1981.

LOS ANGELES/PHILADELPHIA/LONDON 2005
Slive, Seymour. *Jacob van Ruisdael: Master of Landscape*. Los Angeles County Museum of Art; Philadelphia Museum of Art; Royal Academy of Arts, London. London, 2005.

MADRID 1986
Rocha, Francisco J. *Dibujos de los Siglos XIV al XX: Colección Woodner*. Museo del Prado, Madrid. Madrid, 1986.

MUNICH 1982
Renger, Konrad, and Dorothea Schmidt. *Graphik in Holland: Esaias und Jan van de Velde, Rembrandt, Ostade und Ihr Kreis: Radierung, Kupferstich, Schabkunst*. Staatliche Graphische Sammlung München. Munich, 1982.

MUNICH 2014
'Fliessender Wechsel': Alte Meister in der neuen Pinakothek. [Without catalog.] Neue Pinakothek, Munich. Munich, 2014.

MUNICH/HEIDELBERG/BRAUNSCHWEIG/CAMBRIDGE 1995
Scrase, David, and Thea Vignau Wilberg-Schuurman. *The Golden Century: Dutch Master Drawings from the Fitzwilliam Museum Cambridge*. Städtische Galerie im Lenbachhaus und Kunstbau, Munich; Kurpfälzisches Museum, Heidelberg; Herzog Anton Ulrich-Museum, Braunschweig; Fitzwilliam Museum, Cambridge. Munich, 1995.

NEW YORK 1973
Abraham Bloemaert, 1564–1651: Prints and Drawings. Metropolitan Museum of Art, New York. New York, 1973.

NEW YORK 1996
Seventeenth-Century Dutch Drawings in the Pierpont Morgan Library. [Without catalog.] Pierpont Morgan Library, New York. New York, 1996.

NEW YORK 2016
Baum, Kelly, Andrea Bayer, and Sheena Wagstaff. *Unfinished: Thoughts Left Visible*. Metropolitan Museum of Art, New York. New York, 2016.

NEW YORK/BOSTON/CHICAGO 1972
Schatborn, Peter. *Dutch Genre Drawings of the Seventeenth Century*. Pierpont Morgan Library, New York; Museum of Fine Arts, Boston; Art Institute of Chicago. New York, 1972.

NEW YORK/CAMBRIDGE 1960
Haverkamp-Begemann, Egbert, and Felice Stampfle. *Rembrandt Drawings from American Collections*. Pierpont Morgan Library, New York; Fogg Art Museum, Harvard University, Cambridge. New York, 1960.

NEW YORK/FORT WORTH 1995
Bisanz-Prakken, Marian, and Konrad Oberhuber. *Drawings from the Albertina: Landscape in the Age of Rembrandt*. Drawing Center, New York; Kimbell Art Museum, Fort Worth. Alexandria, 1995.

NEW YORK/FORT WORTH/CLEVELAND 1990
Luijten, Ger, and A.W.F.M. Meij. *From Pisanello to Cézanne: Master Drawings from the Museum Boymans-Van Beuningen, Rotterdam*. Pierpont Morgan Library, New York; Kimbell Art Museum, Fort Worth; Cleveland Museum of Art. Rotterdam, 1990.

NEW YORK/LONDON 2001
Liedtke, Walter A., Michiel Plomp, and Axel Rüger. *Vermeer and the Delft School*. Metropolitan Museum of Art, New York; National Gallery, London. New Haven, 2001.

NEW YORK/PARIS 1977
Hasselt, Carlos van. *Rembrandt and His Century: Dutch Drawings of the Seventeenth Century from the Collection of Frits Lugt*. Pierpont Morgan Library, New York; Institut Néerlandais/Fondation Custodia, Collection Frits Lugt, Paris. New York, 1977.

OSAKA 2000
Wheelock, Arthur K., Jr. *The Public and the Private in the Age of Vermeer*. Osaka Municipal Museum of Art. London, 2000.

PARIS 1950
Bruyn, J. *Le Paysage hollandais au XVIIᵉ siècle*. Musée de l'Orangerie, Paris. Paris, 1950.

PARIS 1965
Gorter, Sadi de. *Le Décor de la vie privée en Hollande au XVIIᵉ siècle*. Institut Néerlandais/Fondation Custodia, Collection Frits Lugt, Paris. Paris, 1965.

PARIS 1970
Brejon de Lavergnée, Arnauld. *Le Siècle de Rembrandt: Tableaux hollandais des collections*

publiques françaises. Musée du Petit Palais, Paris. Paris, 1970.

PARIS 1974
Meij, A.W.F.M., Carlos van Hasselt, Maria van Berge-Gerbaud, et al. *Dessins flamands et hollandais du dix-septième siècle: collections musées de Belgique, Musée Boymans-Van Beuningen, Rotterdam, Institut Néerlandais, Paris*. Institut Néerlandais/Fondation Custodia, Collection Frits Lugt, Paris. Paris, 1974.

PARIS 1981
Schnackenburg, Bernhard. *Le Monde paysan d'Adriaen et Isack van Ostade*. Institut Néerlandais/Fondation Custodia, Collection Frits Lugt, Paris. Paris, 1981.

PARIS 1983
Nihom-Nijstad, Saskia, and Claude Wolters-Girard. *Reflets du Siècle d'Or: Tableaux hollandais du dix-septième siècle, Collection Frits Lugt, Fondation Custodia*. Institut Néerlandais/Fondation Custodia, Collection Frits Lugt, Paris. Paris, 1983.

PARIS 1984
Pinault, Madeleine. *Dessins et sciences, XVII–XVIIIᵉ siècles*. Cabinet des Dessins, Musée du Louvre, Paris. Paris, 1984.

PARIS 1985
Hasselt, Carlos van, and Mària van Berge-Gerbaud. *Le Héraut du dix-septième siècle: Dessins et gravures de Jacques de Gheyn II et III de la Fondation Custodia, Collection Frits Lugt*. Institut Néerlandais/Fondation Custodia, Collection Frits Lugt, Paris. Paris, 1985.

PARIS 1989
Hasselt, Carlos van, and Mària van Berge-Gerbaud. *Éloge de la navigation hollandaise au XVIIᵉ siècle: Tableaux, dessins et gravures de la mer et de ses rivages dans la Collection Frits Lugt*. Institut Néerlandais/Fondation Custodia, Collection Frits Lugt, Paris. Paris, 1989.

PARIS 1994
Berge-Gerbaud, Mària van, and Hans Buijs. *Morceaux choisis parmi les acquisitions de la Collection Frits Lugt réalisées sous le directorat de Carlos van Hasselt, 1970–1994*. Institut Néerlandais/Fondation Custodia, Collection Frits Lugt, Paris. Paris, 1994.

PARIS 2004
Alsteens, Stijn. *Regards sur l'art hollandais du XVIIᵉ siècle: Frits Lugt et les Frères Dutuit collectionneurs*. Institut Néerlandais/Fondation Custodia, Collection Frits Lugt, Paris; Musée du Petit Palais, Paris. Paris, 2004.

PARIS 2006a
Schatborn, Peter, Carel van Tuyll van Serooskerken, and Hélène Grollemund. *Rembrandt dessinateur: Chefs d'oeuvre des collections en France*. Département des Arts Graphiques, Musée du Louvre, Paris. Paris, 2006.

PARIS 2006b
Dittrich, Christian, and Thomas Ketelsen. *Rembrandt: les dessins de Dresde*. Institut Néerlandais/Fondation Custodia, Collection Frits Lugt, Paris. Paris, 2006.

PARIS 2007
Bevers, Holm. *Rembrandt: Dessins du Kupferstichkabinett de Berlin*. Institut Néerlandais/Fondation Custodia, Collection Frits Lugt, Paris. Paris, 2007.

PARIS 2009a
Priem, Ruud, and Marc Restellini. *L'Âge d'Or hollandais: De Rembrandt à Vermeer avec les trésors du Rijksmuseum*. Pinacothèque de Paris. Paris, 2009.

PARIS 2009b
Bakhuÿs, Diederik, Jasper Hillegers, Cécile Tainturier, et al. *Tableaux Flamands et hollandais du musée des Beaux-Arts de Rouen*. Collections Flamandes et Hollandaises des Musées de Province. Institut Néerlandais/Fondation Custodia, Collection Frits Lugt, Paris. Paris, 2009.

PARIS 2014
Buijs, Hans, and Ger Luijten. *Goltzius to Van Gogh: Drawings and Paintings from the P. and N. de Boer Foundation*. Fondation Custodia, Collection Frits Lugt, Paris. Paris, 2014.

PARIS/AJACCIO 2012
Berge-Gerbaud, Mària van, Emmanuelle Brugerolles, and Peter Schatborn. *Rembrandt et son entourage*. Carnets d'études, 23. École Nationale Supérieure des Beaux-Arts, Paris; Palais Fesch-Musée des Beaux-Arts, Ajaccio. Paris, 2012.

PARIS/AMSTERDAM 2008
Alsteens, Stijn, and Hans Buijs. *Paysages de France: Dessinés par Lambert Doomer et les artistes hollandais et flamands des XVIᵉ et XVIIᵉ siècles*. Institut Néerlandais/Fondation Custodia, Collection Frits Lugt, Paris; Museum het Rembrandthuis, Amsterdam. Paris, 2008.

PARIS/ANTWERP/LONDON/
NEW YORK 1979
Stampfle, Felice. *Rubens and Rembrandt in Their Century: Flemish and Dutch Drawings of the 17th Century from the Pierpont Morgan Library*. Institut Néerlandais/Fondation Custodia, Collection Frits Lugt, Paris; Koninklijk Museum voor Schone Kunsten, Antwerp; British Museum, London; Pierpont Morgan Library, New York. New York, 1979.

PARIS/HAARLEM 1997
Berge-Gerbaud, Mària van. *Rembrandt et son école: Dessins de la Collection Frits Lugt / Rembrandt en Zijn School: Tekeningen uit de Collectie Frits Lugt*. Institut Néerlandais/Fondation Custodia, Collection Frits Lugt, Paris; Teylers Museum, Haarlem. Paris-Basel, 1997.

PARIS/HAMBURG 1985
Brugerolles, Emmanuelle. *Renaissance et Maniérisme dans les écoles du Nord: Dessins des collections de l'École des Beaux-Arts*. École Nationale Supérieure des Beaux-Arts, Paris; Hamburger Kunsthalle, Hamburg. Paris, 1985.

PARIS/ROTTERDAM/WASHINGTON 2014
Bleyerveld, Yvonne, Albert Elen, and Judith Niesen. *Bosch to Bloemaert: Early Netherlandish Drawings in Museum Boijmans van Beuningen, Rotterdam*. Fondation Custodia, Collection Frits Lugt, Paris; Museum Boijmans van

Beuningen, Rotterdam; National Gallery of Art, Washington. Bussum, 2014.

PHILADELPHIA/BERLIN/LONDON 1984
Sutton, Peter C. *Masters of Seventeenth-Century Dutch Genre Painting.* Edited by Jane Iandola Watkins. Philadelphia Museum of Art; Gemäldegalerie, Staatliche Museen Preussischer Kulturbesitz, Berlin; Royal Academy of Arts, London. Philadelphia, 1984.

POUGHKEEPSIE 1976
Baer, Curtis O. *Seventeenth Century Dutch Landscape Drawings and Selected Prints from American Collections.* Vassar College Art Gallery, Poughkeepsie. Poughkeepsie, 1976.

ROME 2012
Bandera Bistoletti, Sandrina, Walter A. Liedtke, and Arthur K. Wheelock, Jr. *Vermeer: Il Secolo d'Oro dell'Arte Olandese.* Scuderie del Quirinale, Rome. Milan, 2012.

ROTTERDAM 1938
Hannema, Dirk. *Meesterwerken uit Vier Eeuwen, 1400–1800: Tentoonstelling van Schilderijen en Teekeningen uit Particuliere Verzamelingen in Nederland, Bijeengebracht Gedurende de 40-Jarige Regering van H.M. Koningin Wilhelmina.* Museum Boymans, Rotterdam. Rotterdam, 1938.

ROTTERDAM 1985
Meij, A.W.F.M., and J.A. Poot. *Jacques de Gheyn II als Tekenaar: 1565–1629.* Museum Boymans-van Beuningen, Rotterdam. Rotterdam, 1985.

ROTTERDAM 1988
Jansen, Guido, and Ger Luijten. *Italianisanten en Bamboccianten: Het Italianiserend Landschap en Genre door Nederlandse Kunstenaars uit de Zeventiende Eeuw.* Museum Boymans-van Beuningen, Rotterdam. Rotterdam, 1988.

ROTTERDAM 1991
Giltaij, Jeroen, and Guido Jansen. *Perspectives: Saenredam and the Architectural Painters of the 17th Century.* Museum Boymans-van Beuningen, Rotterdam. Rotterdam, 1991.

ROTTERDAM 2005
Elen, Albert J. *Rembrandt in Rotterdam: Tekeningen van Rembrandt en Zijn Kring in het Museum Boijmans van Beuningen.* Museum Boijmans van Beuningen, Rotterdam. Rotterdam, 2005.

ROTTERDAM/FRANKFURT 1999a
Blankert, Albert, Koen Ottenheym, and Arie Jan Gelderblom. *Dutch Classicism in Seventeenth-Century Painting.* Museum Boijmans Van Beuningen, Rotterdam; Städelsches Kunstinstitut, Frankfurt. Rotterdam, 1999.

ROTTERDAM/FRANKFURT 1999b
Blankert, Albert, Koen Ottenheym, and Arie Jan Gelderblom. *Hollands Classicisme in de Zeventiende-Eeuwse Schilderkunst.* Museum Boijmans Van Beuningen, Rotterdam; Städelsches Kunstinstitut, Frankfurt. Rotterdam, 1999.

ROTTERDAM/PARIS 1974
Haverkamp-Begemann, Egbert. *Willem Buytewech, 1591–1624.* Museum Boymans-van Beuningen, Rotterdam; Institut Néerlandais/Fondation Custodia, Collection Frits Lugt, Paris. Amsterdam, 1974.

ROTTERDAM/PARIS/BRUSSELS 1977
Hasselt, Carlos van. *Le Cabinet d'un Amateur: Dessins Flamands et Hollandais des XVI. et XVII. Siècles d'une Collection Privée d'Amsterdam.* Museum Boymans-van Beuningen, Rotterdam; Institut Néerlandais/Fondation Custodia, Collection Frits Lugt, Paris; Bibliothèque Albert I, Brussels. Rotterdam, 1977.

ROTTERDAM/WASHINGTON 1985
Meij, A.W.F.M., J.A. Poot, and Richard J. Judson. *Jacques de Gheyn II als Tekenaar, 1565–1629.* Museum Boymans-van Beuningen, Rotterdam; National Gallery of Art, Washington. Rotterdam, 1985.

SACRAMENTO 1974
Tümpel, Astrid, and Christian Tümpel. *The Pre-Rembrandtists.* E.B. Crocker Art Gallery, Sacramento. Sacramento, 1974.

SACRAMENTO/POUGHKEEPSIE 2010
Breazeale, William. *A Pioneering Collection: Master Drawings from the Crocker Art Museum.* Crocker Art Museum, Sacramento; Frances Lehman Loeb Art Center, Vassar College, Poughkeepsie. London, 2010.

SALEM/SAN FRANCISCO/HOUSTON 2011
Duparc, Frederik J. *Golden: Dutch and Flemish Masterworks from the Rose-Marie and Eijk van Otterloo Collection.* Peabody Essex Museum, Salem; Fine Arts Museum of San Francisco; Museum of Fine Arts, Houston. Salem, 2011.

SAN FRANCISCO/BALTIMORE/
LONDON 1997
Spicer, Joaneath A., and Lynn Federle Orr. *Masters of Light: Dutch Painters in Utrecht during the Golden Age.* Fine Arts Museums of San Francisco; Walters Art Gallery, Baltimore; National Gallery, London. Baltimore, 1997.

STOCKHOLM 1967
Grate, Pontus. *Holländska Mästare i Svensk Ägo.* Nationalmuseum, Stockholm. Stockholm, 1967.

STOCKHOLM 1992
Cavalli-Björkman, Görel. *Rembrandt och Hans Tid: Människan i Centrum / Rembrandt and His Age: Focus on Man.* Nationalmuseum, Stockholm. Stockholm, 1992.

UTRECHT 1961
Swillens, P.T.A. *Catalogue Raisonné of the Works by Pieter Jansz. Saenredam.* Centraal Museum, Utrecht. Utrecht, 1961.

UTRECHT 1965
Blankert, Albert, Maria Elisabeth Houtzager, and H.J. de Smedt. *Nederlandse 17e Eeuwse Italianiserende Landschapschilders.* Centraal Museum, Utrecht. Utrecht, 1965.

UTRECHT 1984
Molen, J.R. ter, and M.I.E. van Zijl. *Zeldzaam Zilver uit de Gouden Eeuw: De Utrechtse Edelsmeden van Vianen.* Centraal Museum, Utrecht. Utrecht, 1984.

UTRECHT 2001
Helmus, Liesbeth M. *Pieter Saenredam, the Utrecht Work: Drawings and Paintings by the 17th Century Master of Perspectives*. Centraal Museum, Utrecht. Utrecht, 2001.

UTRECHT/ANTWERP 1952
Houtzager, Maria Elisabeth, and Emile R. Meyer. *Caravaggio en de Nederlanden*. Centraal Museum, Utrecht; Koninklijk Museum voor Schone Kunsten, Antwerp. Utrecht, 1952.

UTRECHT/BRAUNSCHWEIG 1986
Blankert, Albert, and Leonard J. Slatkes. *Nieuw Licht op de Gouden Eeuw: Hendrick ter Brugghen en Tijdgenoten*. Centraal Museum, Utrecht; Herzog Anton Ulrich-Museum, Braunschweig. Braunschweig, 1986.

UTRECHT/SCHWERIN 2011
Helmus, Liesbeth M., and Gero Seelig. *The Bloemaert Effect*. Centraal Museum, Utrecht; Staatliches Museum Schwerin. Petersberg, 2011.

VANCOUVER 2009
Priem, Ruud. *Vermeer, Rembrandt and the Golden Age of Dutch Art: Masterpieces from the Rijksmuseum*. Edited by Thomas Padon. Vancouver Art Gallery. Berkeley, 2009.

VIENNA 1993
Bisanz-Prakken, Marian. *Die Landschaft im Jahrhundert Rembrandts: Niederländische Zeichnungen des 17. Jahrhunderts aus der Graphischen Sammlung Albertina*. Graphischen Sammlung Albertina, Vienna. Vienna, 1993.

VIENNA 2009
Schröder, Albrecht, and Marian Bizanz Prakken. *Das Zeitalter Rembrandts*. Albertina, Vienna. Vienna, 2009.

WASHINGTON 1995
Grasselli, Margaret M. *The Touch of the Artist: Master Drawings from the Woodner Collections*. National Gallery of Art, Washington. Washington, 1995.

WASHINGTON 1998
Wheelock, Arthur K., Jr. *A Collector's Cabinet*. National Gallery of Art, Washington. Washington, 1998.

WASHINGTON 1999
Wheelock, Arthur K., Jr. *From Botany to Bouquets: Flowers in Northern Art*. National Gallery of Art, Washington. Washington, 1999.

WASHINGTON 2002
Ebert-Schifferer, Sybille. *Deceptions and Illusions: Five Centuries of Trompe l'Oeil Painting*. National Gallery of Art, Washington. Washington, 2002.

WASHINGTON 2006
Master Drawings from the Woodner Collections [without catalog]. National Gallery of Art, Washington. Washington, 2006.

WASHINGTON/DENVER/
FORT WORTH 1977
Robinson, Franklin W. *Seventeenth Century Dutch Drawings from American Collections*. National Gallery of Art, Washington; Denver Art Museum; Kimbell Art Museum, Fort Worth. Washington, 1977.

WASHINGTON/DETROIT 2004
Wheelock, Arthur K., Jr. *Gerard ter Borch*. National Gallery of Art, Washington; Detroit Institute of Arts. Washington, 2004.

WASHINGTON/DETROIT/
AMSTERDAM 1980
Blankert, Albert. *Gods, Saints, and Heroes: Dutch Painting in the Age of Rembrandt*. National Gallery of Art, Washington; Detroit Institute of Arts; Rijksmuseum, Amsterdam. Washington, 1980.

WASHINGTON/LONDON 2015
Sell, Stacey, and Hugo Chapman. *Drawing in Silver and Gold: Leonardo to Jasper Johns*. National Gallery of Art, Washington; British Museum, London. Washington, 2015.

WASHINGTON/LONDON/
AMSTERDAM 2001
Wheelock, Arthur K., Jr. *Aelbert Cuyp*. National Gallery of Art, Washington; National Gallery, London; Rijksmuseum, Amsterdam. Washington, 2001.

WASHINGTON/LONDON/THE HAGUE 2000
Baer, Ronni. *Gerrit Dou, 1613–1675: Master Painter in the Age of Rembrandt*. Edited by Arthur K. Wheelock, Jr. National Gallery of Art, Washington; Dulwich Picture Gallery, London; Royal Cabinet of Paintings Mauritshuis, The Hague. New Haven, 2000.

WASHINGTON/MILWAUKEE/
AMSTERDAM 2008
Wheelock, Arthur K., Jr. *Jan Lievens: A Dutch Master Rediscovered*. National Gallery of Art, Washington; Milwaukee Art Museum; Museum het Rembrandthuis, Amsterdam. New Haven, 2008.

WASHINGTON/NEW YORK 1986
Hand, John Oliver, J. Richard Judson, William W. Robinson, et al. *The Age of Bruegel: Netherlandish Drawings in the Sixteenth Century*. National Gallery of Art, Washington; Pierpont Morgan Library, New York. Cambridge, 1986.

WASHINGTON/NEW YORK/MINNEAPOLIS/
BOSTON/CLEVELAND/CHICAGO 1958
Regteren Altena, I.Q. van. *Dutch Drawings: Masterpieces of Five Centuries*. National Gallery of Art, Washington; Pierpont Morgan Library, New York; Minneapolis Institute of Arts; Museum of Fine Arts, Boston; Cleveland Museum of Art; Art Institute of Chicago. Washington, 1958.

WASHINGTON/NEW YORK/
SAN FRANCISCO 1978
Menzhausen, Joachim, Harald Marx, and Johannes Schöbel. *The Splendor of Dresden: Five Centuries of Art Collecting, an Exhibition from the State Art Collections of Dresden, German Democratic Republic*. National Gallery of Art, Washington; Metropolitan Museum of Art, New York; Fine Arts Museums of San Francisco, California Palace of the Legion of Honor, San Francisco. New York, 1978.

BIBLIOGRAPHY BOOKS & ARTICLES

ACTON 1998
Acton, David. *Master Drawings from the Worcester Art Museum.* New York, 1998.

ADAMS 1985
Adams, Ann Jensen. 'The Paintings of Thomas de Keyser (1596/7–1667): A Study of Portraiture in Seventeenth-Century Amsterdam.' PhD diss., Harvard University, 1985.

AMPZING 1628
Ampzing, Samuel. *Beschryvinge ende Lof der Stad Haerlem in Holland.* Haarlem, 1628.

ANDREWS 1984
Andrews, Keith. 'On Some Drawings by Pieter de Grebber.' *Master Drawings* 22 (1984): 294–298.

ANDREWS 1985
Andrews, Keith. *Catalogue of the Netherlandish Drawings in the National Gallery of Scotland.* 2 vols. Edinburgh, 1985.

ANGEL 1642
Angel, Philips. *Lof der Schilder-Konst.* Leiden, 1642.

AONO 2015
Aono, Junko. *Confronting the Golden Age: Imitation and Innovation in Dutch Genre Painting, 1680–1750.* Amsterdam Studies in the Dutch Golden Age. Amsterdam, 2015.

ASPEREN DE BOER 1970
Asperen de Boer, J.R.J. van. 'Infrared Reflectography: A Contribution to the Examination of Earlier European Paintings.' PhD diss., University of Amsterdam, 1970.

ASPEREN DE BOER 1971
Asperen de Boer, J.R.J. van. 'De Ondertekening bij Pieter Saenredam: Twee Voorbeelden.' *Bulletin van het Rijksmuseum* 19 (1971): 25–31.

BAER 2000
Baer, Ronni. 'The Life and Work of Gerrit Dou.' In *Gerrit Dou, 1613–1675: Master Painter in the Age of Rembrandt*, 26–52. National Gallery of Art, Washington; Dulwich Picture Gallery, London; Royal Cabinet of Paintings Mauritshuis, The Hague. New Haven, 2000.

BAUCH 1960
Bauch, Kurt. *Der frühe Rembrandt und seine Zeit: Studien zur Geschichtlichen Bedeutung seines Frühstils.* Berlin, 1960.

BECK 1957
Beck, Hans-Ulrich. 'Jan van Goyens Handzeichnungen als Vorzeichnungen.' *Oud Holland* 72 (1957): 241–250.

BECK 1966
Beck, Hans-Ulrich. *Ein Skizzenbuch von Jan van Goyen.* Publicaties van het Rijksbureau voor Kunsthistorische Documentatie te 's-Gravenhage. The Hague, 1966.

BECK 1972–1991
Beck, Hans-Ulrich. *Jan van Goyen, 1596–1656: Ein Oeuvreverzeichnis.* 4 vols. Amsterdam, 1972–1991.

BECK 1996
Beck, Hans-Ulrich. 'The Preliminary Drawing for Jan van Goyen's Views of Nijmegen.' *Master Drawings* 34 (1996): 192–194.

BEER 2002
Beer, Gerlinde de. *Ludolf Backhuysen (1630–1708): Sein Leben und Werk.* Zwolle, 2002.

BENESCH 1973
Benesch, Otto. *The Drawings of Rembrandt.* 6 vols. Edited by Eva Benesch. London, 1973.

BERGE-GERBAUD, BLOK, AND BUIJS 2000
Berge-Gerbaud, Mària van, Rhea Blok, and Hans Buijs. *Acquisitions, 1994–1999.* Fondation Custodia, Collection Frits Lugt. Paris, 2000.

BERGSTRÖM 1956
Bergström, Ingvar. *Dutch Still-Life Painting in the Seventeenth Century.* London, 1956.

BERGSTRÖM 1970
Bergström, Ingvar. 'De Gheyn as a Vanitas Painter.' *Oud Holland* 85 (1970): 143–157.

BERNT 1957
Bernt, Walther. *Die niederländischen Zeichner des 17. Jahrhunderts.* 2 vols. Munich, 1957–1958.

BEVERS 2000
Bevers, Holm. 'Review of *Van Eyck, Bruegel, Rembrandt: Niederländische Zeichnungen des 15. bis 17. Jahrhunderts aus dem Kupferstich-Kabinett, Dresden*, by Christian Dittrich.' *Master Drawings* 38 (2000): 70–73.

BEVERS 2006
Bevers, Holm. *Rembrandt: Die Zeichnungen im Berliner Kupferstichkabinett.* Berlin, 2006.

BEVERS 2010
Bevers, Holm. 'Early, Rembrandtesque Drawings by Gerbrand van den Eeckhout.' *Master Drawings* 48 (2010): 39–72.

BIAŁOSTOCKI 1969
Białostocki, Jan. *National Museum in Warsaw Catalogue of Paintings: Foreign Schools.* 2 vols. Warsaw, 1969.

DE BIE 1661
Bie, Cornelis de. *Het Gulden Cabinet van de Edele Vry Schilder-Const.* Antwerp, 1661. Facsimile reprint, Soest, 1971.

BIESBOER 2008
Biesboer, Pieter. 'Jan de Bray: A Most Versatile Artist.' In *Painting Family: The De Brays: Master Painters of 17th Century Holland*, by Pieter Biesboer. Frans Hals Museum, Haarlem; Dulwich Picture Gallery, London. Zwolle, 2008.

BIESBOER 2012
Biesboer, Pieter. 'Cornelis Bega (Haarlem, 1631–1664): Eine Biografie.' In *Cornelis Bega: Eleganz und raue Sitten*, by Peter van den Brink and Bernd Wolfgang Lindemann, 25–26. Suermondt-Ludwig-Museum, Aachen; Gemäldegalerie, Staatliche Museen zu Berlin. Stuttgart, 2012.

BIKKER 2007
Bikker, Jonathan, Yvette Bruijnen, Gerdien Wuestman, et al. *Dutch Paintings of the Seventeenth Century in the Rijksmuseum Amsterdam*. Vol. 1: *Artists Born between 1570 and 1600*. Amsterdam, 2007.

BLANKERT 1967
Blankert, Albert. 'Heraclitus en Democritus.' *Nederlands Kunsthistorisch Jaarboek* 18 (1967): 31–124.

BLANKERT 1986
Blankert, Albert. 'Over Pieter van Laer als Dier- en Landscapschilder.' *Oud Holland* 83 (1986): 117–134.

BOCK 1996
Bock, Henning. *Gemäldegalerie Berlin: Gesamtverzeichnis*. Berlin, 1996.

BOCK AND ROSENBERG 1930
Bock, Elfried, and Jakob Rosenberg. *Die niederländischen Meister: Beschreibendes Verzeichnis sämtlicher Zeichnungen*. 2 vols. Die Zeichnungen alter Meister im Kupferstichkabinett, Staatliche Museen zu Berlin. Berlin, 1930.

BOK 2011
Bok, Marten Jan. '"Een Leven Lang Leren" in Abraham Bloemaert, een Geliefde Meester.' *Kunstschrift* 55, no. 5 (2011): 24–36.

BOLTEN 1979
Bolten, Jaap. 'Het Noord- en Zuidnederlandse Tekenboek, 1600–1750.' PhD diss., University of Amsterdam, 1979.

BOLTEN 1995
Bolten, Jaap. 'Paulus Potter (1625–1654).' *Delineavit et Sculpsit* 53 (1995): 38.

BOLTEN 2007
Bolten, Jaap. *Abraham Bloemaert, c. 1565–1651: The Drawings*. 2 vols. Leiden, 2007.

BOON 1978
Boon, Karel G. *Netherlandish Drawings of the Fifteenth and Sixteenth Centuries*. 2 vols. Catalogue of the Dutch and Flemish Drawings in the Rijksmuseum, 2. The Hague, 1978.

BOON 1992
Boon, Karel G. *The Netherlandish and German Drawings of the XVth and XVIth Centuries of the Frits Lugt Collection*. 3 vols. Paris, 1992.

BRANDT 1687
Brandt, Geeraert. *Het Leven en Bedryf van den Heere Michiel de Ruiter*. Amsterdam, 1687.

BRAUN AND HOGENBERG 1572–1617
Braun, Georg, and Frans Hogenberg. *Civitates Orbis Terrarum*. 6 vols. Cologne, 1572–1617.

BREDIUS 1887
Bredius, Abraham. 'Een en Ander over Caspar Netscher.' *Oud Holland* 5 (1887): 263–274.

BREDIUS 1915–1922
Bredius, Abraham. *Künstler-Inventare: Urkunden zur Geschichte der holländische Kunst des XVIen, XVIIen, und XVIIIen Jahrhunderts*. 8 vols. The Hague, 1915–1922.

BREDIUS 1935
Bredius, Abraham. *Rembrandt Schilderijen*. Utrecht, 1935.

BREDIUS AND GERSON 1969
Bredius, Abraham. *Rembrandt: The Complete Edition of the Paintings*. Revised by Horst Gerson. London, 1969.

BREDIUS AND MOES 1892
Bredius, Abraham, and E. W. Moes. 'De Schildersfamilie Ravesteyn.' *Oud Holland* 10 (1892): 41–52.

BRENNINKMEYER-DE ROOIJ 1990
Brenninkmeijer-de Rooij, Beatrijs. 'Zeldzame Bloemen, "Fatta Tutti del Natturel" door Jan Brueghel I.' *Oud Holland* 104 (1990): 218–255.

BRENNINKMEYER-DE ROOIJ 1996
Brenninkmeyer-de Rooij, Beatrijs. *Roots of Seventeenth-Century Flower Painting: Miniatures, Plant Books, Paintings*. Leiden, 1996.

BRÉTON 2014
Bréton, Etienne, Renaud Jouslin de Noray, and Nicolas Schwed. *Vingt-Sept Dessins de Gerrit van Honthorst (1592–1656)*. Paris, 2014.

BROOS AND SCHAPELHOUMAN 1993
Broos, Ben P. J., and Marijn Schapelhouman. *Nederlandse Tekenaars Geboren tussen 1600 en 1660, Waaronder de Collectie Fodor*. Zwolle, 1993.

BROWN 1995
Brown, Christopher. 'Exhibition Review of *Paulus Potter: Paintings, Drawings, and Etchings*, Royal Picture Gallery Mauritshuis, The Hague, 1994–1995.' *Burlington Magazine* 137, no. 1105 (April 1995): 265–267.

BUIJSEN 1993
Buijsen, Edwin. *The Sketchbook of Jan van Goyen from the Bredius-Kronig Collection*. The Hague, 1993.

BUIJSEN 1995
Buijsen, Edwin. 'Het Archief van een Architectuurschilder: Een Tekenboekje van Daniel de Blieck.' *Antiek, Tijdschrift voor Oude Kunst en Kunstnijverheid* 30, no. 2 (1995): 60–68.

BUIJSEN 1996
Buijsen, Edwin. 'De Schetsboeken van Jan van Goyen.' In *Jan van Goyen*, by Christiaan Vogelaar, 22–37. Stedelijk Museum de Lakenhal, Leiden. Zwolle, 1996.

BURKE 1980
Burke, James D. 'Dutch Paintings.' *Saint Louis Art Museum Bulletin* 15, no. 4 (1980): 5–24.

BURKE 1995
Burke, Peter. *The Fortunes of the Courtier: The European Reception of Castiglione's Cortegiano.* Cambridge, 1995.

BUVELOT 2004
Buvelot, Quentin. *Royal Picture Gallery Mauritshuis: A Summary Catalogue.* The Hague, 2004.

BUVELOT 2010
Buvelot, Quentin. 'Jan Van Kessel in Bentheim?', *Delineavit et sculpsit* 33 (2010): 33–34.

BUVELOT 2015
Buvelot, Quentin. 'A Newly Discovered Letter to Arnold Houbraken on the Life of Paulus Potter.' *Burlington Magazine* 157, no. 1343 (February 2015): 92–96.

CASTIGLIONE 1980
Castiglione, Baldassare. *The Book of the Courtier.* Edited by George Bull. Penguin Classics. Harmondsworth, 1980.

CATS 1642
Cats, Jacob. *Houwelyck, Dat Is, de Gantsche Ghelegentheydt des Echten-Staets.* Amsterdam, 1642.

CHAPMAN 2007
Chapman, H. Perry. 'The Wooden Body: Representing the Manikin in Dutch Artists' Studios.' *Nederlands Kunsthistorisch Jaarboek* 58 (2007): 188–215.

CHIARINI 1989
Chiarini, Marco. *I Dipinti Olandesi del Seicento e del Settecento.* Cataloghi dei Musei e Gallerie d'Italia, n.s., 1. Rome, 1989.

CHONG 1987
Chong, Alan. 'The Drawings of Cornelis van Poelenburch.' *Master Drawings* 25 (1987): 3–62, 85–116.

CHONG 1992
Chong, Alan. 'Aelbert Cuyp and the Meanings of Landscape.' PhD diss., New York University, 1992.

CHRISTIE'S 2012
London, Christie's. *Old Master and British Paintings Evening Sale, 3 July 2012, Sale 5602.* London, 2012.

LE CLAIRE 1998
Le Claire Kunsthandel, Thomas. *Master Drawings, 1500–1900.* Hamburg, 1998.

COENEN 2005
Coenen, Baukje J. L. 'The Drawings of the Haarlem Amateur Leendert van der Cooghen.' *Master Drawings* 43 (2005): 5–90.

COENEN 2012
Coenen, Baukje. 'Experimentierfreudig und Versiert: Cornelis Bega als Zeichner und Grafiker.' In *Cornelis Bega: Eleganz und raue Sitten*, by Peter van den Brink and Bernd Wolfgang Lindemann, 41–59. Suermondt-Ludwig-Museum Aachen; Gemäldegalerie Staatliche Museen zu Berlin. Stuttgart, 2012.

DAALDER 2013
Daalder, Remmelt. 'Van de Velde en Zoon, Zeeschilders: Het Bedrijf van Willem van de Velde de Oude en Willem van de Velde de Jonge, 1640–1707.' PhD, University of Amsterdam, 2013.

DAVIES 1992
Davies, Alice I. *Jan van Kessel (1641–1680).* Doornspijk, 1992.

DAVIES 2014
Davies, Alice I. *Anthonie van Borssom (1630–1677): A Catalogue of His Drawings.* Aetas Aurea, 24. Doornspijk, 2014.

DEKIERT 2004
Dekiert, Marcus. *Rembrandt: Die Opferung Isaaks.* Monographien der Bayerischen Staatsgemäldesammlungen. Munich, 2004.

DELBANCO 1928
Delbanco, Gustav. *Der Maler Abraham Bloemaert (1564–1651).* Studien zur Deutschen Kunstgeschichte 253. Strassburg, 1928.

DOMELA NIEUWENHUIS 2012
Domela Nieuwenhuis, Eric. 'De Vroege Schuttersstukken van de Haagse Sebastiaansdoelen.' In *Face Book: Studies on Dutch and Flemish Portraiture of the 16th–18th Centuries*, edited by Edwin Buijsen, Charles Dumas, and Volker Manuth, 99–108. Leiden, 2012.

DUDOK VAN HEEL 1982
Dudok van Heel, Sebastian A.C. 'Het "Schilderhuys" van Govert Flinck en de Kunsthandel van Uylenburgh aan de Lauriergracht te Amsterdam.' *Jaarboek Amstelodamum* 74 (1982): 70–90.

DUDOK VAN HEEL 2009
Dudok van Heel, S. A. C. 'The Night Watch and the Entry of Marie de Medici: A New Interpretation of the Original Place and Significance of the Painting.' *Rijksmuseum Bulletin* 57, no. 1 (2009): 5–41.

DUPARC 1993
Duparc, Frederik. 'Philips Wouwerman, 1619–1668.' *Oud Holland* 107 (1993): 257–286.

DURANTINI 1983
Durantini, Mary Frances. *The Child in Seventeenth-Century Dutch Painting.* Studies in the Fine Arts: Iconography, 7. Ann Arbor, 1983.

EBERT 2013
Ebert, Anja. *Adriaen van Ostade und die komische Malerei des 17. Jahrhunderts.* Kunstwissenschaftliche Studien, 177. Berlin, 2013.

EEGHEN 2015
Eeghen, Christiaan Pieter van. *Brede Rivieren Langs Hoge Hellingen: Het Stuwlandschap van Midden-Nederland op Zeventiende-Eeuwse Tekeningen.* Utrecht, 2015.

EERENBEEMD 2006
Eerenbeemd, Angelique van den. 'De Italianiserende Tekeningen van Adriaen van de Velde.' *Delineavit et Sculpsit* 30 (2006): 1–64.

EKKART 1985
Ekkart, Rudi. 'Het Portret van Abraham Casteleyn en Zijn Vrouw.' *De Boekenwereld* 1 (July 1985): 13–15.

EKKART 2012
Ekkart, Rudi. 'Dutch Family Ties: Painter Families in Seventeenth-Century Holland.' In *Family Ties: Art Production and Kinship Patterns in the Early Modern Low Countries*, edited by Koenraad Brosens, Leen Kelchtermans, and Katlijne van der Stighelen, 77–84. Turnhout, 2012.

ELLENIUS 1960
Ellenius, Allan. *De Arte Pingendi: Latin Art Literature in Seventeenth-Century Sweden and Its International Background*. Lychnos-Bibliothek, 19. Uppsala, 1960.

FILEDT KOK AND LEESBERG 2000
Filedt Kok, Jan Piet, and Marjolein Leesberg. *The De Gheyn Family*. 2 vols. New Hollstein: Dutch and Flemish Etchings, Engravings and Woodcuts, 1450–1700. Rotterdam, 2000.

FISCHER 1936
Fischer, O. 'Geschichte der öffentlichen Kunstsammlung.' In *Festschrift zur Eröffnung des Kunstmuseums*, 7–118. Basel, 1936.

FOCK AND EKKART 1981
Fock, Willemijn, and Rudi Ekkart. 'De Portretgalerij van de Familie De la Court.' In *Jaarboek Centraal Bureau voor Genealogie*, 1981, 177–230.

FOUCART 2009
Foucart, Jacques. *Catalogue des Peintures Flamandes et Hollandaises du Musée du Louvre*. Catalogue Sommaire des Peintures du Musée du Louvre. Paris, 2009.

FRANITS 2004
Franits, Wayne E. *Dutch Seventeenth-Century Genre Painting: Its Stylistic and Thematic Evolution*. New Haven and London, 2004.

FREISE 1911
Freise, Kurt. *Pieter Lastman, sein Leben und seine Kunst: Ein Beitrag zur Geschichte der Holländ; Malerei im XVII. Jahrhundert*. Kunstwissenschaftliche Studien, 5. Leipzig, 1911.

FUHRING 1998
Fuhring, Peter. *Ornament in Prent: Zeventiende-Eeuwse Ornamentprenten in de Verzamelingen van het Rijksmuseum*. Amsterdam, 1998.

FUHRING 2004
Fuhring, Peter. *Ornament Prints in the Rijksmuseum II: The Seventeenth Century*. 3 vols. Studies in Prints and Printmaking, 5. Rotterdam, 2004.

GASKELL 1989
Gaskell, Ivan. *The Thyssen-Bornemisza Collection. Seventeenth-Century Dutch and Flemish Painting*. London, 1989.

GELDER 1972
Gelder, Jan G. van. *Jan de Bisschop*. The Hague, 1972. Offprint of *Oud Holland* 86 (1971): 201–288.

GELDER AND JOST 1985
Gelder, Jan G. van, and Ingrid Jost. *Jan de Bisschop and His Icones and Paradigmata: Classical Antiquities and Italian Drawings for Artistic Instruction in Seventeenth Century Holland*. Edited by Keith Andrews. 2 vols. Doornspijk, 1985.

GEMAR-KOELTZSCH 1995
Gemar-Koeltzsch, Erika. *Holländische Stillebenmaler im 17. Jahrhundert*. 3 vols. Luca Bild-Lexikon. Lingen, 1995.

GERSON 1968
Gerson, Horst. *Rembrandt Paintings*. Amsterdam, 1968.

GERSZI 1982
Gerszi, Teréz. *Paulus van Vianen: Handzeichnungen*. Hanau, 1982.

GERSZI 2005
Gerszi, Teréz. *Seventeenth-Century Dutch and Flemish Drawings in the Budapest Museum of Fine Arts: A Complete Catalogue*. Budapest, 2005.

GERSZI AND TÓTH 2012
Gerszi, Teréz, and Bernadett Tóth. *The New Ideal of Beauty in the Age of Pieter Bruegel: Sixteenth-Century Netherlandish Drawings in the Museum of Fine Arts, Budapest*. Budapest, 2012.

GIFFORD 1996
Gifford, E. Melanie. 'Jan van Goyen en de Techniek van het Naturalistische Landschap.' In *Jan van Goyen*, by Christiaan Vogelaar, 70–79. Stedelijk Museum de Lakenhal, Leiden. Zwolle, 1996.

GILTAIJ 1977
Giltaij, Jeroen. 'Een Onbekende Schets van Rembrandt.' *De Kroniek van het Rembrandthuis* 1 (1977): 1–9.

GILTAIJ 1988
Giltaij, Jeroen. *De Tekeningen van Rembrandt en Zijn School in het Museum Boymans-Van Beuningen*. Rotterdam, 1988.

GILTAIJ 2007
Giltaij, Jeroen. 'A Newly Discovered Seventeenth-Century Sketchbook.' *Simiolus* 31, nos. 1–2 (2007): 81–93.

GILTAIJ AND LAMMERTSE 2001
Giltaij, Jeroen, and Friso Lammertse. 'Maintaining a Studio Archive: Drawn Copies by the De Braij Family.' *Master Drawings* 39, no. 4 (2001): 367–394.

GILTAY 1980
Giltay, Jeroen. 'De Tekeningen van Jacob van Ruisdael.' *Oud Holland* 94, no. 2–3 (1980): 141–208.

GOEREE 1668
Goeree, Willem. *Inleydinge tot de Algemeene Teycken-Konst*. Middelburg, 1668.

GOEREE 1670
Goeree, Willem. *Inleydingh tot de Practijck der Algemeene Schilder-Konst*. Middelburg, 1670.

GOOSENS 2001
Goosens, Marion. 'Schilders en de Markt, Haarlem 1605–1635.' PhD diss., Rijksuniversiteit Leiden, 2001.

GROEN AND MURRAY 1991
Groen, Karin, and Sarah Murray. 'Underdrawings in Four Early Seventeenth Century Flower Paintings.' In *Le Dessin Sous-Jacent dans la Peinture*, edited by Hélène Verougstraete-Marcq and R. van Schoute, 151–154. Colloque, 8. Louvain-la-Neuve, 1991.

GRUIJS 2003
Gruijs, Marit. 'De Tekeningen van Karel Dujardin (1626–1678).' PhD diss., Rijksuniversiteit Utrecht, 2003.

HAAGEN 1932
Haagen, J.K. van der. *De Schilders van der Haagen en Hun Werk*. Voorburg, 1932.

HABOLDT 1989
Haboldt, Bob P. *Old Master Paintings and Drawings: The First Five Years*. New York, 1989.

HABOLDT 2001
Haboldt & Co. *Northern European Old Master Drawings and Oil Sketches*. New York, 2001.

HABOLDT 2012
Haboldt & Co. *Singular Vision: Haboldt & Co.'s Old Master Paintings and Drawings since 1983*. Amsterdam, New York, and Paris, 2012.

HANNEMA 1961
Hannema, Dirk. *Oude Tekeningen uit de Verzameling Victor de Stuers*. Almelo, 1961.

HASKELL AND PENNY 1981
Haskell, Francis, and Nicholas Penny. *Taste and the Antique: The Lure of Classical Sculpture, 1500–1900*. New Haven, 1981.

HAVERKAMP-BEGEMANN 1976
Haverkamp-Begemann, Egbert. 'The Appearance of Reality: Dutch Draughtsmen of the Golden Age.' *Apollo* 104 (1976): 354–363.

HAVERKAMP-BEGEMANN 2001
Haverkamp-Begemann, Egbert. 'The Beauty of Holland: Albert Cuyp as Landscape Draftsman.' In Washington/London/Amsterdam 2001: 75–85.

HEARN 2015
Hearn, Karen. *Cornelius Johnson*. London, 2015.

HECHT 1997
Hecht, Peter. *Over Rembrandt, Manet, en het Tweede Leven van de Kunst*. Faculty of Arts, University of Utrecht, 1997 (inaugural lecture, September 2).

HELD 1963
Held, Julius S. 'The Early Appreciation of Drawings.' In *Studies in Western Art: Acts of the Twentieth International Congress of the History of Art*, vol. 3, 72–95. Princeton, 1963.

HENKEL 1931
Henkel, Max Ditmar. *Le Dessin Hollandais des Origines au XVIIe Siècle*. Paris, 1931.

HENKEL 1943
Henkel, Max Ditmar. *Tekeningen van Rembrandt en Zijn School*. Catalogus van de Nederlandse Tekeningen in het Rijksmuseum te Amsterdam. The Hague, 1943.

HIND 1931
Hind, Arthur M. *Catalogue of Drawings by Dutch and Flemish Artists Preserved in the Department of Prints and Drawings in the British Museum*. Vol. 4. London, 1931.

HIND AND POPHAM 1915–1932
Hind, Arthur M., and A.E. Popham. *Catalogue of Drawings by Dutch and Flemish Artists Preserved in the Department of Prints and Drawings in the British Museum*. 5 vols. London, 1915–1932.

HINTERDING 2008
Hinterding, Erik. *Rembrandt Etchings from the Frits Lugt Collection*. 2 vols. Paris, 2008.

HINTERDING, RUTGERS, AND LUIJTEN 2013
Hinterding, Erik, Jaco Rutgers, and Ger Luijten, eds. *Rembrandt*. 7 vols. New Hollstein: Dutch and Flemish Etchings, Engravings and Woodcuts, 1450–1700, vols. 71–77. Ouderkerk aan den IJssel, 2013.

HOFSTEDE DE GROOT 1907–1928
Hofstede de Groot, Cornelis. *Beschreibendes und kritisches Verzeichnis der Werke der Hervorragendsten holländischen Maler des XVII. Jahrhunderts*. 10 vols. Esslingen and Paris, 1907–1928.

HOLLSTEIN GERMAN 1959
Boon, Karel G., and Robert W. Scheller, eds. *Hollstein: German Engravings, Etchings, and Woodcuts, 1400–1700*. Vol. 6: *Cranach–Drusse*. Amsterdam, 1959.

HOOGSTRATEN 1678
Hoogstraten, Samuel van. *Inleyding tot de Hooge Schoole der Schilderkonst: Anders de Zichtbaere Werelt*. Rotterdam, 1678.

HOPPER 1991
Hopper, Florence. 'Clusius' World: The Meeting of Science and Art.' In *The Authentic Garden: A Symposium on Gardens*, edited by Leslie Tjon Sie Fat and Erik de Jong, 13–36. Leiden, 1991.

HOPPER BOOM 1975
Hopper Boom, Florence. 'An Early Flower Piece by Jacques de Gheyn II.' *Simiolus* 8 (1975–1976): 195–198.

HOUBRAKEN 1718–1721
Houbraken, Arnold. *De Groote Schouburgh der Nederlantsche Konstschilders en Schilderessen*. 3 vols. in 1. Amsterdam, 1976. Reprint of The Hague, 1753.

HUT 2015
Hut, Margreet van der. *Barend Graat (1628–1709): Zijn Leven en Zijn Werk*. Leiden, 2015.

HUYGENS 1987
Huygens, Constantijn. *Mijn Jeugd*. Translated and annotated by Chris L. Heesakkers. Amsterdam, 1987.

HUYGENS 2003
Huygens, Constantijn. *Mijn Leven Verteld aan Mijn Kinderen*. 2 vols. Introduced, edited, translated, and with a commentary by Frans R. E. Blom. Amsterdam, 2003.

JANSEN 2010
Jansen, Guido. 'Rembrandt's *Joseph Telling His Dreams* and Its Former Owner August Willem Volz (1873–1944).' *Rijksmuseum Bulletin* 58 (2010): 138–143.

JANSEN AND LUIJTEN 1988
Jansen, Guido, and Ger Luijten. *Italianisanten en Bamboccianten: Het Italianiserende Landschap en Genre door Nederlandse Kunstenaars uit de Zeventiende Eeuw.* Rotterdam, 1988.

JUDSON 1988
Judson, J. Richard. 'New Light on Honthorst.' In *Hollandische Malerei im neuen Licht: Hendrick ter Brugghen und seine Zeitgenossen,* by Rudiger Klessmann, 111–120. Herzog Anton Ulrich-Museum, Braunschweig. Braunschweig, 1988.

JUDSON AND EKKART 1999
Judson, J. Richard, and Rudolf E.O. Ekkart. *Gerrit van Honthorst, 1592–1656.* Aetas Aurea, 14. Doornspijk, 1999.

KETELSEN 2006
Ketelsen, Thomas. 'Ein Körper von Gewicht. Rembrandts "Ganymed"-Zeichnung in Dresden.' In *Rembrandt van Rijn: Die Entführung des Ganymed,* by Thomas Ketelsen and Uta Neidhardt, 20–32. Kupferstich-Kabinett, Gemäldegalerie Alte Meister, Dresden, 2006.

KETTERING 1988
Kettering, Alison McNeil. *Drawings from the Ter Borch Studio Estate.* 2 vols. Catalogus van de Nederlandse Tekeningen in het Rijksprentenkabinet, Rijksmuseum, Amsterdam, 5. The Hague, 1988.

KEYES 1987
Keyes, George S. 'Esaias van de Velde and the Chalk Sketch.' *Nederlands Kunsthistorisch Jaarboek* 38 (1987): 136–145.

KEYES AND BOON 1980
Keyes, George S., and Karel G. Boon. *Salomon Savery – Gillis van Scheyndel.* Hollstein's Dutch and Flemish Etchings, Engravings and Woodcuts, 1450–1700, vol. 24. Amsterdam, 1980.

KEYES AND BRIELS 1984
Keyes, George S., and Jan G.C.A. Briels. *Esaias van den Velde: 1587–1630.* Aetas Aurea, 4. Doornspijk, 1984.

KILIAN 2005
Kilian, Jennifer M. *The Paintings of Karel du Jardin, 1626–1678: Catalogue Raisonné.* OCULI: Studies in the Arts of the Low Countries, 8. Amsterdam, 2005.

KLEINERT 2006
Kleinert, Katja. *Atelierdarstellungen in der niederländischen Genremalerei des 17. Jahrhunderts: Realistisches Abbild oder glaubwürdiger Schein?* Studien zur Internationalen Architektur- und Kunstgeschichte, 40. Petersberg, 2006.

KLERK 1982
Klerk, E.A. de. 'De Teecken-Const, een 17de Eeuws Nederlands Traktaatje.' *Oud Holland* 96 (1982): 16–60.

KLOEK 1975
Kloek, Wouter Th. *Beknopte Catalogus van de Nederlandse Tekeningen in het Prentenkabinet van de Uffizi te Florence.* Utrecht, 1975.

KLOEK 2005
Kloek, Wouter Th. *Jan Steen, 1626–1679.* Rijksmuseum Dossiers, 3. Zwolle, 2005.

KLOEK AND MEIJER 2008
Kloek, W. Th., and Bert W. Meijer. *Fiamminghi e Olandesi a Firenze: Disegni dalle Collezioni degli Uffizi.* Gabinetto Disegni e Stampe degli Uffizi, 96. Florence, 2008.

KNEVEL 1994
Knevel, Paul. *Burgers in het Geweer: De Schutterijen in Holland, 1550–1700.* Hollandse Studiën, 32. Hilversum, 1994.

KÖHLER 2006
Köhler, Neeltje, ed. *Painting in Haarlem 1500–1850: The Collection of the Frans Hals Museum.* Ghent, 2006.

KOLFIN 2005
Kolfin, Elmer. *The Young Gentry at Play: Northern Netherlandish Scenes of Merry Companies, 1610–1645.* Leiden, 2005.

KREMPEL 2000
Krempel, León. *Studien zu den Datierten Gemälden des Nicolaes Maes (1634–1693).* Studien zur Internationalen Architektur- und Kunstgeschichte, 9. Petersberg, 2000.

KUZNETSOV AND LINNIK 1982
Kuznetsov, Yury, and Irina Linnik. *Dutch Painting in Soviet Museums.* Leningrad and New York, 1982.

LAMMERTSE 1987
Lammertse, Friso. 'Van Schets tot Schilderij: Naar Aanleiding van Infra-Rood Reflectografisch Onderzoek op Twee Schilderijen van Saenredam in het Rijksmuseum.' *Bulletin van het Rijksmuseum* 35 (1987): 80–90.

LAMMERTSE 1995
Lammertse, Friso. 'Exhibition Review of *Paulus Potter, Schilderijen, Tekeningen en Etsen,* Royal Picture Gallery Mauritshuis, The Hague, 1994–1995.' *Oud Holland* 109 (1995): 222–226.

LAMMERTSE 2008
Lammertse, Friso. 'Salomon de Bray, Schilder, Bouwmeester en Theoreticus.' In *Painting Family: The De Brays: Master Painters of 17th Century Holland,* by Pieter Biesboer, Friso Lammertse, and Fred G. Meijer. Frans Hals Museum, Haarlem; Dulwich Picture Gallery, London. Zwolle, 2008.

LAURENTIUS 2008
Laurentius, Theo, and Frans Laurentius. *Watermarks, 1650–1700, Found in the Zeeland Archives.* Houten, 2008.

LAWRENCE 1991
Lawrence, Cynthia Miller. *Gerrit Adriaensz. Berckheyde, 1638–1698: Haarlem Cityscape Painter.* Ars Picturae, 2. Doornspijk, 1991.

LEEFLANG 2003
Leeflang, Huigen. 'Van Ontwerp naar Prent: Tekeningen voor Prenten van

Nederlandse Meesters (1550–1700) uit de Collectie van het Prentenkabinet van de Universiteit Leiden.' *Delineavit et Sculpsit* 27 (2003): 1–108.

LEEFLANG 2014
Leeflang, Huigen. 'The Sign of Claes Jansz Visscher and His Progeny: The History and Significance of a Brand Name.' *Rijksmuseum Bulletin* 62 (2014): 240–269.

LIEDTKE 1982
Liedtke, Walter A. *Architectural Painting in Delft: Gerard Houckgeest, Hendrick van Vliet, Emanuel de Witte*. Doornspijk, 1982.

LIEDTKE 2007
Liedtke, Walter A. *Dutch Paintings in the Metropolitan Museum of Art*. 2 vols. New Haven, 2007.

LOOTSMA 2007
Lootsma, Hilbert. 'Tracing a Pose: Govert Flinck and the Emergence of the Van Dyckian Mode of Portraiture in Amsterdam.' *Simiolus* 33 (2007–2008): 221–236.

LUIJTEN AND SCHUCKMAN 1989
Luijten, Ger, and Christiaan Schuckman. *Jan van de Velde II – Dirk Vellert*. Hollstein's Dutch and Flemish Etchings, Engravings and Woodcuts, 1450–1700, vol. 33. Roosendaal, 1989.

MANDER 1604
Mander, Karel van. *Het Schilder-Boeck*. 1604. Facsimile reprint, Utrecht, 1969.

MANDER 1604 *Grondt*
Mander, Karel van. 'Den Grondt der Edel vry Schilder-Const.' In *Het Schilder-Boeck*, edited by Hessel Miedema. 2 vols. 1604. Facsimile reprint, Utrecht, 1973.

MANDER 1604 *Lives*
Mander, Karel van. *The Lives of the Illustrious Netherlandish and German Painters*. Edited and translated by Hessel Miedema. 6 vols. Doornspijk, 1994–1999.

MANDER 1604 *Wtleggingh*
Mander, Karel van. 'Wtleggingh Op Den Metamorphosis Pub. Ovidii Nasonis.' In *Het Schilder-Boeck*. (1604) Facsimile Reprint. Utrecht, 1969.

MANUTH 2001
Manuth, Volker. 'The Reputation of the Nude Female Model in the Age of Rembrandt.' In *Rembrandt's Women*, by Julia Lloyd Williams, 47–53. National Gallery of Scotland, Edinburgh; Royal Academy of Arts, London. London, 2001.

MARTIN 1923
Martin, W. 'Jan van Ravesteyn's 'Magistraat en Schutters', 1618, en het ontwerp daarvoor.' *Oud Holland* 41 (1923): 193–198.

MATTESON 1983
Matteson, Lynn R. 'Old Master Drawings from the Woodner Collection.' *Pantheon* 41 (1983): 386–387.

MERWE 2012
Merwe, Pieter van der. *The Queen's House Greenwich*. London, 2012.

DE MEYERE 2006
Meyere, Jos de. *Utrechtse Schilderkunst in de Gouden Eeuw: Honderd Schilderijen uit de Collectie van het Centraal Museum te Utrecht*. Utrecht, 2006.

MICHAŁKOWA 1955
Michałkowa, Janina. *Holenderskie I Flamandzkie Malarstwo Rodzajowe XVII Wicku*. Warsaw, 1955.

MIEDEMA 1981
Miedema, Hessel. *Kunst, Kunstenaar en Kunstwerk bij Karel van Mander: Een Analyse van Zijn Levensbeschrijvingen*. Alphen aan den Rijn, 1981.

MOLTKE 1938
Moltke, Joachim Wolfgang von. 'Salomon de Bray.' *Marburger Jahrbuch für Kunstwissenschaft* 11/12 (1938/1939): 309–420.

MOLTKE 1965
Moltke, Joachim Wolfgang von. *Govaert Flinck, 1615–1660*. Amsterdam, 1965.

MORTIER 2009
Mortier, Bianca M. du. 'Aspects of Costume: A Showcase of Early 17th-Century Dress.' In *Hendrick Avercamp: Master of the Ice Scene*, by Pieter Roelofs, 141–163. Rijksmuseum, Amsterdam; National Gallery of Art, Washington. Amsterdam, 2009.

MOSKOWITZ 1962
Moskowitz, Ira. *Great Drawings of All Time*. Vol. 2: *German, Flemish and Dutch, Thirteenth through Nineteenth Century*. New York, 1962.

MULES 1985
Mules, Helen B. 'Dutch Drawings of the Seventeenth Century in the Metropolitan Museum of Art.' *Metropolitan Museum of Art Bulletin* 42, no. 4 (1985): 3–56.

MURRAY AND GROEN 1994
Murray, Sarah, and Karin Groen. 'Four Early Dutch Flower Paintings Examined with Reference to Crispijn de Passe's "Den Blom-Hof."' *Hamilton Kerr Institute Bulletin* 2 (1994): 6–20.

NAGTEGAAL, MORIEN, AND ZEEDIJK-SACRÉ
Nagtegaal, H. K., H. M. Morien, and L. Zeedijk-Sacré. 'Hollandse Biografieën.' In *Hollandse Genealogische Databank*, www.hogenda.nl, 2014.

NANNEN 1985
Nannen, Henri. *Ludolf Backhuysen, Emden 1630–Amsterdam 1708: Ein Versuch, Leben und Werk des Künstlers zu Beschreiben*. Emden, 1985.

NAUMANN 1978
Naumann, Otto. 'Frans van Mieris as a Draughtsman.' *Master Drawings* 16 (1978): 3–34.

NAUMANN 1981
Naumann, Otto. *Frans van Mieris (1635–1681), the Elder.* 2 vols. Aetas Aurea, 1. Doornspijk, 1981.

NAUMANN 2005
Naumann, Otto. 'Frans van Mieris' Personal Style.' In *Frans van Mieris, 1635–1681*, by Quentin Buvelot, 28–42. Royal Picture Gallery Mauritshuis, The Hague; National Gallery of Art, Washington. Zwolle, 2005.

NEHLSEN-MARTEN 2003
Nehlsen-Marten, Britta. *Dirck Hals, 1591–1656: Oeuvre und Entwicklung eines Haarlemer Genremalers.* Weimar, 2003.

NEUMEISTER AND KREMPEL 2005
Neumeister, Mirjam, and León Krempel. *Holländische Gemälde im Städel Museum, 1550–1800.* Vol. 1: *Künstler Geboren bis 1615.* Petersberg, 2005.

NIEMEIJER 1964
Niemeijer, J.W. 'Een Gestrande Potvis Getekend door Esaias van de Velde.' *Bulletin van het Rijksmuseum* 12 (1964): 20–23.

OVEN 1992
Oven, Thera von. 'Pieter Jansz Invenit.' *Delineavit et Sculpsit* 7 (1992): 5–15.

PALMER AND GIFFORD 1997
Palmer, Michael, and E. Melanie Gifford. 'Jan Steen's Painting Practice: The Dancing Couple in the Context of the Artist's Career.' *Studies in the History of Art* 57 (1997): 127–155.

PASSE 1643
Passe, Crispijn van de. *'T Licht der Teken en Schilderkonst.* Amsterdam, 1643. Facsimile edition with an introduction by J. Bolten. Soest, 1973.

PAUWELS 1984
Pauwels, Henri. *Inventariscatalogus van de Oude Schilderkunst.* Koninklijke Musea voor Schone Kunsten van België. Brussels, 1984.

PEETERS 1990
Peeters, Jan. 'Een Onbekende Tekening van Gerrit Berckheyde in de Atlas Van Eck.' *Koninklijk Oudheidkundig Genootschap Jaarverslag*, 1991, 83–91.

PLIETZSCH 1960
Plietzsch, Eduard. *Holländische und Flämische Maler des XVII. Jahrhunderts.* Leipzig, 1960.

PLOMP 1997a
Plomp, Michiel C. 'Jan Pietersz Zomer's Inscriptions on Drawings.' *Delineavit et Sculpsit* 17 (1997): 13–27.

PLOMP 1997b
Plomp, Michiel C. *The Dutch Drawings in the Teyler Museum.* Vol. 2: *Artists Born between 1575 and 1630.* Haarlem, Ghent, and Doornspijk, 1997.

PLOMP 2006
Plomp, Michiel C. 'Rembrandt and His Circle: Drawings and Prints.' *Metropolitan Museum of Art Bulletin* 64, no. 1 (2006): 1–48.

POTTASH 2005
Pottash, Carol. 'Underdrawings in the Paintings of Frans van Mieris.' In *Frans van Mieris, 1635–1681*, by Quentin Buvelot, 62–68. Royal Picture Gallery Mauritshuis, The Hague; National Gallery of Art, Washington. Zwolle, 2005.

PRINCIPE AND DE WITT 2002
Principe, Lawrence, and Lloyd DeWitt. *Transmutations—Alchemy in Art: Selected Works from the Eddleman and Fisher Collections at the Chemical Heritage Foundation.* Philadelphia, 2002.

REBER 1904
Reber, Franz von. *Katalog der Gemälde-Sammlung der Königlichen Älteren Pinakothek in München.* Munich, 1904.

REGTEREN ALTENA 1942–1950
Regteren Altena, J.Q. van. 'Het Gelaat van de Stad.' In *Zeven Eeuwen Amsterdam*, edited by A. E. d'Ailly. 6 vols. Amsterdam, 1942–1950.

REGTEREN ALTENA 1983
Regteren Altena, I.Q. van. *Jacques de Gheyn: Three Generations.* 3 vols. The Hague, Boston, and London, 1983.

REIFENBERG 1632
Reifenberg, Justus. *Emblemata Politica.* Amsterdam, 1632.

REISS 1975
Reiss, Stephen. *Aelbert Cuyp.* Boston, 1975.

REMBRANDT CORPUS I 1982
Bruyn, Joshua, et al. *A Corpus of Rembrandt Paintings.* Vol. 1: *1625–1631.* Stichting Foundation Rembrandt Research Project. The Hague, Boston, and London, 1982.

REMBRANDT CORPUS II 1986
Bruyn, Joshua, et al. *A Corpus of Rembrandt Paintings.* Vol. 2: *1631–1634.* Stichting Foundation Rembrandt Research Project. Dordrecht, Boston, and Lancaster, 1986.

REMBRANDT CORPUS III 1989
Bruyn, Joshua, et al. *A Corpus of Rembrandt Paintings.* Vol. 3: *1635–1642.* Stichting Foundation Rembrandt Research Project. Dordrecht, Boston, and London, 1989.

REMBRANDT CORPUS IV 2005
Wetering, Ernst van de, et al. *A Corpus of Rembrandt Paintings.* Vol. 4: *The Self-Portraits.* Stichting Foundation Rembrandt Research Project. Dordrecht, 2005.

REMBRANDT CORPUS V 2011
Wetering, Ernst van de, et al. *A Corpus of Rembrandt Paintings.* Vol. 5: *Small-Scale History Paintings.* Stichting Foundation Rembrandt Research Project. Dordrecht, 2011.

REMBRANDT CORPUS VI 2014
Wetering, Ernst van de, et al. *A Corpus of Rembrandt Paintings.* Vol. 6: *Rembrandt's Paintings Revisited: A Complete Survey.* With collaboration of Carin van Nes. Stichting Rembrandt Research Project. Dordrecht, 2014.

REZNICEK 1961
Reznicek, Emil Karel Josef. *Die Zeichnungen von Hendrick Goltzius.* 2 vols. Orbis Artium, 6. Utrecht, 1961.

REZNICEK 1972
Reznicek, Emil K.J. 'Hont Horstiana.' *Nederlands Kunsthistorisch Jaarboek* 23 (1972): 167–189.

ROBELS 1983
Robels, Hella. *Niederländische Zeichnungen vom 15. bis 19. Jahrhundert im Wallraf-Richartz-Museum Köln.* Cologne, 1983.

ROBINSON 1876
Robinson, John C. *Descriptive Catalogue of Drawings by the Old Masters, Forming the Collection of John Malcolm of Poltalloch, Esq.* London, 1876.

ROBINSON 1958–1974
Robinson, M.S. *Van de Velde Drawings: A Catalogue of Drawings in the National Maritime Museum Made by the Elder and the Younger Willem van de Velde.* 2 vols. London, 1958–1974.

ROBINSON 1979
Robinson, William W. 'Preparatory Drawings by Adriaen van de Velde.' *Master Drawings* 17 (1979): 3–23.

ROBINSON 1989
Robinson, William W. 'Nicolaes Maes as a Draughtsman.' *Master Drawings* 27, no. 2 (1989): 146–162.

ROBINSON, 1990
Robinson, William W. 'Early Drawings by Joris van der Haagen.' *Master Drawings* 28 (1990): 303–309.

ROBINSON 1993
Robinson, William W. 'Some Studies of Nude Models by Adriaen van de Velde.' *Nationalmuseum Bulletin* (Stockholm) 17, no. 2 (1993): 53–66.

ROBINSON 1996
Robinson, William W. 'The Early Works of Nicolaes Maes, 1653 to 1661.' PhD diss., Harvard University, 1996.

ROBINSON 2000
Robinson, William W. 'Another Early Drawing by Joris van der Haagen.' *Master Drawings* 38 (2000): 58–61.

ROBINSON 2010
Robinson, William W. 'Another Connected Female Nude by Jacob Backer.' In *Mélanges pour Marie*, edited by Jeroen Giltaij, 57–58. Paris, 2010.

ROBINSON 2015
Robinson, William W. 'The Abrams Album: An Album Amicorum of Dutch Drawings from the Seventeenth Century.' *Master Drawings* 53 (2015): 1–58.

ROBINSON AND ANDERSON 2016
Robinson, William W., and Susan Anderson. *Drawings from the Age of Bruegel, Rubens, and Rembrandt: Highlights from the Collection of the Harvard Art Museums.* New Haven, 2016.

ROBINSON AND WEBER 1979
Robinson, M.S., and R.E.J. Weber. *The Willem van de Velde Drawings in the Boymans-Van Beuningen Museum, Rotterdam.* 3 vols. Rotterdam, 1979.

ROBINSON, M. S. 1990
Robinson, M.S. *Van de Velde: A Catalogue of the Paintings of the Elder and the Younger Willem van de Velde.* 2 vols. Greenwich, 1990.

ROETHLISBERGER 1968
Roethlisberger, Marcel. *Claude Lorrain: The Drawings.* 2 vols. California Studies in the History of Art, 8. Berkeley, 1968.

ROETHLISBERGER 1969
Roethlisberger, Marcel. *Bartholomäus Breenbergh: Handzeichnungen.* Berlin, 1969.

ROETHLISBERGER 1981
Roethlisberger, Marcel. *Bartholomeus Breenbergh: The Paintings.* Berlin and New York, 1981.

ROETHLISBERGER AND BOK 1993
Roethlisberger, Marcel, and Marten Jan Bok. *Abraham Bloemaert and His Sons: Paintings and Prints.* 2 vols. Aetas Aurea, 11. Doornspijk, 1993.

ROLLENHAGEN 1613
Rollenhagen, Gabriel. *Nucleus Emblematum Selectissimorum, Quae Itali Vulgo Impresas Vocant Privata . . . Selectorum Emblematum Centuria Secunda.* Arnhem, 1613.

ROLLENHAGEN 1983
Rollenhagen, Gabriel. *Sinn-Bilder: Ein Tugendspiegel.* Die Bibliophilen Taschenbücher, 378. Dortmund, 1983.

ROYALTON-KISCH 1989
Royalton-Kisch, Martin. 'Rembrandt's Sketches for His Paintings.' *Master Drawings* 27, no. 2 (1987): 128–145.

ROYALTON-KISCH 1991
Royalton-Kisch, Martin. 'Rembrandt's Drawing of the "Entombment over the Raising of Lazarus."' *Master Drawings* 29 (1991): 263–283.

ROYALTON-KISCH 2009
Royalton–Kisch, Martin. *Catalogue of Drawings by Rembrandt and his School in the British Museum.* http://www.britishmuseum.org/research/publications/online_research_catalogues/rembrandt_drawings/drawings_by_rembrandt.aspx

ROYALTON-KISCH 2012
Royalton-Kisch, Martin. 'The Drawings of Rembrandt: A Revision of Otto Benesch's Catalogue Raisonné.' www.rembrandtcatalogue.net, 2012.

ROYALTON-KISCH AND SCHATBORN 2011
Royalton-Kisch, Martin, and Peter Schatborn. 'The Core Group of Rembrandt Drawings, II, the List.' *Master Drawings* 49 (2011): 323–346.

RUSSELL 1977
Russell, Margarita. 'The Iconography of Rembrandt's "Rape of Ganymede."' *Simiolus* 7 (1997): 5–18.

RUSSELL 1988
Russell, Margarita. 'The Artist in His Studio: A Self-Portrait by Michiel van Musscher.' *Apollo* 127 (1988): 9–15.

RUURS 1983
Ruurs, Rob. 'Pieter Saenredam: Zijn Boekenbezit en Zijn Relatie met de Landmeter Pieter Wils.' *Oud Holland* 97 (1983): 59–68.

RUURS 1987
Ruurs, Rob. *Saenredam: The Art of Perspective*. Oculi, 1. Amsterdam and Philadelphia, 1987.

RUYVEN-ZEMAN 2009
Ruyven-Zeman, Zsuzsanna van. 'Onbekend Werk van Pieter Jansz., Glasschilder uit Amsterdam.' *Oud Holland* 122 (2009): 121–144.

RUYVEN-ZEMAN 2011a
Ruyven-Zeman, Zsuzsanna van. *Stained Glass in the Netherlands before 1795*. 2 vols. Corpus Vitrearum the Netherlands, 4. Amsterdam, 2011.

RUYVEN-ZEMAN 2011b
Ruyven-Zeman, Zsuzsanna van, Arjan R. de Koomen, Antonie L.H. Hage, Jan Piet Filedt Kok, eds. *De Cartons van de Sint-Janskerk in Gouda / The Cartoons of the Sint-Janskerk in Gouda*. Delft, 2011.

SCHAAR 1958
Schaar, Eckhard. 'Zeichnungen Berchems zu Landkarten.' *Oud-Holland* 71 (1958): 239–243.

SCHAAR 1959
Schaar, Eckhard. 'Poelenburgh und Breenbergh in Italien und ein Bild Elsheimers.' *Mitteilungen des Kunsthistorischen Institutes in Florenz* 9 (1959): 25–54.

SCHAFFRAN 1957
Schaffran, E. 'Das Dr. W. Wurzbach-Legat an der Galerie der Akademie der bildenden Künste in Wien.' *Oud Holland* 72 (1957): 41–50.

SCHAPELHOUMAN 1985
Schapelhouman, Marijn. 'Tekeningen van Pieter Jansz., "Konstig Glasschrijver."' *Bulletin van het Rijksmuseum* 33 (1985): 71–92.

SCHAPELHOUMAN 1995
Schapelhouman, Marijn. '"Colf" on the River IJsel.' In *The Touch of the Artist: Master Drawings from the Woodner Collections*, by Margaret M. Grasselli, 250. National Gallery of Art, Washington. Washington, 1995.

SCHAPELHOUMAN 2006
Schapelhouman, Marijn. *Rembrandt and the Art of Drawing*. Rijksmuseum dossiers. Rijksmuseum, Amsterdam and Zwolle, 2006.

SCHAPELHOUMAN 2009
Schapelhouman, Marijn. 'The Drawings: Reflections on an Oeuvre.' In *Hendrick Avercamp: Master of the Ice Scene*, by Pieter Roelofs, 85–117. Rijksmuseum, Amsterdam; National Gallery of Art, Washington. Amsterdam, 2009.

SCHAPELHOUMAN AND SCHATBORN 1998
Schapelhouman, Marijn, and Peter Schatborn. *Dutch Drawings of the Seventeenth Century in the Rijksmuseum, Amsterdam: Artists Born between 1580 and 1600*. 2 vols. Amsterdam, 1998.

SCHATBORN 1973
Schatborn, Peter. 'Olieverfschetsen van Dirck Hals.' *Bulletin van het Rijksmuseum* 21 (1973): 107–116.

SCHATBORN 1974
Schatborn, Peter. 'Figuurstudies van Nicolaes Berchem.' *Bulletin van het Rijksmuseum* 22 (1974): 3–16.

SCHATBORN 1975a
Schatborn, Peter. '"De Hut" van Adriaen van de Velde.' *Bulletin van het Rijksmuseum* 23 (1975): 159–165.

SCHATBORN 1975b
Schatborn, Peter. 'Figuurstudies van Ludolf de Jongh.' *Oud Holland* 89 (1975): 79–85.

SCHATBORN 1975c
Schatborn, Peter. 'Over Rembrandt en Kinderen.' *De Kroniek van het Rembrandthuis* 27 (1975): 8–19.

SCHATBORN 1985
Schatborn, Peter. *Tekeningen van Rembrandt, Zijn Onbekende Leerlingen en Navolgers = Drawings by Rembrandt, His Anonymous Pupils and Followers*. Catalogus van de Nederlandse Tekeningen in het Rijksprentenkabinet, Rijksmuseum, Amsterdam 4. Amsterdam, 1985.

SCHATBORN 1986
Schatborn, Peter. 'Tekeningen van Adriaen en Isack van Ostade.' *Bulletin van het Rijksmuseum* 34 (1986): 82–92.

SCHATBORN 1990
Schatborn, Peter. 'Dutchmen Found in Copenhagen: Figure Drawings by Simon Kick and Constantijn Verhout.' In *Festschrift to Erik Fischer: European Drawings from Six Centuries*, edited by Villads Villadsen, 183–204. Copenhagen, 1990.

SCHATBORN 1991
Schatborn, Peter. 'The Importance of Drawing from Life—Some Preliminary Notes.' In *Seventeenth-Century Dutch Drawings: A Selection from the Maida and George Abrams Collection*, by William W. Robinson, 7–12. Rijksmuseum, Amsterdam; Albertina, Vienna; Pierpont Morgan Library and Museum, New York. New York, 1991.

SCHATBORN 1993
Schatborn, Peter. 'Rembrandt from Life and from Memory.' In *Rembrandt and His Pupils: Papers Given at a Symposium in Nationalmuseum Stockholm, 2–3 October 1992*, edited by Görel Cavalli-Björkman, 156–172. Nationalmusei Skriftserie, n.s., 13. Stockholm, 1993.

SCHATBORN 2010a
Schatborn, Peter. *Rembrandt and His Circle: Drawings in the Frits Lugt Collection*. 2 vols. Bussum, 2010.

SCHATBORN 2010b
Schatborn, Peter. 'The Early Rembrandt-esque Drawings of Govert Flinck.' *Master Drawings* 48 (2010): 4–38.

SCHATBORN 2011
Schatborn, Peter. 'The Core Group of Rembrandt Drawings, I, Overview.' *Master Drawings* 49 (2011): 293–322.

SCHATBORN AND DE WINKEL 1996
Schatborn, Peter, and Marieke de Winkel. 'Rembrandts Portret van de Acteur Willem Ruyter.' *Bulletin van het Rijksmuseum* 44 (1996): 383–393.

SCHATBORN AND DUDOK VAN HEEL 2011
Schatborn, Peter, and S.A.C. Dudok van Heel. 'The Core Group of Rembrandt Drawings, III, Supplement.' *Master Drawings* 49 (2011): 347–351.

SCHEYER 1977
Scheyer, Ernst. 'The Iconography of Jacob van Ruisdael's Cemetery.' *Bulletin of the Detroit Institute of Arts* 55 (1977): 133ff.

SCHNACKENBURG 1981
Schnackenburg, Bernhard. *Adriaen van Ostade, Isack van Ostade: Zeichnungen und Aquarelle: Gesamtdarstellung mit Werkkatalo- gen*. 2 vols. Hamburg, 1981.

SCHNACKENBURG 1996
Schnackenburg, Bernhard. 'Isack van Ostade.' In *Dictionary of Art*, edited by Jane Shoaf Turner, vol. 23, 612–615. London and New York, 1996.

SCHNEIDER AND EKKART 1973
Schneider, Hans. *Jan Lievens: Sein Leben und seine Werke*. Supplement by Rudolf E.O. Ekkart. Amsterdam, 1973.

SCHULZ 1978
Schulz, Wolfgang. *Cornelis Saftleven,*

1607–1681: Leben und Werke; Mit einem kritischen Katalog der Gemälde und Zeichnugen. Berlin and New York, 1978.

SCHULZ 1982
Schulz, Wolfgang. *Herman Saftleven, 1609–1685: Leben und Werke; Mit einem Kritischen Katalog der Gemälde und Zeichnungen*. Berlin and New York, 1982.

SCHWARTZ AND BOK 1989
Schwartz, Gary, and Marten Jan Bok. *Pieter Saenredam: The Painter and His Time*. New York, 1989.

SCOTT 1984
Scott, Mary Ann. 'Cornelis Bega (1631/1632–1664) as Painter and Draughtsman.' PhD diss., University of Maryland, College Park, 1984.

SEGAL 1987
Segal, Sam. *Tulips by Anthony Claesz: 56 Seventeenth Century Watercolour Drawings by Anthony Claesz (ca. 1607/1608–1648)*. Maastricht, 1987.

SEIFERT 2011
Seifert, Christian Tico. *Pieter Lastman: Studien zu Leben und Werk: Mit einem kritischen Verzeichnis der Werke mit Themen aus der antiken Mythologie und Historie*. Petersberg, 2011.

SERVAAS VAN ROOIJEN 1881
Servaas, van Rooijen, A.J. 'Het heerlijke stuk van Jan van Ravesteijn van 1618 in het Haagsche Gemeente-Museum'. *Nederland- sche Kunstbode* 3 (1881): 334–335.

SHAWE-TAYLOR 2010
Shawe-Taylor, Desmond. *Dutch Landscapes*. With contributions by Jennifer Scott. London, 2010.

SHOAF TURNER 2006
Shoaf Turner, Jane. *Dutch Drawings in the Pierpont Morgan Library: Seventeenth to Nineteenth Centuries*. 2 vols. New York, 2006.

SHOAF TURNER AND WHITE 2014
Shoaf Turner, Jane, and Christopher White.

Dutch and Flemish Drawings in the Victoria and Albert Museum. 2 vols. London, 2014.

SIEJEK AND KIRSCH 2004
Siejek, Andreas, and Kathrin Kirsch. *Die Unterzeichnung auf dem Malgrund: Graphische Mittel und Übertragungsverfahren im 15.–17. Jahrhundert*. Edited by Ingo Sandner. Kölner Beiträge zur Restaurierung und Konservierung von Kunst- und Kulturgut, 11. Cologne, 2004.

SIGMOND AND KLOEK 2014
Sigmond, Peter, and Wouter Kloek. *Sea Battles in the Dutch Golden Age*. Amsterdam, 2014.

SLATKES 1987
Slatkes, Leonard J. 'Preparatory Drawings for Prints by Adriaen van Ostade.' In *Drawings Defined*, edited by Walter L. Strauss and Tracie Felker, 229–240. New York, 1987.

SLIVE 1973
Slive, Seymour. 'Notes on Three Drawings by Jacob van Ruisdael.' In *Album Amicorum J. G. van Gelder*. 274–276. The Hague, 1973.

SLIVE 1991
Slive, Seymour. 'Additions to Jacob van Ruisdael.' *Burlington Magazine* 133 (1991): 598–606.

SLIVE 2001
Slive, Seymour. *Jacob van Ruisdael: A Complete Catalogue of His Paintings, Drawings, and Etchings*. New Haven, 2001.

SLIVE 2009
Slive, Seymour. *Rembrandt Drawings*. Los Angeles, 2009.

SLUIJTER 1988
Sluijter, Eric Jan. 'Schilders van "Cleyne, Subtile Ende Curieuse Dingen": Leidse "Fijnschilders" in Contemporaine Bronnen.' In *Leidse fijnschilders: Van Gerrit Dou tot Frans van Mieris de Jonge, 1630–1760*, by Eric Jan Sluijter, Marlies Enklaar, and Paul Nieuwenhuizen, 14–55. Stedelijk Museum de Lakenhal, Leiden. Zwolle, 1988.

SLUIJTER 1996
Sluijter, Eric Jan. 'Jan van Goyen als Marktleider, Virtuoos en Vernieuwer.' In *Jan van Goyen*, by Christiaan Vogelaar, 38–59. Stedelijk Museum de Lakenhal, Leiden. Zwolle, 1996.

SLUIJTER 2000
Sluijter, Eric Jan. *De 'Heydensche Fabulen' in de Schilderkunst van de Gouden Eeuw: Schilderijen met Verhalende Onderwerpen uit de Klassieke Mythologie in de Noordelijke Neder-landen, circa 1590–1670*. Leiden, 2000.

SLUIJTER 2006
Sluijter, Eric Jan. *Rembrandt and the Female Nude*. Amsterdam Studies in the Dutch Golden Age. Amsterdam, 2006.

SLUIJTER-SEIJFFERT 2016
Sluijter-Seijffert, Nicolette Cathérine. *Cornelis van Poelenburch (1594/5–1667): The Paintings*. OCULI: Studies in the Arts of the Low Countries, 15. Amsterdam and Philadelphia, 2016.

SMITH 1829
Smith, John. *A Catalogue Raisonné of the Works of the Most Eminent Dutch, Flemish and French Painters*. 9 vols. Vol. 1: *Gerard Dow, Peter van Slingelandt, Francis van Mieris, William van Mieris, Adrian Ostade, Isaac Osta-de, and Philip Wouwermans*. London, 1829–1842.

SMITH 1982
Smith, David R. *Masks of Wedlock: Seven-teenth-Century Dutch Marriage Portraiture*. Studies in the Fine Arts: Iconography, 8. Ann Arbor, 1982.

SNELDERS 1993
Snelders, H.A.M. *De Geschiedenis van de Scheikunde in Nederland*. 3 vols. Vol. 1: *Van Alchemie tot Chemie en Chemische Industrie rond 1900*. Delft, 1993.

SPITS 2013
Spits, Elisabeth, ed. *Het Scheepvaartmuseum: Verhalen over de Zee in 100 Iconen*. Zwolle, 2013.

STARCKY 1994
Starcky, Laure, and Emmanuel Starcky. 'La Fuite de Clélie.' In *Morceaux Choisis parmi les Acquisitions de la Collection Frits Lugt Réalisées sous le Directorat de Carlos van Hasselt, 1970–1994*, by Mària van Berge-Gerbaud and Hans Buijs. Fondation Custodia, Collection Frits Lugt, Paris. Paris, 1994.

STECHOW 1966
Stechow, Wolfgang. *Dutch Landscape Painting of the Seventeenth Century*. London, 1966.

STEFES 1997
Stefes, Annemarie. 'Nicolaes Pietersz Berchem: Die Zeichnungen.' University of Bern, 1997.

STEFES 2011
Stefes, Annemarie. *Niederländische Zeichnun-gen, 1450–1850*. 3 vols. Die Sammlungen der Hamburger Kunsthalle Kupfersichkabi-nett. Cologne, 2011.

STEINER 2004
Steiner, Mary Ann. *Handbook of the Collec-tion*. Saint Louis Art Museum. Saint Louis, 2004.

STRATEN 2005a
Straten, Roelof van. *Rembrandts Leidse Tijd, 1606–1632*. Leiden, 2005.

STRATEN 2005b
Straten, Roelof van. *Young Rembrandt: The Leiden Years, 1606–1632*. Leiden, 2005.

STRAUSS AND VAN DER MEULEN 1979
Strauss, Walter L., and Marjon van der Meulen. *The Rembrandt Documents*. New York, 1979.

SUMOWSKI 1962
Sumowski, Werner. 'Gerbrand van den Eeckhout als Zeichner.' *Oud Holland* 77 (1962): 11–39.

SUMOWSKI 1975
Sumowski, Werner. 'Zeichnungen von Lastman und aus dem Lastman-Kreis.' *Giessener Beiträge zur Kunstgeschichte* 3 (1975): 149–186.

SUMOWSKI 1979
Sumowski, Werner. *Drawings of the Rembrandt School*. 10 vols. New York, 1979–1992.

SUMOWSKI 1983
Sumowski, Werner. *Gemälde der Rembrandt-Schüler in Vier Bänden*. 6 vols. Landau, 1983.

SURH, VAN TUINEN, AND TWILLEY 2014
Surh, Dominique, Ilona van Tuinen, and John Twilley. 'Insights from Technical Analysis on 13 Paintings by Gerrit Dou in the Leiden Collection.' *Journal of Historians of Netherlandish Art* 6 (2014). doi:10.5092/jhna.2014.6.1.3.

SUTTON 1990
Sutton, Peter C. 'Recent Patterns of Public and Private Collecting of Dutch Art.' In *Great Dutch Paintings from America*, by Ben P.J. Broos, 104–119. Royal Picture Gallery Mauritshuis, The Hague; Fine Arts Museums of San Francisco. Zwolle, 1990.

SWAN 2005
Swan, Claudia. *Art, Science, and Witchcraft in Early Modern Holland: Jacques de Gheyn II (1565–1629)*. Cambridge Studies in Netherlandish Visual Culture. New York, 2005.

SWILLENS 1935
Swillens, P.T.A. *Pieter Janszoon Saenredam, Schilder van Haarlem, 1597–1665*. Amsterdam, 1935.

TAYLOR 1995
Taylor, Paul. *Dutch Flower Painting, 1600–1720*. New Haven, 1995.

TERWEN AND OTTENHEYM 1993
Terwen, J.J., and Koen Ottenheym. *Pieter Post (1608–1669), Architect*. Zutphen, 1993.

THIEL 1969
Thiel, P.J.J. van. 'Michiel van Musscher's Vroegste Werk naar Aanleiding van Zijn Portret van het Echtpaar Comans.' *Bulletin van het Rijksmuseum* 17 (1969): 3–36.

THIEL 1974
Thiel, P.J.J. van. 'Andermaal Michiel van Musscher: Zijn Zelfportretten.' *Bulletin van het Rijksmuseum* 22 (1974): 231–249.

THIEL 1976
Thiel, P.J.J. van, et al. *All the Paintings of the Rijksmuseum in Amsterdam: A Completely Illustrated Catalogue.* Maarssen and Amsterdam, 1976.

THIEME AND BECKER 1907
Thieme, Ulrich, and Felix Becker. *Allgemeines Lexikon Der Bildenden Künstler Von Der Antike Bis Zur Gegenwart.* 37 vols. Leipzig, 1907.

TJON SIE FAT AND DE JONG 1991
Tjon Sie Fat, Leslie, and Erik de Jong, eds. *The Authentic Garden: A Symposium on Gardens.* Leiden, 1991.

TRAUTSCHOLDT 1929
Trautscholdt, Eduard. 'Notes on Adriaen van Ostade.' *Burlington Magazine* 54 (1929): 74–80.

TRAUTSCHOLDT 1959
Trautscholdt, Eduard. 'Über Adriaen van Ostade als Zeichner.' In *Festschrift Friedrich Winkler*, 280–305. Berlin, 1959.

TRAUTSCHOLDT 1967
Trautscholdt, Eduard. 'Some Remarks on Drawings from the Studio and Circle of the Van Ostade Brothers.' *Master Drawings* 5 (1967): 159–165.

TRNEK 1992
Trnek, Renate. *Die Holländischen Gemälde des 17. Jahrhunderts in der Gemäldegalerie der Akademie der bildenden Künste in Wien.* Vienna, 1992.

TÜMPEL 1970
Tümpel, Christian, and Astrid Tümpel. *Rembrandt Legt die Bibel Aus: Zeichnungen und Radierungen aus dem Kupferstichkabinett der Staatlichen Museen Preussischer Kulturbesitz.* Berlin, 1970.

TÜMPEL 1974
Tümpel, Astrid. 'Claes Cornelisz Moeyaert.' *Oud Holland* 88 (1974): 1–163, 245–290.

TURNER, HENDRIX, AND PLAZZOTTA 1997
Turner, Nicholas, Lee Hendrix, and Carol Plazzotta. *European Drawings.* Catalogue of the Collections, J. Paul Getty Museum, 3. Malibu, 1988.

VEGA 1975
Vega, L. Alvares. *Het Beth Haim van Ouderkerk: Beelden van een Portugees-Joodse Begraafplaats / The Beth Haim of Ouderkerk aan de Amstel: Images of a Portuguese Jewish Cemetery in Holland.* Assen and Amsterdam, 1975.

VEITH 2011
Veith, Jessica. 'Memorializing the Past: Jan de Bray and the Construction of Identity in Seventeenth-Century Haarlem.' PhD diss., New York University, 2011.

VELDMAN 1993
Veldman, Ilja M. *Maarten van Heemskerck.* 2 vols. New Hollstein: Dutch and Flemish Etchings, Engravings and Woodcuts, 1450–1700. Roosendaal, 1993.

VELDMAN 2001
Veldman, Ilja M. *Crispijn de Passe and His Progeny (1564–1670): A Century of Print Production.* Studies in Prints and Printmaking, 3. Rotterdam, 2001.

VERMEEREN 1986
Vermeeren, Karel. 'Isaac van Ostade (1621–1649) Tekende de Middeleeuwse St.-Catharinakerk van Eindhoven van Twee Kanten.' *Brabants Heem* 38 (1986): 228–236.

VERSLYPE 2005
Verslype, Ige. 'A Preliminary Study on Paulus Potter's (1625–1654) Painting Technique.' *Art Matters* 3 (2005): 97–110.

VEY 1986
Vey, H. 'Willem van de Velde D.Ä (1611–1693): Die Eroverung der "Royal Prince" Wärend der Viertägigen Schlacht.' *Jahrbuch der Staatlichen Kunstsammlungen in Baden-Württemberg* 23 (1986): 153–160.

VEY AND KESTING 1967
Vey, Horst, and Anna Maria Kesting. *Katalog der Niederländischen Gemälde von 1550 bis 1800 im Wallraf-Richartz-Museum und im öffentlichen Besitz der Stadt Köln.* Cologne, 1967.

VOORBEIJTEL CANNENBURG 1950
Voorbeijtel Cannenburg, Willem. 'The Van de Veldes.' *Mariner's Mirror* 36 (1950): 184–204.

WAGNER 1971
Wagner, Helga. *Jan van der Heyden, 1637–1712.* Amsterdam and Haarlem, 1971.

WALFORD 1991
Walford, E. John. *Jacob van Ruisdael and the Perception of Landscape.* New Haven, 1991.

WALLERT AND TAUBER 2004
Wallert, Arie, and Gwen Tauber. 'Over Herhalingen in de Schilderkunst: Het Probleem van Reproductie.' *Bulletin van het Rijksmuseum* 52 (2004): 316–328.

WALLERT AND VERSLYPE 2009
Wallert, Arie, and Ige Verslype. 'Ice and Sky, Sky and Ice: Technical Aspects.' In *Hendrick Avercamp: Master of the Ice Scene*, by Pieter Roelofs, 129–139. Rijksmuseum, Amsterdam; National Gallery of Art, Washington. Amsterdam, 2009.

WEGNER AND PÉE 1980
Wegner, W., and H. Pée. 'Die Zeichnungen des David Vinckboons.' *Münchener Jahrbuch der Bildenden Kunst* 31 (1980): 35–128.

WELLER 2009
Weller, Dennis P. *Seventeenth-Century Dutch and Flemish Paintings.* The Collection of the North Carolina Museum of Art, Raleigh, 2009.

WETERING 2000
Wetering, Ernst van de. *Rembrandt: The Painter at Work.* Berkeley, 2000.

WHEELOCK 1995
Wheelock, Arthur K., Jr. *Dutch Paintings of the Seventeenth Century*. The Collections of the National Gallery of Art Systematic Catalogue. Washington, 1995.

WHEELOCK 2014
Wheelock, Arthur K., Jr. *Dutch Paintings of the Seventeenth Century*. NGA Online Editions, http://www.nga.gov/content/ ngaweb/research/online-editions/ 17th-century-dutch-paintings.html/. Washington, 2014.

WHITE 1964
White, Christopher. *The Flower Drawings of Jan van Huysum*. Leigh-on-Sea, 1964.

WHITE 1982
White, Christopher. *The Dutch Paintings in the Collection of Her Majesty the Queen*. Cambridge, 1982.

WHITE 1999
White, Christopher. *Ashmolean Museum Oxford, Catalogue of the Collection of Paintings: Dutch, Flemish, and German Paintings before 1900*. Oxford, 1999.

WHITE 2015
White, Christopher. *The Dutch Pictures in the Collection of Her Majesty the Queen*. London, 2015.

WIESEMAN 2002
Wieseman, Marjorie. *Caspar Netscher and Late Seventeenth-Century Dutch Painting*. Doornspijk, 2002.

DE WITT 2006
De Witt, David. 'Abraham van den Tempel as a Draughtsman.' *Oud Holland* 119 (2006): 164–196.

DE WITT 2008
De Witt, David. *The Bader Collection Dutch and Flemish Paintings*. Agnes Etherington Art Centre Catalogues. Kingston, ON, 2008.

WUESTMAN 2015
Wuestman, Gerdien. 'Een Onbekende Voorstudie door Frans van Mieris.' *Delineavit et Sculpsit* 39 (2015): 44–49.

YAPOU 1983
Yapou, Yonna. 'Who Was Flinck's Venus?' *Israel Museum Journal* 2 (1983): 58–61.

YEIDE 2009
Yeide, Nancy H. *Beyond the Dreams of Avarice: The Hermann Goering Collection*. Dallas, 2009.

PHOTOGRAPHY CREDITS

Maida and George Abrams Collection, Boston: cats. 2, 71, 93, 95, 117; p. 27 fig. 6: Imaging Department © President and Fellows of Harvard College; cats. 68, 69: © 2016 Museum of Fine Arts, Boston

Albertina, Vienna: cats. 33, 45, 91, 98; p. 41, fig. 15; p. 48, fig. 30; p. 76, fig. 1

Amsterdam Museum, Amsterdam: cats. 116, 121; p. 48, fig. 31

Art Gallery of Ontario, Toronto: p. 174, fig. 15: © 2015 Art Gallery of Ontario

Ashmolean Museum, Oxford: cat. 24; p. 45, fig. 24; p. 227, fig. 1: © Ashmolean Museum, University of Oxford

Bayerische Staatsgemäldesammlungen, Alte Pinakothek, Munich: cat. 127: © RMN-Grand Palais / image BStGS; p. 106, fig. 1 and p. 168, figs. 10, 11: © BPK, Berlin, Dist. RMN-Grand Palais / image BStGS; p. 189, fig. 1: image courtesy of Bayerische Staatsgemäldesammlungen, Alte Pinakothek, Munich

De Boer Foundation, Amsterdam: cat. 15

The British Museum, London: cats. 21, 49; p. 8, fig. 5; p. 42, figs. 17, 18; p. 44, fig. 22; p. 46, fig. 26; p. 47, fig. 28; p. 85, fig. 5: © Trustees of the British Museum. All rights reserved.

The Courtauld Gallery, Courtauld Institute of Art, London: cats. 62, 103: © The Samuel Courtauld Trust, The Courtauld Gallery, London

The Detroit Institute of Arts: p. 22, fig. 5: Founders Society Purchase, Eleanor Clay Ford Fund, General Membership Fund, Endowment Income Fund and Special Activities Fund; p. 231, fig. 2: © Detroit Institute of Arts, USA/Bridgeman Images

The Devonshire Collection, Chatsworth: p. 166, fig. 6 and p. 167, fig. 8: © Devonshire Collection, Chatsworth. Reproduced by permission of Chatsworth Settlement Trustees

École nationale supérieure des beaux-arts, Paris: p. 41, fig. 16 and p. 43, fig. 19: © Beaux-Arts de Paris, Dist. RMN-Grand Palais / image Beaux-arts de Paris

Agnes Etherington Art Centre, Queen's University, Kingston, Ontario: p. 209, fig. 2

Fondation Custodia, Collection Frits Lugt, Paris: cats. 3, 5b, 6, 14, 23, 35, 36, 38, 40, 42, 50, 55, 76, 77, 78, 83, 87, 96, 97, 106, 125, 126; p. 23, figs. 6, 7; p. 36, figs. 4, 5; p. 37, fig. 7; p. 38, fig. 9; p. 40, fig. 14; p. 47, fig. 29; p. 49, fig. 32; p. 51, fig. 35; p. 156, fig. 2; p. 251, fig. 1

Gemäldegalerie der Akademie der bildenden Künste, Vienna: p. 222, fig. 1

Gemäldegalerie Alte Meister, Staatliche Kunstsammlungen, Dresden: p. 6, fig. 1: © BPK, Berlin / Staatliche Kunstsammlungen, Gemäldegalerie Alte Meister, Dresden / Hans-Peter Klut / Art Resource, NY; p. 231, fig. 2: © BPK, Berlin, Dist. RMN-Grand Palais / Hans-Peter Kluth

Gemäldegalerie der Staatlichen Museen zu Berlin-Preußischer Kulturbesitz: cat. 61 and p. 109, fig. 1; p. 161, fig. 4; p. 164, fig. 5: © BPK, Berlin, Dist. RMN-Grand Palais / Jörg P. Anders; p. 257, fig. 1: © BPK, Berlin / Staatliche Museen zu Berlin, Gemäldegalerie /Joerg P. Anders / Art Resource, NY

The J. Paul Getty Museum, Los Angeles: p. 13, fig. 11

Hallwylska Museum, Stockholm: p. 154, fig. 1

Frans Hals Museum | De Hallen Haarlem: p. 110, fig. 2: long-term loan from the Cultural Heritage Agency of the Netherlands, photo: Tom Haartsen

Hamburger Kunsthalle, Hamburg: cat. 16: © BPK, Berlin, Dist. RMN-Grand Palais / image BPK; cats. 74 and 90: © BPK, Berlin, Dist. RMN-Grand Palais / Christoph Irrgang

Harvard Art Museums/Fogg Museum, Cambridge, p. 37, fig. 6: Anonymous fund in honor of John and Anne Straus, and through the generosity of the Fifth Floor Foundation, Howard and Sally Lepow, Leena and Sheldon Peck, Maida and George Abrams and Kathryn and William W. Robinson, 1996.303; cat. 56: Imaging Department © President and Fellows of Harvard College; Kate, Maurice R., and Melvin R. Seiden Special Purchase Fund, Janine Luke, The Louis Agassiz Shaw Bequest, and William and Ami Danoff in honor of Seymour Slive, 1997.5; cat. 57: Imaging Department © President and Fellows of Harvard College; The Maida and George Abrams Collection, Fogg Art Museum, Harvard University, Cambridge, Massachusetts, Gift of George S. Abrams in appreciation of William Robinson's services as Curator of Drawings, 1988–2013, 2013.170; cat. 70: Imaging Department © President and Fellows of Harvard College; The Maida and George Abrams Collection, Fogg Art Museum, Harvard University, Cambridge, Massachusetts, 1999.136; p. 37, fig. 6: Imaging Department © President and Fellows of Harvard College

The State Hermitage Museum, St. Petersburg: p. 77, figs. 2, 3: © The State Hermitage Museum. Photo by T.V. Gorbokoneva; p. 81, fig. 4 and p. 114, fig. 1: © The State Hermitage Museum. Photo by Pavel Demidov

Hessisches Landesmuseum, Darmstadt: p. 271, fig. 1

The Historical Museum of The Hague, The Netherlands: p. 87, fig. 1 (inv. no. 0000-0025-SCH); p. 88, fig. 2: © Redivivus, Conservation and Restoration of Paintings

Kupferstichkabinett, Staatliche Kunstsammlungen, Dresden: cat. 66: © BPK, Berlin, Dist. RMN-Grand Palais / image SKD; p. 7, fig. 2 and p. 8, fig. 4: © BPK, Berlin / Staatliche Kunstsammlungen, Kupferstich-Kabinett, Dresden /Herbert